Praise for Russell Miller

'The excitement, sadness, glory, numbness and terror of warfare sings, screams and whispers through its pages'
New York Times on *Nothing Less than Victory*

'The best account of the reality of photo-journalism I have ever read'
Daily Telegraph on *Magnum*

'Enthralling . . . revelatory' *Daily Mail* on *Behind the Lines*

'Last year, a poll at the National Army Museum to determine Britain's greatest general ended in a tie between Wellington and Slim. This biography will do much more to tip the scales. It pays magnificent tribute to Slim in a very well-informed assessment of what he did to deserve this accolade. It is a most exciting read, full of vivid, even lurid descriptions of the sufferings inflicted by the terrain and the climate as well as by the bestiality of the Japanese enemy . . . [a] forcefully written biography'
Peter Lewis, *Daily Mail* on *Uncle Bill*

'Precision and easy-going style have added appreciably to the historical record of `Uncle Bill` Slim and the extraordinary skill and fortitude of his campaigns'
Andrew Lycett, *Literary Review* on *Uncle Bill*

Russell Miller is an award-winning journalist and script-writer, and the author of fifteen highly acclaimed books, including several works of investigative histories.

By Russell Miller

The Resistance
Bunny: The Real Story of Playboy
The House of Getty
Bare-Faced Messiah
Nothing Less than Victory
Ten Days in May
Magnum
Behind the Lines
Codename Tricycle
The Adventures of Arthur Conan Doyle
Uncle Bill

Uncle Bill

The Authorised Biography of Field Marshal Viscount Slim

RUSSELL MILLER

PHOENIX

To
Aung San Suu Kyi,
Gentle freedom fighter

A Phoenix paperback
First published in Great Britain in 2013
by Weidenfeld & Nicolson
This edition published in 2014
by Phoenix,
an imprint of Orion Books Ltd,
Orion House, 5 Upper St Martin's Lane,
London WC2H 9EA

An Hachette UK company

1 3 5 7 9 10 8 6 4 2

A CIP catalogue record for this book
is available from the British Library.

ISBN 978-1-7802-2082-6

Typeset by Input Data Services Ltd, Bridgwater, Somerset

Printed and bound by CPI Group (UK) Ltd, Croydon, CR0 4YY
The Orion Publishing Group's policy is to use papers that
are natural, renewable and recyclable products and
made from wood grown in sustainable forests. The logging
and manufacturing processes are expected to conform to
the environmental regulations of the country of origin.

www.orionbooks.co.uk

Contents

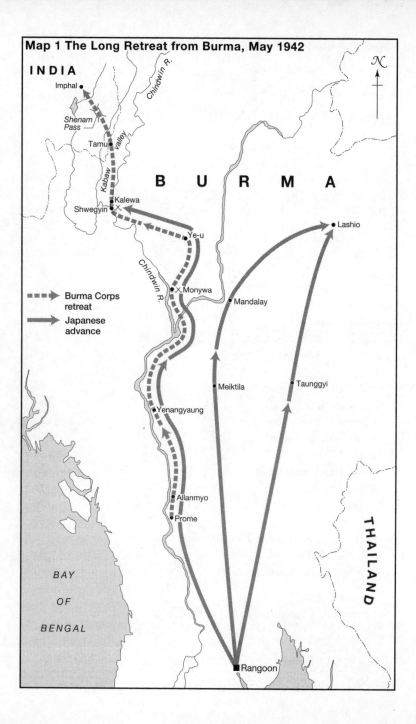

Map 1 The Long Retreat from Burma, May 1942

INDIA

Imphal

Shenam Pass

Tamu

Kabaw valley

Chindwin R.

BURMA

Kalewa

Shwegyin ✗

Ye-u

Chindwin R.

✗ Monywa

Mandalay

Lashio

▬ ▬ ▶ Burma Corps retreat

────▶ Japanese advance

Meiktila

Taunggyi

Yenangyaung

Allanmyo

Prome

BAY

OF

BENGAL

THAILAND

Rangoon

𝒩

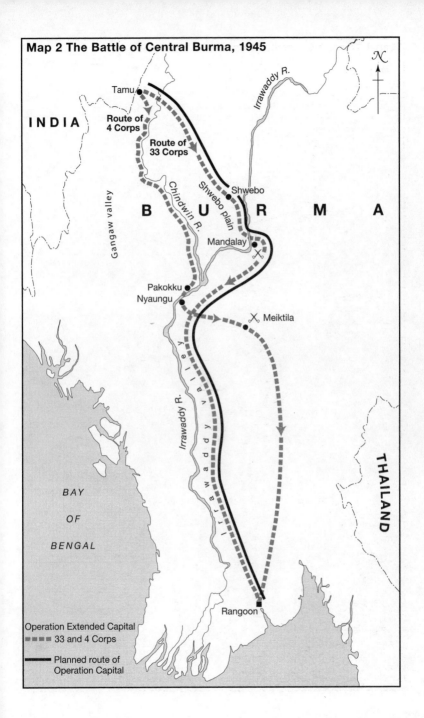

Map 2 The Battle of Central Burma, 1945

INDIA

Tamu

Route of 4 Corps

Route of 33 Corps

Gangaw valley

Chindwin R.

Shwebo plain

Shwebo

B U R M A

Irrawaddy R.

Mandalay

Pakokku
Nyaungu

Meiktila

Irrawaddy valley

Irrawaddy R.

BAY

OF

BENGAL

THAILAND

Rangoon

Operation Extended Capital
▰▰▰ 33 and 4 Corps

━━━ Planned route of
Operation Capital

List of Illustrations

Japanese in September 1945. *(Imperial War Museum)*
20. 'Uncle Bill' as the troops remembered him. *(Viscount Slim)*
21. Bill and Aileen relaxing in the garden of their home in Oxted. *(Viscount Slim)*
22. Bill with Aileen at the state opening of Parliament in Canberra. *(Viscount Slim)*
23. Bill and Aileen at Government House in Canberra in 1958. *(Viscount Slim)*
24. With their new dog, Suzie, on the steps of Yarralumla House. *(Viscount Slim)*
25. A portrait of the Governor-General by the Australian artist Ivor Hele. *(Viscount Slim)*
26. Bill presenting the Victoria Cross to Lance-Corporal Rambahadur Limbu. *(Viscount Slim)*
27. Bill and Mountbatten at a Remembrance Day service in Whitehall. *(Imperial War Museum)*

When you go home
Tell them of us and say
For your tomorrow
We gave our today

Inscription on the 2nd Division
War Memorial at Kohima

Preface

There is a Buddhist school across the road from the cemetery. The road is busy, rumbling with heavy traffic in the searing heat of the midday sun, but you can still hear the children chanting, or perhaps singing. It is a sweet sound, innocent, peaceful. Here in the cemetery, dragonflies jink in the shimmering haze over the graves and butterflies flit among the flowering shrubs. We are walking up and down the rows of engraved tablets set into the neatly trimmed grass, reading the inscriptions from loved ones – mainly parents, for these are predominantly young men buried here. They are heartbreaking, almost unbearably poignant. I can see my wife, two rows distant, is silently weeping.

'Had you known this boy of ours, you would have loved him too.'

'One treasured gift I do retain, your smiling face in a photo frame. Mother.'

'A vacant place to fill, we miss you son and always will.'

'Whatever else I fail to do, I never fail to think of you.'

'You were all I wanted out of life and tho' you have been taken away, my love will never die.'

'To all the world you were only one, to me you were all the world.'

'A loving husband and true friend, one of the best. Goodnight Daddy. Ann and Betty.'

'We shall grow old and weary but he, beyond the reach of time, will always be our lad.'

'Where once there was sunshine, there is now a shadow forever.'

'Tho' we smile and seem care free, no one misses you more than we. Mam and all.'

'My memories are all that are left of a dearly beloved husband, sadly missed.'

'Yours was the courage, laughing soldier. May the fortitude be mine.'

'We had a son.'

Who can know the unfathomable grief which must lie behind those four simple words 'We had a son'? Six thousand, three hundred and sixty-eight men, including seven posthumous holders of the Victoria Cross, are buried in the Taukyyan war cemetery outside Rangoon. Many of them are unidentified. They were moved from scattered battlefield graves across Burma in the Fifties and brought here to rest in the dignified setting of an immaculate Commonwealth War Grave. The names of 26,857 men 'to whom the fortunes of war denied customary rites accorded to their comrades in death' are commemorated in a rotunda in the centre of the cemetery. Some 8,000 men, casualties of the Burma campaign, are buried in other war graves elsewhere in Burma and northern India. Thousands more were cremated, 'in accordance with their faith'.

These men, far from home, fought and died in conditions almost more terrible than can be imagined. They faced a fearless, barbaric enemy devoid of compassion, beyond the reach of humanity. Their battles were waged in the world's most difficult terrain – in mountains, mangrove swamps and jungle – and in the world's worst climate, where malaria was endemic and dysentery commonplace. More men, many more, died of tropical diseases than at the hands of the enemy. What made their plight even worse was that Burma was no one's priority – at the bottom of the list for new equipment, for supplies, for aircraft, for tanks, for everything. No wonder the long-suffering men of the 14th Army called themselves 'The Forgotten Army'.

It required a man of exceptional qualities to transform the miserable fortunes of 'The Forgotten Army' and turn defeat into victory. That man was Bill Slim, a general who came to be idolised by his troops. The British soldiers called him 'Uncle Bill', the Indians and Gurkhas 'Cha Cha Slim Sahib'.

1

Onslaught

The first wave of aircraft attacked the warships at anchor in Pearl Harbor at 0748, Hawaiian time, on 7 December 1941, the 'day of infamy'. A few minutes earlier, nearly 4,000 miles to the east in the South China Sea, where it was the middle of a murky night, Japanese warships opened up an artillery bombardment on the eastern coasts of Thailand and Malaya as landing craft loaded with troops were being silently winched into the heaving sea from a fleet of 20 transports wallowing offshore. Before embarking, each man had been issued with a field manual which glorified the task ahead: 'We Japanese, heirs to 2,600 years of a glorious past, have now, in response to the trust placed in us by His Majesty the Commander-in-Chief, risen in the cause of the peoples of Asia, and embarked upon a noble and solemn undertaking which will change the course of world history ...'

As Japanese troops were fighting their way on shore in Thailand and Malaya, 60,000 troops of the 23rd Army crossed the Shenzhen river in China and fell on the British colony of Hong Kong. Almost at the same time, further to the south, Japanese bombers and Zero fighters attacked the US air base at Clark Field in the Philippines and destroyed half the aircraft of the Far East Air Force in 45 minutes.

By the time the smoke had cleared from Pearl Harbor and a traumatised America began to come to terms with what had happened, it was evident that Japan had embarked on a sweeping armed conquest aimed at domination of Asia and the destruction of European and American imperialism. London and Washington were stunned by the speed and ferocity of the coordinated assault as Japanese forces smashed through Allied defences throughout Asia in one astounding victory after another. Within ten days US air power in the Philippines had virtually been destroyed; the battleship HMS

Prince of Wales and the battle cruiser HMS *Repulse* – the pride of
the Royal Navy – steaming north to intercept Japanese warships,
had been sunk off Singapore with the loss of 840 lives; Hong Kong
was expected to fall at any time; further landings had taken place in
Borneo and the Dutch East Indies.

On 17 December the Japanese 25th Army under Lieutenant
General Yamashita Tomoyuki captured Penang and began advancing down the Malaya peninsula towards the British fortress of
Singapore. British, Indian and Australian troops defending Malaya
found themselves facing a formidable and terrifying enemy – a war
machine, as Churchill put it, of 'hideous efficiency'. Japanese soldiers were well-trained, highly motivated, incredibly resilient, ruthless and utterly fearless, inculcated with a belief there was no greater
glory than to die honourably in the service of the Emperor, 'the Son
of Heaven'. To be taken prisoner alive was a disgrace. As Bill Slim
would say much later, in order to capture a Japanese position held
by 500 men you first had to kill 495 of them and then the final five
would commit suicide.

To the Allied troops the jungle was impenetrable and dangerous; to the Japanese it offered an opportunity to encircle the enemy
unseen. A British historian pointed out after the war, as if it was
somehow ungentlemanly, that the wily Japanese 'did not come
down the road in a straightforward manner'. Time and again,
Japanese troops would emerge from the jungle at the rear of bewildered Allied troops, cutting off their retreat. The Allies were en-
cumbered by heavy equipment, boots and helmets and were largely
restricted to movement by truck on roads or tracks, whereas Japanese
infantrymen wore canvas shoes, cotton shorts and shirts, carried
their own ammunition and four-day ration packs, used bicycles
or animals for transport, and slipped through the jungle like
wraiths.

On 21 December the Thai government signed a treaty of friendship with Japan, effectively providing Japan with a launch pad to
invade Burma. Two days later Japanese aircraft began bombing the
vital strategic port of Rangoon while two divisions from the 15th
Army, under the command of the veteran General Shōjirō Iida,[1]
concentrated in Thailand near the Burma border. The British had
virtually no information regarding enemy intentions – no attempt

had been made to embed intelligence agents inside Thailand partly because of lack of funds and partly because few people had ever expected Burma to be attacked. The Governor-General of the colony, Sir Reginald Dorman-Smith, had confidently reported to London the previous summer his belief that if the Japanese had the temerity to attempt an invasion of Burma the Burmese would rise up against them 'as one man'. (In fact, the very opposite happened – the Japanese invaders were largely welcomed as liberators from the colonial yoke.) After a visit to Rangoon in October 1941, General Archibald Wavell, Commander-in-Chief India, persuaded himself that Dorman-Smith's analysis was correct. Wavell also made little secret of his contempt for the fighting qualities of the Japanese Imperial Army – a crass misjudgement with far-reaching consequences.

On the afternoon of Christmas Day 1941, after 17 days of fierce fighting, Hong Kong fell. The garrison was outnumbered by nearly four to one and had no significant air or naval defences, although the Governor, Sir Mark Aitchison Young, initially rejected an enemy ultimatum to surrender and called on the troops to 'hold fast for King and Empire'. But continued bombing raids severed water mains and the Japanese took control of the remaining reservoir, along with the power station. Faced by the prospect of death from thirst and starvation, the Governor surrendered in person at the Japanese headquarters on the third floor of the Peninsula Hotel, said to be 'the finest hotel east of Suez'. It was a humiliating moment – the first occasion on which a British Crown Colony had ever capitulated to an invading force. Sir Mark was confined to a suite in the hotel for two months before being shipped to prison in Shanghai; 7,000 Allied soldiers and civilians became prisoners of war.

By the end of the first week of January the entire northern region of Malaya was in Japanese hands; Kuala Lumpur, the capital, was captured unopposed on 11 January. Yamashita's 25th Army brushed aside all the Allied defences set up to block its relentless advance towards Singapore. On 27 January the last Allied troops on the Malayan peninsula were ordered to retreat across the causeway linking Johore with Singapore – Britain's 'impregnable' island fortress. Four days later British engineers blew up the causeway to delay the inevitable attack on the island, which began at 2030 on 8 February when the first wave of 4,000 Japanese troops began crossing the Johore Strait in boats. Further landings followed all round the island and within days the garrison was fighting for its life.

On the evening of 10 February, Churchill cabled Wavell in apocalyptic terms: 'There must at this stage be no thought of saving the troops or sparing the population. The battle must be fought to the bitter end at all costs ... Commanders and senior officers should die with their troops. The honour of the British Empire and of the British Army is at stake ... the whole reputation of our country and our race is involved. It is expected that every unit will be brought into close contact with the enemy and fight it out ...'[2] Brave words, but ultimately futile. On the following day Yamashita called on Lieutenant General Arthur Percival, the commander of the garrison, to give up 'this meaningless and desperate resistance'. Percival refused. On 14 February – St Valentine's Day – Japanese troops captured the Alexandra Military Hospital, massacred 321 patients and doctors and raped many of the nurses, a foretaste of the innumerable atrocities to come at the hands of a bestial enemy with utter contempt for prisoners.

By the morning of 15 February, the 25th Army had broken through the last lines of the Allied defences. With food and ammunition running out, Percival held a conference of his senior commanders and all agreed that there was no possibility of mounting a counter-attack and that surrender, no matter how unacceptable and ignominious, was the only option. A photograph of Percival, accompanied by staff officers, one carrying the Union flag and another a white flag, on their way to the surrender ceremony became powerful propaganda for the enemy. At 1715 that afternoon, Percival signed the formal surrender document at the Ford Motor Company factory after Yamashita had thumped the table with his fist when his demands for an 'unconditional surrender' were at first resisted. The Rising Sun was hoisted at the top of the tallest office building on the island and more than 100,000 British troops became prisoners of war (some 12,000 would subsequently die of disease and starvation). It was, one senior commander observed, 'a great disaster for British arms, one of the worst in history, and a great blow to the honour and prestige of the Army'.[3]

Lee Kuan Yew, a future prime minister of Singapore, was then a student at Raffles College and watched the prisoners starting on their long march into captivity: 'I saw them tramping along the road in front of my house for three solid days, an endless stream of bewildered men who did not know what had happened, why it had happened, or what they were doing here in Singapore in any case.'[4]

Meanwhile, some 1,000 miles to the north, Burma, the country least prepared to defend itself against attack, was in desperate straits. For years Burma had been regarded as a remote, and unimportant, outpost of the Empire, an exotic land of golden pagodas, cheerful natives and dusky maidens with almond eyes. Its terrain and its climate were regarded as its best defences – vast tracts of dense, 'impenetrable' jungle covering steep mountain ridges, great rivers striating the country, few roads, monsoon rainfall reaching 200 inches a year, summer temperatures peaking at 115° in the shade and an enervating list of endemic tropical diseases caused by parasites and viruses. 'It could fairly be described,' Bill Slim trenchantly observed, 'as some of the world's worst country, breeding the world's worst diseases, and having for half the year at least the world's worst climate.'

So it was that Burma, a country bigger than France and the Low Countries combined, was, at the time of the Japanese invasion, only protected by a heterogeneous mixture of poorly trained and ill-equipped Indian, Burmese and British troops. The British were mainly homesick conscripts while the Indians and Burmese had little incentive to risk their lives for the perpetuation of the Raj. Wavell visited Burma Army headquarters on 21 December 1941, and was appalled by what he found. The organisation, he decided, was 'so inadequate it might be termed non-existent'. The number of troops, the state of training, their equipment, the intelligence support – virtually nothing was up to scratch. As an immediate result of his visit he appointed the chief of the general staff in India, Lieutenant General Tom Hutton, to take command of the Burma Army and ordered it to be immediately reinforced from India by the 17th Indian Division, which had originally been earmarked to garrison Iraq.

(Further reinforcements which had been promised from Britain and Africa were diverted in a futile attempt to save Singapore and were captured.) Despite his concerns, Wavell nevertheless remained blithely confident that the Japanese were seriously overextended and that any attack would be driven back into Thailand. The reality was that the Burma Army was quite unready in every regard to face an onslaught from the 35,000 battle-hardened enemy troops massing on the border in Thailand and thirsting for blood.

Although Burma possessed useful natural resources – oil, rice, tungsten, manganese and wolfram – the real prize for the Japanese was the prospect of closing the fabled Burma Road, the lifeline to Chiang Kai-shek's Chinese Nationalist Army which was supported by lend-lease aid from the United States. Japan had been at war with China since 1937, had captured many of China's major cities, including Peking, Shanghai and Nanking, and controlled China's coastline, isolating the country from the rest of the world. Virtually all supplies to China made their way by ship to Rangoon then by rail via Mandalay to the railhead at Lashio, from where the 700-mile Burma Road began its hairpin course through high mountain passes across the Chinese border to the city of Kunming. Day and night trucks loaded with goods and war materials ground their tortuous way along the Burma Road, virtually nose to tail, to keep the Nationalists supplied. If Japan could capture Rangoon, all traffic along the Burma Road would cease.

On 22 January 1942, the Japanese launched a full-scale ground invasion of Burma, swarming into the southern province of Tenasserim across the jungle-covered Tenasserim Hills. To the surprise and disgust of Wavell, the Burma Army was outwitted and outmanoeuvred by the enemy's tactics and fell back in disorder from one defensive position after another. By 31 January the Allies had been driven out of the strategically important seaport of Moulmein, Burma's third largest city on the Salween river, less than 200 miles from Rangoon. In two days of fierce fighting the defenders of the city had been forced into a tighter and tighter perimeter with the broad river at their back and eventually escaped across the river by steamer, under a hail of artillery and machine-gun fire, after abandoning a large quantity of supplies and equipment. Wavell flew to the front and excoriated the luckless brigade commander, demanding, 'Take back all you have lost.' In London there was despondency about what was perceived to be the lack of fighting spirit of the troops in Burma.

Major General John 'Jackie' Smyth VC, commander of the 17th Division, despaired at the tactics being forced on him by Hutton to hold as much forward ground as possible. He sent his chief of staff, Brigadier David Cowan – universally known as 'Punch' for his resemblance to the caricature on the cover of *Punch* magazine – to Rangoon to ask Hutton for permission for the 17th Division to fall back and establish a defensive line behind the Sittang river. Hutton, under immense pressure from Wavell not to give ground, refused and set in motion a chain of events that would lead to the Burma Army's greatest humiliation. It was, Smyth would say later, a 'disastrous decision'.

After the loss of Moulmein the division made a stand at the Bilin river and held out for four days of close-quarter fighting between 14 and 18 February. Every reserve formation was thrown into the battle but nothing seemed to be able to counter the enemy's outflanking tactics. With encirclement imminent, Hutton at last gave Smyth permission to withdraw behind the Sittang river. The exhausted division disengaged under cover of darkness and began to retreat along a dusty unmade track leading to the single bridge over the river 30 miles to the west.

The 500-metre iron railway bridge spanning the Sittang was, in effect, the last hurdle on the road to Rangoon and the plan was for engineers to destroy it once the 17th Division was safely across. The Japanese, hoping to capture the bridge intact, raced to cut off the division before it could reach the river. Enemy aircraft strafed and bombed the retreating troops, inflicting heavy casualties and forcing survivors to seek cover in nearby rubber plantations. At five o'clock on the morning of 21 February, Japanese troops infiltrated 17th Division positions and mounted an attack on Smyth's headquarters, but were beaten back. During the day fighting around the bridge intensified, with the Japanese mounting charge after charge against the detachments defending it. By dusk the leading brigade and the division HQ had got safely across but two more brigades were still trying to break through.

In the early hours of 22 February, Smyth, who was by then a sick man, suffering from a painful anal fissure, was faced with a grim decision. He was warned that the bridgehead on the east bank could probably not hold out for more than another hour. If he ordered the bridge to be destroyed more than half his men would be stranded on the wrong side of the river with the bulk of the division's artillery, vehicles and heavy equipment. If he allowed the bridge to stand, the enemy would have a clear road to Rangoon. With a heavy heart, he ordered the bridgehead garrison to withdraw and his sappers to blow the bridge. At 0530 the charges were detonated and a span of the bridge fell into the swirling yellow waters below, stranding two brigades.[5] It was the turning point of the first Burma campaign.

Some of the abandoned soldiers of the 17th Division tried to avoid capture by stripping off their equipment and attempting to swim across the 550-metre-wide river, or float across on crude bamboo rafts. Many drowned or were shot in the water; most of those who reached the temporary safety of the west bank arrived in nothing but their underwear. After the Sittang bridge disaster, the 17th Division was reduced in strength to around 3,500 men (out of 8,500, although it was under-strength at the start), of whom less than half still had their rifles.

Wavell, perhaps looking for a scapegoat for the debacle, fired Hutton and replaced him with General Sir Harold Alexander, one of the last men to leave the beachhead at Dunkirk in May 1940 and said to be Churchill's favourite general. Alexander was brave, but inept. Instructed to make every effort to hold Rangoon, the day after he arrived in Burma he ignored the advice of his staff and rashly attempted to mount a counter-attack with a brigade-sized force as the enemy approached Pegu, a city 50 miles north-east of Rangoon. It was a fiasco: within 24 hours the brigade commander and all three battalion commanders had been killed. With Japanese units now virtually at the gates of Rangoon, Alexander was forced to order the evacuation of the city. Anything that could be of use to the enemy was destroyed, including an £11 million refinery belonging to the Burmah Oil Company, 972 unassembled trucks and 5,000 tyres.

Only a stroke of extraordinary luck prevented Alexander being captured, along with his headquarters and the entire Rangoon garrison. A Japanese divisional commander had been ordered to circle around Rangoon through the jungle to the north and attack the city from the west. In order to protect his flank he had set up a strong roadblock on the only road leading north out of city, apparently not realising that it was the escape route for the Allied troops. The Rangoon garrison, spread out in a 40-mile column along the road, along with Burma Army headquarters, was effectively trapped. Repeated Allied attacks were launched to shift the roadblock but all failed; had the Japanese general kept the roadblock in place, nothing could have saved Alexander. Fortunately Japanese officers tended to follow orders blindly, which is what this one did. As soon as his division was concentrated to the west of the city, and unaware of the prize he had in the bag, he removed the roadblock, allowing Alexander, his staff and the garrison to make a miraculous escape.

When, on 9 March, the Japanese marched into Rangoon they found it deserted. After 75 days of continual air raids, the once bustling port had been turned into a virtual ghost town. The local population had disappeared, Indian police and bureaucrats had abandoned their posts, looting and arson were widespread.

With Rangoon safely in his hands and Burma effectively cut off from the outside world, General Shōjirō was able to turn his attention to the pursuit and destruction of the wretched and bewildered Burma Army, now in full flight from the apparently invincible Japanese on every front. News of what had happened at the Sittang bridge had spread throughout the army like a cancer and destroyed what little remained of morale. The men were exhausted, dispirited and thoroughly frightened, now utterly convinced there was no way the enemy could be defeated. Terrifying rumours abounded of Japanese super-soldiers in disguise who could burrow underground and travel noiselessly through the jungle for days without food. Many of the Burmese recruits had already deserted to return to their villages, and many more were to follow.

It was at this moment that a new man arrived to take direct charge of the Burma Army under Alexander. He was a stocky 51-year-old, newly promoted to acting lieutenant general and possessed of a bulldog tenacity exemplified by a prominent jutting chin which was almost the first thing anyone noticed about him. His name was William Joseph Slim.

Rarely in the annals of military history has an army commander been handed a chalice so virulently poisoned.

2

Playing at Soldiers

The surname Slim emerged in Flanders in the Middle Ages and probably arrived in Britain with Flemish migrants. For some reason, explicable only by the peculiar mechanics of demography, most Slims seem to have congregated in the Midlands, thus Bill Slim's family had strong roots in Birmingham, although he himself grew up in Bristol. Almost every biographical reference to William Slim mistakenly records that he was born in Bishopston, a suburb of Bristol, in 1891. (Indeed, when he was raised to the peerage in 1960, he took Bishopston, 'in the City and County of Bristol', as part of his title.) In fact his birthplace – 72 Belmont Road – was, and still is, in the neighbouring parish of St Andrews.

By the end of the nineteenth century, both parishes had been more or less swallowed by the ever-expanding city and a tram rattled down the middle of the Gloucester Road to take workers into the city centre. Where there was once open farmland and ploughed fields, there were now row upon row of terraced houses built to accommodate the emerging white-collar classes, many of them boasting constant hot water from a kitchen range, an almost unheard of luxury at that time. Today the tree-lined streets of Bishopston and St Andrews have been much gentrified and are popular with young professional couples and estate agents who are wont to describe the terraces of handsome red-brick Victorian houses which predominate as 'highly desirable'.

Much has been made of Bill's rise from humble beginnings; that a field marshal and peer of the realm could emerge from poverty-ridden backstreets in an industrial town. In reality, the Slim family was firmly lodged in the ranks of the rising lower middle class. Bill's father, John Benjamin Slim, was born in Birmingham in 1850 at a time when it was known as 'the City of a Thousand Trades' for the vast variety of goods manufactured there in the wake of the

Industrial Revolution. Hundreds of small workshops turned out buttons, cutlery, nails and screws, guns, tools, jewellery, toys, locks and metal goods of every description. Employment encouraged mass immigration, particularly from Ireland, and by the middle of the nineteenth century Birmingham was Britain's second biggest city.

John was one of six children fathered by William Slim, a successful brewer, and his wife, Eliza, and grew up in a substantial house in Digbeth, in the heart of the city, large enough to accommodate not only the growing family but no fewer than seven lodgers, although it is likely they shared rooms. In the census of 1861 the census taker must have misunderstood their strong Birmingham accent, for he or she registered the family under the name of 'Sline'.

Little is known of John Slim's early life, except for what can be gleaned from the census carried out every ten years. In 1871 he is listed working as a factor's clerk but for some reason he and his older sister, Elizabeth, and younger brother, Benjamin, were all living with their maternal grandfather, John Dutton, who was also a publican, in Montague Street. It may be that the pub his parents were then running – the Greyhound in Holloway Head, a short walk from Montague Street – was too small to accommodate the whole family. In September 1874, William Slim died at the age of 51, a victim of one of the undoubted hazards of his trade, cirrhosis of the liver. Eliza, clearly a formidable woman, took over the running of the pub and by the time of the 1881 census all the children were back living with their mother.

Four of William Slim's children followed their parents into the licensing trade and jointly ran the King's Arms pub in Pershore Street, but John struck out on his own and got a job as a commercial traveller, selling hardware, mainly pots and pans, to the retail trade. He remained living at home until the autumn of 1886 when he married Charlotte Amelia Tucker, the daughter of a Somerset landowner and builder. How and where they met is not known. The bridegroom was 36 and the bride 34, an age at which most women had given up hope of finding a husband (and men, too, perhaps despaired of finding a wife). In the Victorian era it was not unusual for women to be married by the age of 18 and consider themselves to be on the shelf if still unmarried by the age of 25. That her moderately wealthy father, Charles Adams Tucker, a widower with two unmarried daughters, would agree to her marriage to a humble commercial traveller was perhaps an indication of some desperation within the family. (Charlotte's younger sister, Mary, never married.) There was also the problem of religion: Charlotte had converted to Catholicism – John was a Protestant. In this matter the Tuckers clearly prevailed, since the marriage took place on 19 October 1886, 'according to the Rites and Ceremonies of the Roman Catholic Church', at the Church of the Sacred Heart in Lambeth, where Charles Tucker also owned property. He described his occupation on the wedding certificate as 'Gentleman'.

The newly-weds first lived in Burnham, Somerset, where their first son, Charles, was born, but by the time William ('Bill') arrived on 6 August 1891, the family had moved to the outskirts of Bristol and was living at 72 Belmont Road, St Andrews, a three-bedroom semi-detached house faced with locally quarried sandstone. A plaque on the front of the house now commemorates the event:

BORN HERE 6TH AUGUST 1891
FIELD MARSHAL THE VISCOUNT SLIM
OF BISHOPSTON
K.G., G.C.B., G.C.M.G., G.C.V.O., G.B.E., D.S.O., M.C.
1891-1970
A GREAT MILITARY COMMANDER, HE LED THE
FOURTEENTH ARMY IN THE VICTORIOUS BURMA
CAMPAIGN DURING THE SECOND WORLD WAR,
WAS CHIEF OF THE IMPERIAL GENERAL STAFF
1948–1952 AND GOVERNOR-GENERAL
OF AUSTRALIA 1953–1960.

Charlotte's 74-year-old father and her sister, Mary, had moved in with them; Charles Tucker was probably helping to pay the bills. It is likely that brighter prospects for work had persuaded John Slim to move to Bristol with his young family. Towards the end of the nineteenth century, Bristol was booming. A major seaport and the terminus for the Great Western Railway, designed by Isambard Kingdom Brunel, its population had quintupled, supported by new industries, mainly tobacco, paper and engineering, and growing commerce. All around the city farmland was being levelled, hedgerows and trees grubbed out and farm buildings demolished to make way for housing in suburbs like St Andrews.

Like many converts to Catholicism, Charlotte Slim was intensely devout and naturally raised both her sons as Catholics. Bill was christened at the nearby St Bonaventure's Roman Catholic Church, where Charlotte sometimes played the organ. St Bonaventure's was originally a mission founded by Franciscan friars, who were then a common sight in the area. (Bill's christening is included in a tapestry sewn by parishioners recording the history of St Bonaventure's and on display in the church.)

At the age of five Bill was enrolled in the newly opened St Brendan's College in Berkeley Square, Clifton, a two-mile walk from his home, which had been established by the Irish Christian Brothers to develop an educated Catholic laity in and around Bristol. Many of its pupils would eventually enter the priesthood, which was perhaps what Charlotte had in mind for her younger son. (He had other ideas and, incidentally, not much regard for organised religion in later life, despite a rigorous regime of church-going in his youth and education at Roman Catholic schools.)

There was no tradition of military service in the Slim family and Bill's early interest in soldiering extended to no more than playing soldiers with his brother, first using an old set of ivory dominoes, propped upright to represent men and horizontally to represent guns, laid out in ranks in what they fondly believed to be battle formations. When a cannon fired, one boy would say 'Bang' and the other would knock down a soldier on his side. Later they graduated to painted lead soldiers and artillery pieces that fired pellets of chewed paper, but for both boys it was no more than a game. 'The Army was completely outside our contacts and interests,' he would write later. 'As a child I saw, now and then, a few red-coated soldiers in the streets; I never met an officer. Even when, one day, a school friend's elder brother, who had run away and enlisted in the Life Guards, re-appeared, swaggering down the road in tight overalls and white serge pea-jacket, spurs jangling, riding whip under arm, pill box hat over ear, I felt no urge to emulate him. I knew my parents would have been as horrified as his had been at the mere suggestion that a son of theirs should take the Queen's shilling. That I might aspire to be an officer was, of course... quite impracticable.'[1]

(Officers in the British Army needed a substantial private income at that time to meet their social and service obligations and maintain the standard of living expected of them. In a way, young men like Bill Slim could hardly be worse placed to contemplate a military career – not sufficiently well off and not sufficiently high on the social scale to think of Sandhurst and a commission, and not sufficiently low to consider joining as a private soldier.)

In the days before radio and television, when people had to make their own entertainment, the family would gather in the gas-lit parlour at Belmont Road on winter evenings and John Slim would read aloud from works of the popular novelists of the day. Dickens and Thackeray were great favourites and Bill had fond memories of many happy evenings sitting spellbound with his brother while his father read to them. His mother and his Aunt Mary would listen, too, as they sat sewing on each side of the fire. In later life both boys credited their appetite for reading to those cosy fireside evenings in Belmont Road. (During the Great War, Bill carried with him a well-worn pocket edition of *David Copperfield* which always reminded him, 'amid the boredom and beastliness of war', of those gentler times.)

When world events made headlines, John Slim would bring home a newspaper and read out dispatches from foreign correspondents covering thrilling adventures taking place in the far reaches of the Empire. It was in this way that Bill first heard of Kitchener's heroic expedition into the Sudan in 1896, leading British and Egyptian forces up the Nile, building a railway to supply arms and reinforcements, and finally defeating the Sudanese at the Battle of Omdurman. He remembered being puzzled by the constant reference to Kitchener in newspaper stories, since the same name was embossed on their black-leaded kitchen range.

The first book to arouse his interest in soldiering was a fortnightly part work published by Cassell and entitled *British Battles on Land and Sea*. The end of the Victorian era saw a great upsurge in the popularity of magazines publishing both fiction and non-fiction. It was a time when queues would form outside the offices of the *Strand* magazine in London when it was known that a new Sherlock

Holmes story was due, and the publisher George Newnes made a fortune out of a penny weekly called *Tit-Bits*. Books were often published in weekly or fortnightly instalments and Bill's father subscribed to those he thought were educationally worthwhile for his sons. One such was *British Battles on Land and Sea*.

Bill remembered it as not much more than a pamphlet with a green cover but it was full of thrilling engravings which he scrutinised minutely before he could properly read. 'For a small boy they were splendid. Almost every battle, from Saxons and Normans lambasting one another with great axes at Hastings to Wolseley-helmeted British soldiers firing steady volleys into charging Fuzzy-Wuzzies in the Sudan, was there. I pored over these pictures and through them I first began to daydream of myself as a soldier. In my childishly romantic visions I saw myself plunging forward in the most desperate assaults, while somewhere in the background bands played, men cheered and colours waved. Strangely enough, among all these exciting pictures, it was one of a sailor which most riveted my attention. In it a cabin boy, Cloudesley Shovell, was swimming from one three-decker to another bearing a vital message. Above him the great broadsides roared and crashed, the sea all around covered in wreckage was beaten to foam by round-shot and musket ball.'[2]

Bill's older brother, Charles, read the stirring story of Cloudesley Shovell to him, how he rose from cabin boy to be an admiral and Knight of the Bath and in the process became a popular British hero in the eighteenth century, and Bill savoured every word. (Although he could hardly know it at the time, he would eventually follow a not dissimilar path, from lance corporal to field marshal and Knight of the Bath – and twentieth-century British hero.)

Another, rather different, hero lived in a large house nearby – the cricketer W. G. Grace. The great man was in practice as a doctor in Bristol and still playing cricket; in 1895, at the age of 47, he completed his 100th century for Gloucestershire against Somerset. Bill often saw him driving by in his carriage, instantly recognisable by his luxuriant beard, wearing a morning coat and silk top hat. A keen cricketer himself, Bill naturally idolised W. G. Grace and delighted in stories about him. One he liked to tell, almost certainly apocryphal, involved W. G. turning out for a local charity match before an unusually large crowd. When W. G. went out to bat, the first ball thumped on to his pad and the bowler yelled, 'How's that?' The umpire lifted his finger to give W. G. out. Grace took no notice and waited patiently to receive a second ball. 'Dr Grace,' the umpire said, 'I gave you out.' Grace ignored him. The umpire persisted. Grace finally turned to him and said, 'Do you think that all these people have paid their shilling to see you umpire, or me bat?'

In 1897 the family, along with Bill's Aunt Mary but without grandfather Charles, who had passed away, moved two blocks to 12 Maurice Road, overlooking the lawns and trees in St Andrews Park, which had only recently been laid out and was the pride of the parish. It was clear that John Slim was prospering, albeit modestly. (It is possible, of course, that the demise of Charlotte's father may have helped.) Number 12 Maurice Road was a much larger, more substantial house, on three storeys, with a fine bay window on the ground floor and gardens back and front, in an enviable location. John Slim was also able to employ a live-in domestic servant, a 21-year-old local girl by the name of Sarah Chapman, almost certainly a graduate of Muller's, the local orphanage, which trained girls for domestic service and boys for an apprenticed trade.

When the Boer War broke out two years later, the family avidly followed the reports from South Africa in the newspapers, incredulous that the war was going so badly wrong for the British, with garrisons at Ladysmith, Mafeking and Kimberley all under siege. Like many of his countrymen, John Slim was unable to understand how a few rebellious farmers in a faraway country were able to run rings round what everyone considered to be the finest army in the world at a time when much of the globe was coloured red, signifying the overwhelming power of the British Empire.

Young Bill was no less patriotic than his father and was dismayed when his name led to finger pointing at school that he was a Boer sympathiser. In company with nearly everyone else, he viewed the Boers as a cowardly lot who played dastardly tricks such as waving a white flag and then shooting the British soldiers who came forward to accept their surrender. The problem was that in the Boer dialect the word 'slim' meant guile and newspapers frequently referred to the 'slim Boers', 'slim' being applied as an adjective meaning crafty and treacherous. The connection between a boy named Slim and the 'slim Boers' was ludicrous, but it was enough to provoke cruel play-ground teasing which escalated to accusations that, because he was called Slim, he must be on the side of the Boers. Bill did not take it lying down. 'The gibe outraged my pride, my patriotism, my whole being. I remember battering away ineffectually at a bigger boy and blubbering hard, not because he was giving me a hiding, as most of them did, but from sheer frustrated rage and indignation.'[3] (Oddly enough, the prejudice surrounding his name endured. When Slim's name was put forward to the Prime Minister for a senior appoint-ment during the Second World War, Churchill was said to have grunted: 'I cannot think a man with a name like Slim can be any good.' Churchill served as a war correspondent for the *Morning Post* during the Boer War and became something of a national hero when he was taken prisoner and subsequently escaped.)

The trouble at school did nothing to dent Bill's enthusiasm for the war. He collected cigarette cards with pictures of 'Leading Generals', wore their pictures on buttons pinned to his jacket and turned out to cheer when troops on their way to South Africa paraded through Bristol in their new khaki uniforms while bands thumped out tunes like 'Marching to Pretoria' and 'Goodbye Dolly Grey' – the latter one of the most popular songs of the day. When his father burst into his bedroom one morning in May 1900 with the dramatic news that Mafeking had been relieved he was so excited he bounced up and down on his bed in his flannel nightshirt, whooping with joy. Eight months later the death of Queen Victoria, the longest serving mon-arch in British history, would plunge the nation into mourning.

In 1904 the family moved to Birmingham, back to John Slim's home town and the traditional centre of the 'metal bashing' indus-tries, where he had agreed to go into partnership with a friend, Tom Sellers, who was already trading as a wholesale hardware merchant and factor from large premises in Dean Street in the centre of the city. John had spent most of his life in the Black Country and per-haps missed its familiar surroundings, and his extended family still living there. The new firm of Sellers and Slim proudly opened for business in 1905; coincidentally, the premises were very close to the King's Arms, the pub in Pershore Street still being run by John's younger brother, William, and two sisters, Elizabeth and Emily.

John moved his family into a comfortable three-storey house at

72 Poplar Avenue, Edgbaston (later they moved down the road to number 144) and Bill was enrolled at St Philip's Roman Catholic School for Boys on the Hagley Road, a short walk from his home, where the fees were £2 a term. St Philip's had been founded when two priests from the Birmingham Oratory took over the existing grammar school in 1887. School records show Bill had already made his first Confession and first Holy Communion at the time of his enrolment in September 1904. (He was not to be the only famous alumnus – two years earlier J. R. R. Tolkien had joined the same school.)

The school week at St Philip's began with mass at The Oratory on Monday morning and ended with Benediction on Friday afternoon. It cannot be said that young Slim initially excelled at his lessons or, indeed, showed much promise. He had no particular aptitude for sport and was no better than average at most academic subjects, with the exception of English, which he found both easy and enjoyable. He joined the school debating society and discovered a natural talent as a forceful speaker, but according to fellow pupil Philip Pratt he gave no impression of being a 'born leader'.

Meeting Pratt at St Philip's was the start of an enduring friendship; after both boys left school they would correspond regularly for the rest of their lives, although they did not immediately become friends. Pratt remembered having an argument with Bill and calling him names and then feeling rather stupid when Bill refused to respond, but simply walked away smiling to himself. Later they began walking home from school together and learned they had much in common, not least an enthusiasm for stamp collecting. They were sometimes joined by a third boy, William Sewell, the son of the Oratory organist, whom they cruelly called 'the Baggage Animal' because of his willingness to carry both their satchels, a task Sewell apparently cheerfully accepted as the price of their company. (Bill got his comeuppance for his schoolboy cruelty when he bumped into 'the Baggage Animal' in London years later; Sewell was wearing the uniform of a major with four wound stripes on his sleeve. Bill, then a captain, recalled their treatment of him and wanted to hang his head in shame.)

Bill had brought all his copies of *British Battles on Land and Sea* to Birmingham with him and showed them to his new friend. It was possible he was thinking, although perhaps in no more than a boyish way, about a military career as he had taken to studying diagrams of the battlefields and working out other ways in which the action could have been fought. He confessed to Pratt that he often wished he could have been on the scene at the campaigns recounted in *Battles on Land and Sea*, and dreamed of being at the head of a band of soldiers going into an attack into the teeth of gunfire and leading his men to glory. Pratt for his part introduced Bill to the Brigadier Gerard stories by Arthur Conan Doyle and owned up to how much he would have loved to have been a trooper in the 'gay-riding, plume-tossing, debonair' Hussars of Conflans.

Bill was rarely in trouble at school but when he was he usually accepted his punishment stoically, without demur. He had a strong sense of right and wrong, of just and unjust, and when he felt he was being punished unjustly he stood up for himself. On one occasion he had breached some school rule and as punishment the headmaster had forbidden him to attend the forthcoming school play and speech day at the Botanical Gardens. Bill thought it was wrong that the headmaster should attempt to exert control over him outside school hours, so he went anyway. He was spotted by Frank Leighton, the popular deputy head, known at St Philip's as the 'Second Master'. Leighton knew Bill had been banned and asked him what he thought he was doing. 'Well, sir,' Bill replied, 'I don't feel the Head should be able to dictate to me after school hours.' Leighton smiled at his cheek and said: 'All right, you've made your point. Now clear out before he sees you.' Bill left, his honour satisfied. Leighton went on to become the longest serving teacher in the school's history and received a Christmas card from Bill Slim every year until he died in 1950.

When he was 16, Bill surprised everyone, not least himself, by winning a scholarship to attend the venerable King Edward's School, Birmingham, one of the finest in the country, where his brother was already a student. Founded in 1552, King Edward's School was the oldest and greatest of Birmingham's educational institutions; the school building, on New Street, was designed by Sir Charles Barry, who, with A. W. N. Pugin, went on to design the Palace of Westminster, and its striking neo-Gothic splendour made it a landmark building in the city. As a 'Foundation Scholar', Bill was exempt from the fees of £5 a term; he started at the school in July 1908, a month before his 17th birthday.

Philip Pratt believed that at that time his friend was considering a career in teaching. Two years at King Edward's would have been admirable preparation, but Bill did not thrive in the hothouse academic atmosphere of his new school. At the end of his first year, his results were abysmal. Out of a class of 25 boys, the best result he could manage was equal 12th in French. In Latin he was hopeless – 20th in the class – and almost as bad at chemistry (18th). But, curiously, his worst result – 22nd – was in English, which had been by far his strongest subject at St Philip's. (Philip Pratt said Bill 'excelled' at English at St Philip's and that his essay writing was 'exceptional'.) By the spring term of 1910 he had recovered his flair for English, coming third in a class of 28 boys, although he still languished in other subjects. One of his reports suggested that his only academic achievement was the gift of clear thinking and the ability to express himself on paper. His older brother, Charlie, by contrast, was a high-flier and was hoping to study medicine at the University of Birmingham.

During his 22 months at King Edward's, Bill's name never made an appearance in the school magazine, indicating that his prowess on the sports field – the school put great emphasis on sport – was less than dazzling, although he enjoyed cricket and played for the second XV rugby team. Perhaps Bill was not too bothered, because King Edward's had a facility which interested him much more than academic or sporting achievements – an Officers' Training Corps (OTC).

OTCs were established in universities and public schools soon after the turn of the century to provide military leadership training to students with an eye to avoiding a repetition of the critical shortage of officers during the Boer War. King Edward's was one of the first schools to have an OTC and Bill enlisted as soon as he joined the school. It was his first taste, albeit only at weekends and evenings, of military life and he revelled in it, although his name failed to appear in the school's 'Blue Book' which every term listed the boys who had been promoted in what was then called the Cadet Corps.

School records indicate that Bill left King Edward's on 9 April

1910, although his Matriculation Certificate, which showed that he passed in English, Mathematics, French, Chemistry and Geography, was dated July 1910. In an unpublished memoir he began writing late in life, he claimed he had been forced to leave school early: 'I was sixteen when my father's business, in spite of his energy and courage, proved increasingly unsuccessful. He had then, late in life, to find other employment – no easy task. Our whole standard of living was drastically reduced. My brother was still a medical student at the University, and this at a time when all education beyond the elementary school had to be paid for. Obviously I must, and quickly, relieve my parents of some at least of the expense of supporting me, and of my education. The only job I could get immediately was in elementary school teaching, and so, without much thought and with no knowledge at all of teaching, I became a pupil-teacher at seventeen shillings and sixpence a week.'

Bill's memory failed him. His father's business collapsed in 1907 before he enrolled at King Edward's. The *London Gazette* recorded its sad demise on 27 December of that year – that the partnership of Sellers and Slim had been dissolved by mutual consent on 21 December and that 'all debts due and owing by the said firm will be received and paid by the said Tom Henry Sellers and John Slim'. John obviously went back on the road, as the school records at King Edward's note his occupation as 'commercial traveller'. Bill was 18 when he left King Edward's, not 16, and his brother Charles was not a medical student at that time – he did not start at Birmingham University until the summer of 1911, paying £5 5s. a term for his first classes in biology. If it was a financial crisis that forced Bill to leave King Edward's prematurely it was not the collapse of his father's business. Furthermore, the family fortunes could not have been in too bad a state in 1911 since a general domestic servant – 17-year-old Florence Vewman (or, more probably, Newman) – was listed as resident at 144 Poplar Avenue, along with Bill's mother and father and his Aunt Mary.

None of the Slim family today can shed any light on the matter. The current Viscount Slim, Bill's son, vaguely remembers being told that his grandfather was somehow swindled, that an assistant manager ran off with the cash box and tipped the company over the edge. Whatever happened, it is not disputed that after leaving King

Edward's Bill started work as a pupil-teacher in a tough school in one of the worst slums in the city. Steward Street School was off Spring Hill in the heart of Ladywood, an area of squalid back-to-back houses and tenements beset by overcrowding, poverty, violence and disease.

Life in a Birmingham slum was the embodiment of misery. Rats were endemic, toilet facilities primitive, diets inadequate, hygiene impossible; rickets and typhoid were common. Entire families sometimes shared a gloomy single room; many relied on charity to survive. Although plenty of work was available in the city's factories and workshops, wages were very low. (Trade unions had yet to emerge as a powerful industrial force for unskilled workers.) Grinding poverty bred despair, drunkenness, crime and domestic violence.

Bill was shocked by what he found when he arrived at Steward Street School. Many of the children were barefoot, dressed in threadbare rags and largely unwashed. 'Not surprising,' he noted, 'when for most the only water supply was a shared tap at the end of an alley. A few were lousy and it was not wise to lean too closely over them for fear of enterprising fleas seeking fresh pastures.'[4]

Initially standing in for a sick teacher, Bill's first classroom was in the main entrance to the school, so that his class of some forty 14-year-old boys were constantly distracted by visitors coming and going – not that they were much interested in learning in the first place. Such were the conditions that Bill reckoned if he got through the day without having to deal with a riot he was doing reasonably well. He discovered very quickly the need to keep control of his class, but he learned, too, that sympathy and understanding also brought results. He worried about how the barefoot boys would cope in winter and was relieved to find they were supplied with wooden clogs by a charity, which also provided basic sustenance in the form of hunks of bread and dripping.

He spent two years teaching, first as a pupil-teacher then as an uncertified elementary teacher. During that time he developed considerable respect for the boys. He may not have taught them much, he admitted, 'but I learned a lot about the kind of life too many people had to live then in the back streets of an industrial city. At the same time, to have a respect for so many who struggled so hard to be honest and decent through it all. These boys were rough and tough; they knew more about the crude facts of hard life, of sex, disease, drunkenness and petty crime than I did. They daily suffered hardships and deprivations I had never felt. Their enemies to be feared, evaded and outwitted were, generally speaking, rent collectors, school attendance officers, police and sometimes a heavy-handed, not-too-sober parent. Yet these boys, all in all, were cheerful, manly fellows, enduring stoically and taking punishment without whimpering. They had an immensely attractive gamine [sic] humour and a quick-wittedness that was more than a match for me. Loyal to their own standards and their comrades, generous in thought and action to those they accepted, and, when under difficulties, good sons, especially to their mothers.'[5]

It was an experience and education which was instrumental in contributing, later in his life, to the famous rapport he had with his soldiers. Bill understood ordinary people and their problems in a way that conventionally educated officers could not – the rarefied environment of public school and Sandhurst provided few insights into the lives and mores of the working class.

However, two years' teaching was enough to convince him he had no wish to make it his career and in 1912, after some searching, he found a job, for 30s. a week, as a junior invoice clerk in the offices of Stewarts & Lloyds, a steel tube manufacturer, at the corner of Broad Street and Suffolk Street. 'I broke loose,' was how he put it rather grandly, 'and entered industry.' Stewarts & Lloyds had been created only a few years earlier by the amalgamation of two of Britain's biggest iron and steelmakers. The work was less challenging, the hours were longer, the holidays shorter and the pay not much better, but he liked the people he worked with and made two close friends – D. A. O. Mackenzie, a public schoolboy who had worked as a ranch-hand in the United States, and S. H. Lane, a grammar school boy and a brilliant artist who could draw recognisable caricatures Bill thought were quite as good as those of Bernard Partridge, the chief cartoonist at *Punch* magazine.

The three friends liked to go camping in the Clent Hills, 400 acres of forest and heathland to the south-west of Birmingham and less than ten miles from the city centre. After they had finished work at lunchtime on Saturday they would rush home, gather together their camping gear, which included a second-hand army bell tent, and head off on bicycles along dusty roads which led to their camp-site, which they called 'Sinking Can' because they spent much of their time shooting at tin cans floating down a stream. Bill recalled they possessed between them a Colt .45 revolver, an automatic pistol and a .22 rifle and not a single gun licence.

In the winter they all played rugby and attempted to keep fit by attending training sessions in a local community hall where they ran up and down for hours passing a rugby ball from one to another. At the end of the session they stripped off and hosed each other down. Neither Bill nor his friends were much interested in politics, but when they heard that there was a Communist meeting being held in the Town Hall they took the trouble to turn up for no other purpose than to heckle loudly, until the stewards threw them out.

Around the time he started at Stewarts & Lloyds, Bill joined Birmingham University Officers Training Corps. It is generally as-sumed that his brother Charles, who was by then a medical student at the university, somehow pulled strings to get Bill in, but in fact members of Junior OTCs, as at King Edward's School, were allowed to join University OTCs even if they were not undergraduates.

Never was there a more enthusiastic recruit. He attended every parade and all the weekend and annual camps, he practised rifle drill in his bedroom and spent his precious holidays in barracks at the depots of the Royal Warwickshire Regiment or the Worcestershire Regiment. 'I enjoyed the OTC immensely,' he wrote. 'Once or twice a week, as soon as the day's work was done, I would seize my rifle, strap on a leather belt and bayonet and rush down to the Territorial drill hall as soon as the day's work was done to absorb whatever instruction was going. My favourite reading now became *Field Service* and *Musketry Regulations*, all excellent pocket sized manuals.'

His favourite reading also got him into trouble at work, accord-ing to Jim Alford, who worked alongside him in the invoice office at Stewarts & Lloyds. 'Slim and I sat side by side on stools at high desks, with the manager at a table lower down. Invoices had to be written out by hand in indelible ink. I remember Slim was never without his little book of military tactics and exercises. He was en-grossed in it. Once he turned to me and said, "Can you explain this infantry manoeuvre? I would have done it differently." The manager lost his temper and said, "Put that book away and get on." Slim at once apologised and typically saw that he never got caught doing it again.'[6]

Alford recalled that Bill was a lance corporal in the OTC by then, although he was soon to lose his stripe. During a summer camp in Yorkshire, on a blisteringly hot day, he was on a 20-mile route march with his platoon. As they tramped along a dusty lane a woman emerged from her cottage and stood at her garden gate with a jug of beer which she held out to the passing soldiers. Bill, who passed closest to her, succumbed to the temptation. 'I can see her yet,' he wrote years later. 'She was a beautiful old lady with her hair neatly parted in the middle and wearing a black print dress. In her hand she held a beautiful jug, and on the top of that jug was a beautiful foam, indicating that it contained beer. She was offering it to the soldier boys.'

Unfortunately for Bill, as he grabbed the jug the commanding officer, who was riding a horse at the head of the column, turned round and saw him. Apoplectic with rage for what he obviously considered a severe breach of military discipline and good order, he gave Bill a public dressing down, warned him that had they been at war he would have been shot, and relieved him of his stripe on the spot. Bill, unabashed, thought he was a 'damned old fool' – although he wisely kept his opinion to himself.

Bill's single stripe was soon reinstated but his career as a part-time soldier continued to have its ups and downs. Being tested for a proficiency certificate he somehow contrived, while drilling a squad, to manoeuvre the rear rank into a position where the front rank should have been. 'That's not very good, is it?' drawled the examining officer with considerable understatement. Bill looked so crestfallen that the officer took pity on him and said that if he could march his squad to the other end of the parade ground and bellow an order they could hear from where he stood, he would be given a pass. Bill recalled that he got his squad to execute a swift about turn just before they marched straight into a brick wall.

He savoured the homespun military philosophy of senior NCOs and loved to tell a story about how he was poring over The Principles of War in the *Field Service Regulations* when a sergeant major came up to him and, after surveying him with kindly amusement, said: 'Don't bother your head about all those things, me lad. There's only one principle of war and that's this: hit the other fellow as quick as you can and as hard as you can, where it hurts him most and when he ain't lookin'.'[7]

In the archives of King Edward's School there is a photograph of Bill taken at the Birmingham University OTC summer camp in 1912 and captioned by an unknown hand as 'Slim's Lambs'. With five other young blades he is posing in front of a bell tent at an un-identified site. Perhaps they had not yet been issued with uniforms because all of them are dressed in smart suits, with stiff collars and ties, and all have their hair parted neatly and slicked down in the fashion of the day. Bill, in the centre of the group, is instantly recognisable from the shadow cast by his famously pugnacious chin. He was only 21 years old at the time, probably around the same age as his companions, but by today's standards they all look at least ten years older.

Although his responsibilities as a junior clerk were dreary, Bill enjoyed it when he had to visit the steelworks and he developed a similar affinity with the workers that he had had with the boys at Steward Street School. 'The Black Country iron worker was a tough chap, a grown-up edition of the boys I had tried to teach. He had the same solidarity with his mates, shown increasingly through his trade unions; he was cheerful, humorous and worked for long hours at heavy physical labour. Maybe, he gambled a little too much, drank a little too much, and was sometimes a little too ready with his fists, but he and his fellow, the miner, were the salt of the earth. Those men were tolerant, even kind, to an interloper like me.'[8]

Bill was deeply impressed by their skill and stoicism and left a droll description of one of them – 'Billy the Bulger' – in his unpublished memoir: 'A grizzled man of over 50 who, in a disreputable morning coat without collar or tie, but sporting a bowler hat – the badge of superior status – [he] stood beside the press where boiler tubes had the bulge put in one end. There he would stand, hour after hour, in the heat and thunder of the mill, a warning finger upraised, his eye fixed on the glowing end of the tube. Suddenly the finger would fall and instantly with a bang the tube would crash into the press at the exact temperature to take the bulge without splitting. There was oatmeal water for the men to quench their thirst but at intervals a boy carrying a notched stick from which hung cans of beer would approach Billy. The great man would lift a can and, pausing for an instant, refresh himself.' Bill noted that both the boy and the beer came from a nearby pub with the convivial advice that customers who brought their own dinners would be 'supplied with pickles free'. He thought it was probably a good ploy as pickles were likely to encourage a 'raging thirst'.

From the start of his time with Birmingham University OTC, Bill entertained a vague notion of a career in the army which, he admitted, 'nagged' at him. He had discussed it with his father who was implacably opposed to the idea, and advised him to give it up and concentrate on a career in commerce. John Slim's simple ambition for both his sons was that they would grow up to be 'English gentlemen'. When Bill asked his father to explain exactly what an English gentleman was, Slim responded with an uncomplicated definition. 'An English gentleman,' he said, 'is someone who pays up, owns up and shuts up.' Bill never forgot it.

Bill thought he could probably overcome his father's opposition to his embarking on a military career, but a much more insurmountable hurdle remained. Although he was a member of an 'Officers' Training Corps' the chance of his becoming an officer in the British Army was in reality no more than a distant dream. The fees required to attend the Royal Military College at Sandhurst – £150 per annum for the sons of civilians – were quite out of reach for a family like the Slims, not to mention the need for a private income of at least £100 a year once he had been commissioned. (In the more fashionable regiments around £400 a year was required.)

With the prospect of an army career thus curtailed, Bill began casting about for a job that might provide more excitement than sitting on a high stool writing out invoices. He had been promised an overseas posting with Stewarts & Lloyds – in fact his friend Mackenzie had already left for South Africa – but had recently been told he would have to wait until business improved. Meanwhile, he looked around for other opportunities and met a young man who had recently been hired by the Asiatic Petroleum Company, a subsidiary of Shell, and was waiting to be sent out to the Far East. He told Bill that the company was looking to employ more trainees to work abroad.

Although the young man was both a graduate and had personal introductions to senior personnel, Bill, who was not lacking in self-confidence, saw no reason why he should not apply himself. He approached it like a military operation, spending time on reconnaissance into the company, learning everything he could about Asiatic Petroleum from his new friend, reference books and annual reports. Then, armed with the name of the executive who had employed his friend, he bought a day excursion railway ticket to London and made his way to the company's head office, in St Helen's Court, off the Strand. He had no appointment, but his plan was to mount a full frontal attack – simply to knock on the door of the executive whose name he had been given and ask for a job.

Before approaching the office he found a quiet corner and surreptitiously dusted his shoes with his handkerchief. The first obstacle was a uniformed commissionaire in the lobby but he managed to talk his way into the building and hoped that by wandering the corridors he would find the name he was looking for on a door. None of the doors had names. Eventually he heard the clack of typewriters behind a half-open door and pushed it ajar to find himself the object of intense curiosity from the entire typing pool. He swallowed hard and asked the nearest girl if she could tell him where to find Mr X (in his memoirs he never mentioned the man's name). When he confessed he did not have an appointment she warned him that there was no question of his being admitted into the hallowed presence of the executive without one.

But Bill persisted and the girl eventually agreed, with considerable reluctance, to take him to see the great man's secretary, a Miss Smith. Miss Smith was aloof and appeared incredulous that Bill could even think it might be possible to get an interview without an appointment. All she could suggest was that he wrote in, stating his business. 'By the way,' she said, 'what is your business?' 'I want to ask him for a job,' Bill replied.

Bill reported the ensuing exchange with the indignant Miss Smith in his memoirs:

'"You can't walk in off the street like this and ask him for a job. If I let you in he'd throw you out."

'"Oh, have a heart. Just ask if he'll see me. It won't take a minute for him to throw me out, anyway. Please do."

'A glint of amusement came into Miss Smith's eye and turned to a definite and attractive smile.

'"Well, you've got a nerve, at any rate." She paused a moment. "All right, I'll ask him, but," resuming her air of severity, "it'll be no use."

'She disappeared through a door into the holy of holies, to emerge again in a few moments. "He'll see you," she announced, clearly surprised.'[9]

Some time later, Bill emerged, slightly dazed, from the offices of the Asiatic Petroleum Company with the firm offer of a job. He was to start on 1 September 1914. He never did.

From the time he was small boy and his father read aloud reports from correspondents covering the war in South Africa, Bill had always taken the trouble to keep abreast of national and international news. In 1914 the newspapers were full of the troubles in Ireland, the suffragette movement and increasing tension between the great powers in Europe. With Britain and Germany locked into an arms race, shifting international alliances and continuing trouble in the Balkans, there were doom-laden predictions that war was inevitable. Bill's father gloomily prophesied that Britain and Germany were on a collision course and reluctantly admitted it was probably a good idea that his younger son was getting some military experience in the OTC.

In July, despite the growing crisis and the assassination of Archduke Franz Ferdinand in Sarajevo in late June, Bill decided to spend his annual two-week holiday visiting Germany. He made no bones about the fact that he wanted to take a look at the army he assumed Britain would soon be fighting and chose as his destination the historic garrison city of Metz, which had been ceded to Germany after the Franco-Prussian War. (It was returned to France under the Treaty of Versailles after the First World War.) He almost certainly sought advice from his mother, who knew Germany well – before she was married she had worked in Germany as a lady-in-waiting to a German aristocrat. Travelling alone by boat and train, it was his first trip abroad. He could not speak a word of German but with the confidence of youth on his side he was undaunted, arrived safely and found a modest hotel within his even more modest budget.

For the first few days he wandered around looking at everything. Each morning he made a point of joining the small crowd which gathered to watch the changing of the guard at the Kommandantur. He greatly admired their uniforms – black boots, white breeches, blue tunics and shining Pickelhaube helmets. At nights the streets were full of soldiers who were generally smart and well behaved, but it was the officers, 'fine looking fellows' with their swords and gloves and faultlessly cut greatcoats, who really impressed him. At the barracks, with his face pressed against the railings, he found he had a good view of the goose-stepping drill parades. The troops, he thought, seemed well-disciplined, well-trained and well-equipped. He was curious about everything and when he found an open gate unguarded by a sentry he just walked in, unsure of quite what he thought he was going to do. He got as far as the entrance to a barrack block before he was spotted by an enormous red-faced NCO who started shouting at him in German and waving his arms, which Bill wisely took as an invitation to leave.

One morning, to his surprise, the guard at the Kommandantur turned out wearing field service grey uniforms with knapsacks and covers over their helmets. He could not find anyone to ask what was happening but he was aware of much more activity in the town, with horse transport and troops, all, like the guard, in field service grey, moving through the streets. Back at his hotel he met another English guest, a seedy looking little man who said he was a jockey and had been riding in a horse race in Germany. Over a drink his new friend told him he believed that war between Serbia and Austria was only hours away, if it had not already broken out; he was planning to get out of Germany as quickly as possible and advised Bill to do the same.

Next morning Bill left by train for Brussels, where he stayed a couple more days trying to find out what was going on. The few English newspapers available were all out of date, but there was similar troop activity evident everywhere, including, he noticed, ammunition carts drawn by dogs. It was obviously not sensible for him to linger, so he headed for Ostend and caught the first available cross-Channel steamer. The ship was crowded with people

– businessmen, tourists and expatriate families – all desperately trying to get home to Britain before the balloon went up.

Bill confessed to a moment of depression after having observed the German army at close quarters. It looked, he thought, very formidable indeed and he doubted if any army in Europe could stand up to it. His spirits revived, however, when a British destroyer hove into view halfway across the Channel and circled their ship, its white ensign fluttering proudly from the stern.

Back home in Birmingham, Bill found orders waiting for him to report to his OTC camp on Salisbury Plain. Pausing only to change into his uniform, he rushed off to Salisbury by train. He got to the camp just in time to learn that his unit had been instructed to return to Birmingham and await further orders. Arriving back at Snow Hill station, Bill and two others were put in charge of transporting the ammunition safely back to the Drill Hall. It was, he recalled, his first independent command. With war looming, Bill reckoned that military requirements were likely to get top priority. Relying on his uniform and the authority of a single stripe on his arm, he demanded transport from the stationmaster and was instantly provided with a hand trolley and three porters to push it. 'Bayonets fixed, marching to attention, terribly conscious of our importance, the porters pushing and pulling, we escorted the ammunition through the main street of the city. If we did not arouse the admiration of the passers-by, we did at least gain their startled attention. Anyway, I got quite a kick out of my first independent command.'[10]

On 3 August 1914, Germany declared war on France and German troops poured over the border into Belgium. The British Foreign Secretary, Sir Edward Grey, sent an ultimatum to Germany demanding their withdrawal. When there was no response, Britain declared war on Germany on the following day.

For Bill Slim, and hundreds like him, what was to be known as the Great War provided an opportunity to obtain what was formerly unattainable – a commission in the British Army. It was also an opportunity to escape the humdrum life of a clerk in an office. On 22 August 1914, William Slim was gazetted as a temporary second lieutenant in the Royal Warwickshire Regiment.

'When war came our feelings were simple,' he wrote. 'We thought little of high ideals and lofty patriotism, or indeed of what might be in store for us; our country was at war and we took it for granted that we ought to get into the fighting as soon as we could. The war seemed rather like a supremely important football match in which individually we had, by hook or by crook, to get a place in the team. Our only fear was that it might be all over before we got to it.'[11]

3

A First Taste of War

The auguries for a successful military career were not good when newly commissioned Temporary Second Lieutenant William Joseph Slim, number 8709, reported for duty with the 9th (Service) Battalion, The Royal Warwickshire Regiment, at Kandahar Barracks in Tidworth, on the edge of Salisbury Plain, in September 1914. He knocked nervously on the door of the orderly room and almost collided with the assistant adjutant, who was bustling out. The assistant adjutant looked him up and down with considerable distaste and snapped: 'You're improperly dressed.'

Bill was mystified: he had spent hours proudly checking his new uniform. It was clear to the other man that this fledgling young officer had no idea what he was talking about. 'Your whistle cord,' he sneered, as if talking to an imbecile, 'is on the wrong shoulder.' He was right. Mortified, Bill quickly swapped it to the correct shoulder there and then before presenting himself to the adjutant.

His troubles were far from over. A few days later he was walking towards the parade ground and acknowledged the salute of a passing private soldier with no more than a languorous wave of his hand, an affectation that might have been acceptable in the Guards or the cavalry but was certainly not in an infantry regiment. Unfortunately he was observed not only by his commanding officer but by the regimental sergeant major, both of whom (especially the latter) he held in considerable awe.

'Mr Slim,' the Colonel called. Bill turned to face them, his heart in his mouth. 'I see you don't know how to return a salute,' the Colonel continued coldly. 'Sergeant Major, plant your staff in the ground and let Mr Slim practise saluting it until he learns.'

Bill was obliged to spend the next ten minutes marching up and down the parade ground, in full view of the rest of the battalion, throwing up a smart salute each time he passed the RSM's wooden staff. It was a humiliation he would never forget, particularly since it was carried out in front of his grinning fellow subalterns, whom he confessed he could have cheerfully murdered. At the end of his ordeal the Colonel said to him: 'Now remember, Mr Slim, discipline begins with the officers.' Bill, puce with embarrassment, nodded and was dismissed. It was perhaps because of this incident that Bill's choleric company commander routinely referred to him thereafter as 'that damned fool Slim'.

Not long after that, his platoon mutinied. He was sitting in the officers' mess enjoying a cup of tea at the end of the afternoon parade when he was told the orderly corporal wanted to see him urgently. He went out into the lobby and found a very agitated soldier bearing the news that the men in his platoon had barricaded themselves into their barrack room and would neither emerge nor go on duty. Assuming a calmness he certainly did not feel, Bill strapped on his Sam Browne belt and sword – an act which helped steady his nerves – and followed the corporal to the barrack room. On the way he could not help but reflect on the fact that throughout his training in the OTC no one had ever mentioned what to do in the face of a mutiny.

When he arrived he found a small knot of NCOs standing outside the barrack room, the door to which was firmly shut. No one seemed to have any idea what to do. The problem, he was told, was something to do with pay. Most of the men in his platoon were Black Country miners accustomed to going on strike to resolve their grievances. It was the only effective protest they knew; never mind the fact that they were now in the army, and subject to rigid military discipline, they believed they had been defrauded by the army and so had simply gone on strike, regardless of the consequences.

It was a realisation that offered Bill some small comfort. He knew about working men from his time at Stewarts & Lloyds – in fact there had been a strike while he was there – and suddenly felt more able to deal with the crisis. Talking to them through the door, he eventually persuaded them to let him in after he had given his word he would be alone and that no one would try to force an entrance while he was being admitted. He could hear the scrape of beds being drawn back and the door opened just wide enough to allow him to squeeze through.

Once inside, he sat on the edge of a bed, surrounded by a ring of angry faces, while everyone talked at once. When he at last persuaded one of them to put their case while the others remained quiet, it emerged that there was considerable confusion about their pay. They knew, and understood, that they would be earning less than they had as miners, but what they were receiving, after family allotments and compulsory deductions, was derisory. Their conclusion was that they were being cheated and so they had done what they would have done in civilian life – they had withheld their labour.

Bill was sympathetic and aware that many of them did not understand the system of family allotments. He offered, starting first thing the following morning, to sit down with each man individually and go through his pay account, explain where the money was going, make any changes that were needed and correct any errors. On this basis they grudgingly agreed to remove the barricade on the door and return to duty.

'I was congratulating myself on my skill as a conciliator,' Bill wrote later, 'when I was confronted by a demand which my industrial experience should have made me expect – there must be no victimisation. I must promise that no one would be punished. This was a fast one. I had little more familiarity with Military Law than they had, but I did realise that a temporary second lieutenant was in no position to make promises condoning a mutiny.'[1] On this point he dug in his heels and refused to go further than to say that if they returned to duty at once and thereafter behaved sensibly he would do his level best to ensure that no one was punished. With this they had to be satisfied.

Back outside, he discovered that the orderly officer and the regimental sergeant major had been called to the scene. He quickly explained what had happened and somehow got their consent to forget the whole thing. They agreed that if it got to the ears of the commanding officer it was to be presented as a little misunderstanding over pay that the platoon commander had sorted out. Bill worked with the pay clerks for the next three days to resolve the problems to everyone's satisfaction and nothing more was heard of the 'mutiny'.

The incident was an early example of Bill's natural skill at handling men, although in truth in those very early days of the war there was a willingness to forgive raw recruits unaccustomed to the ways of the military, particularly for the elite K1 men (the first 100,000 to enlist were known as Kitchener's First Army, abbreviated to K1). The 9th Battalion, Royal Warwickshires, was a K1 Battalion and intensely proud of the fact. No politician or soldier could boast a hold on the nation's affection rivalling that of Lord Kitchener of Khartoum, then the Secretary of State for War, whose face and accusing pointing finger appeared on thousands of recruitment posters around the country bearing the legend 'Your Country Needs You'. K1 men felt a strong identification with him which bound them together, never mind the fact that they came from all parts of the country, from the 'top drawer' to the working class, and from every conceivable occupation.

Bill had first met his platoon in a bunker on Tidworth Golf Course, where they had been assembled to be introduced to their new platoon commander. They were undoubtedly as curious about him as he was about them: neither was impressed. It was impossible for Bill to conceal – even had he wanted to do so – that he was a novice, a 23-year-old amateur and part-time soldier, a former teacher and clerk with no experience of war who was going to lead them into battle come what may.

For Bill's part, he looked at the raggle-taggle group of men in front of him and wondered how on earth he would ever be able to mould them into a disciplined fighting unit. There were some 70 of them and a more unprepossessing lot would be hard to imagine. Only two had been issued with uniforms; the remainder mainly wore working clothes. A few were in their best suits with bowlers or straw boaters, but cloth caps of every shade and shape predominated, although Bill did notice one man wearing a panama. They were drawn almost entirely from Birmingham and the Black Country, a few farmhands and office workers, but mainly from the heavy industries – iron, coal and steel – the kind of tough, self-confident, resilient men he had got to know at Stewarts & Lloyds. By far the largest contingent were miners who, Bill quickly learned, bore many of the qualities required of a soldier – courage, loyalty, comradeship and a familiarity with danger, fatigue and hardship.

During the months of training that followed, they got to know – and to like, or at least respect – each other. Bill, who had a Birmingham accent himself, would lampoon the laconic backchat between his men – "E ain't polite enough to come from the South; he ain't honest enough to come from the North; 'e must 'ave come from Bermigum.' But it was not long before he could say, with hand on heart: 'I would not have changed them for any platoon in the British, or any other, army.'[2]

Naturally they were all anxious to get into action – they had enlisted to fight, hadn't they? – but Christmas came and went with no sign of them going to war. On 1 February 1915 Bill was promoted to temporary lieutenant, a promotion he would happily have forgone in return for orders to proceed to the front. The first indication that, at last, they would soon be on the move came when they were suddenly issued with drill uniforms and sun helmets and the entire battalion was inoculated with, Bill noted, 'a syringe like a football pump'. Their ultimate destination was the subject of much speculation and rumour but in the end it was decided it was almost certain to be Gallipoli, where a combined force of British, Australian and New Zealand troops was engaged in fierce fighting against the Turks.

On a warm summer evening in June at Blackdown, near Aldershot, the entire battalion paraded in its new equipment and in the gathering dusk the men stood silent as the commanding officer, Lieutenant Colonel C. H. Palmer, recited the Lord's Prayer. They then marched off to Frimley railway station and entrained for the port of Avonmouth, where the troopship *Royal Edward* was getting up steam. As expected, after departure it headed south and then east, through the Strait of Gibraltar into the Mediterranean, while on board bets were taken about their final destination.

During a brief refuelling stop in Malta, Bill found time, on 2 July, to scribble a postcard to his school friend Philip Pratt: 'Dear Phil, Put in here for water. Leave for unknown destination (supposed to be the Isle of Blank) in twenty minutes or so. Uneventful voyage so far. This is beginning to look a little more like business. Bill.'[3]

Business of a sort. The disastrous Gallipoli campaign had been launched in February 1915, to relieve pressure on the Western Front and open a secure maritime supply route to Russia by 'forcing' the Dardanelles, a narrow strait in what is now Turkey connecting the Aegean to the Sea of Marmara and thence to the Black Sea via the Bosphorus. It began with a massive naval bombardment of Turkish forts on the Gallipoli peninsula to the north-west of the Dardanelles. A task force of 18 British and French battleships, with supporting cruisers, destroyers and minesweepers, was assembled for the operation and the main attack was launched on 18 March. Victory was assumed to be inevitable and it was anticipated that the fleet would be in Constantinople within 14 days.

Everything went badly wrong from the start. The strength of the Turkish forces in Gallipoli had been grossly underestimated and the minesweepers were beaten back by sustained fire from the forts on-shore before they could clear the minefields. A French battleship, the *Bouvet*, hit a mine and capsized. Two British battleships HMS *Irresistible* and HMS *Inflexible* both sustained critical damage and HMS *Ocean*, sent to rescue *Irresistible*, was herself struck and both ships eventually sank. The fleet retreated in disarray at a moment when, it later transpired, the Turkish gunners were about to run out of ammunition.

After the failure of the naval attacks, it was determined that ground troops would be required to force the Dardenelles. While the Mediterranean Expeditionary Force, comprising Australian, New Zealand, British and French troops, was being formed, Turkish commanders used the time to prepare defences and bring up reinforcements. Landings began on 25 April on beaches all round the Gallipoli peninsula against fierce resistance. After weeks of savage fighting and heavy casualties on both sides little progress had been made, and most of the invasion force remained on, or close to, the beaches on which they had landed. So many bodies were lying in no-man's-land between the two sides that on 24 May a truce was organised to bury the dead.

In London on 9 June, with the encouragement of Lord Kitchener, the Cabinet authorised sending to Gallipoli three further divisions. One of them was 13th (Western) Division, which included 39 Brigade. The 9th Battalion, The Royal Warwickshire Regiment, was part of 39 Brigade.

The brigade arrived at the Greek island of Lemnos on 9 July and four days later the 9th Royal Warwicks landed in Gallipoli and relieved the Worcesters in the trenches at Cape Helles, where some of the fiercest fighting had taken place. Allied casualties in the previous six weeks had totalled more than 17,000 men dead, wounded or missing, and no more than 500 yards of ground had been won. The Turks were thought to have lost 40,000 men.

Cape Helles, on the southern tip of the Gallipoli peninsula, looked, one veteran wrote, 'like a midden and smelt like an opened cemetery'.[4] The stench of death from unburied rotting corpses was everywhere, the trenches swarmed with bloated flies, sanitation was primitive and the scorching sun was unrelenting; the men, covered with lice, existed on a diet of hard-tack biscuits and bully beef which turned into slime in the heat. As soon as food appeared it was covered with flies, which made it even less appetising, if that was possible.

In addition, there was the enemy, almost on top of them. 'We and the enemy had been so near together,' Bill wrote later in his memoirs, 'that in places we held one part, he another, of the same trench, with a block between us, over which we lobbed our improvised jam-tin – literally jam-tin – bombs and got in return his more sophisticated German cricket-ball and stick grenades. Indeed we did not exaggerate too wildly when we sometimes wryly said we shared the same parapet with the Turk and took turns with him at the loopholes.'[5]

Bill developed a high regard for the courage of the Turkish soldiers and in preparation for hand-to-hand fighting he equipped himself with a large knife, a sawn-off shotgun and a .45 revolver, in addition to his rifle and bayonet. His batman followed him about carrying a large bag of Mills bombs.[6]

During a short break from the line, something happened which cemented Bill's reputation with his men as an outstanding platoon commander. His platoon had withdrawn for a rest to the beach, where they managed to find a single patch of shade under a large rock. The men were utterly exhausted and most of them flung themselves down on the sand and fell asleep, disregarding the fire from Turkish artillery. Bill did not immediately join them but stood in the sun watching the fall of shells from a distant gun. Each explosion was closer than the last on a line heading directly towards them. He quickly calculated the distance between each shell and decided there was a strong possibility shortly that a shell would explode in the midst of his men. He knew how tired they were and how badly they needed to rest and how fortunate they were to have found some shade, but he did not hesitate. Alerting his senior NCO, they set about waking them and getting them to move.

'There was almost a mutiny. Worn out after their long spell in the trenches and heavy with sleep, the men could not be made to realise the need for movement and resented being driven from the only shady spot they had seen for many days. But by dint of persuasion and hard swearing it was achieved at last. The men squatted glumly in the open, sweating profusely and cursing all meddlesome officers with bees in their bonnets while, amid much rejoicing and deaf to all warnings, another platoon from their sister regiment dropped down in their place and were asleep in a moment. In due course the fourth shell arrived and a number of that unlucky platoon never woke again.'[7] None of his men had any more complaints about being made to sit in the sun.

On 29 July the 9th Warwicks were pulled out of the line and shipped back to Lemnos, where they were told to ready themselves for the next big phase of the operation – an attempt to break out of the bridgehead and link up with another landing further to the north. By then they had lost, killed or wounded, 37 men. Among the dead was the CO, Lieutenant Colonel Palmer, who had raised and trained the battalion and who had led them in a recitation of the Lord's Prayer before they left Britain. He had been felled by a sniper's bullet through the head four days earlier.

The troopship SS *Aragon* was moored off Lemnos and was acting as lines of communication HQ. Soon after they arrived, Bill was instructed to go out to the *Aragon*, primarily to collect the unit's mail but secondarily to obtain authority and money to buy eggs, fruit, goats and chickens to supplement the men's rations. It took him some time to find a boat that would ferry him out to the ship and when he did he was confronted with a notice attached to the rails: 'No visiting officers or other ranks will be permitted to board unless they are on duty and wearing correct uniform with jackets and badges of rank'. Bill did not have a jacket, but he managed to borrow one and got on board. He was immediately struck by the contrast between life on board the *Aragon*, where officers lounging in deckchairs were being served pre-lunch drinks with ice (an unheard of luxury), and the wretched plight of his own men, most of whom by then were suffering from various stomach complaints.

No one seemed particularly interested in helping him. 'I got the impression,' he wrote, 'that visitors from the fighting troops, especially those who interfered with the pleasant tenor of staff life, were not really welcome.'[8] By sheer persistence, he finally managed to find the mail and get authority to buy extra rations. On board a water barge on the way back to the harbour, he was reminded of a story circulating in the trenches that the *Aragon* had run aground on the empty gin bottles tossed overboard. It was a lesson he would not forget: staff officers under his command later in his career were left in no doubt that their primary function was to serve the fighting troops.

In early August 20,000 men, including the 9th Warwicks, were ferried on successive nights to a beachhead on the Gallipoli peninsula where they hid in caves and trenches before a planned offensive to capture and secure the Sari Bair Ridge, which dominated the coastal plain and was strongly held by the Turks. The ground between the sea and the crest of the ridge, mainly rock, shale and scrub thorn, was corrugated with deep gullies and ravines in which, as events were to prove, it was easy to get lost.

The 9th Warwicks were part of an assaulting column charged with taking a feature known as Hill Q. Before midnight on 6 August, the troops began moving out of the bridgehead towards their objectives. For three successive nights and two days, with not much food and less water, the 9th Warwicks struggled up and down the ravines and ridges leading to Hill Q. Often lost and obliged to retrace their steps, exhausted in the ferocious heat of the day, and always under persistent Turkish fire, the battalion took heavy casualties and Bill was obliged to assume command of his company when all the more senior officers had been killed or wounded.

By the evening of 8 August, Bill and about 50 remaining men of his company were occupying a cramped and dangerous position on the left of the 1st/6th Gurkha Rifles, led by Major Cecil Allason, who by dint of great skill, courage and enterprise had got to within 200 yards of the summit of Hill Q. Bill had watched their ascent with increasing admiration and under cover of darkness led his men to join them. He shared a dirty packet of raisins with Allason, discussed the situation and agreed that the following morning they should act together as far as possible as a single unit. (Bill was so impressed by the 1st/6th Gurkha Rifles at Gallipoli, their dauntless courage and cheerfulness in circumstances of extreme peril, that he was delighted to join them after the war.)

The advance was due to resume at 0630 next morning. In the early morning light Bill could see his company spread out along the edge of a dry river bed, their grey, weary faces turned towards him as they waited for his whistle. 'I counted the last seconds on my wrist watch and blew my whistle. We clambered out and began to plod very slowly up the scrub-covered spur before us. We were too weary and the slope too steep for speed; even the bullets that began to crack over us before we had advanced many yards could not make us move faster. This fire came mostly from our left and I thought if we inclined more to our right we might, as we went forward, find some shelter behind the spine of our spur. I pushed through the first two lines in which we were moving and turned round to signal the new direction. At that moment someone hit me hard between the shoulders with a huge, flat shovel ...' He had been shot through the chest, the bullet missing his heart by inches.

'The blow pitched me heavily on my face, but after a dazed moment I managed to sit up. I felt no pain and was surprised to see blood spurting from the point of my left shoulder and already spreading in a dark, damp patch over my jacket ... I sat there wonderingly for a second and then Gregson, one of my two surviving officers, was kneeling beside me. The firing was heavier now, clapping just over our heads, and as Gregson leant towards me to speak, he suddenly slumped forward across my feet.'[9] Gregson was dead.

The last remaining officer in the company arrived with the second wave and Bill had enough strength to tell him he was now in command. Bill's batman, Private Greenway, a footman in civilian life, was quickly by his side. 'May I take your equipment, sir?' he asked politely, rather as if he was offering to relieve a visitor to his master's house of his hat and umbrella. Bill nodded and tried to help him but was surprised to find he could not move his left arm.

Greenway was a small, slight man with a very pale face and big eyes who suffered from epileptic fits which he thought his platoon commander knew nothing about (Bill did, but said nothing). He almost certainly saved Bill's life. First he put a field dressing on the wound, then pulled Bill to his feet and half carried him down the steep slope towards a Regimental Aid Post. Bill was spitting blood and several times insisted he could not continue, but Greenway refused to leave him and eventually got him to the post where a doctor stripped the muslin from Bill's topee and used it to bandage him. Greenway did not wait to see what happened to his officer. He gave Bill a rifle-butt salute and staggered back up the hill – to his death.

Several months later an account of the action was published in the *Warwickshire Advertiser* under the by-line 'New Zealander': 'From my own observation I can testify to the imperishable renown which one regiment gained in our eyes during those days, and, as an old Birmingham man, I was proud to shake hands in the after days with the men of the 9th Royal Warwickshires. They had immense difficulties to overcome. They were led the wrong way and had to retrace their steps; they had to attack in full view of the enemy; their left was exposed to enfilading fire ... They held on like grim death; held on when first one and then another unit retired. They asked for reinforcements but were told none were available, and still they stayed ... With their ranks terribly thinned they came back as from parade, parched and hungry but still undaunted ... I saw a quiet-mannered orderly bring his officer [Slim] down the gully and heard the latter telling how his man had seen him fall on the hill and dashing up under heavy fire had carried and slid with him to safety. I saw the same poor fellow a few days later lying in the padre's dugout mortally wounded. Greenway was his name.'[10]

Bill passed out at the Regimental Aid Post and thus recalled nothing of being moved, under fire, to a Casualty Clearing Station. When he regained consciousness he was lying on a stretcher on the deck of barge, vomiting blood and fighting for breath. The barge had been run aground on the beach but was lifting rhythmically on the surf, a motion he did find unpleasant until a slightly larger wave dumped the barge on to the sand with a jarring thud that sent a searing stab of pain through his chest.

'The sun, low down, was shining straight into my eyes and cautiously, without moving my shoulders, and with dawning interest in my surroundings, I rolled my head slowly from side to side to find that I lay in the midst of other wounded men packed close together ... Sitting up on a stretcher touching mine and looking down on me was a lean sunburned man, stripped to the waist, whose right leg below the knee was held together splint-wise by two entrenching tool helves. He looked at me from wrinkled eyes beneath the battered brim of a wide Australian hat. "Poor bastard," he said to himself gently and then realising, I suppose for the first time, I was conscious, he added, "Feeling crook?"[11]

At dusk the barge was towed out to sea and moved from ship to ship, looking for one with space to take on more casualties. Most were already overloaded with the wounded but eventually a ship was found to take them and Bill was lifted on board in a sling. Drifting in and out of consciousness, he was first put under a table in the smoke room and then moved into the saloon, where the walking wounded occupied every chair and the floor was covered by stretchers. The heat of the night and stifling air in the saloon almost overwhelmed him and he became convinced for the first time that he was going to die. He knew he had been badly hit and had lost a great deal of blood but until that moment he had never thought of dying – he also knew he did not want to die down there in that fetid saloon where the smell of death was everywhere. He asked a steward if he could be carried up on to the deck and allowed to die in the fresh air. The steward obliged his first request but not his second.

Being up on deck as the ship ploughed through the night afforded him immediate relief but the steward decided he was not going to allow this young officer to die and literally talked him back into life, telling him sternly it was wrong to want to die and launching into a long story about how he had saved for years to buy a house to settle down in with his wife and when the time came she had died of a heart attack ... Bill was asleep long before the story finished.

Next morning the ship put into Lemnos harbour, where the RMS *Aquitania* was anchored. The *Aquitania* was a new Cunard liner which had been pressed into service at the outbreak of war as a troopship and subsequently converted into a temporary hospital ship. Along with all the other casualties Bill was transferred to the *Aquitania* by barge, and put in one of the luxurious public rooms that had been turned into a ward, with mattresses made up as beds on the floor. The only hitch was that when they tried to lift him off his stretcher the stretcher came too – he was stuck to the canvas by congealed blood. Cleaned up by the nurses, he slept in clean white sheets for the first time for weeks.

Under sedation through much of the voyage home, Bill remained critically ill and at one point was given the last rites by a Catholic priest on board. He was lying in a bed next to an Irishman, similarly critically wounded, and each expected the other to die in the night. His only diversion was a tattered copy of Kipling's *Kim*, which gave him his first taste of a country he would soon get to know extraordinarily well – India.

When the *Aquitania* docked at Southampton, lines of motor ambulances were waiting on the quayside along with dozens of women Red Cross volunteers ready to minister to the casualties as they were carried off the ship. Bill, lying on a stretcher on the quay, actually found the attention of these 'well meaning ladies' rather trying and wished they would go away. It was an effort to be polite, he explained, when refusing a cigarette or a cup of tea for the sixth or seventh time. He knew it was ungrateful, but he excused himself by explaining that he was 'not feeling too bright'.

At the 2,500-bed Royal Victoria Military Hospital at Netley, on the shores of Southampton Water, Bill was examined by a senior army doctor who, after scrutinising the rudimentary x-ray photographs of those days, announced to the two younger doctors in his entourage with considerable satisfaction that Bill was 'really good clinical material'. Bill, who was being held in a sitting position on his bed not without some discomfort, would have preferred a diagnosis that recognised him as a patient rather than 'clinical material' but the doctor, a colonel, appeared more interested in explaining Bill's injuries to the two other doctors than worrying about his patient's feelings: 'The left lung is completely collapsed, with lesions. The heart is displaced into the resulting cavity some three inches. It is evident from the track of the bullet and the area of local paralysis and insensitivity, that the bracheal plexus has suffered injury. The scapula is fractured and the head of the humerus is shattered.'[12]

When the 'clinical material' ventured to ask what the future held for him, in particular if he would be able to stay in the army, the colonel breezily replied: 'No, not a hope. You've finished with soldiering for good.' Bill was devastated. It was, he would write many years later, a 'morale shattering defeat' worse than anything he had ever suffered in battle.[13]

The colonel's advice was that Bill should undergo major surgery which would fuse his upper arm and shoulder. It might possibly allow him to raise his hand to his mouth, but it would almost certainly result in a medical discharge from the army. Fortunately a younger doctor, a Territorial acting without authorisation of any kind, came to see him later that evening and persuaded him to refuse to have the operation. His argument was that the operation would leave him physically disabled for the rest of his life; whereas without the operation he would be no worse off and perhaps stood a reasonable chance of getting back the use of his arm with new treatments, like therapy and massage, becoming available. Undoubtedly what swung the argument for Bill was the prospect, no matter how remote, of being able to stay in the army.

He was undoubtedly warned by the colonel of the dire consequences of refusing the operation but he stuck to his guns and slowly began to recover. On 26 August he was well enough to write to his friend Philip Pratt from the Sick Officers' Quarters, Netley: 'I suppose you heard I got pipped. It was a bit of a knockout – thro' the lung, smashed the left shoulder to blazes and bust the top of my arm. I couldn't breathe for a few days … We had some real war out there. I'm afraid there isn't much of the poor old regiment left. I was in command of the company when I was knocked over. Both Captains hit at the beginning of the battle. Anyhow I've seen a little of most kinds of fighting from trench mortars to aeroplane duels. I've lost every stitch of kit and don't suppose I shall ever see it again. More expense. I don't suppose a grateful country will do anything about it … Write as soon as you can. Yours, slightly damaged, Will. PS. I haven't told my Mother the wound is serious but I wrote Charlie a letter to the University Club. You might tell him in case he didn't get it. W.'[14]

He was not exaggerating when he wrote that there was not much of the regiment left: in four days of fighting during the abortive assault on Sari Bair all the officers of the 9th Royal Warwicks had been killed or wounded, 57 other ranks died, 227 were wounded and 117 listed as missing.

Bill's reference to the expense of replacing his kit was telling – he would be dogged by money worries for much of his life. Ten days later he wrote again to Pratt with good news: 'There seems little doubt I shall get back at least part of the use of the arm. They give me a terrific doings every morning – so far they have succeeded in getting my wrist to work as well as the hand and incidentally they have given me hell.' He did not tell his friend about an embarrassing little incident with a nurse a few days earlier when he was sitting in the garden of the hospital enjoying the sunshine. She stopped by him in her red cape to tuck a rug over his knees and as she bent over him he was suddenly and unwisely prompted to lean forward and kiss her lightly on the cheek. She was, he noted, 'young, fresh as the day, pretty as the garden'. If he thought his chutzpah might be re-warded, perhaps, with a shy smile, he was very much mistaken. The girl was furious, drew back immediately, glared at him and snapped, 'I don't like that.' She stalked off, leaving Bill, shame-faced, wonder-ing what on earth had motivated him do it.[15]

On 24 September Bill appeared before a medical board and was declared 'permanently disabled but fit for active service in three months', a verdict presumably comprehensible to the army, if no one else. The following week he was discharged from hospital and sent to London to recuperate at the home of Georgina, Countess of Dudley. Owners of large London houses anxious to do their bit for the war effort had agreed that they should be used as temporary con-valescent homes for wounded officers. Lady Dudley, a noted beauty in the Victorian era, offered to arrange for Bill to convalesce further at a sanatorium in Switzerland if required, but it was deemed not necessary by the War Office. While he was resident at Lady Dudley's he met an officer from the Black Watch and during a convivial night on the town the other man bet Bill he would not walk up the Strand in a kilt. Of course he did, and won a free dinner from the Scot.[16]

The August offensive in Gallipoli during which Bill had been wounded ended in failure and resulted in much criticism of the hand-ling of the campaign in the newspapers at home. Ellis Ashmead-Bartlett, a war correspondent for the *Daily Telegraph*, portrayed it as 'the most ghastly and costly fiasco in our history since the battle of Bannockburn'. Ashmead-Bartlett's dispatches are said to have con-tributed to the dismissal of General Sir Ian Hamilton, the British commander-in-chief in Gallipoli, after which Kitchener reluctantly decided to abandon Gallipoli and ordered the evacuation of all Allied troops. Nothing had been achieved and around 130,000 men (from all sides) had died.

Bill's battalion, the 9th Royal Warwicks, was among the last Allied troops to be evacuated. They were withdrawn on the night of 8/9 January 1916, first to Lemnos and then to Port Said in Egypt. The battalion was brought up to strength by drafts from England before being sent in February to Mesopotamia (modern-day Iraq, with parts of Syria, Turkey and Iran), where the forces of the Ottoman Empire had laid siege to the British garrison at Kut-al-Amara, 100 miles south of Baghdad.

In January 1916, Bill was assigned to 'light duty' – he had regained most of the use of his left arm – and posted, to his considerable displeasure, to the 12th (Holding) Battalion, The Royal Warwickshire Regiment, at Bovington in Dorset. 'I am most annoyed with the WO,' he wrote to Pratt on 2 February 1916. 'They have transferred me to this Battalion, strafe 'em, without consulting me in the least. I don't want to join this blank regiment. The old 9th was good enough for me ... The prospect of stopping here for the duration of the War fills me with gloom.' He added, with mock horror, that there were not only a number of officers in the battalion who would never go out and get killed but furthermore '*they did not even want to*'.[17]

On 18 February a medical board reported that he was 'not fit for service at present'. He was re-examined on 23 March and again declared 'unfit at present' with a recommendation he be seen again in three months. Kicking his heels in Bovington and fretting at being so far from the action, Bill began writing short stories and sending them to Philip Pratt for friendly criticism. It was evident in his letters to Pratt that he was already thinking of trying to market his literary efforts; or, rather, that he hoped Pratt could be persuaded to market them on his behalf as his unofficial agent. Pratt, too, was writing and sending his work to Bill for reciprocal assessment, although he seemed rather more ambitious since, in March 1916, he was apparently working on a film script – more than a decade before the first 'talkies' appeared on cinema screens.

The best thing to come out of Bill's frustrating posting to the 12th Battalion was a friendship with another young officer in the battalion, Lieutenant R. E. Barnwell. The two men often went out riding together in the Dorset countryside and in the course of conversation Barnwell casually mentioned that while he was serving in France he had heard the War Office was handing out regular commissions to temporary officers on a very limited basis. Barnwell himself had already applied; in fact, he had been told his name was shortly being forwarded to the Commander-in-Chief, Home Forces, who was allotted just two recommendations a month, and he was very hopeful he would be one of them.

It was the first Bill had heard of it. He had no idea what he was going to do after the war and the thought of being able to stay on in the army with a regular commission, despite his wound, was like a dream come true. The problem, he explained to Barnwell, was that he had no private means. 'Neither have I,' the other man replied, but he was hoping to be able to join a regiment that did not require its officers to be independently wealthy. Bill did not even know such regiments existed. Inspired by his new friend, he began to trawl through the more obscure and distant reaches of the regular army and learned that the West India Regiment was looking for officers.

Raised in 1795, the West India Regiment normally recruited in the Caribbean, although it was part of the British Army. What mainly interested Bill was the fact that officers in the regiment were said to be able to live on their pay. Thus it was that the West Indian Regiment would unwittingly provide the portal through which Bill Slim could realise his ambition to become a regular officer in the British Army. He applied to join and, on 1 June 1916, the *London Gazette* recorded that Lieutenant W. J. Slim had been formally commissioned into the West India Regiment. In reality, he would never serve with it.

In the meantime he had been roped in to conduct reinforcement drafts to France. The British Expeditionary Force, six divisions strong at the start of the war, had been virtually wiped out by the end of 1915 and in March 1916 the government had authorised conscription to make up the appalling losses being suffered in the trenches on the Western Front.

Not all conscripts were suffused with a desire to fight for their country. 'Dear Phil, I leave for France in three hours,' Bill wrote to his friend on 3 April 1916. 'Sounds awfully dramatic but it only amounts to this – I'm conducting a draft of 38 men to Etaples or somewhere. Not a very exciting job but a rather aggravating one as half the men aren't a bit keen on going and two at least I'm sure are going to try to cut in London when it's a bit difficult to shepherd them ... They are a pretty tough lot when the drink is in 'em, too, bless 'em.'[18]

When he returned from France, Bill was put in charge of training a company of about 120 conscripts, one of whom, an 'incorrigible rogue', tested his talent as a manager of men to the full. The man – Bill called him Richard Chuck but that may not have been his real name – claimed to have been a tramp in civilian life; he could hardly read or write and was greatly displeased at being conscripted. He was morose, insolent, insubordinate and so boneheaded that his platoon commander suggested he should perhaps be discharged as mentally deficient. Most officers would have given up on him and been glad to get rid of him, but not Bill. He was sure that Chuck was deliberately playing dumb to get out of the army. Bill made it clear to Chuck he knew what his game was and there developed between them a kind of mutual respect. While Chuck remained a rebel – he was later court-martialled for striking an NCO – he also became a fearless fighting man, an inspiration to his comrades on the battlefield and testimony to Bill's natural skill in handling men. (During a frontal assault on an enemy position in the face of devastating fire in Mesopotamia, Chuck rallied his faltering comrades by shouting over the deafening din of battle, 'Heads up, Warwicks. Show the blighters your cap badges.' The men were actually wearing helmets, but the call to regimental pride was sufficient to stiffen their resolve and carry them forward. Bill, who was standing close to Chuck, often told that story as an example of what morale can achieve.)

In August 1916, Bill learned of a draft that was being sent out to his old unit, the 9th Warwicks, in Mesopotamia and immediately volunteered to conduct it. They embarked on a merchant ship converted into a troop transport and hit heavy storms crossing the Bay of Biscay which resulted in the 'usual horrors of mass sea-sickness'.[19] Passing through the Strait of Gibraltar into the Mediterranean, lookouts were posted throughout the ship to warn of enemy submarines. One evening Bill was just stepping into a bath when alarm bells began ringing throughout the ship. Imagining it was just another practice drill and cursing under his breath, he wrapped a towel round his waist, put on the topcoat he used as a dressing gown, grabbed a lifejacket and headed for his muster station on deck. As he did so, he heard the gun on the stern of the ship open fire and realised it was not a drill.

Up on deck one of the ship's officers told him the pale green track of a torpedo had been seen crossing the bows a few minutes earlier. He joined his men, who were drawn up in two ranks, all wearing lifebelts, along the rail on the forward deck. The stern gun was still firing rapidly but they could not see its target. All at once there was a whistling sound over their heads and a shell burst in the sea on the far side of the ship. It was evident that the submarine had surfaced somewhere nearby. Shell after shell screamed over the ship while the soldiers stood in massed ranks along the deck, helplessly waiting for the one that would explode in their midst.

At this moment, with the tension inexorably rising among the men, a draft of Welsh Territorials bound for India and drawn up alongside the Warwicks, began to sing a hymn, 'Nearer My God to Thee'. They seemed to start together as one man; it was, Bill recalled, almost as if they were a choir and their choirmaster had just brandished his baton. 'As an example of steadiness and discipline it was strange and moving,' he wrote, 'yet somehow the hymn with its melancholy cadences made me think of the sinking of the *Titanic*.'[20] It made him shiver – 'Nearer My God to Thee' was said to have been the last melody the band played on the *Titanic* before the ship went down in the North Atlantic on 15 April 1912.

When the Welshmen had finished, another shell hurtled overhead so low that men flinched and ducked instinctively. Suddenly a voice piped up from among the Warwicks with a boisterous rendition of an apposite and popular music hall song, 'I don't care if the ship goes down, it doesn't belong to me', which made everyone laugh. It was Private Chuck. Almost immediately afterwards the shelling stopped and the submarine crept away into the gathering dusk, although the men remained at muster stations for another hour, singing heartily. Bill returned to his cabin still clad in nothing but a towel and coat, but in a strangely cheerful mood.

A few days later a radio message to the ship informed him that his father had died suddenly of a stroke at his home in Birmingham at the age of 64. Bill had been close to his father but took the news stoically, in the knowledge that there was no possibility of his returning for the funeral. There were no further incidents on the voyage, and after leaving the Mediterranean via the Suez Canal they headed north up the Persian Gulf, crossed the bar at the mouth of the Shatt-al-Arab waterway, dropped anchor in the port of Basra, in what is now Iraq, and disembarked. After two days sweltering in fly-infested tents at the British reinforcements camp, Bill was anxious to get his draft to the battalion, but they were obliged to wait three more days on rust-stained barges moored on the Tigris river while an old paddle steamer that was to tow them upriver was refloated after it had run aground.

The circumstances of what happened when Bill arrived with his draft at the 9th Warwicks' camp in Mesopotamia are murky. In *Unofficial History*, a light-hearted account of his adventures as a young officer first published in 1959, he claimed he had been passed as fit and was simply rejoining his battalion. But the reality was that he was a draft conducting officer who was expected to return to Britain after delivering his draft to its destination. Instead, Bill simply stayed with the battalion. It may be that from the start it was Bill's intention to use the draft as an opportunity to return to his unit; certainly the battalion would have welcomed him, since it was desperately short of officers. Bill himself never divulged what happened, either in his memoirs or to his family. 'He would never tell me how he got back to the battalion in Mesopotamia,' said his son, John, the second Viscount Slim, 'but it was pretty obvious he disobeyed every rule and command just to get there.'[21]

4

A Premonition of Death

When Bill arrived at the 9th Warwicks' tented camp in Amara, Mesopotamia, in October 1916, with badly needed reinforcements, the battalion had been withdrawn for rest and retraining after eight months in the front line. As part of the 13th Division, the regiment had taken part in abortive attempts to relieve the British garrison which had been besieged at Kut, 100 miles south of Baghdad, by Turkish forces since December. Once again, it had suffered grievous losses during hand-to-hand fighting – by April, after less than a month's combat, the battalion had lost nearly all its officers and was reduced to no more than 200 men.

Some 23,000 Allied troops were killed or wounded trying to relieve Kut, all for nothing. When negotiations to buy the garrison's freedom for £2 million failed, the garrison commander, Major General Charles Townshend, surprisingly surrendered, on 29 April, after a siege that had lasted 147 days. It was, according to one British military historian,[1] 'the most abject capitulation in Britain's military history'. The entire garrison of 13,000 men was marched into imprisonment at Aleppo, where more than half would die of disease or their treatment at the hands of their captors. After the Kut disaster the 9th Royal Warwicks, greatly weakened and demoralised, held part of a blockhouse line against the Turks for the next five months.

Bill was not the kind of man to enjoy rest and retraining while a war was going on. 'Resting in Mesopotamia,' he wrote, 'meant that, instead of sitting in trenches dug in the desert, one sat in tents in the same desert. It was just as hot, just as uncomfortable, just as depressing, and more monotonous. But it was something to be back with the battalion again and to find myself commanding my old company.' (He had been promoted to temporary captain on 2 September 1916.)

He was, of course, acutely aware of the poor state of morale following the humiliation at Kut. 'Failure lay heavy on them [the troops]. A campaign that had once been carried forward on a wave of optimism was now sunk in stagnant despondency. In Mesopotamia in that summer of 1916 men felt they were far, very far, from home, forgotten of their friends and deserted by God.'[2]

But things were changing rapidly. Almost all the generals involved with the Kut debacle had been dismissed and in July 1916 the energetic General Sir Stanley Maude had been appointed commander of all Allied forces in Mesopotamia. Despite being instructed to do no more than hold the existing line, Maude set about reorganising and resupplying his army and making plans for a major new offensive. Even junior officers like Bill were soon aware of a new spirit re-energising the men. Rations, comforts and replacement of worn-out equipment appeared on a scale previously unheard of. (Poor supplies had previously bedevilled operations in the country.) The port at Basra was greatly improved so that ships could be unloaded more rapidly and improved river steamers were put into service to move supplies upriver. New hospitals were established to provide better care for the sick and wounded. 'There was not a man in the Force who did not feel the renewed energy and hope that were vitalising the whole army,' Bill wrote. 'To watch an army recovering its morale is enthralling; to feel the process working within oneself is an unforgettable experience.'[3] It was a lesson he would put to good use many years later in Burma when he was called upon to regenerate an army similarly demoralised.

General Maude's plan was to advance in strength up both sides of the Tigris river, sweep away the Turkish fortified positions along the way and avenge the humiliation of Kut. The offensive was launched on 13 December 1916, by which time the 9th Warwicks, under a new CO, Lieutenant Colonel Edward Henderson, were in position at Sheikh Saad, where they joined the front line.

Over the ensuing weeks Bill's company was frequently in the thick of the action and he was not too proud to admit that he was often terrified. On one occasion, shortly before an expected enemy counterattack, he was sent with two men to try and make contact with the Gloucesters, who it was hoped were still on the left of their position. Worming their way across open ground from one fragment of cover to the next, they eventually dropped into a trench which had been badly smashed by shellfire. With his revolver in his hand, he scrambled over the fallen earth from one bay to another, finding nothing but wreckage and dead bodies. For a moment he considered turning back but decided he was as frightened to go back as he was to go forward, so he went on, not knowing whether he would encounter friend or foe round each bend. Eventually he heard voices and stopped in his tracks, straining to listen, his heart in his mouth. He heard a clearly agitated soldier proclaiming that another attack was on its way and that they would all be wiped out. There was a pause and then, to his great relief, a voice with a rich West Country accent replied: 'Aw, don' 'ee worry. Us'll beat they.' He knew he had found the Gloucesters.[4]

Bill's innate pragmatism also helped him cope with the manifest irritations the army wrought upon young officers. Early one morning, tired, soaking wet and covered in mud, he was about to enter the trench which led to the brigade headquarters dugout, but hastily stepped aside when an officer with the red and gold tabs of a general bustled out followed by two staff officers. Bill saluted and pressed himself against the sandbagged wall to let them pass. The general stopped, looked him up and down with disgust and snapped: 'Your name and unit, sir?' Bill told him.

'How do you think your men can have any respect for you?' he demanded. Bill, dumbfounded, said nothing as the general continued with mounting fury: 'You're filthy, sir, your uniform is disgusting, you're unshaven, you look as if you haven't had a wash for a week. Don't you understand that an officer must at all times in appearance be an example to his men? How can they respect you looking as you do? Report at once to your commanding officer and tell him what I have said. I hope he'll know how to deal with you.' With that, the general stomped off, followed by his staff officers, who gave Bill similarly disapproving looks.

Bill was amazed by their insensitivity. 'I could not help thinking how much more sensible it would have been if, instead of biting my head off, he had asked me why I was such a disgusting sight. Then I might have told him that, difficult as it was to be well turned out in the trenches when it had been raining for the last 24 hours, it was even more so if you had been out on patrol between the lines half the night, lying flat in the mud as Very lights went up, trying to see what the Turks were doing on their wire. I had got back to our lines, soaked, mud-plastered and not a little shaken by a near squeak or two in the darkness. When I reported to my Colonel, he thought one piece of information I had gleaned was important enough to be telephoned at once to Brigade. I gathered they doubted that it was, but wanted to cross examine me to make sure. So here I was at Brigade Headquarters just when the general was paying an unusually early visit. However, after a couple of years of war I had grown philosophical about unpleasant encounters, even with generals. I shrugged and went in, mud and all, and made my report.'[5]

By and large, Bill did not have a high opinion of senior officers; in fact, he had concluded that his own CO was possibly 'windy'. In Bill's view Lieutenant Colonel Henderson had an overworked, not to say vivid, imagination and was always fussing about dangers that did not exist. Once when Bill and his company were holding a forward position he became so annoyed by a day and a half of false alarms that he disconnected the telephone line in order to get some sleep. Half an hour later Bill was woken with the news that the CO, convinced by the lack of telephone communication that the post had been overrun by the enemy, had turned up with a reserve company to retake it.

Bill was obliged to revise his precocious assessment of his CO when Henderson won a Victoria Cross. On 25 January 1917, on the west bank of the River Hai, near Kut, a heavy Turkish counter-attack had driven the leading British troops out of their trenches. At around noon the 9th Warwicks were ordered into the front line to recapture the position. Colonel Henderson, who had been shot in the arm moments earlier, nevertheless jumped on to the parapet in front of the trench and, shouting to his men to follow him, led them across 500 yards of open ground under intense enemy fire. He was shot down again, but somehow got to his feet. He was hit twice more yet brought his men to within 100 yards of the enemy trench before finally falling, mortally wounded. The 9th Warwicks then charged with fixed bayonets and recaptured the position. Lieutenant Robert Phillips, who had already shown great courage in the attack, went out under very heavy fire and with the help of a comrade dragged the colonel back to the trenches, where he died. Both Henderson and Phillips were awarded the Victoria Cross. Besides

Colonel Henderson, the 9th Warwicks had five officers killed and six wounded in the action; 52 other ranks were killed, 118 wounded and 11 missing. Bill was greatly saddened by their losses, but could not help but wonder at the advisability of leading men across open ground in a direct frontal assault on enemy guns.

The Allied forces under General Maude made good progress up the Tigris river despite incessant rain, which made the ground almost impassable and resupply very difficult. On 7 February Bill's company was on advance guard duty with orders to keep in contact with the Turkish rearguard but not to engage. The enemy was strongly entrenched on a ridge between the Allies and the Euphrates river. Bill had a good eye for assessing ground and spotted a break in the ridge some distance to his left which he thought might lead to a position from which the Turkish trenches would be vulnerable to enfilading fire. He decided his orders were sufficiently flexible to allow him to make a reconnaissance (it was drummed into every officer then, and still is, that 'time spent in reconnaissance is never wasted'). He discovered the break was a wadi that appeared to be undefended; it was an opportunity too good to be missed. Leaving one platoon to hold their present position and engage the attention of the enemy, he led his remaining men into the wadi, hoping to be able to encircle the Turkish troops holding the ridge. The going was much more difficult than he anticipated (which was probably why the area was undefended), but he persisted. When, eventually, they reached the point where they could overlook the enemy trenches, his quarry had flown. To avoid being outflanked, the Turks had withdrawn; Bill could see them scurrying down the far side of the ridge towards the river. His men took their place on the ridge and Bill ordered his signal section to make contact with the battalion and to tell them he was in sight of the Euphrates. 'You can't be,' was the reply, 'the Turks are holding all the high ground in front.'

'Well,' Bill said, 'I'm looking down at it now.'

'Then where are all the Turks?'

'They seem to have gone. Perhaps someone told them I was coming.'

'All right. Continue your detail but slowly – and don't get into trouble. I expect a general advance will be ordered.'[6]

For this action, Captain William Slim, 9th Battalion, The Royal Warwickshire Regiment, was awarded the Military Cross.

Early one morning several days later, as the Allied forces were pressing north towards Baghdad, it suddenly occurred to Bill that the stirring picture on the cover of one of his favourite boyhood books, *The Boy's Book of Battles*, which his Aunt Mary had given him when he was eight years old, had not only suddenly come to life, but he was right in the middle of it. The cover of the book showed, in glorious colour, a fictional battlefield with a squadron of cavalry galloping across a plain, massed ranks of the infantry waiting to advance, the artillery behind them spewing forth smoke and fire and ships of the Royal Navy floating in the distance on an impossibly blue ocean.

Even as a boy, Bill had suspected it was a somewhat glamorous depiction of war, but as he looked around him in Mesopotamia nearly 20 years later, he realised it was not so far from the truth. On his right was a division of cavalry with glittering lances and red and white pennants, just like in *The Boy's Book of Battles*. Alongside him two batteries of 18-pounders were preparing to fire and behind him the dust was rising from the columns of infantry on the move. Completing the picture he could see, through the early morning mist, gunboats moving up the Tigris river.

(All the preparations that day came to nought, since the Turkish rearguard had slipped away in the night. The only enemy they found was a squad of dejected Turkish gunners who had somehow been left behind, crouched apathetically around their guns waving dirty white rags tied to the cleaning rods of their rifles.)

It was characteristic of Bill to be reminded, during an operation, of a picture in one of his childhood books; unlike many young officers, he was not desensitised by war and was still captivated by the romance of exotic, faraway countries. Many years later, in *Unofficial History*, he penned a vivid description of a dawn reconnaissance on horseback in Mesopotamia: 'We left the palm groves, still dark against the lightening sky, and trotted out into the flat, featureless plain. It was a lovely morning, the air fresh with almost a nip in it, the sky a gentle, unclouded blue with the last pale rear-guard of the stars retreating as the red rays of the advancing sun, straight as sword blades, pierced the misty curtains of the horizon. As we rode, the dull brown earth ahead seemed to take a faint opalescent sheen, and then, suddenly, our horses' hoofs were among flowers – tulips and tiny blue grape hyacinths. I had not seen a flower, hardly a green thing, for a year; it seemed unbelievable that the Mesopotamia I had known, so arid, harsh and cruel, should suddenly grow gentle with spring flowers. I slipped from the saddle and picked a little bunch. When I caught up with the rest again they had passed beyond the flowers and were back to bare brown earth. As the sun climbed, the freshness went out of the air, and I felt an increasing stickiness between my bare knees and the saddle. I looked at my flowers; they had wilted in my hand. Regretfully I let them fall. We were back in the old Mesopotamia, and I had better begin thinking of other things than flowers.'

By the beginning of March, Allied troops, including the 9th Warwicks, were on the outskirts of Baghdad. To his great satisfaction Bill had been given command of a mixed force of two companies of infantry, a machine-gun section mounted on mules and two horse-drawn 18-pound guns. 'I do not believe,' he wrote, 'Napoleon himself ever felt so Napoleonic as I did that early spring morning in 1917 when I watched the first mixed force I had ever commanded defile before me.'7

After a precarious crossing of a fast-flowing tributary of the Tigris on a rickety bridge built by engineers only the night before, Bill learned his force was to be in the vanguard of the advance up the east bank of the Tigris. 'Remember,' his CO told him sternly, if rather pointlessly, at the end of the briefing, 'the first duty of an advance-guard is to advance.' Astride his horse, Anzac, Bill led his men across ground strewn with the detritus of a retreating army – shredded uniforms, discarded boots, abandoned equipment, broken guns, scattered shell cases and innumerable bodies already bloated by the sun. Among them Bill noticed a single Arab, a giant of a man, who he rather uncharitably assumed, for no other reason than that he was an Arab, had been shot while trying to loot from the dead.

The advance had not progressed far before a machine gun opened up on them from the cover of a dense date palm grove on the bank of the river. Bill, horribly conspicuous on his horse, scrambled to the ground with undignified haste, uncomfortably aware of the critical gaze of his groom, Private Bronson, who seemed completely un-bothered by the gunfire. When his own 18-pounders had dealt with the machine gun, they got on the move again, only to be held up once more by more Turkish soldiers firing through loopholes from behind a high mud wall enclosing an orange grove. Bill was told there was a possibility the river end of the wall was undefended so he ran there with his orderly, Private Francisco Ferrero, the English-born son of an Italian hairdresser, and found an unpainted wooden door. He put his eye to a crack in the wood and as he did so the door swung open. Bill and Ferrero both sprang back and took cover on each side of the opening. No bullets whistled through. Bill saw Ferrero release the safety catch on his rifle and brace himself to jump into the garden. Thinking he should probably take the lead, Bill leapt into the opening at precisely the same moment as Ferrero, with the result that they collided and became jammed for a few seconds, each silently cursing the other.

Still nothing happened. There was no sign of the enemy. Bill thought the garden, with its deep green trees heavily laden with or-anges, was full of menace but Ferrero gasped, 'Oh, sir, isn't it beau-tiful.' More troops were pouring in through the gap and within a short time the few Turks inside the garden were rounded up. The next phase of the advance was marked by a trail of orange peel as his men worked out how to eat an orange while simultaneously carry-ing a rifle with a fixed bayonet.

The operation ended with a fierce firefight outside the village of Um-ul-Baqq, which was briefly suspended by both sides when two black-robed women emerged to round up a herd of goats grazing in the firing line. At one point Bill realised to his dismay that he was much too far forward to direct the action, particularly the machine guns and 18-pounders, but fortunately a signaller was nearby and semaphored his orders. Once the 18-pounders opened up, the shells kicked up so much dust that the Turks could no longer fire accu-rately and they made a run for it, hotly pursued by the Warwicks. At the end of the day, Bill sent a triumphant, not to say grandilo-quent, signal to his CO: 'I have carried Um-ul-Baqq at the point of a bayonet.' The CO was unimpressed and replied: 'How many Turks have you killed?'

On 11 March the Union flag was hoisted above the citadel in

Baghdad while more than 15,000 Turkish prisoners were being rounded up. On the following day, the 9th Warwicks conducted house-to-house searches throughout the city looking for enemy soldiers who might have gone into hiding. On 15 March, Bill sat down and wrote an eight-page letter to his brother describing his adventures, while a dust storm whirled outside his tent:

Dear Charles,

We got here four days ago as I suppose you know. I expect the papers talk of the triumphal march to Baghdad but altho' there was plenty of marching there was a good deal of scrapping too. The old Turk is rather good at a rearguard action. Our Bde was in every scrap but one and our crush [?] weren't at the back every time. In fact we had rather a bloody time in more ways than one but it's worth it to get to this place. The men marched and fought marvellously. It's no joke to march across broken country with a pack for ten miles on small rations and then bump into the Turk sitting in a trench. We did enjoy one day tho' – the 10th. We were in the last scrap before the city – about four miles out. The regt. was vanguard to the force and I had the job of clearing the river bank – its all palm groves and gardens – with an Arab village or two. The Turks had piquets of 20 or 30 men stuck in the trees and villages all over the place and they made it rather hot at times for our fellows in the open. We had a supporting battery that had shoved right up and came into action about 1000' behind us – jolly good. We got forward under this and pushed old Johnny out of the trees. We went back to a nullah and as he seemed rather jumpy and we saw one or two of his fellows looking it I did a bit of a charge. I could only get half the Coy. together in time, the rest were held up by walls, but they all howled like sin and we went like good 'uns. The Turks didn't wait for us but ran for a village about 200' away. Pearson [a fellow officer] had come up to support me by then and his fellows joined in. We got a few with the bayonet but our fellows were tired and couldn't run the whole distance so I stopped in the nullah to pull them together – we had some pretty shooting from here.

As soon as a line was up I gave five rounds rapid and hell for leather for the village. Old Johnny had had enough and bolted. We got in and couldn't get any further as we had three machine guns on us from his trenches then so we put two or three Lewis guns on him off the roofs of the houses and had tea. He shelled the village hard but it was rotten shooting altho' it made it rather difficult to get water from the river. The shelling frightened the wounded prisoners we had no end. The Turks cleared in the night and we came in next morning.

This was the most interesting scrap I have ever been in as I was all on my own – unfortunately one of our officers was killed and that of course spoiled it. I had a rather unique experience. I shot a young Turk as he was getting to the village and a moment afterwards saved him from being bayoneted by an excited Tommy. When we had the place I came back, had him bandaged, gave him a drink and shook hands with him. His leg was smashed – not very good shooting on my part, what?

I've visited the city once or twice – it's not all that fine. We marched thro' part of it the other night and all the lousy Jews came out and clapped and cheered and said 'Velcome'. They were having a thin time until we came, being chucked into the river, etc. There's a topping village near our camp with a fine mosque – I rode in with two of my officers the other morning – caught two Turks hiding in a café and got 30 rifles. We were then invited to visit the principal of the University and the chief priest of the Mosque – we went and found them both charming old boys – we had an Arab breakfast with them. The secretary of one of them spoke French awfully well so we got on splendidly. They wanted to tell us how glad they were the Turks had gone and they wanted to know if the Chief of Police would be hanged – he seems to have been rather unpopular with everybody. I was very struck with the courtesy and knowledge of these people. All the chief men of the town came to see us and we were all awfully polite. They thought there were French troops with us. I have visited them once or twice since and am great pals with the old birds. It's very useful because when we go shopping in the village some old fellow in a green turban comes with me and sees I am not done down. It's awfully funny – he called down the most fearful malediction on a man who tried to charge too much for oranges. I also got some special dates called honey dates which are a perfect dream. I wish I could send a skin of them home. I eat them all day long – they say they never send them out of the country. I have never tasted any to touch them. They are a light yellow colour like honey and melt in the mouth. When you think that ten days ago I was

offering 10/- for a pot of jam and not getting it you can guess how we
log into this sort of stuff. Of course prices are going up – we are such
fools at paying … It's been an awfully interesting month but I'm glad
it's over and we're here. It's getting hot.

  How's the navy? [Charles had joined the Royal Navy as a medical
officer] … *Have you done any stunts lately? Hope to hear from you.*
  Love to all at home,

  Your loving brother, Bill [8]

Less than two weeks after writing to his brother, Bill experienced for
the first time what he called a premonition of death. It happened
at Duqma, on the Marl Plain, a vast flatland, 20 miles by 20 miles,
of hard-baked white clay crossed by a rutted track along which the
Turkish army was retreating. In truth it was not so much a premonition as a presumption – a certainty that he was going to die. It
came upon him as he was walking away from the divisional commander's conference, where he had sat at the back as a junior officer
while the plans for the attack the following day were outlined. He
wished he had had the moral courage to voice an objection, but in
those days junior officers were, like small boys, occasionally seen but
rarely heard.

The plan, such as it was, was for the assault troops to march
through the night to start lines parallel with the enemy trenches
and then to launch a frontal attack at dawn. Bill could never understand the fondness of generals at that time for hurling troops
directly at enemy defences in gigantic frontal assaults, which were
horribly costly in lives and often yielded little. He described it, with
admirable restraint, as 'blinkered'. He would have sent a detachment to 'make faces' at the enemy on their most southerly position
and taken the rest of the force round to the north and rolled them
up from the flank or the rear. But he was a captain, not a general,
and he had to do what he was told.

He kept his opinions to himself – there was certainly no justifica-
tion for sharing his reservations with his men – and in the half-light
before dawn next morning he concentrated on getting his company
into position for the attack. After marching all night the men were
tired and hungry, but not necessarily daunted, he thought, by what

lay ahead – a 3,000-yard trek across open ground with no cover of any kind into the teeth of the Turkish guns. Bill assumed that, as his troops had beaten 'Johnny Turk' again and again in the preceding months, they simply took it for granted that they would do so again. In truth they were more bothered by the flies, which had materialised out of nowhere as soon as they arrived, than by the forthcoming battle. Bill lined his men up on a compass bearing, six paces apart, and positioned his little headquarters of NCOs, signallers and runners in the middle of the line. As he looked along the line left and right, the horizon was lightening behind them, ensuring, he ruminated bitterly, that they would all be nicely silhouetted for the Turkish gunners. He waited, his eyes glued to the luminous dial of his watch. At the appointed time he blew his whistle to signal the start of the assault.

Nothing happened until after they had covered several hundred yards. Turkish guns started firing sporadically and shrapnel shells began bursting overhead, fortunately falling well short of their line. Bill was in no doubt their aim would improve rapidly. When the artillery on both sides opened up in earnest, creating a deafening tumult for the troops on the ground, men began falling here and there and cries of 'Stretcher-bearer' could be heard above the racket. As the sun rose a heat haze began to shimmer across the plain, fortunately making it difficult for the enemy gunners to find their range.

When the line had advanced about a mile, a halt was suddenly called, taking everyone by surprise. The men lay down in their ranks and most fell asleep in a matter of minutes, despite the blistering sun and the torment of the flies which crawled all over them. At two o'clock an order came to resume the advance. Officers and NCOs went up and down the line, shaking and prodding the men awake and once more they began plodding across the plain in a line that was now beginning to waver.

'As we drew nearer to the Turkish emplacements we began to lose men at an increasing rate. One of my four officers had already been killed and we were getting perilously near to our own shell bursts when our guns lifted on to the enemy second line. This was always the crucial moment, would our infantry overrun the first trenches before the enemy could man his parapet and get his machine guns into action? We began to move faster. Suddenly, as the dust cloud drifted sideways like a travelling curtain before us, there, not a hundred yards away, I could see the neat sandbagged back of a trench with heads bobbing about against it. There came a deafening crack-crack of bullets about our ears and the horrid slurred shriek of shrapnel balls as they thudded around and into us. Just for an instant, through a clear gap in the dust, I saw, for the only time in my life, to the left of the mound, half a mile beyond the trenches, not only the flashes of the guns firing at us, but there in the open the actual guns themselves.

'We were running now, hunched up, with bayonets at the charge. I reached across my body with my right hand to draw my revolver. Amid that infernal din, dust and flashes something hurtled out of the sky and, missing my knee, hit the ground beside my foot with a thud that even in that pandemonium I heard. I looked down and there was the case of a shrapnel shell embedded in the earth. I saw too my arm and realised for the first time that the case had hit me. Its open end had just caught my forearm at its thickest part and like an old fashioned cheese taster had scooped out quite a large chunk of sleeve and flesh. There was practically no blood but my arm did not look good.

'We were now through the odd strands of broken wire and our men were shooting down into the trench or leaping across it after Turks who were running hard. Somehow I jumped over where the gap was narrow at a traverse and found myself in the general melee on the other side. My revolver was still in its holster and it would have been hard with me if any of the Turks still milling about had come for me and when I saw one heading straight at me I thought my premonition was about to be fulfilled. Then I saw that he was unarmed and had slung round his neck a big leather box with a red crescent in a white circle painted on it. He at once opened the box, produced a large pair of scissors and began to cut off my sleeve.'[9]

Bill was sickened by the size of the hole in his arm and the fact that the bone – a curious blueish colour – was exposed. After being treated by the Turkish medical orderly, he was weak from loss of blood and realised he could take no further part in the action. He walked back to a field dressing station, stopping to examine those corpses he recognised. One of them was a subaltern in his company, lying on his back as if asleep in the sun. Bill knelt beside him, opened his breast pocket and took charge of a packet of photographs and letters until he could return them to his family. He learned later that the 9th Warwicks had captured their objective and put the Turks to flight on their segment of the line, but at the cost of three officers killed and seven wounded, and 140 casualties among the other ranks.

After being patched up at the dressing station, Bill was taken by motor ambulance to a steamer on the Tigris, which chugged downstream to Amara and from there he was transferred to Basra to await evacuation. The news that Captain W. J. Slim of the 9th Warwicks had been wounded in Mesopotamia sent penpushers in Whitehall into something of a panic. Captain Slim had not been passed as fit for active service by a medical board. What was he doing in Mesopotamia? Worse, what was he doing in the front line? Who had authorised him to rejoin his battalion? A flurry of angry signals passed between London and the hospital in Amara where Bill was being treated for his wounds and where the medical staff were anxious to avoid further trouble. (The inadequate treatment of casualties earlier in the Mesopotamia campaign had been described in the House of Lords as a 'scandal'.)

He was only made aware of his curiously special status by the extraordinary number of doctors that seemed to be conferring over his case; they were not, it transpired, discussing his medical condition but deciding how quickly they could get rid of him, since no one wanted to take responsibility for him. 'With my bundle of incriminating papers round my neck like the Ancient Mariner's albatross,' he wrote, 'nobody wanted me; no one would have me in his hospital.'[10] It was decided he would be dispatched, post haste, to recuperate in India.

On 24 April 1917, Bill's mother received the following letter at her home in Birmingham from the British Red Cross and Order of St John:

'Dear Madam,

'The War Office has just informed us by telephone that Captain W. J. Slim of 9 Royal Warwicks is at the Officers' Hospital, Beit Naawa, suffering from a gunshot wound in the forearm and that it is expected he will shortly be invalided to India.'[11] (Although he probably did not appreciate it at the time, being evacuated to India was the best thing that could have happened to him since it would facilitate his transfer to the Indian Army, which he greatly admired and respected, and his eventual posting to the Gurkhas, an ambition he had cherished ever since Gallipoli.)

Bill's move to India was held up by his wound inconveniently turning septic, but he was eventually transferred to a hospital ship bound for Bombay, which tossed and pitched in rough seas for the whole of the 1,500-mile voyage and added seasickness to his misery. He did discover, though, that he could count himself fortunate only to have been wounded in one place: some of his fellow officers had seven or eight separate wounds.

In the disembarkation shed on the quayside in Bombay he was met by a medical officer and told to report to the Lady Willingdon Hospital, which had the reputation of being the best in India but was also notorious for its strict discipline and was known through-out the East as the 'gilded cage'. Bill, in no mood to be ministered to by nursing martinets, cannily suggested that as he was classified as walking wounded it would be entirely wrong to deprive a more deserving case of a bed; was there not some other place he could go? The medical officer thought about it for a moment, then had the bright idea of sending him to the Byculla Club, which had offered to take in wounded Allied officers. The Byculla, founded in 1833, was the oldest and snootiest gentleman's club in Bombay (it was where the Prince of Wales was entertained during a visit to India in 1905) and was famous for its prawn curry dinners and the exotic Byculla cocktail, a lethal concoction made up of generous quantities of sherry, port, Curaçao and ginger-flavoured brandy.

So it was that later that day Bill, dressed in none too clean crumpled khaki drill and scruffy ammunition boots, with his arm in a sling, entered the imposing porte cochère of the Byculla Club to find the members gathering for dinner, as usual, in immaculate white dinner jackets, silk cummerbunds, black evening trousers and patent leather shoes. He was, nevertheless, afforded a warm welcome and instantly introduced to the delights of the Byculla cocktail with the warning words of the doctor on the quayside ringing in his ears: 'Under no circumstances exceed two chota pegs a night.' During the excellent dinner, an obliging neighbour cut up his food for him when he saw what difficulty he was having managing with only one hand.

Bill left a wry account of the studied eccentricity of the members at the Byculla, most of whom were middl-aged or older: 'In the dining room half a dozen tables were arranged along one wall [each] with only one chair. Gradually they were occupied in solitary state. One [member] moved with measured dignity to his table, sat down, clapped his hands for a khidmatgar [waiter] and without a word pointed to the electric fan whirring above his head. The servant vanished and the fan stopped. Another khidmatgar entered with an embroidered silk guidon on a polished staff with which he proceeded to fan the gentleman, a hand punkah wallah obviously being more agreeable than the mechanical kind.'[12]

Bill attended the Lady Willingdon Hospital every day for treatment to his arm, which was slow to heal, but doctors seemed more concerned about the damage caused to his lungs and shoulder by his earlier injury. Eventually it was decided to send him to a hill station to convalesce. His knowledge of hill stations was restricted to what was contained in Kipling's *Plain Tales from the Hills* and stories he had been told of the delights of a hill station called Mussoorie, known as 'The Queen of the Hills', and the kindness of its ladies. Naturally he asked to go to Mussoorie but was brusquely informed that it was reserved exclusively for officers of colonel's rank or above, and so he was sent to Simla, the summer capital of the British Raj. He never for a moment regretted it.

Perched on a ridge 2,205 metres above sea level in the foothills of the Western Himalayas, surrounded by dense forests of cedar, rhododendron and oak, Simla (now called Shimla) had been 'discovered' by the British early in the nineteenth century and proved, as Lord William Bentinck, the Governor-General of India at the time, noted, 'a very agreeable refuge from the burning plains of Hindoostan'.[13] So agreeable, in fact, that many army officers, civil servants and entrepreneurs built large summer cottages there, favouring traditional designs that reminded them of home. Intent on turning Simla into an approximation of a comfortable suburb in the Home Counties, they gave their homes nostalgic names like 'Richmond Villa' or 'The Briars' or 'Woodbine Cottage' and created 'English' gardens planted with roses, lupins and hollyhocks.

Simla soon acquired a handsome town hall, library and theatre, none of which would have looked out of place in Surrey, and a reputation for 'frivolity, gossip and intrigue'.[14] Large numbers of un-attached wives and daughters whiled away their summers in Simla and the presence of not quite so large numbers of similarly unat-tached young men inevitably created a propensity for deliciously shocking scandal. Those not involved in intrigue had much else to occupy them – the expatriate community spawned clubs, cinemas, churches and even a general store that stocked English preserves, Cheddar cheese and sponge cakes.

In 1903 a narrow gauge railway line was opened to Simla (it is still operating) from Kalka, a little town at the base of the mountains on the road from Delhi. Until then, Simla could only be approached by horse, rickshaw or cart along a winding mountain track. The railway greatly facilitated the annual transfer of the government and army headquarters from Delhi, 170 miles to the south, for the summer months. The Viceroy and his staff moved into the massive neo-Gothic Viceregal Lodge on Observatory Hill; the Commander-in-Chief (Kitchener in 1903) also had his own official residence, a vast, rambling 'Tudorbethan' house called Snowdon maintained by 856 servants. Towards the end of the summer – winters in Simla are cold, with frequent snow – the whole caravanserai moved back to Delhi, a process which took about a week to accomplish.

Bill arrived in Simla in May 1917 and was provided with ac-commodation at The Crags, a large 'English' villa which had been turned into a convalescent home for officers. The Crags not only offered residents magnificent views over the mountains but was said to possess one of the best ballrooms in Simla (not, perhaps, much of an attraction for all-male occupants suffering from a variety of incapacities). On 18 June, Bill wrote rather gloomily to his friend Philip Pratt from The Crags: 'I'm about as fit as I shall ever be. The lung is as you were. I no longer spit blood and chunks of lung – the sands of Mesopot I suppose made that start on the way to Baghdad. The arm has healed at last, there's only a scar left now. It was rather beastly at one time at Amara and Basra – very septic all down my arm. But that's all over – of course I didn't tell Mother so there's no cause to tell her at all ...'[15]

He soon brightened up as he became involved in Simla's hectic social life. 'Simla is a fairly gay place these days,' he wrote to Pratt on 2 August, 'dinner parties, lunches, picnics, dances, tennis, skating rink, riding, etc. I'm not up to tennis or dancing but manage quite well, thank you. At any rate, I've spent most of my back pay.'[16] Some of his money went on hiring a horse which, he confessed to Pratt, bolted with him three times in one day, resulting in an order being published stating 'Officers will not gallop in the streets of Simla'.

In November he was finally passed as fit to return to duty but to his dismay he was given a desk job in Delhi – as a GSO III, a general staff officer, at army headquarters. Nothing could have pleased him less, but he accepted his lot and knuckled down to work, despite his increasing boredom. 'I'm still stuck up here getting fedder and fedder up daily,' he wrote to Pratt in June 1918. 'It's an appallingly dull existence – I'm reduced to reading Shaw to keep awake.'

Like every other officer in the headquarters, Bill anxiously followed newspaper reports of the progress of the war in Europe and was aware by the summer of 1918 that the end was at last in sight. He was still at his desk in Delhi when the news came through that an armistice had been signed with Germany in a railway carriage in the Compiègne Forest on 11 November 1918, bringing the Great War to an end with a complete victory for the Allies. Some 16 million lives, both military and civilian, had been lost. Many of those lives, Bill thought sadly, had been wasted in fruitless frontal attacks to gain ground of no tactical importance. It was a lesson that would shape his leadership philosophy for the rest of his career.

By the time of the Armistice, Bill had decided to apply to join the Indian Army. Originally raised and paid by the East India Company, the Indian Army formally came into being when the Crown took over direct rule of British India after the mutiny in 1857. Largely recruited from the so-called 'martial races' – Marathas, Rajputs, Sikhs, Gurkhas, Pashtuns, Garhwalis and Balochis – with British officers, it was responsible for the defence of the Raj and internal security, particularly on the wild and rebellious North-West Frontier. Some 1.3 million Indian Army soldiers had served with great distinction in the Great War and won 17 Victoria Crosses; almost 75,000 were killed or reported missing.

It was by no means a foregone conclusion that Bill's application to join the Indian Army would be successful. Despite his disaffection with his staff job, he had received consistently good reports ('chits' in the Indian Army), praising his energy, initiative, resourcefulness and common sense, and had been promoted to temporary major, but commissions in the Indian Army were much sought after, since promotion was quicker, responsibility was greater (there was always action on the North-West Frontier) and the pay was so much better that officers in the Indian Army could actually live on it. Cadets at the Royal Military Academy Sandhurst who wanted to join the Indian Army needed to pass out in the top 30 to be considered; a young cadet by the name of Bernard Montgomery, later to become Viscount Montgomery of Alamein, was bitterly disappointed when he failed to join the Indian Army – he passed out 36th in 1908.[17]

A further problem for Bill was that after the Armistice all such applications were at that time being routinely refused because of an excess of officers. He persisted, nevertheless, and garnered support at the highest level. On 8 January 1919, the Viceroy's office in Delhi sent a signal to Edwin Montagu, Secretary of State for India in London, recommending Bill's application: 'This officer has an excellent war record and exceptional qualifications. He has done consistently good work in his present appointment and we consider him suitable in every respect for Indian Army.' Montagu replied on 26 February: 'In consideration of Commander-in-Chief's strong recommendation I reluctantly agree to the acceptance of Slim. As I have been rigidly rejecting all similar applications since Armistice unless acceptances had been actually issued, Slim's acceptance will cause embarrassment here ...' Montagu accepted that Bill was a 'special case' but nit-picked, and argued he should be transferred with the rank of lieutenant rather than captain. Delhi replied with another strong recommendation that he should retain his rank 'as a reward for good service'.[18]

On 22 May 1919, Bill was gazetted as a lieutenant in the Indian Army, but he was obliged to remain at his desk job for almost another year. His annual report for 1919 concluded that 'before being trained for further staff work, at which he should eventually do well, he requires a thorough grounding in regimental work'. His Brigadier concurred and scribbled a note at the end of the report: 'Yes, a good spell of regimental work will do him more good than anything.'

Bill most heartily agreed and on 27 March 1920, after considerable lobbying on his part – he told everyone he met that it was his ambition to join the Gurkhas – he was posted as a captain to the

1st/6th Gurkha Rifles, the regiment he had first met on the ridge at Sari Bair in Gallipoli four years previously. He could not have asked for a better posting. It was the start of a love affair with the Gurkhas that would endure: for the rest of his life he thought of himself as a Gurkha first, a soldier second.

In a preface to the Battalion's official history, written when he was a field marshal, Slim recalled: 'I spent many of the happiest, and from a military point of view the most valuable, years of my life in the Regiment. The Almighty created in the Gurkha an ideal infantryman, indeed an ideal Rifleman, brave, tough, patient, adaptable, skilled in field-craft, intensely proud of his military record and unswervingly loyal. Add to this his honesty in word and deed, his parade perfection, and his unquenchable cheerfulness, then service with the Gurkhas is for any soldier an immense satisfaction.'

5

A Recruit for the Gurkhas

In 1920 the 6th Gurkha Rifles were based at Abbottabad, a pleasant garrison town set in a lush green valley in the hills north of Rawalpindi which gained brief notoriety in 2011 when it emerged as the final hiding place of Osama bin Laden. There were many worse places to start a regimental career in the Indian Army than Abbottabad (now, of course, in Pakistan). Founded by Major James Abbott of the Bengal Artillery in 1853, it was 1,200 metres above sea level, escaped the fearsome heat of summer in the Punjab, was verdant with parks, gardens and eucalyptus trees and was generally viewed as the best of the so-called frontier stations. In stark contrast to the filth and chaos of Indian towns, the cantonment was neat and clean and was laid out in a grid system with tree-lined roads connecting the various barrack blocks, parade grounds and sports fields. The goal posts on the football pitch were meticulously painted with the regimental colours; a swimming pool was available along with tennis courts, a polo ground and even a golf course and a cinema. Saint Luke's Church ministered to the Europeans, but there was also a mosque, a gurdwara for the Sikhs and a temple for the Hindus. In the centre of the cantonment was a small *sadar*, or bazaar, where soldiers and their families could do their shopping.

The 6th Gurkhas officers' mess, guarded at the portal by two regimental cannon, seven-pound mountain guns irreverently known as 'Bubble' and 'Squeak', was the pride of the cantonment and was run rather like an Edwardian gentleman's club. It featured oak-panelled public rooms with leopard and tiger skins stretched out on the floor, heavy mahogany furniture, open fireplaces with carved wood mantels where log fires burned in the winter and a large verandah overlooking the garden. Electricity had recently arrived in Abbottabad and flickering electric light bulbs now replaced candles in the candelabras. The mess servants wore white starched uniforms with green cummerbunds and the *havildar* (sergeant) in charge sported a black velvet waistcoat with a Kilmarnock hat and a jaunty peacock feather.

Officers were expected to dress for dinner in full mess kit, except on Sundays when black tie and dinner jacket was acceptable, although gentlemen continuing to a dance after dinner were allowed to wear white tie and tails. Tweeds ('tinker's mufti') were greatly frowned upon and never worn in the mess and if an officer arrived for dinner in uniform straight from duty he was obliged to eat alone at a separate table laid for him in the card room. After dinner, bridge, billiards or 'slosh' (snooker) were played. On Guest Nights (*burra khana*) the Regimental Band and the Pipes and Drums would play on the lawn in front of the verandah before the evening degenerated into boisterous, alcohol-fuelled games, unsteady highland dancing, indoor rugger practice and sometimes a frenetic race around the building pushing 'Bubble' and 'Squeak'.

For young officers interested in field sports, Abbottabad was a paradise: there was shooting, mainly for black partridge and chikhor; fishing for mahseer, an excellent game fish, in local rivers with trout available in nearby Kashmir; pigsticking and polo at a fraction of the cost at home; big game shooting for the more adventurous; and in the case of the 6th Gurkhas, mountaineering, very much encouraged by the Honourable Charles Granville Bruce, former CO of the 1st/6th Gurkhas, who led British expeditions to Mount Everest in 1922 and 1924.

Bachelor officers were accommodated in bungalows within the mess compound but their living conditions were hardly luxurious. Each item of furniture, including the thunderbox and the zinc bath tub, had to be rented at a rate of one rupee per calendar month. There was no piped hot water and water for shaving and bathing was heated outside over an open fire, usually in old kerosene oil drums, and brought into the bungalow by the officer's *bhisti* (water carrier).

The working day began before dawn when officers made their way to the company lines, on bicycles or on horseback, and joined their men on physical training, drill, or dry practice manoeuvres, either within the cantonment or on the steep forested hills behind Abbottabad. Newly joined officers found it extraordinarily difficult to keep up with the wiry and sure-footed Gurkhas, who seemed to be able to run up and down hills all day without tiring or stumbling. A hearty breakfast – several courses, usually including mulligatawny soup and a fruit salad – was served in the officers' mess between nine and ten o'clock after which training resumed until the midday parade.

In the afternoon all officers were required to join their men playing sport – football, cricket or basketball. After the games parade they were free to go to the Gurkha Club for a swim, or a game of tennis. Most evenings around sunset the young officers of the 6th Gurkhas could be found sitting in wicker chairs on the verandah of the mess in sweat-stained tennis clothes, swilling Murree beer from silver tankards while punkah wallahs listlessly tugged at the cords of slowly waving fans.

This was the life to which Bill was introduced when he reported to Abbottabad and was put in charge of A Company that summer day in June 1920. His welcome was polite but reserved. The Gurkhas were family, a very close-knit family, and despite his war record and his Military Cross he was going to have to win their trust before he could earn his place in that family.

The 6th Gurkhas also had their own way of doing things, which had to be rapidly learned by newly arrived officers. There was little room for individuality or idiosyncrasies: whether it was pitching camp or organising a parade, there was a set procedure, a *kaida*, which everyone followed for the greater good. 'This institutional manner gave the regiment an uncompromisingly purposeful character,' the military historian John Mackinlay pointed out. 'There was no affected casualness about the 6th Gurkhas; no perfume-wearing, limp-wristed slackers were to be found draped over the mess furniture, which was significant in those post war days when the long cigarette holder and a slight lisp were de rigueur in gentle society.'[1]

Bill had, of course, mugged up on the history of the regiment before he arrived. He knew it had started life as the Cuttack Legion, raised in Orissa in 1817 and recruited from plainsmen as part of the army of the East India Company, that it had gone through many manifestations before transferring to the Indian Army, becoming a Gurkha regiment in 1886 and being renumbered the 6th Gurkha

Rifles in 1903. He knew, too, that after he had been wounded and carried from the battlefield at Sari Bair in Gallipoli in 1915, the 1st/6th Gurkhas, with the few remaining Warwicks, had stormed and briefly held the ridge before being driven back by a Turkish counter-attack. Of all the battalions in the brigade which took part in the attack, only the Gurkhas succeeded in reaching the crest of the ridge.

His admiration for the Gurkhas was already firmly rooted in his mindset after Sari Bair and it was not in the least diminished by close contact with them as a company commander. 'I got here without incident and am leading a strenuous but unexciting life in command of a company …' he wrote to Pratt soon after he arrived. 'They are topping little fellows and awfully keen. Of course I'm rather stuck on the language question and I seem to have forgotten most of the regimental soldiering I ever knew. Still, it's coming back slowly. Nearly all my kit has been held up or lost in the railway strike – curse it. My gramophone, books and bicycle have vanished and I can't get any news at all. Damned annoying. For some reason I bought a nice Bokhara rug the other day – that's the only piece of decent junk I've got in my quarters now.'[2]

The 'language question' was a problem he was required to tackle rather urgently, since his men would not respond to orders delivered in English or in faulty Gurkhali (the language spoken by the hill Gurkhas) and required confirmation from an officer who could speak a language they could understand before they would act. He described his problems to his friend in a letter dated 26 June: 'It's ten o'clock in the morning now but to my thinking putridly hot. In ten minutes I've got to go down to my office and stop there until midday parades – trying to understand complaints and try criminals in an utterly unknown language with an interpreter. It makes me much hotter than taking violent exercise, this trying to understand what they say. I know about three words of *khas kura* (Gurkhali) and a lot of their words are like Hindustani so we get on somehow. I don't know what an Englishman would say if he were tried by a Chinaman who only spoke Chinese and a little French – but that's what it amounts to.'[3]

In fact Bill was being overly modest with his 'three words' – he was quick to master both Gurkhali and Urdu, at least well enough to command his company, and his evident affection for his men was soon reciprocated. His Gurkhas gave him a private nickname, 'Slimbo', a sure sign of his acceptance into the regimental family. Nicknames were frequently uncomplimentary and officers were discouraged from inquiring too diligently about their own nicknames or those of their brother officers. The Gurkhas loved to mimic and lampoon the mannerisms and quirks of their commanders in the privacy of their barrack rooms and Bill was certain he was no exception, although in public he was always respectfully referred to as 'OC sahib'. As in most Gurkha regiments, Bill was the only British officer in his company and quickly developed a close working relationship with his Gurkha colleagues, known as VCOs – Viceroy Commissioned Officers. (More than two-thirds of the officers in the Indian Army were VCOs.)

He had not been long in Abbottabad before his company was ordered into action on the North-West Frontier, where the fierce and warlike border tribes, mainly Pathans, had never accepted British sovereignty (or, indeed, any authority other than their own) and had been fighting an elusive guerrilla war for close on 100 years in the Frontier's harsh and lonely wilderness of jagged peaks, scrub and desert interspersed with rocky outcrops. The threat from the border tribes had increased greatly after the brief Anglo-Afghan War in 1919. The Afghanistan army was quickly repulsed after invading India but not before the local tribesmen had taken the opportunity to equip themselves with modern weapons – notably Lee-Enfield rifles – captured from the retreating Afghans.

The military was frequently deployed in an attempt to dominate the area, which stretched hundreds of miles from Quetta to the Khyber Pass, but the bleak and distant terrain, familiar home ground to the tribesmen, made the task extremely perilous. Units deployed to the Frontier reached their operational area by a series of route marches, camping overnight, digging in tents to thwart snipers and sleeping in shell scrapes. Because they were tied to their cumbersome lines of communication – columns of pack transport carrying food, water and ammunition on which their lives depended – their movement was restricted to the valley floors while their lightly equipped enemy operated with comparative freedom on the hills and ridges, flitting from rock to rock and waiting for an opportunity to attack. So it was that the troops were subjected to constant sniper fire, ambush, booby traps on roads and hit and run attacks on outposts and isolated forts. It was little wonder that the Frontier was referred to by soldiers as 'the Grim'.

Bill liked to tell a story about an incident on the Frontier when one of his platoons was being sniped at and he went forward to investigate. He had to cross a stretch of open ground and as he did so he was fired at on several occasions and was obliged to dodge from cover to cover. When he finally arrived at the platoon's position he found the VCO grinning from ear to ear and when Bill demanded, a mite tetchily, why he had not been given covering fire, the other man replied: 'You looked so funny dodging about in the open.' Bill had some difficulty seeing the funny side of it.

Fighting in hostile terrain against cunning and courageous tribal war parties posed a range of difficulties very different from those encountered in conventional warfare and for young officers the learning curve on the North-West Frontier was steep, particularly since mountain warfare techniques were still in their infancy. For want of a better strategy, or indeed any coherent strategy at all, the military countered the insurgency with a series of 'butcher and bolt' punitive expeditions designed to terrorise the local population into submission, a strategy that, inevitably, bolstered their opposition and hatred of the Raj. ('Hearts and minds' had yet to be adopted as a means of winning over locals.)

In October, Bill took part in one such raid, against the fortified Wazir village of Char Kahn, while his company was camped in the desert at Thal, on the Kurran river. At the briefing in the civil rest house, one of Bill's favourite theories about British military operations was confirmed. There were, he had decided, two characteristics common to every operation – first, that it would be fought uphill, and second, that it would be fought on terrain covering the junction of at least two map sheets. For the raid on Char Kahn, some 11 miles south of their camp, four separate sheets of maps were required. The Wazirs – a warrior tribe with a notorious reputation for blood feuds – had recently been causing the authorities more than the usual difficulties and as a result it had been decided that their village should be burned down as a reprisal.

A mixed force of Sikhs, Punjabis and Gurkhas was assembled

for the operation – the 1st/6th Gurkhas were to provide the rear-guard. The column set off after dark following what was described as a 'made camel road', a rutted track full of stones and potholes and difficult to follow in the dark. After crossing the wide, fast-flowing Kurran with some difficulty, the Gurkhas in the rearguard lost contact with the troops in the main column and Bill was sent ahead, on his horse, Darkie, to find them and request that they halt to enable the rearguard to catch up. For a while he thought he was lost. Riding alone through hostile territory in the dark was not an experience he would want to repeat, but he eventually found the column and was given a reprimand by the Brigadier in com-mand, who seemed to hold him personally responsible for the delay. He returned to his regiment to receive another tongue-lashing from his CO for not asking the Brigadier why the blazes the column had not halted after crossing the river to prevent them falling behind.

By first light the column was within sight of Char Kahn and the first shots were exchanged with the tribesmen. 'The first shot of a fight affects people in different ways,' Bill wrote. 'The Gürkhas halted around us, fell suddenly silent, then a low buzz of talk came from them. Our old Subadar-Major sighed gently ... he breathed in a mixture of mild interest and satisfaction. The colonel let his false teeth fall to his lower lip and recovered them with an audible click. For myself, I had momentarily an uncomfortable cross-channel feel-ing where my breakfast should have been. Why do battles always start at dawn on an empty stomach?'[4]

Initially, the raid went relatively smoothly and the troops set fire to the village before the tribesmen could organise any proper de-fence. It was the retreat from such operations that often presented the greatest danger, as Bill was quickly to discover. Barely had the column evacuated the smoking ruins of the village before a Wazir war party was in hot pursuit, intent on killing every soldier it could find. The rearguard was very soon in action, with one line retiring while the line behind provided covering fire – a gruelling process of leap-frogging which sometimes required the retiring line to make a run for it under intense fire from the hillsides all around.

Bill was always amazed by the casual behaviour of the Gurkhas under fire. At one point as they were hastily splashing across a river with the tribesmen closing in on them Bill noticed that one of his men had stopped and was staring intently into the water. Bill shouted at him to move on, but he took no notice, bent down, put a hand in the water and then with a sudden flick tossed a silver fish on to the bank. He picked it up and shoved it in his haversack with a broad grin. A little later, a mule was wounded, broke loose and bolted towards the pursuing Wazirs, casting its saddle and scattering bits of machine gun across the ground. The subadar in command of the retreating platoon immediately put his men to work gathering the gun parts regardless of the fire from the hills and the spurts of dust springing up around their feet. The subadar himself picked up the mule's heavy pack saddle and began running back to cover.

Bill watched what happened next with a mixture of astonishment and admiration. 'After a hundred yards he slowed to a walk, and himself halting, faced towards the enemy, raised the saddle high above his head, the broken girth streaming loose, and roared "M'lai her. Look at me, Subadar Ratanbahadur Rana, I.-D.-S.-M." and he fairly rolled the initials of his decoration, the Indian Distinguished Service Medal, off his tongue. He then did a couple of press-ups with the saddle and resumed his retirement. As a bit of bravado it was worse than foolish – but there was something magnificent about it. It pleased the men tremendously; the Gurkha is a simple soul who likes people to behave in character. So do I, when it is Ratanbahadur's sort of character.'[5]

Bill calculated at the end of the operation that they had marched 32 miles in 23 hours over very difficult terrain, across several rivers, much of the time harried by the Wazirs. By the time they got back to their camp they were utterly exhausted. But it was, he would have been the first to admit, very valuable experience. Active service on the North-West Frontier was a challenge for any junior officer and a proving ground for individual soldiering skills and leadership. Often isolated in remote outposts and left to their own resources, they faced a resourceful enemy quick to take advantage of tactical mistakes or weak defences. They had to think quickly, on their feet, and their decisions were frequently a matter of life or death. They had to win the confidence of their men, learn how to get the best out of them and deal with any number of fast-changing crises. Bill enjoyed his service on the Frontier, although he was not afraid to admit there were many occasions when he was 'frightened to death'.

It could also be a lonely life. 'The hour of my solitary dinner approaches,' he wrote to Pratt from Miranjani Camp in the Murree hills. 'I have dined alone every night for a month now, except once. My Gurkha Officer comes in after dinner sometimes to drink whisky Macdonalds with me, our conversation is either business or stories of some of his twenty-two brothers – I don't think he knows how many sisters he's got. Females don't count for much in this part of the world – at least not sisters. Some other fellow's young *swashnie*, or Gurkha wife, is possibly another thing ...

'I generally get bored with my own company at about half past nine and go to bed. There's a bit of a wind getting up tonight. We had some tents blown down the other night but my 80-pounder will stand a good deal. I'm typing this by the light of a hurricane *bhuttie*, or India lamp, which is waving about in the breeze. Consequently I can't see what I have written and I'm not good enough to type in the dark. I think I had better chuck it and go to bed ...'⁶

When the regiment was not deployed on the North-West Frontier it was kept busy on 'aid to the civil power' duties, dealing with local disorder, largely caused either by ethnic tensions between the majority Hindu and minority Muslim communities or by increasing resentment against British rule. The Amritsar Massacre, in April 1919, when 50 Indian Army soldiers were ordered to fire on the crowd at a religious festival, killing between 379 and 1,000 men, women and children (the first estimate is British, the second Indian), had prompted widespread disturbances across the country and boosted the movement for non-cooperation with India's British rulers led by the scrawny figure of Mahatma Gandhi, whose uncompromising rhetoric thrilled the Indians as much as it alarmed the British. The goodwill and loyalty engendered in India towards Britain by the Great War quickly dissipated in the Amritsar aftermath and when Gandhi assumed leadership of the Indian National Congress in 1921 the campaign for Swaraj – independence of India from foreign dominance – gathered pace, until around a third of the army in India was deployed on internal security duties.

At Bill's level, 'aid to the civil power' was trammelled by India's notorious bureaucracy. Before he could take action of any kind, he first had to obtain the signature of a magistrate, or some other authorised official, on Indian Army Form D.908, which was headed 'Instructions to Officers Acting in Aid of the Civil Power for Dispersal of Unlawful Assemblies' and contained detailed instructions about what he could, and could not, do when faced either with mobs screaming for each other's blood or from a unified mob screaming for his blood and that of his men. The sparks that ignited trouble on the streets usually flew off a flint of simmering resentment. Bill was duty officer when he was called out to quell a riot in Gurampur, set off because a Muslim meat market had been built within sniffing distance of the Hindu quarter, thus outraging the sensibilities of the strictly vegetarian residents.

Not long afterwards he was commanding a night patrol through the town to enforce a dusk to dawn curfew which had been imposed to deter further trouble. When the headlights of the leading vehicle picked out a figure in a white suit scurrying down a side street he was ordered, at gunpoint, to halt. In the murky half-light Bill thought he recognised him, from his suit and the bag he carried, as a little Hindu doctor he had seen treating the injured at an earlier riot. The man confirmed that he was, indeed, a doctor, explained he was on his way to deliver a baby and showed Bill his pass signed by the local police superintendent. Bill warned him to be careful as he was close to the Muslim area, but the doctor said he was almost at his destination and pointed to a house a few doors along the road. Bill allowed him to continue and climbed back into the leading truck. From the cab he watched the doctor, still visible in his white suit even away from the glare of the headlights, step up to a doorway in the street and rap on the door. As he went to knock again a shadow detached itself from the gloom on the other side of the street and flitted towards him. Before Bill could do anything he saw the glint of a knife and a bare arm raised to strike. The little doctor never stood a chance as the knife was plunged into his back; he gasped and crumpled to the ground as his assailant slipped away up a side street.

Bill leapt down from the lorry, assigned two men to tend to the doctor then set off in pursuit with the remainder of the patrol. They

chased the culprit through a warren of back alleys and turned a
corner just in time to see him scramble over a high mud wall. Bill
attempted to follow but as he was heaving himself up the wall it
crumbled and he fell back to the ground. While he was picking
himself up, one of his Gurkhas reported that their quarry had disappeared into a house across a courtyard on the other side of the
wall. Now more than ever determined not to let him get away, Bill
clambered over what remained of the wall, crossed the courtyard
and banged on the door. When there was no response, he drew
his revolver, told his men to stand back and fired at the keyhole.
Absolutely nothing happened – the door remained firmly shut. (He
admitted later that perhaps he had been reading too much Bulldog
Drummond.)

Eventually an upstairs window opened and an angry voice demanded to know what was going on. 'I am a British officer,' Bill
shouted. 'Open the door.' The reply was unconvincing – there was,
it seemed rather improbably, no key. At that moment four of his
men appeared with a heavy wooden bench which they began to
use as a battering ram. After three or four crashes against the door
there was the sound of bolts being drawn and it was opened by an
enraged old man who wailed in protest as the soldiers barged in.
He was joined by other male members of the family, all shouting
and waving their arms as the search began. There was no sign of
the assailant in any of the rooms on the ground and first floors but
when Bill went to lead his men to the top floor the way was barred
by a carpet hanging across the stairs, signifying purdah. More importantly, standing in front of the carpet was a large woman who
began screaming at him from behind a strip of muslin she held over
her mouth. Above the uproar, the elderly man who had reluctantly
answered the door shouted, in perfect English, that the top floor
was the *zenana*, the area of the house reserved for women that men
could not enter.

There followed a furious argument, with Bill insisting that he had
the right to search the top floor and the men in the house equally
insistent that he could under no circumstances breach the sanctity
of the *zenana*. Bill suggested that the women waited in a room on a
lower floor while his men searched their quarters but they refused to
give way. In the end, increasingly angry, he gave them an ultimatum

– either the women be brought downstairs, or his men would search the floor with them present. Very unwillingly, with much cursing and muttering, they agreed to give the soldiers access to the top floor once the women had been removed. A procession of about a dozen women, all dressed in burqas, traipsed silently down the stairs under the watchful eyes of the soldiers. When they had been closeted in a side room, Bill led the search party upstairs into a suffocating sanctum reeking of stale perfume. They looked every-where, under beds and furniture, in every closet, and still they found nothing.

Bill had posted men all round the property to ensure that no one climbed out of a window or slipped away through a side door and so was convinced the assailant was still in the house. The only hiding place was among the women but he knew that asking the women to show their faces to him was out of the question. It was his sergeant who suggested that checking the women's hands might be quite as revealing as their faces. (In an account he left of the incident, Bill pointed out by way of curious explanation that the sergeant was 'a married man'.)

Back downstairs, Bill told the elderly man who seemed to be in charge that they believed the man they were pursuing might be among the women. The old boy began to splutter that it was quite impossible but Bill cut him short. He explained that their quarry had a finger missing from one hand (the fictitious tale he and his sergeant had devised) and if the women would show him their hands as they returned upstairs he would be satisfied; he and his men would leave the house and not return. After urgently confer-ring with the other menfolk in whispers, the man finally consented, fulminating all the while that it was an outrage, bringing down the wrath of Allah on all infidels and in particular those that had in-vaded his home.

One by one the women passed between Bill and his sergeant with their hands held out. All were small and obviously feminine until the seventh or eighth 'woman', whose hands were unusually large and calloused. Bill glanced over to where the men of the house were huddled in a corner and saw how tense and strained they appeared, and then looked across at his sergeant, who nodded imperceptibly. Still, he hesitated. If he was wrong and ripped the veil from a woman it would be a disaster and would inflame the entire Muslim community. Fortunately, his sergeant rose to the occasion and 'accidentally' dropped his rifle butt on to the 'woman's' slippered foot, producing a deep-throated howl of pain from under the burqa that could only have come from a man. Before he could make a dash for it he was grabbed by the soldiers and taken into custody. All the other men in the house were also arrested as accessories; the story caused a great deal of entertainment later in the officers' mess.

In February 1921, Bill wrote to Pratt to tell him he was returning once more to the Frontier, affecting the world-weary disdain of the seasoned warrior: 'I'm off back to jolly Daramsand in about ten days. Can't say I want to go a bit – it will be getting hot and fly-blown again soon. Besides, the war is still going on. Our friends the Wazirs have taken advantage of the reduction of the Daramsand force to two battalions to get uppish. They scuppered the escort to the surveying party that is drawing maps of the delightful district last week. Only one wounded man got away – the bodies of the rest were recovered that night having been subjected to what we call "the usual Eastern indignities". Luckily, our battalion was not on escort duty when it happened or we should have been for it. The blighters tried a raid on us just afterwards but beyond the loss of one greatcoat, and pair of boots and the side of our tennis court the affair was merely a huroosh and some shooting. I hope they'll calm before I go back.'[7]

The following month Bill was appointed adjutant of the 1st/6th Gurkhas, the second most important commissioned post in the battalion, after the commanding officer, and a position he would hold for the next three and a half years. It was clear evidence that his worth as an officer was appreciated and recognised by his peers. The adjutant was responsible for the behaviour and discipline of the junior officers, the training of new recruits and the day-to-day running of the battalion. It was a job that required a firm hand tempered with humanity at a time, after the war, when some officers were finding it difficult to settle down to peacetime soldiering. Bruce Scott joined the regiment as a captain shortly after Bill was appointed adjutant: 'Without being sergeant-majorish, Bill, through his firm and tactful handling, kept everybody in their right place and anybody who tended to be "bolshie" was quickly sat upon, with the result that we were a very happy crowd. He was a perfectionist – under his eye the guard mounting and bugles very quickly became as good as they had ever been; he spoke the language well, knew men intimately and they in turn had a respect and affection for him. Once a Gurkha orderly brought him a cup of tea with a fly in it. Bill pointed it out and the orderly just flicked it out with his finger on to the ground and stamped on it. That was the kind of story he loved to tell.'[8]

Coincidentally, Herbert Gibbs, the battalion Quartermaster (known to all his friends as 'Gibbos') had attended the same school as Bill – St Philip's in Birmingham – and they became close friends. Gibbs asked Bill to be his best man when he married and remembered Bill as a fine adjutant who never threw his weight about. 'He was the best officer in the regiment. He would leave you under no misapprehension if you made a mess of something. You knew you would not get away with it but at the same time you never felt it would be held against you, but he did tell you off good and proper. He also passed on praise when it was due.

'He was always a soldier but extraordinarily human the whole time. When one of the men lost his false teeth, Bill paid for the top row and I paid for the bottom. The man came into my office some time later and I asked how his teeth were and he pulled them out, put them on my desk and said, "This set is yours and these are the Adjutant's."

'Bill worked like hell but he had plenty of time for fun; he was always ready to join in the fun and games in the mess. Like all of us, he enjoyed horseplay. We had two old guns outside the mess, Bubble and Squeak, and on mess nights we use to have gun drill and Bill was always Number One gunner. It was childish but fun. He was not much good at games. He was handicapped because of his wounds and couldn't really play tennis because he couldn't get his arm up. He could shoot, but he was out of games really.'[9]

When Philip Pratt, who by then was an NCO in the Warwickshire Yeomanry complained in a letter to Bill that his social life within the Yeomanry was rather staid, his friend was prompted to describe the rumbustious life in the 1st/6th Gurkhas officers' mess on a *burra khana*: 'The last we had was when we won the Peshawar District Football Cup – most of us were "mellow" before we had christened the cup – several of us having been to the Gurkha Officers' Club where one eats large curried chickens and drinks raw rum in tumblers. After Mess we had all the Gurkha officers in and I think even your low taste would have been satisfied. Normally we are almost Pussfoot [cautious] – can't afford anything else with whisky at ten rupees a bottle – but on great occasions we do break out.'[10] Bill might have been putting a gloss on the evening for his friend's benefit, because his colleagues mostly recalled that he was a comparatively modest drinker.

While at Abbottabad, Bill acquired a dog, Peggy, a wire-haired terrier which became a great favourite with the Gurkhas after an incident that caused a lot of amusement in the battalion. Bill was invited one evening to dinner with a colleague who had recently married; naturally he took Peggy along. He was the first guest to arrive and was, of course, offered a drink. Other guests arrived and more drinks were served with no sign of dinner appearing. Eventually Bill inquired of his hostess if there was perhaps a problem. She admitted there was. 'Your dog,' she said, 'has pinched the dinner.' Peggy was last seen disappearing down the road as fast as her legs would carry her with a leg of mutton – dinner – in her mouth.

Bill did not have much luck with animals generally. In his letters to Pratt he often referred to his 'charger' or his 'fiery steed' as if he was an enthusiastic rider but the reality was that he did not much like horses and the feeling was mutual. When he first arrived at the 1st/6th Gurkhas he was informed that all officers were required to attend riding school and pass the school's stiff examination in horsemanship: Bill failed three times before he got through. Bill, said Scott, was a 'thoroughly bad' rider, would regularly fall off his horse and once achieved the distinction of falling off a water buffalo carrying him across a river, emerging covered in mud with only the whites of his eyes showing.

On a New Year's Day parade after he had been made adjutant he was sitting on his horse waiting for an inspection when it suddenly reared up on its hind legs and deposited him unceremoniously on to the parade ground. Luckily he managed to clamber back on before the Brigadier General turned up, but there was hardly an officer on the parade who was not smirking. Later, on a visit to a cavalry brigade at Meerut, his horse bolted. 'I distinguished myself by choosing the fiercest [horse],' he explained in a laconic letter to Pratt, 'and being bolted with for a start and, having regained control more or less, getting pitched on my head at the third jump.'[11]

Bill's letters to his friend were usually light-hearted and self-effacing and rarely mentioned the multitude of problems with which he had to deal as adjutant. The job required him to maintain a fine balance between being a tactful diplomat and firm disciplinarian, especially when his brother officers were involved. There was considerable disgruntlement among young officers commanding companies in the battalion, for example, when they were usurped by more senior men rejoining the regiment after long spells of staff or extra-regimental duty. The junior officers felt they knew their men far better than the newcomers and resented being forced to give up their commands, but when they began to air their resentment in the mess Bill stopped it immediately, bluntly telling them to cut out the bellyaching and get on with their jobs. Although he was undoubtedly sympathetic to the young officers' complaints, he would never countenance backstabbing in the mess and his ruling was accepted without question.

A trickier situation arose when a new commanding officer, Lieutenant Colonel G. M. Glynton, arrived from the 3rd Gurkhas in 1922. Bill got off to a somewhat shaky start with his new CO by mistaking him for a piano tuner. He was expecting a tuner to show up at his office and when an unprepossessing stranger put his head round the door he demanded, unceremoniously, 'Who might you be?' It was Glynton. A short, punctilious man, he managed to exasperate all the officers of his new regiment by constantly harping on about the superior methods of his old one. Bill's friend Herbert Gibbs was aware that Bill was as irritated by the new CO as everyone else (although he would never allow a word to be spoken against him in the mess) and greatly admired the way his friend went about 'reforming' him.

'It came to a head over a trivial matter,' Gibbs recalled. 'We were told [by the new CO] that the men did not know how to pitch tents in the correct way. If there was one thing we could do it was just that. The battalion had marched from the end of Mesopotamia to the shores of the Caspian Sea, 589 miles, between 18 September and 28 November, 1918, and during the hot weather of 1919 marched most of the way back – as far as Kut. On return to India the battalion was for most of the next two years under canvas. The men were so used to pitching tents that they could have done it with their eyes shut.'

Bill decided the time had come to set the new CO straight on certain matters related to the 6th Gurkhas by arranging, with Gibbs' help, a discreet demonstration for him of the way the 6th Gurkhas pitched tents as opposed to the method he proposed. (Glynton had even drawn a sketch of the way it was done in the 3rd Gurkhas and circulated it to the officers.) It was clear from the demonstration that there was nothing to choose between the two techniques. Afterwards, in the CO's office, Gibbs sat with his heart in his mouth as Bill informed Glynton, very politely but firmly, that much as the 6th Gurkhas admired the 3rd Gurkhas, they did not feel the need for any instruction from that regiment and that the Colonel should understand that the 6th Gurkhas were not the 3rd Gurkhas and never would be. Glynton coloured and Gibbs expected him to explode with fury at being addressed so candidly by a junior officer. 'For a moment it seemed that the storm would burst,' Gibbs wrote, 'and that we were for the high jump.' However, after a brief and tense silence, Glynton swallowed and said, 'Right, I understand, so that is now settled, thank you.'[12] The matter was never mentioned again.

Relations greatly improved thereafter and Bill came to like and respect Colonel Glynton, not least for his belief that his young officers should be offered every opportunity and inducement to attend the Indian Army Staff College at Quetta. Many Indian Army officers thought going to staff college was a 'very poor show', that officers should stay with their regiments rather than become 'staff wallahs'. Glynton fundamentally disagreed: he encouraged all his young officers to compete for a place, set practice papers for them, marked their efforts and organised discussion groups and tutorials. The result was that the 1st/6th Gurkhas under his command produced an unprecedented number of generals from a single battalion – Bill Slim, Bruce Scott and David 'Punch' Cowan – who were all friends in Abbottabad and who, by extraordinary chance, would end up together fighting the Japanese in Burma.

In November 1922 the 1st/6th Gurkhas were redeployed to Malakand, a frontier station guarding the Malakand Pass, where they would remain for the next two years. Malakand acquired some notoriety when in 1897 an army of 10,000 Pashtun tribesmen laid siege to the tiny British garrison there; the relief force included a Second Lieutenant Winston Churchill, who wrote an account of the action for the *Daily Telegraph*, articles which later became the basis for a book, *The Story of the Malakand Field Force: An Episode of Frontier War*.

'Malakand isn't a bad spot – it's easily the pick of the Frontier Stations,' Bill reported in a letter to Pratt. 'Awfully windy and getting very cold now. But what with stone houses to live in with electric light installed it's almost too good to be true. I always wanted as a small boy to live in a fort and here I am. It's just like a toy fort – with a round tower on top and a big flag flying over all – and I'm certainly living right inside it. Actually it's very peaceful here at the moment and if I only had a few minutes to myself during the day I could continue to fix up a very decent quarter for myself. I am doing so gradually only it's devilish difficult getting everything carted up the road.'[13]

To judge by his letters to his friend, Bill's life in India could have been featured in the pages of *The Boy's Own Paper*, but he forbore to mention the hard slog – the work he put in at nights studying for the interminable examinations that were the bane of every young officer's life in both the Indian and British Armies. All Bill's colleagues at the time commented on his dedication to study and his determination to advance his career. He would play a full part in the fun and games in the mess, but alone in his room the lights would burn late as he worked at his books. Scott remembered Bill sitting up half the night reading and writing, although he allowed himself the indulgence of regularly reading a scurrilous Sunday newspaper, the *People*, which he joked was his 'dirt ration'. At the end of 1923 he was rewarded in his annual report with a recommendation for the Staff College. Endorsing the recommendation, General Lord Birdwood, Commander-in-Chief, Northern Command, India, added: 'A first class officer. Best of his rank in the Battalion.'

In 1924 Bill became eligible for home leave – officers in the Indian Army were allowed to return to Britain for six months every three years. In March, in the company of his friend Gibbos, he travelled by train to Bombay where he boarded a ship bound for England, a country he had not seen for seven years.

6

Bill in Love

B ill had planned to spend much of his leave studying for the Staff College examination, but in fact a great deal of time was consumed moving his elderly mother, then 71, and two equally elderly aunts, from the grimy environs of industrial Birmingham to the balmy climes of Bournemouth on the south coast – a famously genteel location for the retired and those wishing to see out their days in a deckchair on the promenade. Afterwards Bill confessed to his friend Gibbos that he would rather have moved 'a blooming Division' than those three old ladies.[1] Bill and his brother Charlie, now a GP in Wolverhampton, bought the house – 7 Arcadia Avenue – jointly with the proceeds of their war gratuities. It boasted all modern comforts, including electric light, but their mother insisted on continuing to use oil lamps on the basis that they had served her very well thus far and she saw no earthly reason to change. In pride of place in the sitting room was her harmonium, on which she liked to play her favourite hymns.

After settling the ladies into their new home, Bill caught a train for London where he ran into an old friend, Tony Ayrton, whom he had last seen in Mesopotamia. Bill was standing outside the Cavalry Club in Piccadilly when a striking mustard-yellow Rolls-Royce drew up at the kerb with his friend at the wheel. Bill's first thought was that his friend's 'rich uncle' must have died, but Ayrton scoffed at the notion and breezily informed Bill that the car, which he called Elizabeth, was a one of the 'spoils of war'. Over a drink in the club he explained further.

In Mesopotamia, Ayrton was the dashing commander of a Light Armoured Motor Battery, equipped with Rolls-Royce armoured cars, which had frequently crossed the path of the 9th Warwicks. The battery was part of the Machine Gun Corps, a unit which frequently fought in advance of the front line and suffered such heavy casualties that it was given the nickname 'the Suicide Club'. Ayrton had a happy habit of turning up at critical moments: on one occasion when the 9th Warwicks were advancing on a Turkish position a sudden gust of wind swept away the dust screen set up by an artillery barrage leaving Bill and his men horribly exposed several hundred yards from their objective. Just as Bill braced himself for the Turkish guns to open up, Ayrton appeared leading a column of eight armoured cars which swept into the gap, their machine guns firing continuously. Within minutes it was all over and Bill had nothing to do but round up the prisoners.

Sitting together in leather armchairs in a London club, Mesopotamia must have seemed very far away, but Ayrton brought it all back, telling Bill how it was that very action that provided him with an opportunity. As they roared in front of the Turkish lines one of his cars was hit by a shell and virtually destroyed, although the chassis was miraculously undamaged. By salvaging the engine and other bits and pieces from a car wrecked earlier and written off by the pen-pushers, his engineers managed to create an extra vehicle, not on the battery's strength. 'Pure buckshee', as he put it. The problems came in 1919 when the battery was due to be shipped home and the embarkation officer refused to accept the surplus car. Ayrton was undaunted. The battery establishment included a Ford van which was used to carry spares – it was promptly driven into desert and abandoned to make space for the 'buckshee Rolls'.

But what happened at the other end, Bill inquired, when you arrived back in Britain minus a van but plus a Rolls? Ayrton grinned. Simple, he said. He wired his brother from Aden and arranged for him to buy a replacement Ford van, second-hand, which was waiting on the quayside in Southampton when they got back. So the battery returned to its base with its full complement of vehicles and Ayrton's brother drove off in the 'buckshee Rolls', subsequently fitted with a new body and painted yellow and now parked outside the club, no doubt attracting admiring glances from passers-by totally unaware of its provenance in the Mesopotamian desert.

It was on this same trip that Bill encountered his erstwhile troublesome recruit, Private Chuck, the soldier he described in

Unofficial History as 'an incorrigible rogue'. He was walking alone through Kensington late one night and, as he stepped off the pavement to cross a deserted square, a car screeched round the corner at high speed, forcing him to leap out of its path. The car stopped with a squeal of brakes and a man in rough clothes, a cap and muffler, jumped out. Bill was about to remonstrate with him when he recognised him as Private Chuck. Although Chuck had caused him all kinds of difficulties in the 9th Warwicks, he had got to like and respect the man and was pleased to see him.

To Bill's disappointment, his pleasure was not reciprocated. Chuck grudgingly shook Bill's outstretched hand, but was edgy and obviously anxious to get away. Bill asked him what he had been doing since the war. He was evasive and kept looking over Bill's shoulder. Bill persisted, asking if he had found a job. Chuck shook his head, said he had to be on his way, muttered something about meeting a girl and hurried off on foot. Bill watched him go, hurt that he had not been willing to spend a minute or two with his former company commander.

No sooner had he disappeared than an explanation for his haste materialised: a police car tore into the square and pulled up alongside the car Chuck had left behind. Three men jumped out, one of them a uniformed police constable. When they had checked there was no one in the other car, they approached Bill and asked him if he had seen anyone driving it. Bill said yes, a man had got out and walked off. He asked what was going on and the plain clothes police officer told him the car had been stolen and used in a smash and grab raid half an hour earlier.

When Bill was asked if he could describe the man who had got out of the car, he thought about all the trouble he had had with Chuck in the 9th Warwicks; but he also thought about the song he had sung when their troopship was being attacked, and his spirit and courage under fire, and the fact that they were in the same regiment and bound by loyalty to the same cap badge.

'Describe him?' he finally said. 'No, I'm afraid I couldn't do that.' If Bill ever suffered a pang of guilt about failing to assist the police with their inquiries, he never mentioned it. Indeed, the fact that he included the anecdote in *Unofficial History* rather indicated that he felt more pride than guilt.

The most significant aspect of Bill's first home leave occurred not in Britain but on the ship returning to Bombay when he met, and fell in love with, the young woman who would become his wife. Aileen Robertson was 23 years old, one of three children of a minister in the Church of Scotland. Aileen's father, the Reverend John Anderson Robertson, ministered to his Presbyterian flock from a beautiful church in Corstophine, an affluent suburb of Edinburgh. Her mother, Jeannie, was a member of the wealthy Mathewson family, well-known linen manufacturers in Dunfermline.

The reverend met his own future wife when the Mathewsons were renting Killiecrankie House, near Pitlochry, for the summer and John was the new young minister at the nearby Tenandry Kirk, where the family worshipped. Jeannie's mother disapproved of their burgeoning friendship and so they were obliged to conduct their romance clandestinely by mail. (It was said within the family that Mrs Mathewson wanted her daughter to stay single so that she would have someone to look after her in old age, but perhaps she simply wanted more for Jeannie than an impoverished minister, or was worried that John was five years younger than her daughter.) The morning post was delivered to Killiecrankie by a Crimean war veteran who had lost an arm and who carried letters tied in bundles hanging from a hook on his prosthetic arm. Jeannie would sit on a grassy bank up the lane from the house, waiting for the postman's pony and trap, grab the bundle for Killiecrankie House and extract the love letters from John before her parents could see them. When John proposed marriage, Jeannie's mother only gave her reluctant approval to the match after her two older brothers intervened on their sister's behalf, warning their mother that she 'had to let Jeannie go'. Jeannie Mathewson and John Robertson married in June 1895 and moved into Tenandry Manse, where their first child, Athol, was born in 1897. Another boy, Douglas, followed eighteen months later; Aileen arrived in 1901.

In May 1903 the Robertsons and their three young children moved to Corstophine, where John became the minister at St Anne's, then known as 'the Tin Kirk' for its corrugated iron roof. (In 1913 the Tin Kirk was replaced by a new church designed in the style of Romanesque churches in north-east Italy. The central memorial window is now dedicated to Athol Robertson, who was killed on the Somme; his brother Douglas won a DSO and MC in Flanders before he was 21 and went on to have a distinguished career in the colonial service.)

Aileen was a gifted musician – she took piano and singing lessons as a child, became a leading voice in the church choir and performed in amateur recitals in Edinburgh. Her life might have been very different had not her wealthy Aunt Nellie, who had married into the Mathewson family and lived in a large house in Dunfermline with a butler and retinue of servants, invited her to join her on a trip to India in the autumn of 1924. Nellie was recently widowed and had lost two of her sons on the Western Front; she was planning to visit her remaining son, Dick (William Richard Mathewson), who was a medical missionary in Kashmir, but she did not want to travel alone and suggested to the Reverend Robertson that Aileen would be an admirable travelling companion. Nellie would, of course, pay all the expenses. Initially Aileen demurred; she did not want to leave home, particularly if it was thought she was joining what was then rudely known as 'the fishing fleet' – girls looking for husbands in India or the Far East. She was also enjoying life in Edinburgh. It was her father who persuaded her to change her mind, pointing out the benefits of travel – broadening the mind, et cetera – and the simple reality that he would never be able to afford to send her abroad, quite apart from the fact that it would have been ill mannered to turn down Aunt Nellie's generous offer.

A passage to India was arranged for the two ladies on a ship leaving from Marseilles in France, to avoid the long sea passage across the Bay of Biscay and through the Gibraltar Strait into the Mediterranean. Coincidentally, a young Gurkha captain returning to duty in India had made the same arrangement. It is not definitively recorded how and where Aileen and Bill first met – one version asserts that it was on the cross-Channel ferry from Dover, another that it was on a train heading south through France to Marseilles. George Mathewson, Nellie's grandson, has researched the family history and written a short account entitled 'The Courting of Aileen Robertson by Captain Bill Slim' which includes the following: 'The elderly aunt [Nellie] was fastidious about being in good time for appointments and so it was that the two ladies were aboard the boat at Dover (?) in very good time before its departure. Thus it was that

Aileen was able to go up and stand on the deck above the gangplank and survey the passengers as they came on board. Among them was a young Gurkha captain, Bill Slim, who happened to look up, their eyes met and thus began a high seas romance …'[2]

However they met, there is little doubt that Bill was captivated from the moment he first set eyes on Aileen. A quiet word with the purser on board the ship in Marseilles secured for him a place on her table, but unfortunately Aunt Nellie took her self-imposed duties as an unwitting chaperone very seriously and insisted on sitting between them. Nevertheless, Bill contrived to spend as much time as possible with Aileen, strolling the decks, playing deck games or sitting in adjoining deckchairs and talking. Bill had a great sense of humour and could always make her laugh. Every moment convinced Bill that Aileen was the girl for him and three days out from Marseilles, uncharacteristically impetuous, he asked her to marry him. She, sensible girl, said she needed more time, but the voyage to Bombay was a long one, through the Suez Canal and across the Indian Ocean, and Bill pursued his suit with determination, despite Aunt Nellie's equal determination to keep an eye on them. On the rare occasions when they thought they might be alone Bill would invariably hear a discreet cough, which was Aunt Nellie announcing her vigilant presence.

Dick Mathewson was waiting to greet his mother and cousin when their ship docked in Bombay and escort them to their hotel. As soon as she had a moment Aileen told her cousin, bubbling with excitement, that she had found *the* man. Mathewson was unimpressed. 'There's always a man,' he replied warily, 'when you're about.' Nevertheless, Aileen insisted that this was *the one*. Bill risked overstaying his leave by four days to spend more time with her in Bombay, still under the strict supervision of Aunt Nellie. He was introduced to Mathewson and when they were alone announced that he intended to marry Aileen. Mathewson liked Bill and was sympathetic, but pointed out that there would be difficulties, since he was a Catholic and she was the daughter of a Scottish Presbyterian minister. Bill made it clear he did not think it would be a problem. He also complained about what he saw as Aunt Nellie's overprotective behaviour towards her niece. 'Does she think,' he asked plaintively, 'I am going to try to seduce the poor girl?' Given Bill's ardour, it was highly probable that was exactly what Aunt Nellie did think.

Back in Abbottabad, by then thoroughly lovesick, he applied for a further ten days' compassionate leave to visit Aileen in Kashmir. By chance his friend Bruce Scott was temporarily in command in the absence of the CO and signed Bill's leave chit, almost certainly making himself liable for a roasting when the Colonel returned. Bill had to borrow money from a friend to make the trip to Kashmir, where he hired a houseboat close to the one in which Aileen and her Aunt Nellie were staying. His persistence finally paid off: Aileen said 'yes' and they became unofficially engaged. Her happiness was only slightly dented when, setting out to meet Bill one day in her best dress and silk stockings, she slipped on a plank crossing a ditch, fell into the ditch and returned to her aunt plastered in mud and sobbing with frustration.

As a sensible precaution, since Aileen knew next to nothing about soldiers or soldiering, Bill arranged for her to visit Abbottabad to introduce her to the Gurkhas and to see where she would be living after they married. Aileen stayed with Punch Cowan and his wife, Poppy, in their bungalow, and liked everything she saw. As Bill would write many years later, dedicating *Defeat Into Victory* to her, she became 'a soldier's wife who followed the drum and from mud-walled hut or Government House made a home'. But first there remained the not inconsiderable matter of parental approval.

The Reverend Robertson was frankly appalled when his daughter returned home to Edinburgh to announce she had fallen in love with an officer in the Indian Army, since he not unnaturally assumed the officer concerned was an Indian. (A mixed-race marriage was not a popular concept in the straitlaced Presbyterian Church.) Her mother, learning that her daughter's putative fiancé was a Roman Catholic, promptly rushed upstairs and locked herself in her room for 24 hours.[3] Once the Reverend Robertson had been reassured that Bill was white and his wife had finally come to terms with his Catholicism, they then had to swallow the fact that he was penniless and his prospects were unknown. To press his case, Bill had himself photographed in Abbottabad standing legs apart and staring into the middle distance with mouth set firmly and prominent chin jutting forcefully. In his pith helmet, polished boots, spurs and jodhpurs, a row of medal ribbons above the pocket on his tunic, one hand on his Sam Browne belt, the other hanging by his sword, he looked the very epitome of an English officer and gentleman. But he was still a Catholic and still faced uncertain prospects. It was a tribute to the good reverend's tolerance, or possibly an indication of how much he loved his daughter, that he finally gave the union his blessing.

On 23 November 1925, Bill wrote delightedly to his friend Philip Pratt: 'The great news – which I expect you have heard – is that I'm engaged. Aileen didn't want to tell anyone until she had squared her people. They weren't a bit keen on her marrying a penniless captain of mercenaries and asked most pointed questions about my bank balance – or rather lack of one. However, she's soothed them down and it's all fixed up.'[4]

Aileen's return to Edinburgh had at least enabled Bill to knuckle down to his studies for the Staff College at Quetta which, like its counterpart at Camberley in England, was designed to single out future high-fliers, those officers with the potential to be army commanders. When the list of successful candidates was published in June 1925, Bill's name was at the top, with 6,225 marks. 'There must have been an awfully dud lot this year,' he wrote to Pratt with his usual diffidence, 'or else I've got someone else's marks.'

Bill took three months' leave towards the end of 1925 to be able to spend some time with Aileen when she returned to India alone – a big step for a young woman making a new life in a strange country far from home. On New Year's Day 1926, in the appropriate setting of St Andrew's and St Columba's Scottish Church, Bombay – built in 1815 and known as 'the Scottish Kirk' – Bill and Aileen became man and wife. He had no more qualms marrying in a Protestant church than his father had, 40 years earlier, marrying in a Roman Catholic one. In fact the ceremony was followed some time later by a blessing in a Catholic church, but it was no more than a formality, or possibly a sop to placate his devout mother, because by then Bill's faith had more or less lapsed.

The newly-weds had little time to put down roots in Abbottabad: as soon as Bill's leave ended in February he was due to begin his two-year course at Quetta, 1,000 miles away. The Command and Staff College, Quetta, established in 1905, remains the most prestigious institution in the Pakistan army. The emblem of the college was an owl, representing learning and wisdom, perched on crossed swords and the motto when Bill was a student was 'By the Pen as much as by the Sword'. (In 1950 it was changed to the Persian couplet '*Pir sho, beyamoz – Saadi*' – grow old by learning.)

Now the capital city of Pakistan's Balochistan province, Quetta was then capital of British Baluchistan, a garrison town ringed by mountains and straddling the entrance to the picturesque Urak valley, close to the border with Afghanistan. Known as 'the fruit garden of Pakistan' for its almond and peach orchards, it is situated 1,600 metres above sea level and is prone to earthquakes and hailstorms of stunning ferocity, generating flash floods capable of sweeping away everything in their path. Summers were pleasantly warm, but winter could be bitterly cold when the wind blew off the snow-capped mountains to the north. With polo, racing and hunting readily available, Quetta was considered by many to be the most agreeable cantonment in India.

Bill and Aileen moved into one of the comfortable bungalows furnished with chintz-covered sofas and armchairs and reserved for married officers. He quickly settled down to his studies, soon creating a reputation for himself as something of a loner and a man of forthright, original and independent views, unafraid to air them. On occasion he scandalised fellow students by surreptitiously reading a novel in class if a lecture failed to engage his attention. That never happened in the classes given by Lieutenant Colonel Percy Hobart of the Royal Tank Corps, who had unusual and innovative ideas about mobile armoured warfare that Bill found both exciting and interesting. Nicknamed 'Hobo', the future Major General Sir Percy Hobart detested the 'you're not paid to think' doctrine that was prevalent in the military, and would later be recognised as a true pioneer whose specialised armour played a major role in helping the troops ashore in Normandy on D-Day 1944. Bill and 'Hobo' became friends at Quetta, bonded by a mutual belief that, on the contrary, they *were* paid to think.

Although the course was demanding on all the students and required a great deal of after-hours reading and writing – not a chore for a bookworm like Bill, who was frequently described by his friends as being one of the best-read men they had ever met – there was a vibrant social life, with regular dances in the Officers' Club, organised picnics in the hills during the summer and parties with games of sardines and charades. Formality was the order of the day – wives and girlfriends wore long dresses to dances and the men wore dinner jackets. There were jackal hunts with a pack of fox-hounds, point-to-points and duck shoots. Snow was not unusual in the winter and at Christmas bands of carol singers went around the married quarters in the cantonment.

Sport played a big part in the curriculum and gave students an op-portunity to demonstrate their leadership abilities and team spirit; Bill was obliged to stand on the sidelines since his war wounds pre-vented him from taking any active part. It did not bother him in the slightest as he showed little aptitude for games and almost caused a riot in the mess one day by daring to question the character-building value of polo – an attitude close to heresy and one that he would later joke almost got him thrown out of the college. Hunting and polo were considered suitable accomplishments for ambitious young officers between the wars and remarks like 'a good rider to hounds' would occasionally appear in annual reports. The Quetta Hunt was subsidised by the college, which paid for grooms and a forage allowance for the horses.

At the end of his first year, Bill's annual confidential report probably came as something of a shock as it suggested he was lazy. 'Captain W. J. Slim is much above average,' it started promisingly, but then continued: 'Could do very well if he worked – which he has not. Might be brilliant. Has ideas and originality. Does not play games, but is sufficiently active.'[6] (It was perhaps understandable that Bill – normally the most diligent and dedicated of men – was not working as hard as he might since he was newly married. Not only that, but Aileen had discovered towards the end of the year that she was pregnant.)

Bill was never going to take kindly to being accused of being lazy and while Aileen coped as best as she could with her pregnancy he threw himself into his work. Among his other duties he took over as editor of *The Owl*, the college magazine, and also won the Bertrand Stewart Military Prize for an essay on amphibious warfare which was later published in the *Army Quarterly*. By the time their son, John Douglas (both his grandfathers were named John), was born on 20 July 1927, he was widely accepted as one of the most gifted students in the college. 'Everyone seemed to know he was outstanding,' said his friend and fellow student Henry 'Taffy' Davies. Another student, Michael Roberts, remembered running into a friend outside the Gurkha mess and being invited to go inside to 'meet a man who is going to be Commander-in-Chief' – it was Bill. Both would eventually serve under Bill in Burma, Taffy Davies as his chief of staff and Roberts as a brigade commander.

Punch Cowan, his friend from the 6th Gurkhas, followed Bill to Quetta in 1927 and was impressed both by his knowledge and spirit and the fact that he was writing satirical articles for *The Owl* exhibiting a robust independence which the directing staff occasionally found hard to stomach. 'If he did not agree with what was happening, he made no bones about it,' Cowan recalled. 'One of the instructors used to refer to him as "that bloody man Slim". He did a lot of reading and writing and was very difficult to beat in an argument. When he was angry he stuck his chin out and looked grim, but he never shouted, always talked in a very soft voice and chose his words carefully.'[7] Bill wrote his thesis on the history of British India and Cowan borrowed his research notes, which were all perfectly organised and indicated his complete mastery of the subject.

Bill graduated from Quetta in December 1927 with an A grade, conferred on 'officers of exceptional merit and outstanding ability'. In his final report the commandant of the college was slightly guarded in his praise, perhaps because Bill had exhibited a little too much independence of character: 'He is an original quick thinker, with very decided views and personality. He is critical, has apparently read widely and can take a broad view on any subject. He is a good speaker with considerable powers of command and not afraid of expressing his own views. He is not always tactful, but an interesting man to have dealings with.'

Before leaving Quetta, Bill asked Donald MacDonald, the chaplain of the 2nd Battalion, The Cameronians, to christen his infant son. MacDonald was surprised; he knew Bill was a Catholic and imagined the boy would be baptised a Catholic. They had a long discussion during which Bill confessed that for some time he had become disenchanted with many of the tenets of his religion, in particular the obligatory dogmas clustered around the core faith. At the start of his marriage they had always said prayers before meals, but he no longer did so. MacDonald felt that Bill's disquiet was founded more on intellectual aversion than spiritual reformation. Bill leaned towards basic Christianity; as a soldier he approved of the direct simplicity of the Ten Commandments and the Lord's Prayer, rather than dreamy, abstract, ruminative theories about faith or the rubric of the Church. He was also completely unbothered by denomination. 'As a family,' his son John explained, 'we were perfectly happy praying in a mosque, a church, or a temple.'[8]

MacDonald became a good friend and they would have many talks about religion over the years. The chaplain visited Bill frequently when he was commanding the 14th Army in Burma and remembered one occasion when Punch Cowan's 17th Division was fighting to take a vital town called Meiktila. MacDonald was the division's chief padre and they were sitting together outside Bill's quarters when he suddenly turned to his friend and said, 'Now Donald, get your chaps to pray flat out for this victory.' Donald liked that – the idea of praying 'flat out' was so typical of Bill.

After graduating from Quetta, Bill was posted to Army Headquarters, Delhi, as a General Staff Officer. He would have much preferred to return to Abbottabad, to his beloved 6th Gurkhas, but his career demanded a staff appointment. He was promoted to brevet major in June 1929 and served as GSO 2 in the Directorate of Military Operations for the next four years, a period of intense frustration during which he felt his career had stalled. Promotion was painfully slow: he was 41 years old before he was made a substantive major on 19 May 1933.

Bill and Aileen's second child, a daughter, Una, was born at the Hindi Raj Hospital in Delhi on 1 December 1930. In March 1931 Bill was due for a second spell of home leave and the whole family – Aileen, four-year-old John and four-month-old Una – embarked on a ship in Bombay for the long voyage home and a round of family visiting in Scotland and England. It was the first time the Reverend Robertson and his wife had seen their son-in-law – and, of course, their grandchildren. In Corstophine the good reverend was able to reassure himself that while Bill was sun-tanned he was, very definitely, not Indian and Aileen's mother was pleased to discover that her son-in-law was charming, even though he was a Catholic. Bill's 79-year-old mother, still living in Bournemouth, was thrilled to see her grandchildren. Bill and Aileen also called on Philip Pratt in Birmingham and stayed for some time with Bill's brother, Charlie, who was by then married, to another doctor, and both were in practice in Wolverhampton. In November Bill returned to duty in Delhi and to some familiar, and unwelcome, problems.

To all intents and purposes the Slims were living comfortably in India – they had a spacious house on Queensway (now Jan Path) in the centre of the city with a large garden, stables, a full complement of servants and a governess for the children. Aileen was a frequent visitor to the Delhi Flying Club, where she usually found a member to take her joyriding. When the headquarters moved up to Simla for the summer they enjoyed the hill station's hectic social life – dances and dinners and parties at the USI Club and picnics and lazy afternoons at the swimming pool or tennis courts (Aileen loved tennis and played a great deal). John Slim can remember as a small boy seeing his parents go out for dinner. 'We lived on horses in India. My father would be wearing full evening dress mess kit and my mother in a long dress riding astride. As she mounted her horse – she never rode side-saddle – all the servants would avert their gaze in other directions and the ayah would put a big quilt round her.

'We were very much an Indian family. One of my first memories was when we lived in tents, although I'm not sure where it was. There was a tent for my parents' bedroom, another for the drawing room and another for the dining room. There was a bathroom attached to the bedroom tent but no running water. A man called a *bhisti* brought you water heated in tins on a fire. In hot weather we had fans but no refrigerator. Ice was stored in a hole in the ground.

'We all had servants, but they were part of the family; I used to play with the servants' children in the courtyard of our house. Generally there was not much social mixing with the locals, but my father and mother were very pro getting to know them. There was definitely a barrier between us and them but I don't think we Slims paid too much attention to it. A very nice Sikh used to come to our house with his wife. My father had a great respect for India and the Indians.'[9]

A popular trip in Simla was to ride, walk or take a rickshaw out to Wildflower Hall, a hotel owned by a Mrs Hotz, a formidable German lady, some six miles from the centre of Simla. Sunday

lunch at Wildflower Hall was famous and started with mulligatawny soup, followed by chicken curry and rice, roast pork, cold
meats and salad, apple tarts, cheese and coffee – all for two and a
half rupees (£2.50 in today's money) per head. In the centre of the
dining room was a grand piano always topped by a huge bouquet
of fresh flowers. (Wildflower Hall was burned to the ground in 1993
but was completely rebuilt and is now run as a luxury hotel by the
Oberoi group.)

What appeared to be an idyllic and largely carefree existence for
the summer residents in Simla concealed an anxiety that would dog
Bill all his life – he had serious financial problems. With a wife and
two children to support, not to mention a costly lifestyle, he simply
could not manage on his pay, particularly as Aileen was hopeless
with money. 'He was always worried about his finances,' said Phil
Vickers, a fellow staff officer with whom he shared an office at army
headquarters. 'He said the difficulty was that Aileen had absolutely
no sense of the value of money. One year at Simla Bill moved the
family to an hotel some miles outside the town as an economy. I
remember Bill being appalled when the telephone rang in our office
and it was Aileen saying she was coming in for lunch, which meant
expensive transport for her and an expensive lunch. Bill usually only
had sandwiches or a cheap lunch in the mess. Another time Aileen
bought herself a fur coat which later disappeared and Bill was quite
pleased because he had insured it for more than its purchase price.'[10]
(Years later Bill told Gwendolen Mathewson, Aileen's cousin, that
he hoped when he retired he would be able to get an appointment
on a board of directors somewhere, but that 'however much money
I make Aileen will spend it'.)[11]

Bill urgently needed to find a way to supplement his pay which
would not compromise his professional life as an army officer and
he discovered it by writing fiction – short stories – for publication.
In 1930 he had taken over the editorship of the quarterly *United
Services Institution Journal* and seen the abysmal standard of con-
tributions. He had always enjoyed writing and had a natural ability
to express himself lucidly and concisely – essential qualities for a
short story and an attribute that made him such an effective speaker
when he was called upon to address large bodies of troops. He also
had a keen insight into human nature and a dry sense of humour

– he once joked that 'Any girl in any walk of life who isn't a complete fool and whose face is distinguishable at five yards from the flap of a saddle can get married in India'. All he needed was an agent and he found one in the shape of his friend Philip Pratt, who good-naturedly undertook the tedious business of circulating Bill's work around newspapers and magazines in the short-story market, dealing with rejections – there were many – and collecting the fees, which he deposited in a 'literary account' set up in a bank in Bournemouth, where Bill's mother still lived. Pratt was also writing stories and plays on his own account, under the faintly bizarre pen-name Strawsom Fletcher, but would not have the same success as his friend.

Writing under the pen-name Anthony Mills (Slim loosely spelled backwards) Bill quickly acquired the knack of capturing the attention of readers early, then weaving a tale of drama and adventure with a snappy, unexpected ending. His output was prolific, even if acceptances were initially few and far between. Punch Cowan's wife helped by typing his handwritten manuscripts (sometimes correcting grammatical or spelling mistakes) but no one but Aileen was allowed to post his submissions because she 'brought him luck'. In anticipation of rejection, he cannily sent Pratt duplicates of the cover and the first and last pages so that a 'tired manuscript could carry on without re-typing'. The same story was sometimes offered to seven or eight outlets before Pratt gave up.

From 1930 onwards, Bill's regular letters to Pratt, while still full of news, often included a business element and instructions as to where to send his latest story: 'I've sent it first to *Britannia and Eve*, who will no doubt return it in due course to you. Will you then be kind enough to circulate it as follows: *Women's Journal, Good Housekeeping, Pearson's Magazine, Windsor, Cassell's, London, Cornhill, Cover Magazine* and *20 Story Magazine*? After that anywhere you like ...'

Bill paid Pratt what he could afford and when he could afford it, but was always appreciative of his efforts and effusive in his praise. In June 1933 he sent his friend a cheque for three guineas 'with which I suggest you take the most attractive woman you know out for the evening or, failing that, buy yourself a cigarette holder or some small thing that will remind you of how you have helped the deserving and struggling author'. He should not, Bill added sternly, use the money to pay debts or insurance.

Always self-deprecating, he liked to affect a world-weary expectation that his stories would be turned down. 'I've sent "The Leopard's Spots" to Associated Newspapers. It's not a very bright one I'm afraid. When it comes back try it on *The Tatler*, *National Geographic* and that bunch. When they've turned it down, *Truth* might take as look at it. After that, God knows ...' When the *Daily Mail* accepted 'The Leopard's Spots' Bill's offhand reaction was to suggest that the editor 'didn't seem very particular'.

In many ways Bill was lucky, since the short story market in the thirties was flourishing, perhaps as an escape from the Great Depression which followed the Wall Street Crash in 1929. People wanted to get away from relentless headlines about poverty and unemployment and many newspapers customarily ran short stories; the *Daily Mail* was one of Bill's best customers (Cecil Hunt, the literary editor, became something of a mentor and encouraged Bill to keep writing). He had plenty of material from which to draw – like Kipling before him, he recognised that to most people in Britain India was a land of unimaginable and exotic mystery, so most of his work was set in India, often on the Frontier where unrestrained swashbuckling was believed to be the order of the day and brightened innumerable dreary lives back home.

Not all his fiction had a military theme. On 25 July 1934, the *Daily Mail* published a story by Anthony Mills under the title 'Do I Tell?'. It was a sad little tale of unrequited love in which, unusually, the good guy does not come out on top. The narrator, Pargeter, is hopelessly in love with the beautiful Adela, but she has given her heart to another – the heroic Robert, who is about to return from overseas. That night Pargeter, who is staying with Adela and her aunt, hears an intruder downstairs. Hoping to prove himself a hero, he creeps down and discovers the intruder is Robert. He also sees that the door of the family safe is open and that it is empty. At that moment Adela appears and Robert, all bonhomie, quickly steps in front of the safe and surreptitiously closes the door. Adela is thrilled to have her boyfriend back but Pargeter knows the truth about him. The story ends with a cliffhanger, Pargeter's dilemma: should he tell?

Bill kept a meticulous account of how much he earned each year, where each story had been submitted, where it had been published (he always tried *Blackwood's Magazine* first because he thought it was the best) and how much he had been paid for it. The sums were far from enormous – in 1931 he earned a total of £38 18s. 6d., rising little by little each year to £79 13s. in 1935 – approximately £3,000 in today's money – just about enough to pay his son's school fees, which was a major concern. 'Financially things are rather grim,' he had written to Pratt in August 1932. 'How I am going to pay for John's schooling, to say nothing of Una's, beats me.' Eight years' hard labour as a part-time fiction writer, usually toiling late at night long after the children had been put to bed, netted Bill the grand total of £554 17s. 6d.

At army HQ Bill rarely mentioned his literary activities and few of his colleagues knew what he was doing. It was not that Major W. J. Slim was ashamed of being Anthony Mills in another life – on the contrary, he was rather proud of it – but his natural reticence prevented him from boasting about it. Phil Vickers, who worked with Bill in the Operations Directorate, remembered him as a highly professional officer. Vickers was on the Q staff, responsible for supply, and recalled long discussions with Bill on how to improve the situation for troops on the North-West Frontier, who were required by supply constraints to move along the bottom of the valleys, leaving the hostile tribesmen to occupy the high ground. They agreed that the problem could be resolved if the troops could be supplied by air, but Vickers pointed out that the Royal Air Force was 'not geared to that kind of thinking'. To his astonishment, Bill promptly reached for a telephone, rang a staff officer in the RAF, airily announced the army was thinking of developing air supply and asked if he had any views.

'The consequences were disastrous,' Vickers said. 'The staff officer got on to AOC Air, who blew his top and got on to the Commander in Chief, who naturally knew nothing about it. He thought who could have started this business, sent for Slim and tore him off a strip.'[12] Nevertheless, experiments began with 'free drops' in Frontier conditions and packaging was developed to protect supplies dropped from the air into mountain areas. No credit was attributed to Major Slim and none was claimed, although he perhaps thought back to that incident when air supply became a vital component of his victory in Burma. This incident did not seem to have any effect on his reputation since the Chief of the General Staff for the Indian Army noted on Bill's annual report for 1932: 'By reason of his special qualities I would like to bring his name to the notice of those under whom he will serve in the future as one who, in the interests of the Service, is worthy of special attention.'[13]

In February 1933, Bill was mercifully released from staff work and returned to 1st/6th Gurkhas as second in command – a happy event that unfortunately coincided with an outbreak of cholera in Abbottabad. The regimental history[14] recorded that only three large hypodermic needles were available to inoculate the battalion and that as the needles got blunter those at the end of the queue suffered badly inflamed arms and were admitted to hospital, 'among them Major Slim'.

Bill had only been back with his battalion for a year when he was offered the post of Indian Army representative at the Staff College in Camberley, Surrey. His name had been put forward by the incumbent, 'Jackie' Smyth VC, whose military career would end at the Sittang river bridge nine years later. At the time the Commandant of the College, Major General John Dill, said he'd never heard of Bill Slim. 'You will,' Smyth replied with undoubted prescience. Bill never hesitated to accept the appointment, even though it meant a drop in his pay. (His automatic promotion to brevet lieutenant colonel was not accompanied by a pay rise.) The directing staff at Camberley only included one officer from the Indian Army and to be chosen was both a great honour and a tacit recognition of an officer with enormous potential. It was also an opportunity for Bill to make his name in the British Army, where he was virtually unknown. He felt time was running out – in 1934 he was 43 years old and already fretting that he was getting too old for further promotion, notwithstanding the fact that his annual reports, year on year, invariably referred to him as 'outstanding'.

The Slim family – Bill, Aileen, seven-year-old John and his four-year-old sister, Una – sailed for England in January 1934 and moved into his predecessor's old quarters at No. 6 Bungalow – not much more than a wooden hut, but perfectly comfortable and much cheaper than any other accommodation – in the college grounds.

Before starting at Camberley, Bill visited Birmingham to look up old friends. He found Jim Alford still working at Stewarts & Lloyds, took him out to lunch at the Midland Hotel and gloomily confessed that he did not think he would get any further in the army and that his career as a soldier was virtually over. This streak of pessimism, perhaps exacerbated by his financial problems, characterised Bill's life around this period, despite the fact that he impressed everyone he met with his personality, integrity and intellect.

Jackie Smyth sent Bill an encouraging note when he started his new job and Bill replied in his usual unassuming way:

Dear Jackie,

It was awfully nice to get your note wishing me luck on my first day at the Staff College. Everybody is so kind and you have left me such complete notes etc, that if I do make a mess of it, it will be my own fault. Again, thanks for all your help. I feel apart from myself my only handicap is that I have to succeed you.

Yours, Bill.[15]

Bill would later claim he used Smyth's lecture notes word for word during his first year as an instructor, but as he made the claim during an after-dinner speech at a City livery event hosted by Smyth, it may be that he was bending the truth somewhat. Those who knew Bill well found it hard to believe that he would not want to put across his own very forthright views on the art of war in preference to those of a friend, no matter how well respected.

By all accounts Bill was a brilliant success as a member of the directing staff at Camberley, both with his students, his fellow instructors and superior officers. Major Charles Dunphie (later Major General Sir Charles Dunphie) was a student at Camberley from 1935 to 1936: 'We had a most able and later highly distinguished batch of instructors and we were all of the opinion that Slim was one of the best. He tackled every subject in a down to earth manner and presented it in simple, straightforward language. He also had the knack of making any lecture interesting by introducing enough of the personal side and by including a sufficient degree of humour. In the mess he was always natural, affable and tremendously interested in all kinds of subjects other than military. I don't think I have ever learned more from anybody.'[16]

One of Bill's fellow instructors, Lieutenant Colonel Archibald Nye (later Lieutenant General Sir Archibald Nye and Vice-Chief of the Imperial General Staff) remembered him as 'probably the best all-round officer of his rank in the Army'. Nye and Bill had much in common. Both (mistakenly) felt they were badly placed for promotion and were consequently downcast about what prospects the army held for them. Both were broke, although Nye, a bachelor, admitted that as a married man Bill probably had more financial worries.

None of this affected his work. 'Although he represented the Indian Army,' Nye recalled, 'nobody regarded him merely in that capacity and his standing as an instructor was very high indeed among his contemporaries. This rating sprang mainly from his complete sanity and soundness, for he was a man who always had his feet on the ground. He had a sense of stability, solidity and reliability, but if you said only that you might give the impression of a good, solid to God, reliable old carthorse. The point about him was that he had an outstandingly clear mind and moved in a careful, logical way toward problems. I thought at the time, and said so, that as far as the Indian Army was concerned he was in a class by himself.

'One could not fail to respect him for he imbued one with confidence since he had two qualities at a very high degree: quality of character, which included complete integrity, and at the same time the quality of a very good intellect. One does not often come across a man with both these qualities so well developed.

'He was not a phrase-maker but always gave the impression that whatever he had to say was thoroughly sound. Although universally popular, he was not a back slapper, but to call him reserved would be untrue, because it would infer he was the type of man who said little about anything. In fact he gave the impression that before he spoke about something he had already given a great deal of thought to the subject – there was little spontaneity in his views about things and what emerged was the result of careful and mature thinking. I think it was quite noticeable that when asked a question he might pause for a moment, think and then give an answer in carefully chosen words. With all this, he combined a great sense of humour and was a shrewd judge of people and things.'[17]

It was typical of Bill that he would put some backs up at the College by frowning on the practice of allowing students a day off to go hunting (it was claimed it gave young officers an 'eye for country'). He also frequently and loudly declared himself of the opinion that it was far more difficult and dangerous to ride a motorcycle flat out from Marble Arch to Camberley than it was to spend a day hunting on a horse. This was not a view calculated to win him friends among the cavalry, but he was not in the least bothered.

For Bill's family, his tour of duty in the United Kingdom was a welcome change from the heat and dust of India and his children saw a great deal more of him than they had ever done before. John remembers his father reading him bedtime stories, usually G. A. Henty and Arthur Ransome, just the way that Bill's father had read to him when he was the same age. He was very proud of the fact that his dad marched in the funeral cortège of King George V in January 1936 and delighted when the family got front row seats on the Mall to watch the Coronation procession of George VI a few months later. (There was no Durbar celebration in Delhi, as there was for his predecessor, because of rising Indian nationalism and the looming prospect of war in Europe.)

At the end of Bill's first year in Camberley, the Commandant reported that he was 'one of the best instructors I have had' and at the end of his tour of duty in 1936 the then Commandant, Major General Clement Armitage, recommended Bill for rapid preferment: 'His work has been beyond praise and of a high class ... He is old for his rank and should be given rapid promotion to full Colonel, command or any 1st grade staff appointment.'[18] Shortly before he was due to leave Camberley, Bill learned he had been nominated for a year-long course at the Imperial Defence College, where the science of warfare was studied and inter-service officers were groomed as future commanders by developing their analytical powers, knowledge and strategic vision.

Bill should have been delighted to have been selected for the IDC but he was not. He felt the longer he stayed in the UK the more likely it was that he would be forgotten in India. Friends who met him around this time found him unusually depressed and troubled about his future. Taffy Davies, his friend from Quetta, was then a GSO2 at the War Office and lunched with Bill two or three times a week. 'In those days he was very fed up with life. He was heavily in debt and talked about getting out of the army. He was old – 46 – and did not think he would get anywhere.' Davies and his wife ran into Bill and Aileen at the Criterion Grill in Piccadilly soon after he had been appointed to the IDC. 'Bill said he was trying to put off the IDC course until he had done a spell of regimental soldiering. He was due for command and was afraid he would miss it and become a permanent staff officer.'[19]

In the event, Bill was unable to defer his IDC course. He rented a flat at 11 Nevern Square, Earls Court, for the family and joined the stellar group of IDC students who would, like Bill, go on to great things. They included Sir Keith Park, flying ace and hero of the Battle of Britain, Captain Bernard Warburton-Lee RN, who won a posthumous Victoria Cross attacking German destroyers in Norway, Admiral Sir Guy Russell, commander of the battleship HMS *Duke of York* when it sank the *Scharnhorst* at the Battle of North Cape, General Sir Alan Cunningham, architect of the victory over Italian forces in East Africa, and the future chiefs of both the Australian and New Zealand General Staff.

Bill's name would become quite as illustrious as those of other alumni but, curiously, he failed to shine at the IDC. One reason was that he missed much of the summer term when he went into hospital to have a gallstone removed. More importantly, he was bored. After the dynamic and stimulating debate that was routine at Camberley, he found the IDC course to be muted, timid and hidebound by convention.

Strategic thinking in the military in Britain between the wars was less than impressive, despite the fact that Germany was gearing up for war, and this was inevitably reflected in the IDC syllabus. It was perhaps significant that 1937 was Bill's most successful year as a short story writer; he earned £171 11s. – more than twice what he had made in any other year. His final report blandly noted that he was 'an officer of marked ability with sound views' who did not hesitate to criticise opinions with which he disagreed.[20]

Bill's despondency about his future was very nearly justified: he had been put on the retirement list. Despite his impressive record and a clutch of recommendations, when his name came up before a Promotions Board in Delhi a majority was initially in favour of passing him by on the grounds of age. Only after an impassioned argument by a member of the board who knew Bill well was his promotion to lieutenant colonel approved.

Bill returned to India – alone – in early 1938 to take a three-month course at the Senior Officers' School in Belgaum, a garrison town in the Mahratta district known in the Indian Army as 'The Cradle of Infantry', before taking command of the 2nd Battalion, 7th Gurkhas, which had gone through a bad patch. He would, of course, have preferred to return to the 6th Gurkhas, which he viewed as his 'own' regiment, but there was no vacancy available. On 2 May 1938 his promotion to substantive lieutenant colonel was confirmed and in July he travelled to Shillong, the pictur-esque hill-station capital of Assam in the north-east of India, with its pine-forested hills and tea plantations, where the 2nd/7th was based and where he also discovered on arrival that he would be acting as Shillong garrison commander, responsible for assisting the local police. One of his duties was to impose some order on the native bazaar, which as far as he could make out consisted entirely of brothels and illicit stills producing fiery liquor. He told Pratt that he 'dearly longed to burn it down' and glumly characterised his job as 'a cross between the chairman of a Parish Council and a brigadier'.[21]

The rolling hills around Shillong were said to remind early European settlers of Scotland, but Bill never felt at home there; he considered he was in a backwater, was lonely and exasperated by problems left behind by his predecessors – primarily the poor state of the troops' training (many of the VCOs and NCOs were grossly overweight). A month after his arrival he wrote a long letter to Philip Pratt: 'I know no one here – not a single officer of my new battalion even and so I'm rather on my own. There are a lot of unpleasant jobs to be done as my two predecessors were all for a quiet life and peace in their time. Today for instance I had to tell two worthy Gurkha *havildar* majors (i.e. sergeant-majors) that they could not become officers because they were over 40 years old. Unfortunately before I arrived they had been told they would be promoted – it's forbidden by regulations to promote after 40 and of course they ought to have

been told. Now, poor devils, they think it's entirely due to the arrival
of a shit of a new Colonel. They would willingly kill me and I don't
altogether blame them – but people who put off unpleasant duties
so that their successors will have the unpleasantness and the blame
want a particularly warm corner of the next world.'[22]

Momentous events in Europe appear not to have impinged greatly
on Bill's daily life in the Indian Army except that the Munich crisis
in September obliged him to cancel, to his intense irritation, an
all-expenses paid trip to Java to observe Dutch army manoeuvres.
By then Aileen had arrived back in India to join her husband.
They moved into a thatched cottage, with electric light and running hot and cold water, in the grounds of the 'remarkably decent'[23]
Stonylands Hotel and began to enjoy a busy social life with parties
and weekly dances at the club. The children remained behind in the
UK – Una had been enrolled in a school near her maternal grand-
parents in Scotland and John was a boarder at Ashdown House
school in Forest Row, Sussex. They would not return to India until
after the war had started.

Polo was the most popular game in Shillong, but Bill's principal
recreation was golf, once he had found a fellow officer who was as
mediocre a player as himself. They played on the local links with
their own set of idiosyncratic rules, which included being allowed
up to five shots off the tee and then choosing the best. Meanwhile,
Aileen slipped comfortably and happily into the role of the CO's
wife, helping with the families and babies while her husband 'made
an unpleasantness of himself' – Bill's words – to their fathers.

In fact, he did not have much time for spreading 'unpleasantness' – hardly long enough to get to know his men – because in
April 1939, after less than a year with the 7th Gurkhas, he was promoted to the local rank of brigadier and sent back to Belgaum to
become the Commandant at the Senior Officers' School. Shortly
after taking over his new job Bill made a prescient change in the
curriculum. Although he recognised that the main enemy in any
future conflict was likely to be Germany, he nevertheless decided to
introduce into the syllabus a study of the Japanese invasion of China
in 1937 and the organisation and capabilities of the Japanese army, at
least to the extent of the very limited intelligence available, and set
jungle warfare exercises to deal with an imaginary Japanese invading

force – this at a time when such an eventuality was generally considered not just unlikely but downright absurd.

Like most of his brother officers in the Indian Army he followed events in Europe with increasing concern. He had been disgusted by the British government's policy of appeasement towards Nazi Germany after Austria had been annexed by Anschluss in March 1938 and was deeply sceptical when Neville Chamberlain, the British Prime Minister, returned to London in brief triumph in September 1938, after his third meeting with Adolf Hitler had apparently secured a peace agreement with Nazi Germany. A huge, cheering crowd greeted his famous 'peace in our time' speech delivered from the first-floor window of 10 Downing Street. It was, of course, a chimera. In the early hours of 1 September 1939, Germany invaded Poland. Two days later, Britain and France, followed by the countries of the Commonwealth, declared war on Germany.

So began the deadliest conflict in human history. Any thoughts Bill might have had about retiring, or ending his military career, vanished that day.

7

A Battle in the Sudan
and a Bullet in Eritrea

As soon as war had been declared, Bill hurried to the Indian Army headquarters in Delhi determined to find himself an active service command; he had no intention of remaining stuck running a school in Belgaum while there was a war going on. He was rewarded, two weeks later, by being given command of the 10th Indian Infantry Brigade then being formed at Jhansi, in what is now Uttar Pradesh, for service in the Middle East. Bill saw it as a golden opportunity for proper soldiering after the years he had spent in lecture rooms and playing soldiers on exercise.

Jhansi, some 250 miles south-east of Delhi, was an ancient walled city and the home of Lakshmi Bai, a legendary warrior queen and firebrand who led the local rebellion against British colonialism at the time of the Indian Mutiny and became a symbol of resistance to British rule after her death in battle in 1858. Among her many feats she was said to be able to jump from the walls of Jhansi's seventeenth-century fort directly on to her horse.

Bill's brigade, which was destined to become part of the 5th Indian Division, was a mixed bag of Baluchi, Garhwali and Punjabi troops, each with their own battalion – the 4th/10th Baluch, the 3rd/18th Royal Garhwal Rifles and the 3rd/2nd Punjab – each requiring to be handled differently, and each speaking their own language, although all orders were given in Urdu. Most were raised in the warrior tradition, with their fathers and grandfathers having served the King-Emperor before them. The Baluchis hailed from the barren, rugged mountain territory in the west of what is now Pakistan, close to the borders of Iran and Afghanistan; the kingdom of Garhwal was a princely state in the Indian Himalayas; and the Punjab was a vast area with a long history and rich cultural heritage close to Kashmir in the north of the country. Bill was delighted to find that his old friend Taffy Davies was in command of the Garhwali battalion.

Operations on the North-West Frontier and internal security duties had dominated the tactics and strategic thinking of the Indian Army for more than two decades and it was ill equipped for active service outside India against modern, mechanised armies. Bill learned his raggle-taggle brigade was earmarked for Iraq as a motorised unit, but it had no motor transport and none of the soldiers could drive. Its transport comprised only the mule carts and pack mules used routinely on the Frontier. In every other way, the brigade's equipment was similarly deficient – no wireless sets, no armoured fighting vehicles, no anti-tank or anti-aircraft guns and obsolete automatic weapons. It was said that all the new equipment was being sent to the British Army in France and that the Cabinet had decided that the Indian Army would be allocated low priority as it would not be taking part in 'first-class war'.[1]

Bill first addressed the problem of transport. He scrounged three very old three-ton trucks for driver training and then, with the help of the local District Commissioner, he hired every driving instructor he could find in Jhansi to start teaching his men to drive. Civilian owners of private cars were also roped in to help. At the same time he began a rigorous programme of retraining to prepare his brigade for whatever lay ahead.

'Slim was a forceful trainer and the exercises he set us were full of imagination,' said Davies. 'He had completely overcome his pessimism regarding the future of his career. He was now sure of himself. He had the ability to see into the future and his comments on training were both instructive and very much to the point. He made it quite clear what he wanted and his impact on the soldiers was great. Although the staff and the units had been collected from many parts of India and did not know one another, by his personality, the confidence he inspired and his friendly manner, he very soon welded the brigade into a happy and enthusiastic team.'[2]

In March 1940 the brigade began receiving new equipment, most importantly motor transport, by which time it had a substantial cadre of fully trained drivers. Iraq remained its destination until June when Italy declared war on France and Great Britain; a month later

Italian troops crossed from Eritrea and Ethiopia into the Sudan and captured the frontier posts of Karora, Kassala, Kirmuk and Gallabat. At that time Eritrea and Ethiopia formed part of Italian East Africa; the Sudan was jointly administered by the United Kingdom and Egypt and was known as Anglo-Egyptian Sudan. Urgent reinforcements were needed to protect the Sudan and in August the 5th Indian Division was switched from Iraq to the Sudan.

The division left Jhansi for Port Sudan at the end of August, shortly before Bill's children were due to arrive back in India and join their mother in Simla. Bill missed them sorely, as he explained in a letter written to Una in a train en route to Bombay on 8 September:

Poons darling, [he had called Una 'Unapoons' ever since she was a baby]

I am afraid I shall have left Bombay before you and John get there. I am more sorry about it than I have been about anything for a long time. I did so much want to see you and John and see what a big girl you have got since I saw you last. But it can't be helped.

I hope you had a nice voyage but I expect you are glad it is over and you must be thrilled to see Mummy again. I bet she is thrilled too. I wish I were with you all.

I think you will like Simla and it will be lovely living in a wee house – Three Bridges – with Mummy. Now you are so much bigger you will be able to help her in all sorts of ways. I know you will.

Work hard at school because when you go Home again you will not want to be behind other girls of your age who stayed in England.

Give Judy [the family dog] *a pat for me when you see her at Jhansi and look after her in Simla.*

I shall be thinking of you and Mummy and John all the time at the war. Write me often and I'll write to you when I can.

Lots and lots of love, my Poons from Daddy
xxxoooxxxoooxxoooxxxooo[3]

No matter what horrors he was facing at the front, Bill always found time to write warm and loving letters to Aileen and the children throughout the war, as well as corresponding regularly with his friend Philip Pratt. His letters to John and Una are full of gentle admonitions to help their mother at home and work hard at school, but his humanity and love for them shines through on every page – he never fails to tell them how much he misses them and how much they are always in his thoughts and how he often wonders what they are doing. When he heard that Una had contracted measles from her brother as soon as she arrived in India he wrote to her immediately at Simla:

Poons darling –

I got your nice letter dated 30th Sept written on the pretty Bo-Peep paper and loved reading it.

I am so glad you are better. Was it nasty having measles? I should have liked to see you covered in spots. Did you have lots?

What do you think of Judy? Is she behaving well? There isn't much room, I'm afraid, to throw balls for her in Simla and that's what she likes best of all.

Mummy tells me you weren't sick in the car going up to Simla, I think that is pretty clever of you because nearly everybody is sick on that windy road. I've often felt like it myself there. So if you weren't, you need never be sick again in a car.

How do you like Mummy's flat in Simla? Which room have you got? How are you furnishing it? What dresses have you got? Write and tell me all about it and what you do. Letters from you and John and Mummy are the nicest presents I get here.

When are you starting school? I hope you will like it. Work hard and don't forget to help Mummy with the house and things.

I wish I was with you all, but I think of you three in the little house up the hill at Simla and I wonder often what you are all doing.

Lots and lots of love, my Poons, from Daddy

PS. Give Mummy a hug from me.[4]

Not long after the 5th Indian Division landed at Port Sudan on the Red Sea in September, Bill learned to his dismay that the divisional commander, Major General Lewis Heath, had ordered each brigade to replace one of its Indian battalions with a British battalion – a ludicrously outdated custom stemming from the days of the Mutiny, when it was thought that the presence of a British battalion would 'stiffen' the native troops. Bill protested strenuously at losing a battalion he had personally trained, which he knew well and in which he had complete confidence, but he was overruled. With great reluctance he accepted the 1st Battalion, The Essex Regiment, as a replacement for his Punjabis. A few days later, on Wednesday, 6 November 1940, his brigade went into action, to recapture the fort at Gallabat.

Oddly enough, this little operation would go down in history as the first British land offensive of the Second World War. Even though more than a year had passed since the declaration of war against Germany, the Axis powers had made all the running, invading and occupying the Low Countries, France and Norway and ejecting the British Expeditionary Force at Dunkirk. So it was that to Temporary Brigadier W. J. Slim fell the honour of leading the fightback by attacking a small mud and stone fort in the desert on the frontier between the Sudan and Ethiopia. Since capturing the fort in June the Italians had greatly improved its defences with coils of barbed wire, anti-tank mines and a perimeter wall of stones and logs cemented with mud. Tall elephant grass as high as a man restricted visibility around the redoubt. Two miles beyond, on the other side of a dried-up river bed and on the lower slopes of Jebel Mariam Waha, a mountain ridge, was Metemma, a native village also heavily fortified and occupied by the Italians. Bill's orders were to capture both and block any attempt by the Italians to advance into the Sudan. The secondary aim of the operation was to open a supply route to rebel patriots in Ethiopia loyal to the Emperor Haile Selassie and encourage a revolt against the Italians.

The brigade bivouacked for several days in a dirty little town called Gedaref and then moved 90 miles south-east towards Gallabat along a deeply corrugated road across a monotonous landscape studded with camel-thorn scrub and largely populated by giraffes and ostrich. On 28 October, accompanied by his senior commanders on ponies borrowed from the Sudan Defence Force, Bill carried out his first reconnaissance, interrupted only by a low-flying enemy aircraft which obliged them all to dismount temporarily and shelter under their ponies. From an observation point known as Signal Hill he had an excellent view of the terrain and the defences of Gallabat and Metemma, and watched Italian working parties marching in and out of the fort.

Bill made his plans with typically meticulous care, relying on speed, surprise and shock to carry the day. Intelligence indicated that the Italians were at about the same strength as the 10th Brigade, but they held the advantage since they were so well entrenched in defensive positions. They had constructed mutually supporting firing positions and could also call on strong reinforcements based at Gondar, 100 miles to the east, if necessary. Bill hoped to even the balance by keeping from the Italians the fact that he had in support a regiment of field artillery and a squadron of tanks. He ordered the guns and tanks to be held far back while gun pits were dug at night in great secrecy, hidden by camouflage and stocked with ammunition. The men from the Royal Tank Regiment were instructed to replace their distinctive black berets with pith helmets lest they were spotted by the enemy and recognised.

Bill's plan was to use low-flying aircraft to hide the noise as the tanks and artillery were moved into position. Timing and coordination was of the essence to avoid unnecessary casualties. The Baluchi battalion and a detachment of the Sudanese Defence Force would be deployed to protect the flanks and the battle would begin with a bombardment from the air, using every available aircraft, to disrupt enemy communications and create confusion. At the same time the artillery would open up, then lift the barrage on to Metemma as the tanks battered through the outer defences of Gallabat, closely followed by the Garhwali battalion. Once the fort was taken the tanks were to break through the wire surrounding Metemma and open the way for the 1st Essex to capture the village.

Anthony Eden, the Secretary of State for War, was on a visit to Khartoum and was on hand to wish Bill luck a few days before the operation was due to begin. It was obvious to Bill afterwards that Eden knew all about it and he felt faintly embarrassed that, following the precept of absolute secrecy, he had made no mention of it. Eden also made no direct reference to it, but after thanking Bill for showing him around the brigade he added, with a twinkle in his eye, 'and the best of luck on Wednesday'.

'Like all commanders on the eve of battle, much as I might try to appear calm and confident, I was inwardly anxious and restless …' Bill wrote. 'As darkness fell on the Tuesday night, I made for my command post on a small hill just above the track that ran gently uphill straight towards Gallabat, about a mile and a half away. Standing there, I listened to the muffled sounds of troops and guns moving up and the last loads of ammunition being dumped. The tramp of the Garhwalis, as company by company they passed up the road to their deploying positions, came up to me muted by the thick dust.

'I could even hear a faint swishing murmur away out on the right where some of the Baluchis were pushing through scrub and thick grass towards a hill overlooking Gallabat to secure our flank. Then all other sound was blotted out by the roar of an aircraft flying low to drown the engines of the tanks as they rumbled forward. By ten o'clock all was silent; our outposts gave no sign. Once or twice a white Very light had soared up from Gallabat as some nervous Italian peering over his ramparts thought he heard a stealthy move in the darkness beyond, but no burst of fire followed and all sank to quiet again. Our plans were made, the attacking troops had reached their start lines, and guns and tanks were ready with their crews sleeping beside them. I felt as I lay down and pulled a blanket over me that while like other mortals we could not command success, we had done all we could to deserve it.'[5]

Bill was woken before dawn by his Garhwali batman with a cup of piping hot tea in an enamel mug. He threw off his blanket, stood up and was sipping his tea when the brigade major loomed out of the darkness and reported that all units were in place. Bill never forgot watching the sky lighten behind the distant hills and the colours change from pale lemon to a dazzling gold as the sun appeared. There was no indication from the Italians that they suspected an attack but there was also no sign of the Royal Air Force. Minutes ticked by and Bill became increasingly nervous (later it transpired that heavy rainfall in the night had delayed the take-off of the bombers). Finally, he heard the faint hum of aircraft approaching from the west.

Every face turned to the sky as the aircraft – Wellington bombers escorted by Gladiator fighters – swept overhead. A moment later Bill heard the distinctive crump of the first bombs crashing on Gallabat and the rattle of machine guns as the Gladiators joined the attack, but the din of the air strike was immediately drowned by the artillery, as the 18-pounders and 4.5-inch howitzers of 28 Field

Regiment unleashed their fury. The smell of cordite filled the air and the fort almost disappeared in billowing clouds of brown dust from the shells bursting in and around it. Through his field glasses Bill could see little sign of enemy retaliation and assumed his careful plans to surprise the Italians had paid off.

After the aircraft had left – the plan was for them to return to base before the Italians could scramble their superior Fiat CR42 fighters – his Royal Air Force adviser gave him the satisfying news that they had all returned and that a direct hit had been scored on the enemy wireless station, one of the principal targets. Meanwhile, he could see that the tanks had emerged from their hiding places and were lurching towards the fort followed by lines of Garhwali infantry in slouch hats who had risen from the ground as if by magic and were pushing through the waving elephant grass. As the tanks and infantry closed on the fort, the artillery lifted on to Metemma. For a while Bill could see nothing of the battle from his command post. From within the swirling clouds of dust came the sounds of machine-gun and rifle fire punctuated by booms from the tanks' two-pounders, but he could only imagine the scene as, hopefully, the Garhwalis were sweeping over the fort's defences with fixed bayonets.

At 0730 a Very light curved into the sky above the fort and burst into green and red stars. It was the success signal: Gallabat had fallen. Absolutely delighted that his initial plans had worked so well, Bill jumped into a Bren carrier with his batman and 'Welcher' – Lieutenant Colonel G. de V. Welchman, commander of 28 Field Regiment (who as a brigadier would be Bill's chief artillery officer in Burma) – and headed for the fort, as the guns moved forward and the men of the 1st Essex trudged along the side of the road to get into position to attack Metemma.

Some way short of the fort they were stopped by an NCO and warned that the road ahead was mined. They were directed to a roughly marked diversion to the left, but Bill was anxious to press on. Convinced that only the road was mined, he ordered the driver to turn off the road to the right and head directly for the fort. It was a mistake. Within minutes they discovered they were in the middle of a minefield: an infantry carrier ahead of them suddenly blew up and two or three soldiers close by triggered anti-personnel mines.

'Everything that is shot or thrown at you, or dropped on you, in war is most unpleasant,' Bill confessed, 'but of all horrible devices the most terrifying – at least to me – is the land mine. A man ought to be able to plant his feet on his Mother Earth with some confidence; when instead, on his footfall, she erupts into flame, blast, and hurtling steel, it is unnatural and very, very frightening.'[6]

Their carrier stopped. A young officer in the 1st Essex approached the vehicle and promptly stepped on a mine, losing most of his foot. Bill and Welcher jumped down and tended to his wounds as best they could with field dressings while a medic was summoned. Other soldiers began slowly moving forward again, heads bowed, intently scrutinising the ground in front of them to try and get out of the minefield. Bill and Welcher followed suit, leading the carrier. When there were no further explosions they assumed they must be out of the minefield, climbed back on board and made a dash for the fort.

Just outside the walls of the fort they were greeted by a small group of Garhwali soldiers sheltering behind a rock outcrop, waving their hats and shouting. The noisy engine of the infantry carrier and continuing gunfire prevented Bill from hearing what they were shouting, but he not unnaturally assumed he was being welcomed, that his gallant troops were cheering their commander in his moment of victory. As he stood up in the carrier to acknowledge their acclaim he suddenly realised they were shouting at him to get away and, as if to emphasise the point, a prolonged burst of machine-gun fire spattered the rocks in front of them. The driver of the carrier stamped on the accelerator and swerved behind the same rocks. 'I began to wonder,' Bill mused, 'if the officer who had fired the success signal had not been a trifle premature.'

It did not take the Garhwalis long to dispatch the Italian machine-gunners with grenades and Bill was at last able to enter the fort, where there were bodies and dead mules everywhere, already crawling with flies. It was clear from intensive gunfire to the east that the battle was far from over – the Italians had mounted an unexpected counter-attack, which was eventually driven back.

From an embrasure on the eastern wall, Bill was able to survey the next objective – Metemma. Although a few native huts were burning fiercely, he was surprised to see that the village seemed to have suffered little damage and the coiled wire perimeter remained intact. He was not too worried, since the tanks would easily breach it, but then the tank squadron commander appeared with the worst possible news. He reported that only three of his twelve tanks were still operational. Five of his cruiser tanks and four of his light tanks had been disabled either by mines or from hitting boulders concealed in the elephant grass.

Furthermore, there had been a tragedy of mistaken identity which had needlessly cost the lives of several of his men. Going into action, the tank crews had resumed wearing their traditional black berets. On more than one occasion, when a tank had been disabled the crew dismounted to attempt repairs and found themselves being fired on by their own side in the mistaken belief that they were Italians. The squadron sergeant major, whom Bill knew well and liked enormously, had been killed.

While Bill was digesting this, the tank commander explained that a truck loaded with spare parts was on its way; it might be possible to repair six or seven of the broken tanks but it would take several hours after the truck arrived. Bill knew that any opportunity of storming Metemma before the Italians could recover from the shock of the initial assault was irrevocably lost.

From that moment, disaster piled upon disaster. Bill returned to his command post to make arrangements to postpone zero hour for the second phase of the operation, cheering himself up on the way by swiping two bottles of Chianti he found in the ante-room of what had been the Italian officers' mess. He was looking at a map and talking on the telephone to the commander of a Sudanese Defence Force attachment posted on the flank when he first heard the distant drone of aircraft approaching from the east – from the direction of the Italian air base 100 miles behind the border. He stepped outside and saw a considerable number of aircraft approaching – a formation of about ten Caproni medium bombers escorted by at least double that number of CR42 fighters. He watched helplessly as the Capronis flew in single file over Gallabat, disgorging their bombs and sending up great gouts of smoke and fire.

Two British Gladiator fighters appeared and were almost

immediately shot down by the CR42s. Three more arrived and suffered the same fate, without the loss of a single Italian aircraft. Bill was furious – it had been agreed that if the Gladiators were needed they would only be deployed in strength, never singly or in pairs when they were most vulnerable to the superior CR42s. (The squadron in Eritrea was led by the Italian ace Capitano Mario Visintini, who was said to have shot down 20 enemy planes before he crashed his aircraft and was killed in February 1941, aged 27.)

Worse was to come. Barely had the skies cleared before a *jemadar* (the lowest ranked VCO) on traffic control duty arrived breathless in the command post to report that lorries loaded with British soldiers were leaving Gallabat, tearing down the road and refusing to stop. The men were shouting that the enemy was coming and they had orders to retire. At first Bill did not believe him. He thought the *jemadar* probably misunderstood what was going on and that the lorries were returning empty from Gallabat to reload. The *jemadar* shook his head and invited Bill to see for himself.

Bill walked out to a promontory overlooking the road and saw that there were indeed two trucks racing away from the fort at high speed about 100 yards apart. Each of them was apparently packed with men from the 1st Essex Regiment. Two sepoys stood in the road, waving their arms to get the trucks to stop, and were forced to leap for their lives as both vehicles swept on regardless.

Seriously alarmed, Bill ran down to the road with the *jemadar* and a staff captain just as another truck appeared, loaded with gesticulating British soldiers shouting that the enemy was coming. The driver ignored Bill's frantic signals to stop. With a sinking heart, Bill guessed that the 1st Essex had panicked, presumably as a result of the bombing raid. He instructed the *jemadar* to construct a barrier across the road and sent the staff captain back to the command post with orders to telephone all posts further back to block the road with vehicles. Then he started walking alone along the deserted road towards the fort with no very clear idea of what he was going to do.

After about a quarter of a mile he came across a small group of 1st Essex men marching in his direction. All, except one, still carried their rifles. He stopped them and asked them what they were doing. They had a garbled story about a massive ground attack on the fort involving heavy casualties. The Italians had reoccupied the position, they said. They suggested that they might be the only survivors. Bill listened patiently, but with mounting anger, and eventually ordered them to retrace their steps. A little further up the road they encountered more stragglers – one of them, to Bill's fury, was an officer – which he similarly rounded up. When he saw one or two men slip away into the bush, he took to walking at the rear.

At the minefield which they had blundered into earlier in the day, Bill found sections of Indian sappers and miners occupying defensive positions along the road. The sight of these well-disciplined and determined troops seem to steady his nervous party, which now included a few bemused Garhwalis who had no idea what they were doing. They had been told by the British soldiers that a general retreat had been ordered and when Bill explained it was a mistake they were perfectly happy to go back.

A few hundred yards from the fort Bill discovered the guns still in position and the battery commander standing in the centre of the road with a revolver in his hand, guarding more fugitives from 1st Essex whom he kept together by the simple expedient of threatening to shoot anyone who tried to bolt. There had been no ground attack, he said, but the bombing had caused many casualties.

Inside the fort, Bill found a scene of carnage, with wounded everywhere, some of them terribly mutilated. His brigade major grimly explained what had happened. The bombing began soon after the 1st Essex had arrived. It had been heavy and made doubly worse by the ground, which was solid rock. Shrapnel and rock splinters combined to terrible and lethal effect. The British troops had little time to find cover and when, at the height of the bombing, an ammunition truck exploded near the reserve company it tipped some of them over the edge. They fled, shouting to others to join them, to save themselves. The panic spread rapidly and before the officers could regain control the demoralised and terrified men had seized trucks parked at the bottom of the hill and driven away. Bill felt he had no alternative but to relieve the colonel of the 1st Essex of his command. The morale of the battalion was so badly shaken that he later recommended its withdrawal from the front.[7]

As if all this was not bad enough, the Royal Tank Regiment commander reported to Bill that the lorry with vital spares had turned
up shortly before the aerial attack and had suffered a direct hit.
Almost all the spares and tools had been destroyed. It would now be
days before the damaged tanks could be put back on the road. Bill
was further depressed when he toured the fort and saw for himself
the state to which the troops had been reduced by the ordeal of the
bombing. At one point he stopped at the embrasure from where he
could see Metemma. It suddenly seemed very far away.

Back at the command post he gloomily considered his options.
First, he recognised it would be madness to attempt an assault on
Metemma without the tanks and he had no real idea of when sufficient tanks would be available. Second, he considered it unwise to
use what remained of the 1st Essex; they would need to be relieved
by the Baluchi battalion and that, too, would take time. Third, the
inevitable delay meant that the Italians would have plenty of opportunity to bring up reinforcements, making a direct assault that
much more difficult. Fourth, the enemy now had overwhelming air
superiority after the loss of five Gladiator fighters out of a total force
of only 19.

While his situation seemed hopeless, being Bill he was not
minded to give up. After the melancholy assessment of his own
position, he turned his thoughts to that of the Italians and tried to
imagine how his counterpart in Metemma was feeling. He had lost
Gallabat and must have been shaken by the sudden appearance of
British artillery and tanks. He probably had little idea of what forces
he was up against – he might think the entire 5th Indian Division
(which he would undoubtedly know had arrived in the Sudan) was
waiting in the wings. He probably had little idea that most of Bill's
tanks were out of action. He was very unlikely to know that the 1st
Essex had run away and he had similar problems himself – native
informers had told Bill's intelligence staff that most of the soldiers in
the colonial battalion which had garrisoned Gallabat had fled into
the countryside. Finally, apart from a single abortive counter-attack
earlier in the day, the Italians had shown little inclination to go on
the offensive.

'I had the idea,' Bill concluded, 'that the enemy was sitting behind
his barbed-wire in no very happy frame of mind. Could I play on

that, gamble on it? Even if I could not fight him out of Metemma, could I not frighten him out? The more I thought about it, the more I thought I might.'[8]

Only one opportunity presented itself – the Jebel Mariam Waha, the long mountain ridge running north to south behind Metemma. If his Baluchi battalion marched at night, round the flank of Gallabat and Metemma, it could seize Jebel Mariam Waha at dawn and threaten the Italians from the rear. It was true that without tanks an assault could no more be mounted from Jebel Mariam Waha than it could from Gallabat, but the Italian commander would not know that and might well consider it prudent to withdraw without a fight. Bill knew it was a gamble, but he convinced himself that it was one worth taking.

That night the Italian air force returned to bomb Gallabat once more; they were back again shortly after dawn the following morning. Bill realised that the troops could not endure the bombing indefinitely and later that morning he convened a conference of his senior officers – Welcher, his brigade major, and the colonel of the Garhwalis – by the embrasure overlooking Metemma and put his new plans to them. He had little time for what he called 'the "what-I-have-said-I-have-said" type of commander', dictating what was going to happen without consultation, and was more than ready to listen to their views. To his dismay, all three of them were deeply pessimistic that his plans would be successful. They thought it was too much of a gamble; it would be impossible to supply the troops on Jebel Mariam Waha and it was very likely there was no water there; with total air supremacy the Italians would be able to bomb them off the ridge; and it was known that reinforcements were on their way and might arrive that night, making it difficult for the troops on the ridge to extract themselves.

Bill still believed the gamble was worth taking. 'I still had a hunch my idea would work,' he noted, 'but these three men were each of them braver than I was. Would they hesitate if the risk was a reasonable one? If it were such a gamble, was I justified in taking other men's lives on what I had to admit was just a hunch?'

But then his brigade major produced the clinching argument, reminding Bill that his paramount orders were to prevent an Italian advance into the Sudan, which would become difficult with the troops so widely scattered. Very reluctantly, he acceded to their advice. It was promptly agreed between them that without taking Metemma there was little point in hanging on to Gallabat, incurring more needless casualties and wearing down morale. Gallabat without Metemma was of little strategic value and Bill gave orders for the troops to withdraw under the cover of darkness that night.

'In the dark I stood beside the track just below Gallabat and saw the guns go past back to their original positions; then the infantry, silent and depressed, followed them, so different from the men who had hopefully moved up two nights ago. And all the time beating in my brain was that same torturing thought, "You ought to have tried it".'[9]

The failure of the operation was a bitter pill for Bill to swallow and he was the first to take responsibility for the mistakes that had been made: proper reconnaissance of the terrain the tanks were to cross would have minimised losses; the fiasco of the tank crews in black berets being shot by their comrades was preventable; poor liaison with the Royal Air Force was partly responsible for Bill losing his air cover; and the panic which had gripped 1st Essex was disastrous to his plans. When he had first been informed that a British battalion would replace his Punjabis, he had asked if the change could be delayed until after the Gallabat operation but was refused.

There were extenuating circumstances for the battalion's dishonour. It had largely been employed on internal security duties in the Sudan. Ill-equipped for a pivotal role in the operation, it should probably have been deployed on the flank rather than leading the second phase of the battle. Bill might have been trying to avoid accusations from the Indian troops that their British comrades were being spared at their expense. Nevertheless what happened at Gallabat was an indelible stain on the Essex Regiment's otherwise fine record and led to rancorous recriminations. Some Essex officers blamed Bill for poor planning, allowing the battalion to crowd into the fort thus making it a sitting target, and bore him an enduring grudge. Many years later when he came to write about the operation in *Unofficial History* he agonised for some time about whether or not he should identify the regiment. In the end, characteristically, he decided not to do so.

Equally characteristically, he blamed himself when, ten days after the withdrawal, he was shown intercepted Italian signals from Metemma, after the fort at Gallabat had fallen, which strongly indicated that the enemy was more than ready to retreat had he gone ahead with his plan to occupy the Jebel Mariam Waha. The Italian colonial troops had suffered heavy casualties and their commander, who believed he was heavily outnumbered, reported on 7 November that he could not hold out much longer. 'Like so many generals whose plans have gone wrong, I could find plenty of excuses for failure, but only one reason – myself,' Bill concluded. 'When two courses of action were open to me I had not chosen, as a good commander should, the bolder. I had taken counsel of my fears.'

It was a lesson he would never forget. Bill withdrew to a position close enough to constantly harass the Italians – he called it 'annoying the enemy' – with artillery and night patrols and prevent them reoccupying the ruins of Gallabat. In training notes issued after the battle he highlighted the difficulties they had faced: 'The majority of the troops who assaulted Gallabat had hardly seen an aeroplane or tank, let alone co-operated or been attacked by them; they had never seen or heard an artillery bombardment or had a shell pass over their heads. The noise alone, heard for the first time, is distressing and bewildering.'[10]

In January 1941, the Allies launched a major offensive against the Italians in East Africa and 10th Indian Brigade was ordered north to Kassala, on the Eritrean border, where Bill got his revenge for the humiliation of Gallabat by cutting off the retreat of the Italian 41 Colonial Brigade and capturing the Commandant with his staff and some 800 troops.

Shortly afterwards, advancing into Eritrea with the Italians in full flight, his brigade was suddenly ordered to disengage from the action and race south to cut off an enemy force retreating on his flank. Bill sent a Sudanese armoured car company ahead to reconnoitre the ground and followed in his own truck with a single escort vehicle. Bill was driving, with Welchman sitting beside him and Bill's batman in the back. The heat was stifling, the vehicles threw up huge clouds of dust and he was exhausted from lack of sleep. He thought he might possibly have dozed off for a second – in any case he saw nothing of the two CR42 fighters which suddenly appeared overhead. The first he knew they were being attacked was when the dashboard exploded in front of him. He stamped on the brakes and shouted 'Get out'. Somehow he remembered to switch off the engine and then he threw himself out of the truck as the two fighters turned for another pass, but his foot became jammed in the spare wheel clamped to the side of the truck. In the seconds it took to disentangle his foot and fling himself to the ground the fighters were on him and bullets were spraying everywhere. He felt what he described as a huge kick which seemed to propel him several feet across the ground, face first.

'I lay still in what seemed a sudden and extraordinary silence. I felt no pain but I was certain I had been shot to pieces, that my back was broken, my legs paralysed, my vital organs destroyed. I would never move again. Strangely enough I was no longer frightened. "What a pity" I thought, gently sorry for my wife, my children and myself. "What a pity." And I lay quite still.'[11] While he was lying face down in the sand, he picked up a still-hot bullet and slipped it in his pocket as a 'souvenir' for his son, John, should he survive.

In fact Bill was not paralysed and neither was his back broken. He had been shot in the backside, an ignominious and embarrassing wound that would cause great hilarity among his friends for months. After the fighters had disappeared, he was able to pull himself to his feet, although bleeding profusely and in great pain, and take stock. The escort truck had been completely destroyed and eight men in their party had been wounded, three seriously. Welchman had been hit in the arm during the first strike. Bill's truck was still serviceable. The wounded, patched up with field dressings, were loaded into it – Bill, ashen-faced, reclining with his back arched, rather than sitting, on a seat – and driven back at 50 miles an hour along the same track to a dressing station at brigade headquarters.

As soon as the forlorn little party arrived, medics took over. Bill was given a double shot of whisky laced with morphine and, with Welchman was put directly into an ambulance which set off immediately for the casualty clearing station at Malawiya Pools, in the Sudan. It was a long and agonising journey along a very bumpy road: Welchman, sitting in the front, tried to help by shouting: 'Another bad bump coming, sir' whereupon Bill would raise himself by the straps hanging from the ambulance roof. From Malawiya Pools they were sent on to the hospital at Gedaref, where an Indian surgeon operated on Bill immediately. The machine-gun belts on CR42 fighters were loaded in groups of three – first an armour-piercing bullet, then incendiary, then explosive. Bill had been hit by all three. The first two had burrowed into his flesh, but the third had gone right through him, exploded on the ground and peppered him with shards of metal. The surgeon also removed fragments of Turkish shrapnel he had been carrying round in his body since Mesopotamia.

When Bill came round groggily from the anaesthetic he called for Welchman who was in the same ward, and gave him detailed instructions about the disposition of the brigade. Welchman, realising his commander was delirious, said he would attend to it right away, whereupon Bill murmured, 'Thanks awfully, that's grand', and lapsed back into unconsciousness. Next day Welchman sent a telegram to Aileen on Bill's behalf: 'Wounded. Nothing to worry about but shall not sit down comfortably for some weeks.' Weeks later Bill discovered, to his intense irritation, that it had not been dispatched because the censor's office had strict instructions not to send private cables unless their meaning was absolutely clear.

When Bill was fit to be moved he was transferred by train and Nile steamer to Gordon College in Khartoum, which had been converted into a hospital and where two sympathetic nurses manoeuvred hand mirrors to enable him to inspect the surgeon's handiwork on his rear end. 'Doesn't it look beautiful?' one of them suggested. 'No,' Bill grunted, 'it looks to me like a cross between a night watchman's fire bucket and my aunt's string bag.'[12]

Not long after he had arrived in Khartoum, Bill was sent a consolation present by his brigade. A procession entered his ward escorting a stretcher. He was given a note stating that on the stretcher he would find, with the compliments of his brigade, the commander of the Italian force he had set out to intercept. When the escort stepped aside to allow him a view of the stretcher, he saw a woeful Italian officer lying face down with very similar wounds to his own, but inflicted by a British anti-tank gun.

After his discharge from hospital Bill was not fit enough to return to his brigade and was given convalescent leave in India. On his way home he stopped in Cairo where he was summoned to a meeting with General Wavell, the General Officer Commanding-in-Chief Middle East Command, and Sir John Dill, the CIGS, who was visiting from London. No doubt Bill was questioned about events at Gallabat and in Eritrea. When one of these two very senior officers inquired as to the nature of Bill's wounds, it was said to have been one of the very few recorded instances of Wavell heartily laughing out loud.

Happily reunited with his family at Simla, Bill found the hill station covered in snow, a stark climatic contrast to his recent experiences in East Africa. He had not seen his children, John and Una, by then 14 and 11, for two years and enjoyed a snowball fight with them on the day of his arrival.

Bill eventually returned to duty as Director of Operations and Intelligence at army HQ in Delhi with responsibility for planning operations in the event of a German victory in the Caucasus, or the possibility that Iraq would switch allegiance from the Allies to the Axis. He was not happy about being back at HQ – he wanted another active command – but he was given no choice and at least was offered a desk at which he could stand, no doubt to the amusement of many junior officers. Events, however, moved swiftly in his favour. On 1 April 1941, the very event for which Bill had been asked to make contingency plans – the defection of Iraq to the Axis powers – looked very much more likely when the Arab nationalist Rashid Ali al-Gaylani seized power in Iraq in a coup d'état, supported by four senior military officers known collectively as 'The Golden Square'. Rashid called for the withdrawal of all British forces and his National Defence Government was immediately recognised by Nazi Germany. The British response was to assemble an expeditionary force in India, designated Force Sabine, to seize and secure the port of Basra and protect the Anglo-Iraqi oilfields and RAF bases operating under treaty at Shaibah and Habbaniya. General Edward Quinan was appointed to command Force Sabine and Bill was offered the job as his Brigadier, General Staff (BGS). 'I think the combination should be a good one,' General Sir Claude Auchinleck, C-in-C of the Indian Army, wrote to Wavell.[13] Auchinleck, known as 'the Auk', had joined the Indian Army in

1903 and knew Bill well – they had worked together at GHQ ten years earlier.

Quinan and Bill left for Basra on 4 May 1941. A week later Major General W. A. K. Fraser, commander of the newly raised 10th Indian Division, which had already arrived in Iraq, asked to be relieved of his command. He was in poor health and felt he no longer had the confidence of his subordinate commanders. On 11 May, Auchinleck sent a cable to Wavell suggesting replacing Fraser with Bill Slim. 'I have every reason to expect that Slim's energy, determination and force of character generally will prove equal to the task.'[14]

On 15 May 1941, 49-year-old Brigadier William J. Slim was appointed commander of the 10th Indian Division with the temporary rank of major general.

8

An *Opéra Bouffe* in Persia

By the time Bill arrived in Baghdad to take command of the 10th Indian Division on 12 June 1941, the brief rebellion led by Rashid Ali al-Gaylani had been crushed; Rashid had fled to Persia, an armistice had been signed and a pro-British government restored. Almost a quarter of a century had passed since Bill's previous visit to Baghdad as a young captain in the 9th Warwicks during the Great War. Then, with the Turks retreating in disarray, his task was to conduct house-to-house searches for enemy soldiers in hiding; this time his division was to be responsible for the defence of the whole of northern Iraq.

He had barely begun to assess the problems involved before his orders were changed. In early June a mixed force of British, Indian, Australian and Free French troops from Palestine had attacked Syria and Lebanon, then under control of Vichy France, to prevent Nazi Germany from using the area as a springboard for an assault on the Allied stronghold of Egypt. Two weeks after Bill reached Baghdad his division was ordered to advance into Syria and join the attack from Iraq.

The 10th Division had only been formed, at Ahmednagar, a few months earlier (in January 1941) and Bill was concerned that some of the officers and men under his command were newly recruited and had little combat experience and so he embarked on a series of briefings for the officers about what lay ahead. John Masters, the adjutant of the 2nd Battalion, 4th Prince of Wales's Own Gurkha Rifles, (later to become famous as the author of *Bhowani Junction* and many other novels about the Raj) recalled that the new divisional commander had a rare ability to connect with his audience. Masters was among the officers of 21 Brigade gathered together to meet Bill in a hangar at Habbaniyah airfield 50 miles west of Baghdad. They knew almost nothing about him except that he had been recently promoted from a brigade on the Abyssinian front 'where, we heard, his preferred command position was within whispering range of his leading riflemen, and where he had received a burst of machine gun bullets fired into his rear elevation'. Many such gatherings, Masters noted, ended with those present, having heard it all before, concluding their General was a 'pompous old blatherskite', so the quiet that fell on the hangar when Bill entered was not 'entirely of awed expectation'; more, he said, of a 'judicial hush'. But Bill would prove to be very far from a blatherskite.

'Slim was squarely built, with a heavy slightly undershot jaw and short greying hair. He began to speak, slowly and simply, with no affectation. He told us first that we had done a good job in the Iraqi campaign. But no one could call that a very serious business. He had already seen enough of our fighting spirit and our technical competence to know that we needed little teaching there. What he wanted to do was to prepare us, practically and above all mentally, for the heavier fighting that we must soon meet.

'By now he had our whole attention. He talked a bit about matters that still needed attention – road discipline, defence against air attacks, battle drills to speed up the execution of orders ... Then he began to talk about the nature of modern war, of what it was really like when you engaged an enemy as determined, as numerous, and perhaps better armed than yourselves. Then, he said, tactics and strategy, important though they were, became less central. Situations develop which no tactical or strategical move can alter ... "We make the best plans we can, gentlemen, and train our wills to hold steadfastly to them in the face of adversity, and yet to be flexible and change them when events show them to be unsound, or to take advantage of an opportunity that unfolds during the battle itself. We have already trained our men to the highest possible level of skill with their weapons and in their use of minor tactics. But in the end every important battle develops to a point where there is no real control by senior commanders. Each soldier feels himself to be alone. Discipline may have got him to the place where he is, and discipline may hold him there – for a time. Co-operation with other men in the same situation can help him to move forward. Self-preservation will make him defend himself to the death, if there is no other way. But what makes him go on, alone, determined to break the will of the enemy opposite him, is morale. Pride in himself as an independent thinking man, who knows why he's there, and what he's doing. Absolute confidence that the best has been done for him, and that his fate is now in his own hands. The dominant feeling of the battlefield is loneliness, gentlemen, and morale, only morale, individual morale as a foundation under training and discipline, will bring victory."

'I went back to our camp in a thoughtful mood.'[1]

The advance into Syria was given the code name 'Deficient', which could hardly have been more appropriate given that the 10th Division was desperately short of transport, fuel, arms and ammunition. A shortage of rifles meant that many drivers were unarmed, leaving them highly vulnerable to marauding bands of Arab brigands skilled at setting ambushes and looting whatever they could lay their hands on. Before jerrycans became widely available, fuel was usually carried in thin four-gallon tin cans, fittingly known as 'flimsies', which invariably leaked and added enormously to supply difficulties.

Luckily for Bill he had acquired on his staff a man with a positive genius for somehow finding whatever supplies were needed in the time available. Lieutenant Colonel Arthur Snelling of the Royal Indian Army Service Corps, always known as 'Alf' and later 'Grocer Alf', was the Quartermaster General of the division. A small, slight man, his stature belied his drive and energy and he quickly gained a reputation for masterly improvisation, what Bill called conjuring – 'producing rabbits out of hats, making bricks without straw'.[2] (He would later be a vital member of Bill's team in Burma.) His greatest asset was trust – he never promised what he was unable to deliver. Snelling's favourite response to a request from Bill was usually: 'What you ask is, of course, impossible with the resources we have available, but I will arrange.'

The first objective of the 10th Division was to capture a bridge over the Euphrates at the strongly defended town of Deir-ez-Zor, in eastern Syria, before advancing on to Aleppo, the largest and oldest city in Syria and the end of the fabled Silk Road. The bridge was a vital strategic target since it was the only crossing point over the Euphrates for some 500 miles. The division first concentrated at Haditha, a ramshackle mud village on the banks of the Euphrates

150 miles north-west of Baghdad, from where it faced a 200-mile trek across a waterless desert wilderness, plagued by sandstorms, to reach Deir-ez-Zor. It was, Bill liked to say, 'Miles and miles of sweet Fanny Adams, with a river runnin' through it'. (He had heard a disgruntled soldier in the Great War use the same words to describe Mesopotamia and never forgot it.) He set up his headquarters in a deserted bungalow built by an oil company for its employees at a pumping station on the then defunct Iraq–Libya pipeline. Meanwhile, Snelling, using every form of transport he could lay his hands on, including native boats on the Euphrates, civilian trucks hired in Baghdad and even village donkeys, was busy stocking Haditha with fuel, rations and ammunition.

It was evident to Bill from the start that he would be unable to attack Deir-ez-Zor with his entire division – the distances were too great and the lines of communication too vulnerable, even though Snelling had acquired 300 lorries by persuading Iraq Command to strip all its formations, except one brigade, of second-line transport. RAF pilots, overflying Deir-ez-Zor at great risk, brought back aerial photographs showing that the town and airfield were most strongly protected in the south and west, with concrete gun emplacements and machine-gun posts protecting all the approach roads. Intelligence provided by local informers indicated there were between two and four thousand troops in the garrison, including the Foreign Legion, three or four artillery batteries and a number of armoured cars. In addition the defenders had total air supremacy – Bill's entirely inadequate RAF 'squadron' of four Gladiators and four Hurricanes was no match for the innumerable Vichy French fighters and bombers on call from nearby airfields.

As at Gallabat, Bill decided that a quick surprise attack was his best hope. His plan was to move the bulk of the 21st Brigade to within striking distance of Deir-ez-Zor, while a motorised column, comprising the 13th Lancers in elderly armoured cars, a troop of field guns and the 4/13th Frontier Force Rifles, made a wide sweep round to the west of the town, moving at night and halting on the Aleppo road to the north, poised to make a simultaneous attack at dawn with 21 Brigade. The commander, Brigadier Charles Weld, was a friend of Bill's and, like him, a veteran of operations on the North-West Frontier.

A high-walled fort on the outskirts of Abu Kamal, a farming town just across the Syrian border, was selected as the operational base. On the night of 27/28 June, two companies of Gurkhas with armoured cars went forward to seize the fort, which was believed to be garrisoned by a detachment of Syrian gendarmes. Reconnaissance parties in the area had earlier been fired on and encountered enemy mounted patrols, but when the Gurkhas arrived they found the garrison had decamped, leaving behind only two surprised and very frightened gendarmes, who fired off a few wild volleys before surrendering.

Over the next three days the assaulting brigade group concentrated around Abu Kamal, 84 miles from Deir-ez-Zor, while supplies were poured into the area. Bill did not interfere. Having made a plan and issued his orders, he firmly believed in letting his subordinate commanders get on with the job without him breathing down their necks. Instead he occupied his time trying to improve the lines of communication from Baghdad. Large numbers of supply trucks were being lost, literally. To save fuel and time, drivers avoided the winding track which ran alongside the Euphrates and followed a direct route laid out across the desert marked by empty petrol cans. But at night, especially in a dust storm or sandstorm, it was easy to lose your way and hard to locate the marked trail again.

An even greater danger was posed by bandits, particularly when it became known locally that many drivers were unarmed. (Bill estimated that around 500 drivers in his division had not been issued with a rifle, partly because India had shipped so many weapons from its reserve stock to Britain to make up for losses incurred at Dunkirk.) The desert was littered with trucks that had been hijacked and picked clean, stripped down to the bare bones of the chassis, their crews murdered – either by local brigands or the followers of Fawzi al-Qawuqji, an Arab terrorist leader who was operating in the area and who had caused the British considerable discomfort in Palestine. Bill visited all the staging posts between his headquarters and Baghdad, urged the tightening of convoy discipline, more escorts and continued raids on native villages searching for loot.

On the afternoon of 1 July, Weld reported that his brigade group had made good progress towards Deir-ez-Zor, despite several bombing raids by the French. The motorised column would leave that night and the attack would begin at dawn the following morning. Bill wanted to be present when the battle began, so he grabbed the opportunity for a rest, leaving instructions that he should be roused in time to drive across the desert and meet Weld at his tactical head-quarters at dawn the following day.

He had just been woken and was dressing by electric light – a rare luxury, courtesy of the oil company which had not bothered to switch off the power supply – when Ouvry Roberts, his chief staff officer, put his head round the door with bad news. Although wireless reception was patchy and hard to decipher, Weld seemed to have sent a message to say that he had recalled the flanking column. Bill was dismayed. 'I seemed fated, once again, just when I thought my plans were developing nicely, to be brought up with a jolt.'[3]

Bill left immediately with his ADC to find out what was going on. They drove through the night in a station wagon, bouncing and jolting along a rough track deeply rutted and strewn with boulders. Twenty miles from Deir-ez-Zor they came across the bulk of the brigade's transport attempting to disperse before first light and ten miles further on, just as dawn was breaking, they reached Weld's headquarters on the banks of the Euphrates.

Over breakfast, Weld, who had always impressed Bill by his calm, unshakeable demeanour, explained what had happened. Halfway through his account they were all obliged to run for the trenches when Vichy bombers droned overhead, but although the raid kicked up a lot of dust and smoke and made a great deal of noise it did little damage. When the planes had disappeared they clambered out of the trench and Weld coolly continued his report after ordering the teacups, which were by then covered in dust, to be removed.

The previous day his brigade group had made good progress along the river track, although they had been spotted by the French air force and attacked several times. The RAF had done its best to intervene, but Weld thought that all four Gladiators had been shot down and two of the Hurricanes were missing. In the end the convoy had been saved by a ferocious dust storm which blew up out of nowhere and made life hell for the troops on the ground but prevented further attacks from the air. The flanking column had set off at dusk, as planned, but had not fared well. The terrain was much tougher than anticipated; there was another dust storm which exacerbated the difficulties of keeping the column together; vehicles got out of touch with each other; the need for all the transport to grind along continuously in low gear had used much of their fuel reserves; the dust, atmospherics and terrain had played havoc with radio communications, which were intermittent at best.

When Weld finally got a message warning him there was no possibility of the column being in position to mount an attack on Deir-ez-Zor from the north at dawn, he had little choice but to temporarily abort the operation. He believed that, without a diversion from the north, a frontal attack with the two battalions at his disposal would have little chance of success. He ordered the column to return and sent a message to that effect to divisional headquarters.

After relaying all this dismal news to Bill, Weld then spelled out his new plan: he intended to make another stab at an attack that night. He had had a small delivery of fuel, not enough for the flanking column to mount an assault from the north but enough to strike from the west. Bill was not happy about it. The western approaches to Deir-ez-Zor were much more heavily defended. With virtually no air cover and limited artillery, he did not feel the flanking column would be able to cause sufficient confusion and alarm in the enemy ranks to improve the brigade's prospect of success in the south. On the other hand, they could not stay where they were for very long without being bombed to smithereens.

What he most wanted to do was to stick to his original plan and the only man who might be able to make it work was Alf Snelling. He sat down and wrote what he later described as 'the most urgent signal I could compose', instructing Snelling to gather together every drop of petrol he could find, even if it rendered every vehicle in the base immobile. The signal ended with the command 'the petrol must, repeat must, repeat must' reach the brigade by 1800 hours that evening.

Thereafter Bill could do little but wait to see if Snelling could pull off a miracle. He talked to the troops in the flanking column and warned them to get some sleep as they had another long night ahead of them and with Weld he visited the leading Gurkha battalion dug in alongside the road to Deir-ez-Zor waiting for the order to advance. At various times during the day the French artillery on hills to the north of the town opened up and a few Vichy bombers flew

over the brigade, but both targeted the wrecked and burned-out vehicles littering the road. In the early afternoon, to Bill's great relief, a
signal arrived from divisional HQ to say that a convoy carrying fuel
was on its way and in the late afternoon the first of a motley collection of trucks began straggling into the brigade group. Snelling had
surpassed himself: the convoy delivered no less than 5,000 gallons
of fuel. By seven o'clock the flanking column was ready to move
and Weld ordered his second Gurkha battalion to prepare to move
forward.

At this late juncture Bill was suddenly assailed by doubts. So
much could go badly wrong and the risks were very considerable.
He was acutely aware, for example, that if the attack failed the flanking column would be marooned. It had insufficient fuel to return to
the brigade and would be at the mercy of the enemy; its destruction
or capture was inevitable. Such a disaster, he thought, could cost
him his command. He began to wonder if he should not have accepted Weld's revised plan, or even played safe and postponed the
operation until more supplies had been brought forward.

'Fears and doubts began to creep in on me. Then I remembered
Gallabat, eight months before, when I had taken counsel of my
fears, and missed my chance. This time I would not. I would listen
to my hopes rather than to my fears. I would take the risk. I felt
in my bones that if we got that column coming in from the unexpected and ill-defended north just as we attacked in the south, we
should catch the French off balance and topple them.'[4]

Bill watched as the flanking column set out across the desert
in the gathering gloom, kicking up clouds of sand and dust as it
departed. The gunners brought up their 18-pounders to firing positions within range of the Vichy defences and Weld ordered the
leading Gurkha battalion to move forward under cover of darkness.
Since all the troops involved had been cautioned to maintain strict
radio silence, Bill could see no point in staying up waiting for news.
He got a camp bed from his station wagon, set it up with the help
of his ADC and settled down to sleep under the stars, leaving orders
to be woken in plenty of time to observe the action.

Before dawn next morning, Bill, Weld and a signal officer trudged
across the desert to their observation post on a bluff from where
they could see the road into Deir-ez-Zor, a corner of the airfield and

part of the town, although most of it was screened by a ridge which ran to the north-west and sloped down to within a few hundred yards of the river bank. There followed, for Bill, some of the most agonising hours of his life as he waited for news that the flanking column was in position.

If all had gone well the news would have come through at first light, but first light only brought the distant drone of approaching enemy bombers which flew low overhead, just out of small-arms range, and emptied their bomb holds. After they had departed the French artillery opened up and the division's 18-pounders responded immediately. For a while there was a lively artillery duel, but then the guns fell silent, as if waiting for the battle proper to begin. As minutes and then hours passed, Bill paced up and down with Weld, pretending to reminisce about India and mutual friends while surreptitiously checking his watch every few seconds.

By nine thirty he was convinced his plan had failed and was silently blaming himself for pushing Weld and his brigade into a far worse position than they were when he had arrived the previous day. He considered ordering the frontal attack to go ahead anyway, but Weld's advice was to hang on. The attack could be launched in a matter of minutes. They had waited this long already, another half an hour or an hour would make no difference.

Bill, more and more despondent, resumed his moody pacing until, shortly before ten o'clock, he saw the brigade signals officer hurrying up the hill waving a piece of paper. The column had at last, at long last, made contact. It was a couple of miles north of the town and advancing rapidly; the leading troops were already on the outskirts of the town. Bill wanted to say something momentous like 'Let battle begin', but Weld and the signals officer were already sliding down the hill towards the signals truck. Fifteen minutes later, the division's artillery opened up in earnest. 'I dare say,' Bill recalled, 'there have been bigger and better bombardments, before and since, but no general ever listened to one with more relief than I did on that mount.'[5]

From the observation post Bill could soon see, through his field glasses, lines of Gurkhas, some firing from the hip, moving up the ridge before vanishing into the clouds of smoke and dust created by the artillery. When the smoke suddenly cleared, Vichy troops were abandoning their trenches and disappearing over the crest, pursued by the Gurkhas. Bill switched his glasses to the airfield, where he could hear heavy machine-gun fire. His troops were advancing steadily towards the airfield on both sides of the road. Meanwhile, from the north of the town there was more machine-gun and rifle fire, along with the dull crump of shells – the column was clearly engaged.

It was not long before two Very lights soared into the sky – one from the ridge and one from the airfield – signalling success. Bill decided to see for himself what was going on in the town and to ascertain that the precious bridge over the Euphrates had been saved. He jumped into his station wagon with his ADC and set off for the town, standing in the open roof to get a better view. He waved to the CO of the Gurkha battalion which was moving up in support and the CO waved back cheerfully before disappearing into a cloud of dust churned up by the station wagon. Level with the airfield they came upon an extraordinary sight – hundreds of Syrian troops tearing off their uniforms, khaki jackets and baggy Zouave trousers, and running away in their underwear in an apparent attempt to merge back into civilian life without being captured.

Bill did not stop, but ordered his driver to continue into the town, where a large cheering crowd had gathered. He spotted Sikh turbans among the soldiers, indicating that the flanking column had already joined up with the Gurkhas in the main assault. They turned down a deserted road that seemed to lead to the river and came across a young British officer leading a party of Frontier Force riflemen towards the bridge. He told Bill that he thought the French still occupied it as it was their only escape route. Confirmation was supplied by a burst of light automatic fire up the street in their direction. Bill took cover in the nearest building then ran up to the roof to watch the action from there. When the firing had died down somewhat, he continued on foot to the bridge with his ADC and discovered that it had been captured intact before French sappers had been able to trigger the demolition charges. A squadron of armoured cars was sent across the bridge to pursue the last of the retreating French forces.

Bill headed back into town, where locals were pouring on to the streets to celebrate the departure of the Vichy French. A Frontier

Force platoon helped him force a path through the mob as he was swept towards the municipal offices for an impromptu, yet official, handing over of the town. In an upstairs room at the municipal offices the Syrian deputy governor (the governor was the recently departed French commander) introduced Bill to the city councillors and officials then delivered a formal speech welcoming the British as deliverers and rendering the town into his keeping. Bill was rather hoping that a key might be proffered on a velvet cushion, but had to be content with a speech. In reply, he assured the deputy governor that as long as the citizens kept the peace, obeyed the orders of his troops and gave no succour to the enemy, they would be safe.

After coffee had been served Bill left for the governor's house in the station wagon and suffered a moment of unease as they turned into the gates and found it apparently occupied by the Foreign Legion, but they turned out to be the household staff in Legion uniforms. None of them appeared to have any difficulty in switching allegiance and Bill was welcomed by the major-domo and offered the lunch that had been prepared earlier in the day for the departed governor. His predecessor had clearly left in a hurry – Bill found his personal effects, his sword, medals and photographs all in place and correspondence neatly piled on his desk. Only the key to the safe was missing but when it was blown with gelignite no top-secret plans were discovered – just a collection of pornographic photographs and a set of black silk woman's underwear.

Brigadier Weld and some of the other officers joined him for an excellent celebratory lunch, by which time the scale of their victory had become clear. All the French guns, bar two which had slipped over the bridge, had been captured, along with large quantities of arms, ammunition and, most importantly, fuel. A bombing raid during the morning, presumably aimed at destroying the stocks of ammunition and fuel, failed.

The battle at Deir-ez-Zor was a significant turning point not just for the campaign in Syria but for Bill's confidence and ability to learn from his mistakes. At Deir-ez-Zor he proved the effectiveness of manoeuvre warfare; refused to be cowed by unquestionably daunting logistical problems; kept his nerve when his plans began to unravel; remained focused on his task and purpose; declined to take counsel of his fears after the disappointment at Gallabat and from planning to execution chose the bolder course of action. It set a blueprint for the remainder of his military career: a steadfast belief that, once he was satisfied his plans were correct, nothing must be allowed to erode them.

Two weeks after the fall of Deir-ez-Zor, all Vichy French resistance in Syria ended and the 10th Indian Division, part in Syria and part still at Habbaniyah in Iraq, had the opportunity for a brief rest. Bill, summoned to a conference in Jerusalem, was very much looking forward to a few days of luxury and comfort at the five-star King David Hotel, where the British Mandate maintained its headquarters. He never made it. Half an hour into a flight to Jerusalem, the pilot handed him an urgent signal ordering him to return to Baghdad immediately and report to the army commander, General Quinan.

He wondered, at first, if he was in hot water again. Bill's relationship with his army commander had not been helped by two unfortunate incidents which had not endeared him to Quinan. The General was returning by air from Jerusalem and was irritated to find his aircraft cluttered with odd-shaped packages and when he inquired what the hell they were he was informed that they were instruments for a jazz band. General Slim, he was told, had authorised their purchase and transport, even though army HQ had issued strict orders that only items essential for operations were to be carried by the RAF.

Bill had barely recovered from the roasting he had received from the army commander when a captured French lorry barrelling down the centre of the road towards Habbaniyah forced the General's car off the road and into a ditch, with the General inside. Further inquiries established that the truck was loaded with beer destined for men of the 10th Indian Division. Beer was hard to find in Syria and Iraq but the resourceful Snelling had discovered there was plenty available in Haifa, 600 miles away. After the French had fled Deir-ez-Zor, Bill had plenty of captured transport and fuel, so he approved a substantial overdraft from the Division's contingency account and sent a convoy to Haifa to buy refreshment for his troops, sweltering in the midsummer heat in the desert. In doing so, he incurred the General's wrath on several accounts, apart from his division's lamentable road discipline: why was he using transport to carry unauthorised supplies, why was he holding undisclosed captured enemy vehicles, why had he not obtained the required higher authority approval for such an overdraft?

In fact, Bill had not been called back for another reprimand, to his great relief. He was told he was to take charge of a scratch force, comprising a brigade from his own division, the 2nd Indian Armoured Brigade and 4th British Cavalry Brigade, and invade Persia in three days' time. 'It seemed,' he noted laconically in *Unofficial History*, 'a fairly tall order.'

After Operation Barbarossa, the German invasion of Russia in June 1941 by more than 4.5 million Axis troops, the situation within Persia became critical for the Allies. There were thought to be between 1,000 and 3,000 Germans in Persia working assiduously for the Axis with the connivance of the Shah. Britain was concerned about the Abadan Oil Refinery, owned by the Anglo-Persian Oil Company, which was crucial to the Allied war effort, and Russia desperately needed to keep open the corridor by which it was receiving lend-lease supplies from the United States through the Persian Gulf. In mid-August, amid increasing tension, the British government and its new ally, the Soviet Union, presented a demand to the Shah that all German nationals in Persia be expelled. When he refused, a joint invasion was agreed, with three Soviet armies striking from the north, part of the 8th Indian Infantry Division moving to secure the Abadan oilfields in the south and Bill's brigade group crossing the border from Khanaqin in the west to capture the ancient city of Kermanshah, 75 miles inland.

Bill did not arrive in Khanaqin until 24 August, the day before the invasion was scheduled to begin. He knew nothing of the place, apart from a well-remembered popular rhyme in the Great War:

> *The Qaimaqam of Khanaqin,*
> *Is versed in every kind of sin,*
> *For all the grosser forms of lust,*
> *He makes a gorgeous bundobust.*

Fortunately, Brigadier John Aizlewood, commander of the 2nd Indian Armoured Brigade, had made meticulous plans for the operation; Bill sat down with him and went over his proposals in great detail and was happy he could approve.

Shortly before dawn on 25 August, Hussars in obsolete Mark VII tanks armed with a single Vickers machine gun led the brigade group across the border into Persia. It encountered very little opposition apart from a few desultory shots from frontier guards, who promptly fled. Bill, following, noted that it was the fifth frontier he had crossed in the last 12 months. The first major obstacle they faced was the Kai Tak Pass, a formidable escarpment rising 3,000 feet from the flat plans of the Tigris and Euphrates and running from north to south across their path 30 miles from the border.

Pressing forward with the advance guard, by mid-morning Bill and Aizlewood were at the entrance to the Kai Tak Pass. Standing on the roof of the station wagon he could see the road to Kermanshah snaking and looping up the face of the escarpment before disappearing into a series of gorges. Intelligence reports indicated the Persian army was holding the pass in strength, with some 5,000 troops, although there was no sign of them. In some ways the enemy strength was academic – Bill estimated a handful of men could have held the pass against a force many times the size of his brigade group.

With not a sign of movement anywhere, Bill ordered his driver to proceed cautiously up the road, stopping every now and then so that he could sweep the area with his field glasses. They passed a white-painted *chai khana*, tea shop, completely deserted, and drove slowly round the next bend so that Bill could see up the pass: at that moment they heard the rattle of small-arms fire and a shell burst some way off the road in a cloud of dust, smoke and stones. The driver rapidly reversed back round the bend just as another shell smashed into the road where they had stopped.

Further back down the road, John Masters, advancing in battle formation with the 2nd/4th Gurkhas, was astonished to see a khaki station wagon heading towards them from the direction of the pass. 'The leading riflemen dropped and prepared to open fire. But the car was obviously unarmed and flying a red divisional flag from the radiator cap. It stopped beside us and General Slim got out. "How the hell did he get past us?" I muttered. Willy [the CO, Lieutenant Colonel William Weallens] hurried forward. "Morning Willy", the general said. "There's nothing until you get round the fourth hairpin. They've got an anti-tank gun there." There was a large hole through the back of the car body. Slim climbed back into his car, we saluted and he drove on.'[6]

Unwilling to sacrifice men's lives needlessly in a frontal assault on the Kai Tak Pass, Bill discussed the options with Aizlewood, who pointed out on the map a route up the escarpment some 20 miles to the south, which avoided the pass and joined the main road to Kermanshah at a village called Shahabad. It was long, some 90 miles, but said to be passable by wheeled vehicles and only lightly defended. Bill decided to send a brigade along this alternative route to attack the troops in the pass from the rear.

On the following day the Royal Air Force carried out a number of heavy bombing raids along the escarpment. Before dawn on 27 August, as two Gurkha battalions began to head up the pass, Bill received a signal from the flanking column to say that it had captured Shahabad and the Persians, obviously unnerved by the bombing, had withdrawn and were in full flight. Early that morning Bill drove unmolested to the top of the pass and found about 50 sorry-looking Persian prisoners squatting beside the brigade HQ; it seemed their officers had decamped in the night without a word to any of them.

Bill wanted to press on to Kermanshah, where there was concern for the safety of some 50 British subjects employed at an oil refinery, but 15 miles beyond Shahabad their progress was halted by a strong Persian force occupying a line of hills straddling the road. Reconnaissance patrols indicated that it was an army corps of two divisions plus a cavalry brigade. Bill used the halt as an opportunity for his strung-out formation to close up and shelter behind a ridge for the night.

Next morning, while he was squatting on the forward face of the ridge and surveying the scene through his field glasses, the Persian artillery opened up with modern 155mm guns which, frustratingly, far outranged his old 18-pounders. As the shells whistled overhead Ouvry Roberts made Bill laugh by grunting, 'Damned cheek.' Bill had no great opinion of the Persian army but was still reluctant to attempt an attack against such superior numbers. It was the possible plight of the British employees at the oil refinery, however, which swung the balance and he ordered a general advance to begin at ten o'clock.

As the final preparations were being made, a large black saloon car emerged from a village halfway across the valley and headed in their direction with white flags fluttering from the windows on both sides. It stopped at the foot of the ridge and a dapper Persian officer stepped out. He was, Bill later observed, immaculate from the high heels of his field boots to the top of his smart kepi, 'a credit alike to his tailor, his bootmaker, and his batman'.[7] Bill stepped forward in his scruffy khaki drill to meet his visitor who announced, in French, that he had a message from the Persian commander-in-chief for the British commander. Bill admitted, in his schoolboy French, that he was the commander. A look of incredulity, quickly suppressed, twitched across the visitor's face.

He had come, he explained, to offer a ceasefire. The Shah wanted no more bloodshed: the terms were that all hostilities were to cease immediately and the British were to remain in their present positions until a peace agreement had been hammered out by their governments. Bill demurred. Under no circumstances, he said, could he accept any limitation on the movement of his forces. He would agree a ceasefire if the Persian forces withdrew by two o'clock that afternoon, if he was given unfettered access to Kermanshah and if all British subjects in Persian hands were delivered unharmed and well treated.

The visitor was indignant and complained that Bill was demanding a surrender rather than a truce. Bill agreed, but refused to budge. He sensed, correctly as it turned out, that the Persians had no stomach for a fight, even though they considerably outnumbered Bill's force. A great deal of Persian bluster ensued, particularly when Bill added a demand that all British subjects be produced at his headquarters safe and well by four o'clock that afternoon. When Bill suggested the Persian officer might return to his headquarters and discuss the matter with his commander he (the Persian) was obliged to admit that it was not the custom in the Persian army for the general to be in the front line. In the end, he accepted all Bill's terms with some reluctance, saluted and departed in his car with the white flags still protruding from each window.

Later that morning the first reports began arriving that the Persian troops were withdrawing from their positions. Bill's next visitor was the English manager of the oil refinery, who had driven out from Kermanshah to assure Bill that all the British subjects were in good health and invited him to return with him to the town to see for himself. They drove back through the retreating files of Persian soldiers on each side of the road and, after tea served on fine china in the drawing room of the manager's bungalow, Bill sought out the Persian commander at his headquarters in the centre of the town and insisted all his troops should be clear of the area within the next 48 hours. This, too, was agreed.

'Next morning we marched into Kermanshah in style and formally occupied it. Large crowds clustered along the sides of the streets and although I cannot say anyone cheered, there was no doubt that the bulk of them were friendly and even those, who, I suspected, would have liked to be hostile, were at least resigned. Our troops had smartened themselves up, and as they moved through the city on their way to their bivouac areas they looked, in spite of their not very large numbers, workmanlike and, as I meant them to, formidable enough not to invite liberties.'[8]

For the next few days Bill was busy establishing a presence in what had been agreed as the British zone and occupying the important towns of Senneh and Hamadaon before the the Russians, who were advancing rapidly from the north, could get there. By 30 August, British and Soviet forces had linked up (Bill was the first British general in the war to meet a Russian general face to face), the Persian army had been defeated (in total, 15 divisions had surrendered without much resistance), the oilfields secured and the Trans-Iranian railway was in Allied hands, opening a crucial supply route to the Soviet Union.

Bill described the campaign thereafter as an '*opéra bouffe*' (farce). It certainly had elements of Gilbert & Sullivan about it: the elaborate courtesies of pompous Persian officers in immaculate Ruritanian uniforms vainly attempting to maintain their dignity in defeat; the machinations of slippery, obsequious and excessively polite petty bureaucrats; the suspicious peasants with no knowledge of anything beyond their daily lives; the wary Russian officers with an alarming taste for vodka and caviar and a surprising love of parties; the humourless Commissars and brutalised Russian troops.

At one point Bill Slim and Ouvry Roberts were required to undertake a secret mission to Tehran disguised in civilian clothes. To prevent the collapse of the Persian government, the Allies had refrained from occupying Tehran on condition that all remaining German nationals in the capital be handed over, but the government was prevaricating and Bill was sent to meet the British ambassador, Sir Reader Bullard, to find out what was going on. By then his division had moved to Arak, an industrial city on the Trans-Iranian railway 170 miles from Tehran.

Bill and Roberts visited Arak's biggest store to kit themselves out with Persian civilian outfits, including the cloth cap worn by almost every Persian male since the reforming Shah had banned traditional clothes in favour of Western dress. 'We emerged a couple of desperate looking thugs, as little like British officers as it is possible to imagine,' he recalled. His confidence in his disguise was rather shaken when, shortly after setting out by car, they passed a Persian post and the sentry presented arms – as did every other sentry along the road. To Bill's gratitude, Sir Reader forbore to laugh when they arrived at the embassy. After a briefing, they returned to Arak and were once again punctiliously saluted by every sentry.

With the Persian government still showing no sign of meeting the Allied terms, an ultimatum was delivered on 10 September requiring the surrender of all Germans and Italians within 48 hours. No Germans appeared and the British and Soviet governments ordered Tehran to be occupied. By 16 September elements of the 10th Division had assembled a few miles south of the city. Bill was told that Germans were collecting in their embassy, claiming diplomatic privileges, and as women and children were among them it was presumed he would hesitate to fire. His reply was robust. As the Germans had bombed his 90-year-old mother at her home in Bournemouth and his children at their school, he said, he would have few scruples about returning the compliment. To prove the point, he ordered his 6-inch Howitzers to be brought forward. At the last minute, the Germans in the embassy surrendered, although it was later discovered that a number of the most dangerous agents had escaped.

On 17 September, British and Soviet forces occupied Tehran. Bill did not remember it as a particularly triumphant or spectacular affair; the troops simply marched into their previously allotted areas watched by indifferent locals in shabby European clothes. In truth, they may have been more concerned with internal politics than foreign armies – the previous day Reza Shah had been forced by the Allies to abdicate in favour of his 22-year-old son, Mohammad Reza Shah Pahlavi, who would rule the country until his overthrow by the Iranian Revolution in 1979.

In the following weeks Bill was required to work closely with the Soviets and he got to know his Russian counterpart, General Novikov, well. Although Soviet troops were not encouraged to socialise with their British and Indian counterparts, different rules applied for the officers as long as the Russians could be hosts rather than guests. Very early on General Novikov invited Bill and about 30 of his officers to visit the Soviet headquarters at Kazvin, 100 miles north-west of Tehran, and to spend the night there. The visitors arrived at midday and were immediately served shots of vodka with delicious canapes and heaped spoons of caviar; each round of drinks was accompanied by an extravagant toast to which Bill felt obliged to respond in equally effusive terms. When all the toasts were exhausted, General Novikov announced it was time for lunch. Bill had assumed the canapes were lunch and had never felt less like eating in his life. To his dismay, he discovered it was not so much a lunch as a banquet with many courses, at the end of which there were more toasts. By then Bill had learned not to sip from any one of the glasses in front of him, since the moment he did so it was instantly refilled.

Lunch did not finish until late in the afternoon, but the entertainment continued: a Russian officer played on a grand piano in the corner of the room and then a military choir was ushered into the room to perform soulful Georgian ballads. The singers were highly professional and Bill inquired, through an interpreter, how such talent had been gathered together. The choir turned out to be the male chorus from Tbilisi Opera House, which had been pressed into service as General Novikov's headquarters defence company. Novikov asked Bill if there was anything he would like the choir to sing and he requested 'The Volga Boatmen', the only Russian song he knew, which was performed by a young officer with a magnificent bass voice. After the songs there was energetic dancing to the accompaniment of balalaikas.

Bill's feeling of conviviality turned to alarm when Novikov rose to his feet and said: 'Now the British officers will sing.' He protested

through the interpreter that none of them could match the quality
of what they had just heard; that British officers were by and large
unmusical and that any attempt at singing could only offend the
ears of their hosts, but the genial Novikov would have none of it:
the Russians had sung for their guests, the British must sing for their
hosts. Bill conducted a hurried conference with his fellow officers
and discovered that not only was there only one song they all knew,
but they only knew one verse. As none of their hosts seemed to
speak English, they decided there was nothing to be lost by singing
the same verse over and over again. Thus primed, Bill announced
that they would perform a traditional English folk song. So it was
that the senior officers of the 10th Indian Division took to the floor
and embarked on a faltering single-verse rendition of 'Daisy, Daisy,
Give Me Your Answer Do' ...

    Bill would later be awarded a DSO for 'gallant and distinguished
service' in Iraq, Syria and Persia. In January 1942 the new Shah of
Persia signed a treaty of alliance with Britain and the Soviet Union
and the 10th Division was withdrawn back to Habbaniyah in Iraq
with orders to prepare for the possibility of another German offensive. Bill set up his headquarters in a bombed-out flying-boat
station on the lake and the division settled down to a period of
intensive training.

    It was at his headquarters, in early March, that he was summoned
to take a telephone call from the army commander in Baghdad.
General Quinan told him he was to relinquish his command and
leave for India within three days. Bill's first reaction, typically, was to
assume he had been sacked, but Quinan assured him that this was
not the case; he was to be given another job.

    Bill's heart sank. He said he did not want another job; he wanted
to stay with his division. 'A good soldier goes where he's sent and
does what he's told,' Quinan snapped and slammed down the telephone. Bill called his staff together to give them the news, then
cabled Aileen in Simla and asked her to meet him in Delhi. His
departure was held up for several days by continual sandstorms but
eventually the weather cleared sufficiently for a flying boat to take
off from Habbaniyah lake. They landed on a lake at Gwalior in
central India, where Bill had to wait for a train for the 200-mile
journey to Delhi. Aileen was waiting for him on the platform when

he arrived; almost a year had passed since they had last seen each other.

Bill reported to General Headquarters the following day and was informed that he would be flying to Burma with Lieutenant General Edwin Morris, the Chief of the General Staff in India, who was visiting the front to assess what was a fast-deteriorating situation after the Japanese invasion in mid-January. Rangoon had fallen only a few days earlier, on 9 March, and the Allies were attempting to reorganise to block the Japanese advance. No one seemed willing to tell Bill why he was travelling with General Morris. He resigned himself to being a 'good soldier' and do what he was told without asking too many questions.

They left early the next morning, spent the night in Calcutta, and flew on next day across the sparkling Bay of Bengal to the Allied air base at Akyab, on the Arakan coast of Burma. Bill was struck by how clean and tidy Akyab appeared compared with similar towns in India. There they were briefed by Air Vice-Marshal Donald Stevenson, the Air Officer Commanding in Burma. Stevenson, who had won a DSO and MC and bar with the Royal Flying Corps in the Great War, painted a grim picture of how things stood. It had been estimated that 14 fighter squadrons would be needed to meet a Japanese attack; in the event, there were two. Without the assistance of the American Volunteer Group, an extraordinary unit of mercenary volunteer pilots loaned by China to assist in the defence of Rangoon, Allied air power would have been immediately overwhelmed at the time of the invasion. During the bombing of Rangoon – there were 31 raids during the first two months – 130 enemy aircraft had been destroyed, but the disparity between both sides remained. At the time Stevenson was speaking 14 regiments of the Japanese air force had been deployed against Burma; the Allies could muster a daily operational force of around 45 aircraft, as against the enemy's 260. They talked late into the night and little of what Stevenson had to say offered any encouragement.

Next day they flew over the Arakan mountains into central Burma. It was Bill's first opportunity to get a look at the terrain – the seemingly endless ridges covered with jungle which looked, he thought, like a thick green carpet rucked into folds. Suddenly the ridges opened out into a fertile valley with a silver river snaking through it – the Irrawaddy. They landed at Magwe, then the Allies' main air base in Burma, where they had another briefing, before continuing to Mandalay, landing on a rough airstrip cleared on the rice paddies outside the town. From Mandalay they took the winding road up to Maymyo, a hill station in the Shan Highlands named after a Colonel Rupert May of the Bengal Regiment in the nineteenth century, where Army Headquarters, Burma, had been set up in the incongruous surroundings of Maymyo's dusty streets lined by orange-flowered flame trees and its 'English cottages' and gardens planted with sweet peas, morning glory, hibiscus, poinsettia and fuschia.

At Maymyo, Bill had a brief meeting with General Sir Harold Alexander, recently appointed GOC Burma. Bill knew that Alexander's chief of staff was shortly to return to India and worried that he was perhaps being considered as his replacement, but Alexander made no mention of it during their meeting. Although he liked and greatly respected Alexander at that time (he would change his opinion later), he had no desire to become his chief of staff. He had never seen himself as a staff officer and had never been particularly happy when he had been obliged to take staff jobs earlier in his career.

What Bill did not know was that it had been decided a corps commander and corps headquarters would be essential to conduct future operations in Burma while Alexander handled administrative and political problems and that his name had been put forward as a suitable candidate. Neither Alexander, nor Field Marshal Sir Alan Brooke, the new Chief of the Imperial General Staff, knew Bill particularly well, but Brooke's deputy, General Nye, did – Bill had made a big impression on Nye when they were instructors together at Camberley and it was probably Nye who was instrumental in Bill's appointment.

Bill left Maymyo with his future still unclear to him although he was gloomily pondering the prospect of being offered another staff job in India. He imagined he would be returning to Delhi but instead he was told to report to Calcutta, where he was driven through the dense traffic to Government House to meet General Archibald Wavell, who had swapped jobs with Auchinleck to become the Commander-in-Chief, India. Wavell questioned him briefly about his trip to Burma, responding to everything Bill said with a curt 'I see'. Then he said, without further preamble, 'I want you to go back to Burma to take command of the corps that is to be formed there.'

Wavell didn't wait for him to accept. He simply told him he would be taking on a very difficult job and that the sooner he left, the better.

Bill was ecstatic. 'I'll start tomorrow morning,' he replied.

9

The Corps Commander

After his brief meeting with Wavell, Bill found a map of Burma and retired to his sweltering room at Government House, where he sat under an ineffective fan and tried to familiarise himself with the country. He had learned the trick of turning the map of a strange country into a rough diagram with the principal features and distances marked – once he had got the diagram into his head he found it easier to visualise the entire country. Apart from what little he had learned during his brief visit, and the map on his lap, he was painfully conscious of the fact that he knew very little about Burma, or the Japanese, or jungle warfare. When he was commanding the 2nd/7th Gurkhas he had, during their annual training in Shillong, cast the Japanese in the role of enemy and at the Senior Officers' School he had introduced a study of the Japanese invasion of China into the syllabus, but in reality he knew precious little of their tactics or their senior officers.

In the meantime, he cabled Aileen with the good news of his appointment and promotion to lieutenant general, but if she was less than thrilled she might have been forgiven; she would undoubtedly have preferred her husband to have been offered a nice, safe posting at headquarters. The majority of his kit was somewhere between Iraq and Delhi, but a local tailor was called in, measured him up and was able to produce, overnight, three sets of khaki drill uniforms. That evening, after dinner, Bill joined a jolly party on a visit to an air-conditioned cinema in Calcutta. It was, he admitted, an odd way to spend his last night in civilisation but he sensibly thought there was nothing to be gained by sitting in his room and fretting.

Early next morning Acting Lieutenant General W. J. Slim, newly appointed commander of 1st Burma Corps (Burcorps), left for the front with three shirts, three pairs of khaki slacks, his Gurkha hat and a bedding roll. He was due to fly to Burma from Dum Dum aerodrome north of Calcutta, but when he arrived at the chaotic terminal, typical of India, no one claimed to have any knowledge of who he was or where he was going. After a great deal of confusion, head wobbling and shouting, a Sikh pilot from the Indian Air Force appeared with orders to fly Bill to Burma in a two-seater Lysander. Bill strapped on a parachute and clambered into the observer's seat behind the pilot, who then discovered the engine would not start. After 30 frustrating minutes trying to get it to fire, he gave up and went off to look for another aircraft, which he eventually found and they took off, several hours behind schedule.

They stopped for refuelling (and a welcome cup of tea) at the airstrip near Chittagong, in what is now Bangladesh, and sunset was approaching by the time they crossed the Irrawaddy. Bill was able to make out a number of white pagodas, curiously luminous in the smoky dusk, as they circled the airfield at Magwe, waiting for a signal from the ground to land. There was no signal. With his fuel running low, the pilot had no alternative but to land while he could still see the runway. He taxied to a group of huts where there were other parked aircraft; no one appeared to greet them and when Bill clambered down from the Lysander he found the place deserted. Vigorous ringing on a field telephone discovered in one of the huts produced no answer. Eventually they stopped a military truck on the perimeter road of the airfield and hitched a lift to the RAF officers' mess, where they were provided with a meal. After dinner Bill chatted to some of the RAF officers and suggested that perhaps it was unwise to leave the airfield and aircraft completely unprotected at night, but was airily informed that it was nothing to do with the RAF – it was the army's job. He would recall this conversation, bitterly, a few days later when the Japanese attacked the airfield with devastating effect.

Very early the following day they took off through the dawn mist and headed south to Prome, a bustling river port established by the British Irrawaddy Flotilla Company in the late nineteenth century, 180 miles upriver from Rangoon, where Burcorps was to be head-quartered. On this occasion a driver and an ADC were waiting to meet him at the airfield and take him straight to a conference with General Alexander, recently appointed commander of the Burma Army, and Burcorps' two divisional commanders, Punch Cowan and Bruce Scott, both of whom, by an extraordinary twist of fate, were old friends, having served with Bill in the 1st/6th Gurkhas. Cowan had taken over command of the 17th Indian Division after the Sittang bridge fiasco and Bruce Scott had been in command of the 1st Burma Division since its formation the previous year. Bill was delighted to see them. 'We had served and lived together for twenty-odd years; we – and our wives – were the closest friends; our children had been brought up together in the happiest of regiments. I could not have found two men in whom I had more confidence or with whom I would rather have worked.'[1]

With no need to introduce Bill to his divisional commanders, Alexander launched directly into a review of the current situation. What remained of the 17th Division was re-forming some 30 miles south of Prome and was thus not at that time in contact with the enemy. The 1st Burma Division was stationed in and around the town of Toungoo, some 80 miles to the east, waiting to be relieved by the Chinese 5th Army, at which time it would be transferred to the Irrawaddy front and join 17th Division. The initial plan was to stabilise the front and deny Upper Burma to the Japanese by hold- ing the two main routes north, through the Sittang and Irrawaddy valleys – the Chinese would cover the road and railway through the Sittang valley; Burcorps would be responsible for protecting the road alongside the Irrawaddy through Prome. The weak link in the plan was that the two routes were 80 miles apart, separated by the rugged mountain wilderness of the Pegu Yomas, which not only formed a barrier between the Chinese and Burcorps but was vulner- able to infiltration and encirclement, tactics in which the Japanese excelled.

Alexander flew out of Prome immediately after lunch and Bill, who had driven straight to the conference from the airfield ear- lier that morning, turned his attention to his headquarters, which was already being set up in the courthouse, a handsome terracotta building a few yards from the river bank. There he had a reunion with another old friend, Brigadier Taffy Davies, who had met Bill at Staff College and commanded a battalion in the 10th Infantry Brigade at the beginning of the war and was now Burcorps' chief of staff. Davies was busy trying to create a headquarters out of virtually nothing – there was very little office equipment or transport, few tents and no proper messing arrangements. Bill was told that the cooking pots, crockery and cutlery in the officers' mess had all been 'borrowed' from abandoned European bungalows and the mess staff had been recruited from the streams of refugees pouring into the town. Communication was provided by a small detachment from the Burma Signals equipped with just four wireless sets and pedal-operated battery chargers. There were virtually no maps, apart from those picked up from evacuated government offices, and place names were often, confusingly, pronounced very differently from the way they were spelled. Transport shortages were beefed up by using civilian cars left behind in Rangoon; Taffy Davies rode about in a large American limousine, gangster-style, with a bullet hole in the windscreen just level with his eyes.

Later in the afternoon Cowan drove Bill in an armoured carrier to visit his division. Cowan, a powerfully built man with a ruddy complexion and a fondness for cigars, had a talent, like Bill, for inspiring great loyalty and affection from his men. On the road, he explained what had happened in the campaign so far and the events at the Sittang bridge; he said the division had drawn on the last reinforcements available in Burma but was still well under strength with around 7,000 troops, less than half its establishment. When they arrived, Bill was shocked by their lack of equipment and the wretched state of their uniforms, although he was careful not to show it. Nevertheless he felt they were in good heart, despite what they had been through. The division also had under command the 7th Armoured Brigade, equipped with American Stuart and Honey tanks. 'They had had plenty of fighting in the Western Desert before coming to Burma,' Bill observed, 'and they looked what they were – confident, experienced, tough soldiers.'[2] They would certainly prove their worth in the weeks ahead.

At divisional headquarters, set up in a Burmese village of huts built on stilts, almost the first man Bill ran into was Godfrey Welchman – 'Welcher' – now a brigadier, still carrying a spear he had picked up in Eritrea. They had last seen each other when they occupied adjoining hospital beds in Khartoum. Bill decided on the spot to poach Welcher for his own headquarters, blithely explaining to Punch Cowan that as they (Cowan and Welchman) were both superb morale-raisers it was wrong they should be in the same headquarters. By and large Bill disapproved of generals bringing preferred staff officers with them to a new appointment (he dismissed it as 'travelling with a circus'), but Welcher was an exception.

That evening, Bill was 'dined in' at the home of *teakwallah* Philip Howe, the forest manager of Steel Brothers, a huge British-owned timber conglomerate set up to ship Burmese teak to Europe, which had offices in Prome. Steel Brothers had chartered a ship to evacuate their employees from Rangoon the previous month, but Howe, who knew Burma and the Burmese extremely well and could speak the language, had stayed behind and been recruited by Cowan as an intelligence officer, part of a scratch force of expatriate civilians employed in the faint hope they could garner information about the enemy's whereabouts and intentions. Howe also provided Bill with accommodation in a comfortable company-owned house.

Over the next few days Bill spent most of his time working at the courthouse in the judge's room, still lined with bookshelves and leather-bound law books, which he had taken over as his office, or visiting the troops. A born leader, he knew how important it was to show himself to the men and he had a natural ability, rare among Second World War generals, to communicate with soldiers at all levels. This talent, combined with an abundance of common sense, a complete lack of pretension or humbug and a soldier's salty humour, would generate astonishing loyalty and affection among the troops. One famous story about Bill's pep talks had a little Cockney sergeant (sometimes it was a Jock, sometimes a corporal), carried away by his rhetoric, jumping to his feet and shouting, 'Don't worry, sir, when the day comes, we'll all be behind you.' 'Don't you believe it, sergeant,' Bill is said to have retorted with a twinkle in his eye. 'When the day comes, I'll be a long way behind you.'

George MacDonald Fraser, who served in Burma as a private in The Border Regiment and after the war became famous as the author of the Flashman novels, said Bill had 'the head of a general but the heart of a private soldier'.[3] (For years after the war, many Burma veterans persisted in the mistaken belief that Bill had risen from the ranks as the only possible explanation for his common touch.) Those who knew him well were not fooled by the impression he liked to give of just being a simple soldier; behind his bluff exterior was a shrewd brain, notable self-knowledge and a profound understanding of human nature.

One of Bill's main concerns while he was finding his feet in his new job was that army HQ in Delhi had not yet identified Burcorps' ultimate objective. Was he going to be required to defend and hold part of the country, oversee an organised retreat into India, or attempt a counter-attack in concert with the Chinese? He did not know. What he did know was that whatever Burcorps' objective, it – and he – faced formidable problems. Firstly, he was getting virtually no intelligence about Japanese strength, movements or intentions. (Ultra[4] intercepts were not widely available at that time.) The speed and ferocity of the enemy onslaught on Burma had allowed no time for the organisation of 'left behind parties' to report on Japanese activities. His only reliable source of information was from documents found in the pockets of dead Japanese (prisoners were rarely captured alive), but they needed to be translated and he had only one officer in the entire corps who could speak Japanese.

In Burcorps' outposts often the first intimation of enemy action was a stream of tracer bullets rattling from the jungle and the unnerving babel of Japanese soldiers shrieking and howling like animals as they attacked. Bill likened his situation to being a blind boxer trying to strike an unseen opponent and parry blows he did not know were coming until he had been hit.

Compared to the enemy his troops were ill trained and ill equipped for fighting in the jungle. Even if the 17th Division had been up to strength, the reality was that it had been trained for operations in Africa and the Middle East. The 1st Burma Division was, as its name implied, recruited locally, mostly from the hill tribes, but had only been formed in July the previous year, was inexperienced in battle and the reliability of the lowland Burmese troops was known to be questionable. The enemy, in stark contrast, was able to deploy crack troops in overwhelming numbers – tough, ruthless, savage fighters with a total disregard for human life, their own or others' – their morale boosted by an unbroken series of victories since the start of the war. Japanese tactics sought to induce panic, fear and paralysis in the enemy and succeeded to the extent that the Imperial Japanese Army, in the first few terrible months of the Burma campaign, had quickly gained a reputation for being invincible.

Mechanised transport meant Burcorps was tied to roads – unable, as Bill put it, to 'shake loose from the tin can of mechanical transport tied to our tail' – and the Japanese had developed the roadblock into almost an art form, sending small vanguard units to move through the jungle – jungle considered impenetrable by British, Gurkha and Indian troops – at remarkable speed, emerging far to the rear of their enemy to block the escape route with felled trees or burned-out vehicles, then fiercely defending the position with machine guns, mortars and mobile artillery. In addition, the Japanese could usually count on help from native Burmese, who were largely hostile to the Allies after years of colonial domination (the invaders had presented themselves, and initially been welcomed, as 'liberators' from the yoke of the Empire).

Allied casualties had been heavy, sickness was increasing and with Rangoon in enemy hands there was little or no prospect of Burcorps being re-equipped, resupplied or reinforced. Most worrying of all, morale was, unsurprisingly, plummeting. 'This was not the first, nor was it to be the last, time that I had taken over a situation that was not going too well,' Bill noted with characteristic understatement. 'I knew the feeling of unease that comes at such times, a sinking of the heart as the gloomy facts crowd in ...'[5]

In his favour, he had plenty of experience of combat, of managing and inspiring men in difficult circumstances, of making do with inadequate support and services and of working in hostile environments. He also possessed an instinctive, bulldog reluctance to be daunted by problems, no matter how intimidating or demoralising.

Bill was convinced that what was needed to restore morale and the troops' fighting spirit was a solid success in battle to wrest the initiative from the Japanese. He had never forgotten his old sergeant major's philosophy in the OTC: 'There's only one principle of war, me lad, and that's this: hit the other fellow as quick as you can and as hard as you can, where it hurts him most and when he ain't lookin'.' He believed it would be possible to mount an effective counter-attack once the 1st Burma Division had been released from the Toungoo area by the arrival of the Chinese and reunited with Punch Cowan's division and it was to this end that he made his plans.

In the meantime he encouraged small-scale offensive operations against the Japanese. On 17 March, Major Mike Calvert, who would later become one of the best-known Chindits and thoroughly deserve the soubriquet 'Mad Mike', put together a small force of commandos and led a daring raid by riverboat on the port of Henzada, behind Japanese lines, inflicting heavy losses on the enemy. Two days later, a company of the 1st Battalion, The Gloucestershire Regiment, which had arrived in Burma from India in 1938 as a garrison unit, staged a night raid on the town of Letpadan the day after it had been occupied by the Japanese, killing a large number of the enemy and chasing the remainder into the jungle. It was, Bill thought, 'a most sprightly affair'.

When advance elements of the Chinese 5th Army arrived in Toungoo, Bill ordered Bruce Scott to start moving his division across the Pegu Yomas to Allanmyo, a town that straggled along the east bank of the Irrawaddy some 40 miles north of Prome, where it would have time and space to assemble without interruption – it was estimated it was going to take between ten days and a fortnight for the entire division to gather at its new location. At the same time, Bill brought Cowan's division and the 7th Armoured Brigade closer to Prome to ease transport problems and close the gap with the Burma Division. (He subsequently admitted in *Defeat Into Victory*, with the searing honesty which was so much a part of his character, that he made a mistake and that it would have been better to leave 17th Division forward where it was and concentrate the Burma Division closer to Prome.)

On the morning of 21 March, after aerial reconnaissance had revealed a large concentration of Japanese aircraft on the airfield at Mingaladon, near Rangoon, a small force of nine British bombers and ten Hurricanes – all the available Allied aircraft from Magwe and Akyab – mounted a raid which resulted in the destruction of 16 Japanese fighters on the ground and 11 in the air. Despite anti-aircraft fire from the ground and fierce dogfights in the air, all the British planes returned safely, except for one Hurricane.

So successful was the operation that a second raid was planned for that afternoon, but before the aircraft could get off the ground the Japanese retaliated with a massive attack on Magwe airfield. Over a period of 25 hours, wave after wave of Japanese bombers and fighters in large numbers blasted Magwe. The overwhelming strength of the enemy – some 250 aircraft were deployed in total – forced the

RAF and the American Volunteer Group to abandon the airfield. The AVG withdrew to its base at Lashio, in the north-east of the country, and the RAF to the island of Akyab, on the west coast, but the Japanese then hit Akyab airfield in the same strength and with the same ferocity, forcing it, too, to be abandoned and transferred to Chittagong. From that moment, there were no flyable RAF aircraft anywhere in Burma, with the exception of a single ancient Tiger Moth.

Even at moments of dire peril, Bill always did his best to maintain an air of cheerful unconcern in front of his subordinates, but the news from Akyab was just too much. 'I so well remember Slim's dismay,' recalled the then Major Brian Montgomery, one of his staff officers and the younger brother of the future commander of the Eighth Army, 'and Taffy Davies' rage, when the news reached us at Prome that our air cover had vanished overnight. We sensed it had gone for good, and so it had.'[6]

The departure of the Royal Air Force from Burma was not only another serious blow to morale, but left Burcorps, and indeed Burma itself, at the mercy of enemy aircraft, which were free to range far and wide unmolested, reducing town after town to blazing ruins (the most common building material in Burma was wood). Widespread chaos and confusion ensued. 'Many of the essential services of Burma have collapsed,' Alexander's chief of staff reported on 26 March. 'Even several hundreds of miles from the front, the services have ceased to function, personnel have disappeared and orders are disobeyed or ignored. This applies to both superior as well as subordinate personnel.'[7]

George Rodger, a British photojournalist on a roving assignment for *Life* magazine and one of the future founders of the Magnum agency, described the transformation of one village after a Japanese bombing raid: 'Thazi was a sleepy little Burmese village as colourful and gay as any. There were the usual picturesque little thatched or tin-roofed houses and open-fronted shops all covered by flowering creepers. Doll-like children played in the road and bright-skirted girls strolled in twos and threes from shop to shop or stood gossiping in the doorways of their homes. Ox-carts lurched down the street with creaking unoiled axles, the drivers lolling under their wide bamboo hats, half asleep in the sun.' After the raid, he wrote, 'frail houses were flattened, rubble covered the streets, trees stood stripped of their boughs and the shattered bodies of the villagers lay twitching in the dust'.[8]

Prome, now packed with Indian refugees trying to get out of the country, was bombed almost daily, an experience Bill did not enjoy: 'I had been bombed often enough before, but never in a town, and I found it much more frightening than in the desert or the bush.'[9] All public services in the town had broken down, disease was rife and garbage piled up on the streets. When an epidemic became a serious risk, Bill authorised the release of prisoners from the local jail, who were given their liberty in return for a few days of (strictly supervised) street cleaning.

Meanwhile, the position of the Chinese 200th Division, which had relieved Bruce Scott's Division in Toungoo, became critical when the Japanese encircled and cut off the town. On 28 March, General Alexander, who was in Chungking having discussions with Generalissimo Chiang Kai-shek, sent a signal to Bill ordering him to launch an immediate offensive from Prome to relieve the pressure on the Chinese. Privately, Bill was appalled: he thought it had been agreed that Burcorps would not start major offensive operations until the entire corps was concentrated and ready for action and that was far from the case. Burma Division was still assembling north of Prome and the 17th Division had not yet been fully re-equipped. He also had grave doubts that anything he could do would be likely to divert Japanese forces from Toungoo. In his usual tactful way, he did not vent his anger in *Defeat Into Victory*. 'General Alexander,' he wrote diplomatically, 'was in a much better position to judge the effects than I was.' (It would not be the first time he disagreed with Alexander's decisions. Their respective memoirs are instructive about the nature of their relationship – Alexander felt no need to dwell on Bill's contribution to the Burma campaign, while Bill only included two anecdotes about Alexander, both rather disapproving, about his foolhardy courage under fire.)

Despite his misgivings, Bill had no alternative but to follow orders. He instructed Punch Cowan to put together the strongest mobile force he could assemble and strike south against the Japanese, destroy the enemy wherever they were encountered and exploit any local successes. The only help he could offer from headquarters was a small armed flotilla of marines, commandos and Burmese military police, which would patrol the Irrawaddy and prevent the enemy from crossing the river behind 17th Division's strike force, which Cowan put under the command of Brigadier John Anstice of the 7th Armoured Brigade.

All Bill could do then was sit back and wait for news. When it came in, it was all bad. Contact was quickly made with the enemy and fierce, confused fighting followed. While the troops and tanks of Anstice's force were fully occupied, more Japanese moved around the flank of the battle and seized the village of Shwedaung, blocking the only road leading back to Prome. The first Anstice knew about it was when a liaison officer was returning to divisional headquarters and discovered, to his horror, that Shwedaung was full of Japanese. Anstice had no choice but to turn round and try to fight his way back. Throughout the evening and night of 29 March and most of the following day, Anstice's troops threw themselves at the Japanese block with little effect, taking heavy casualties from enemy snipers hiding in the village and in bamboo groves at the side of the road and from fighter aircraft strafing the column from the air. When it became evident there was no way to smash through, Anstice ordered his troops to break off the engagement and make their way back to Prome across country as best they could. Around 400 men never made it back, many more were wounded, two guns and ten tanks were destroyed or captured. They were losses Bill knew he could ill afford, particularly as nothing had been achieved.

At a time when he was trying to build morale, he was also keenly conscious of the fact that the ill-fated expedition would do little for his reputation as a commander, particularly as the operation had provided further evidence of what captured Allied prisoners could expect at the hands of the Japanese. A detachment from the armed flotilla was sent to occupy Padaung village, on the west bank of the Irrawaddy, where the villagers welcomed them with gifts of food and drink. Unknown to the troops, Japanese were hiding in bamboo huts in the village. While they were enjoying a rest, the Japanese sprang out from their hiding places and surprised them. In the brief firefight that followed, a few escaped but most were killed or wounded. Twelve British soldiers and marines, all wounded, survived the night but were tied to trees the following morning and used for bayonet practice. Such bestial incidents, which would become commonplace, inculcated in Bill a hatred for the enemy that never left him.

To top it all, Bill learned that 17th Division's valiant but fruitless efforts had made not a scrap of difference to events at Toungoo, which was swiftly captured by the enemy. The 200th Chinese Division was put to flight, having abandoned all its vehicles and guns and suffered more than 3,000 casualties. The loss of Toungoo was a major setback for the Allies since it provided the enemy with more forward airfields and left Burcorps isolated, much too far forward, in the west.

With the Japanese closing on Prome, now almost burned to the ground after continuous pattern bombing, and cholera breaking out among the hapless refugees, Bill ordered the back-loading of stores from the town and moved his headquarters 35 miles north, to a large house with a garden at Allanmyo. It was there that a young major in the Burma Frontier Force first met Bill in circumstances he would never forget.

Major I. C. G. Scott had been given what he considered to be incomprehensible orders to patrol the Irrawaddy. 'The orders were so vague and ridiculous that I decided to go to Corps HQ to seek clarification. I was feeling like death with malaria and dysentery so I was quite ready to have a fight with the first staff officer I met ... On arrival I went in through a door into semi-darkness and started to feel my way up a narrow staircase. I was more or less blind, having come in from bright sunlight. I sensed rather than saw someone coming down the stairs, we met, and a voice said, "And who are you?" I was unable to distinguish the person speaking but saw that he was wearing a bush hat and he certainly did not look very important. "I am OC FFR4," I replied, "and I am looking for the half-wit who gave me these bloody stupid orders which I want to discuss." There was a silence. The figure in the bush hat turned and started to go upstairs saying, "Follow me". I followed and he entered a well-lit room where, to my horror, I saw that he was wearing the insignia of a general – he was in fact General Slim, the Corps Commander. He said to the G1, "This young man is looking for the half-wit who gave him some bloody stupid orders. Must be you, old boy." He gave me a pat on the back and said, "Give him hell" and resumed his descent of the stairs. I duly had my orders modified and returned to my command having met the great man himself, which gave me great satisfaction.'[10]

On 1 April, Generals Wavell and Alexander arrived in Allanmyo for a crisis meeting with Bill. After reviewing the grim state of affairs, Wavell decided there was no point in continuing to hold Prome and that Burcorps' priority must now be the protection of the oilfields at Yenangyaung, further to the north, on which the Allied army depended for its fuel. Present at that meeting, in a very junior capacity as a young staff officer, was Captain James Lunt of the 4th Burma Rifles. It was the first opportunity he had had to see his new corps commander: he was both impressed and reassured. 'He was wearing an ordinary Army issue topi, without embellishment, an ill-pressed khaki shirt without medal ribbons, and a pair of khaki slacks that looked as if he had slept in them (which he probably had). There was none of that trimness in appearance I always associated with Alexander, and yet, without any obvious effort, Slim dominated the scene. I was to meet him many times in the years to come and he always recalled to mind that remark by Oliver Cromwell: "If you choose goodly, honest men to be captains, honest men will follow them" ... Slim did not make promises ... which, if they failed to materialise, might damage morale. Nor did he convey the impression that our difficulties were only temporary, as Alexander might have done. Slim just gave one confidence that everything that could be done to provide us with a fighting chance would be done. If his effect on my personal morale was any guide, I can only say he stiffened my resolution, and this after only a few minutes' conversation.'[11]

While the meeting was still going on, three officers turned up in the garden and encountered Philip Howe, the *teakwallah* who was now travelling with the corps headquarters, in his own Morris 8 car. Howe was concerned to stay out of the way of the top brass and was reading a book on a swing seat in a quiet corner. 'My peace was rudely shattered by three army captains bursting into the garden and demanding beer. "We know it's here and we intend to get it", they said. "Where is it hidden?"'

Howe could not resist the opportunity to bait them. Oh yes, he said, there's beer here all right and it's very easy to obtain: '"All you have to do is go upstairs where you'll find Generals Wavell, Slim and Alexander in conference on the verandah. I'm sure they'll be only too happy to give you a bottle of beer each. They may even give you a case. Why don't you go and ask them?" I have never seen three men more amazed and crestfallen. They would not believe me until they had asked the sentry, after which they crept out of the garden on tiptoe and in utter silence.'[12]

That night, the Japanese attacked Prome in strength and drove the 17th Division out of the town. Neither Bill nor Taffy Davies slept a wink, but stayed up all night listening to reports from the battlefield to keep abreast of what was going on. At 1030 on the morning of 2 April, Cowan telephoned Bill from his headquarters in a forest off the Prome–Allanmyo road to say that he had received reliable reports of a strong enemy force moving round his rear to cut him off. He asked Bill if he should hold his present position or withdraw to Allanmyo. Bill could see no point in him holding on and in any case needed to concentrate Burcorps – he ordered Cowan to withdraw. To reach Allanmyo the dog-tired men of 17th Division faced a long march in the torrid heat of the day. They had been fighting all night, there was no water en route and they were constantly machine-gunned by Japanese fighters; nevertheless they arrived complete and, Bill thought, in not too bad shape. In some ways they were lucky – the Japanese had not pursued them on the ground, presumably, Bill concluded, because they, too, were exhausted.

Concerned to maintain contact with the Chinese on the left flank, General Alexander next ordered Burcorps to hold the small market town of Taungdwingyi, on the east side of the Yomas, which presented Bill with another dilemma. He did not feel he could hold Taungdwingyi – 'in strength', as Alexander had decreed – as well as both banks of the Irrawaddy at Allanmyo without his line becoming overstretched. After sending a brigade of the 17th Division to cover Taungdwingyi, he reluctantly decided on another withdrawal to the south of Magwe, where there was open ground in which he could better deploy the 7th Armoured Brigade. 'I did not like the idea ...' he wrote, 'we were fast approaching the dangerous state when our solutions to all problems threatened to be retreat, but I hoped it would be the last.'[13] It was a hope unfulfilled.

Bill visited 17th Division troops in Taungdwingyi to explain what was happening. 'You've probably been wondering why we have had these everlasting withdrawals,' he told them, 'and I sympathise with you. I've loathed them too. The reason, however, is that I must have good open country where the tanks can operate with good effect against the Japs, and this is it. You, 63 Brigade, are to hold Taungdwingyi, 1st Burma Division is in Magwe, 48 Brigade and the tanks are in the middle. Now, wherever the Japs attack, the other two will close in and we'll really knock him this time.' He then went on to spell out his plans in detail. His words had an electrifying effect on morale. 'I don't remember feeling more elated in the whole campaign than I did that day,' said Captain John Hedley of the Burma Rifles. 'Thank God, we all thought, now we know what is expected of us.'[14]

The final elements of Burcorps evacuated Allanmyo on 8 April, after demolishing a small oilfield on the opposite side of the river. A new defensive line was set up in the 'dry belt' of Burma, where the dense jungle gave way to arid dusty plains, dotted with cactus and intersected by dried-up river beds. American war correspondent Darrel Berrigan described the scene as the troops headed north: 'Men, mules and horses were strung out across the dusty hills under a white, blazing sun. They were collapsing, dog-tired, in the sand for a rest, then heaving themselves to their feet again and marching forward. Bearded, dust-caked men, with the sweat-salt dried white across their shirts, their water bottles clanking dry against their hips.'[15]

The availability of water now determined the disposition of the corps as much as strategic considerations – 40-gallon drums filled from a Burmah Oil Company swimming pool were used to set up water points. Bill was still hoping, despite all the setbacks, to launch a counter-attack, even though Burcorps was hardly fighting fit – its two divisions were continually reduced in strength, partly due to casualties and sickness and partly to desertions. Many of the soldiers in the Burma Division were recently recruited Burmese; in the face of the Japanese onslaught more and more of them slipped away back to their villages, their loyalty to their wives and families greater than that to their regiment.

Nevertheless, Bill pressed General Alexander to ask the Chinese to take over from the 17th Division at the eastern end of his line at Taungdwingyi in order for him to assemble sufficient troops to mount a counter-offensive. Alexander raised the issue with Joe Stilwell, the cantakerous American general recently arrived in Chunking as Chief of Staff to Generalissimo Chiang Kai-shek, who promised to send a Chinese division (equivalent to a brigade in the British Army) to relieve the 17th Division. While waiting for it to arrive (it never did – Chiang secretly cancelled Stilwell's order), Bill finessed his plans for an offensive, completely unaware that he was preparing for an event that was never going to happen.

Stilwell, universally known as 'Vinegar Joe' for his acerbic temperament, was one of the most idiosyncratic and controversial characters to emerge in the Burma campaign. Nearly 60 years old, he wore steel-rimmed spectacles and his grey hair cropped short and once described himself as 'unreasonable, impatient, sour-balled, sullen, mad, hard, profane and vulgar'.[16] He had spent 13 years in China as a military attaché and was fluent in Cantonese, but singularly lacked the tact and patience needed to deal with the Chinese, although in his defence he faced maddening and frustrating obstacles that would have tried the patience of a saint, which he was certainly not. The Nationalist army was four million-strong, but poorly supplied, badly trained and abysmally led. Although Stilwell was nominally in command in Burma, Chiang initially refused to invest him with an all-important seal of office, the vermilion Kuang-Fang, and thus Chinese generals felt they were at liberty to ignore his orders, or at least delay acting on them until receiving confirmation from Chungking. In addition, many Chinese generals were more or less autonomous warlords with a marked reluctance to commit their resources to the battle against the Japanese, preferring instead to hoard their artillery and armour for the upcoming internal struggle they expected against the Communists.

While Stilwell contrived to alienate almost everyone he encountered, he reserved a visceral loathing, which he rarely bothered to conceal, for the British. Philip Mason, secretary of the Chief of Staffs Committee, recalled a memorable meeting in Delhi at which it was explained to Stilwell that his plans for recapturing Burma were unworkable. Wavell asked Stilwell if he was satisfied.

'I am,' he replied, his face like stone.

'Are you satisfied on purely military grounds?'

'I am.'

'And what shall you say to Chiang Kai-shek?'

'I shall tell him the bloody British wouldn't fight.'

After a shocked silence Wavell said quietly 'I see' and closed the meeting.[17]

When Stilwell flew to Maymyo for his first meeting with General Alexander, he was, perhaps predictably, unimpressed. Handsome, debonair, the son of an earl, ex-Harrow and Sandhurst, commissioned into the Irish Guards, Alexander exemplified the kind of languid, upper-class Englishman with polished manners that Vinegar Joe detested. The feeling, it seems, was mutual, as Stilwell wrote sourly in his diary on 13 March: 'Alexander arrived. Very cautious. Long sharp nose. Rather brusque and *yang ch'i* [stand-offish] ... Astonished to find ME – mere me, "a goddam American" in command of Chinese troops. "Extrawdinery." Looked me over as if I had just crawled out from under a rock.'[18]

Oddly enough, Bill was one of the few Brits Stilwell actually liked. (Whereas Stilwell usually referred to the British in his diary as 'Limeys' and 's.o.b.s', Bill gets a mention as 'Good old Slim – maybe he's all right after all'.) The first time they met, Stilwell took Bill aback by announcing: 'Well, General, I must tell you that my motto in all dealings is "Buyer Beware"', but Bill had few complaints about working with him. He respected Stilwell as a tough, courageous leader who, while often downright rude, would keep his word once he had given it. He also suspected that Stilwell liked to play up to his bombastic 'Vinegar Joe' nickname when he had an audience, since in private he was quite a different person. The American had a sense of humour, too. On one occasion, Stilwell was sitting with Bill sadly watching the retreat when he suddenly said: 'At least you and I have an ancestor in common.' Intrigued, Bill said, 'Oh yes, who?' 'Ethelred the Unready,' Stilwell replied.[19] Bill burst out laughing.

Enemy bombing attacks continued with increasing intensity. One morning the alarm sounded at the corps headquarters as Bill and his senior officers, who had assembled for a conference, were finishing breakfast. 'In a group we walked towards the slit trenches, I still carrying a cup of tea. Looking up, we could see the usual tight wedge of twenty or thirty bombers coming straight over. The mess servants and others saw them too and began to run for shelter. I had been insistent on stopping people running at these times as it had led to panic, so continuing our move at a slow and dignified pace, I called out to them to stop running and walk. I remember shouting in Hindustani, "There's plenty of time. Don't hurry", a remark that almost qualified for the Famous Last Words series [a popular feature in *Reader's Digest*]. At that instant we heard the unmistakeable scream of bombs actually falling. With one accord two or three generals and half a dozen other senior officers, abandoning dignity, plunged for the nearest trench. Scott, being no mean athlete, arrived first and landed with shattering impact on a couple of Indian sweepers already crouching out of sight. I followed, cup of tea and all; the rest piled in on top, and the whole salvo of bombs went off in one devastating bang. Poor Scott, crushed under our combined weight, feeling warm liquid dripping over him, was convinced that I had been blown into the trench and was now bleeding to death all over him.'[20]

During this period Bill visited both divisional headquarters in the company of General Alexander, travelling in the latter's shiny black saloon car with a flag flying from the bonnet, perhaps unwisely ostentatious since the roads were regularly patrolled by Japanese aircraft. While they were at Bruce Scott's headquarters, which although well hidden in a forest was probably betrayed from the air by vehicle tracks leading in and out, they were machine-gunned by Stukas. Bill scrambled into a slit trench, but Alexander refused to follow his example and stood casually behind a tree until the aircraft had disappeared. Bill had to admire his imperturbable courage, but was furious with him at the same time for setting a bad example to the men, who were constantly badgered to use the trenches for shelter. Japanese fighters carried small anti-personnel bombs and, had one been dropped near Alexander, he would certainly have been killed or very seriously injured. On the way back to corps headquarters they had to cross a bridge that was being shelled by the enemy. Bill suggested they should each cross in a tank, but Alexander wanted to know how their car was going to get across. When Bill said their driver would just have to take his chances, Alexander said it would be just as dangerous for the driver as it would be for him. 'Yes,' Bill

72 Belmont Road, Bristol, Bill's birthplace in 1891.

Bill (centre, standing) at the University of Birmingham's OTC annual summer camp, 1912.

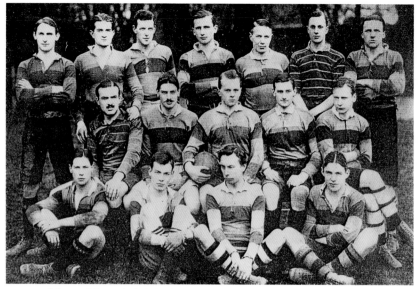

Bill (second from the left, back row) in the Old Edwardians rugby team, 1913.

Second Lieutenant Slim (centre, middle row) with his platoon in the 9th Battalion,
The Royal Warwickshire Regiment, 1914.

Out for a ride in Dorset, 1915. He didn't like horses and horses didn't like him.

The adjutant of the 1st/6th Gurkha Rifles in Abbottabad. Bill had this photograph taken in an attempt to impress his future father-in-law.

On operations (standing, right) with the 1st/6th Gurkha Rifles on the North-West Frontier.

On a rare visit to his family in Simla in 1943 after the retreat from Burma.
Left to right: John, Aileen, Bill and Una, and Judy, the family dog.

The Burma campaign, according to Bill, was fought in 'the world's worst country, breeding the world's worst diseases and the world's worst climate'.

Bill and Wingate probably photographed at Lalaghat airfield before the second Chindit expedition in 1944.

Being knighted by Wavell at Imphal in December 1944.

With Aileen after the ceremony; Aileen wears her Red Cross uniform and carries Bill's KCB insignia.

Broadcasting to the troops after the fall of Mandalay in April 1945.

Inspecting the troops at the Mandalay victory parade. Talking to the troops was what Bill enjoyed most.

replied patiently, 'but he's not the army commander.' 'Very well,' said Alexander, 'you go in a tank and I'll go in the car.' They both went in the car.

On 10 April, the Japanese began probing Burcorps' defences, pushing small groups of infiltrators through the line, some in creaking bullock carts disguised as Burmese villagers or refugees. On the following day battle was engaged all along the extended front and that night, which was pitch black and lit only by flashes of lightning during violent thunderstorms, the Japanese mounted a fanatical attack in strength. After fierce hand-to-hand fighting – Bill described it as 'one of the bitterest fought actions of the whole campaign' – the enemy was flung back by dawn.

Over the following nights, the Japanese resumed their attacks with undiminished ferocity. By the morning of 14 April it was clear that Burcorps' position was so precarious that the precious oilfields at Yenangyaung, which had already been prepared for demolition, could not be saved. With Burcorps headquarters packed and ready to withdraw, at 1300 on 15 April Bill gave the order for the demolition of the refinery and hundreds of derricks in the oilfield to prevent them falling into enemy hands. A million gallons of crude oil erupted in an explosion that sent flames 500 feet into the air as machinery and buildings disintegrated and billowing clouds of dense black smoke blotted out the sun, turning day into night. It was, Bill recalled, a fantastic and horrible sight.

The following day, as the exhausted Burma Division was withdrawing through Yenangyaung, a strong enemy force circled round to its rear at night and set up a roadblock on the only driveable route leading north. The division was effectively trapped within sight of the burning oilfields, with the air fetid from the smoke and fumes. 'The situation,' Bill noted drily, 'was not encouraging.' He was greatly relieved when he learned that a regiment of the 38th Chinese Division had arrived in the area, at the village of Kyaukpadaung. (The division, originally intended for the defence of Mandalay, had been diverted to the Irrawaddy to assist and was placed under Bill's command.) He jumped in a jeep, drove to Kyaukpadaung and found the regimental commander in an upstairs room in one of the few houses still standing in the village. A British liaison officer with the regiment who could speak perfect Chinese effected introductions and Bill got straight down to business with a map, explaining, with the help of the interpreter, what he wanted the regiment to do.

At the end he asked the Chinese officer if he understood and he acknowledged he had, but made no sign that he intended to get moving. Bill asked the interpreter what was happening and after a considerable back and forth in Chinese the interpreter informed Bill that the regiment could not move until it had received orders from the divisional commander, General Sun Li-jen. Bill patiently explained that, as the division was now under his command, there was no need for his orders to be confirmed by General Sun. The Chinese officer readily agreed but still insisted he had to wait. This went on for about half an hour, at the end of which Bill could cheerfully have shot the man with his own enormous Mauser pistol. 'At last, just when I was feeling desperate, he suddenly smiled and said "All right, I will do it." Why he changed his mind I do not know.'[21]

Later that day Lieutenant General Sun Li-jen himself arrived. Sun was a graduate of the Virginia Military Academy in the United States, as he proudly informed Bill within minutes of being introduced, and spoke excellent English, with an American accent. Bill liked him instantly and, after discussing the plans to extricate Burma Division, offered to put Burcorps' artillery and armour under his command for the attack scheduled to take place the following morning, a smart diplomatic move on Bill's part that delighted Sun but horrified Anstice, the commander of 7th Armoured Brigade, who shot Bill a wounded look that spoke volumes about what he felt.

The plan was for the Chinese to attack the roadblock from the north while the Burma Division attempted to fight its way out. Bill watched the attack go in the following morning and was impressed by Sun's troops, but, despite their courage and determination, the assault faltered when the tanks became bogged down in the soft ground. The Burma Division fared no better. Hampered by a shortage of ammunition, exhaustion, lack of water and the blistering heat (the temperature peaked at 114 degrees), the division failed to break out. An American war correspondent watched the 1st Royal Inniskilling Fusiliers charge with fixed bayonets but reported that 'they were so worn out that they stumbled forward like drunken men hardly able to hold their rifles'.[22]

By the afternoon the situation was extremely dangerous and Bill was facing the prospect of perhaps losing half his corps. At 1630, Bruce Scott called Bill on the radio. They spoke in Gurkhali and used a private code made up of information only they would know from their long friendship, like the ages of their children or the number of the bungalows in which they had lived in Abbottabad. Scott's message was stark: his troops were worn out by continuous fighting and desperately short of water. He asked Bill for permission to destroy their guns and transport and fight their way out that night.

Bill faced the worst possible personal dilemma. Bruce was his long-time friend; their wives knew each; their children knew each other. It was Bruce who had wangled him unauthorised leave to go to Kashmir when he was courting Aileen. He knew that Bruce was the last man in the world to dramatise his situation; that if he had asked permission to withdraw he badly needed to withdraw. But at the same time there were considerable risks involved in exfiltrating at night; losses could be considerable if the troops got mixed up and the Chinese failed to recognise their Burmese comrades. On top of that he badly needed the division to save its guns and transport. He had ordered the Chinese to mount another attack next morning with all available artillery and tanks. He told his friend the division would have to stay put, endure the night and try to break out the next morning, when the Chinese would make another attempt to clear the roadblock. Scott took it well, as Bill knew he would. 'All right,' he said, 'we'll hang on and we'll do our best in the morning, but, for God's sake, Bill, make those Chinese attack.' (Later that night Scott scribbled a note to his friend. 'If I don't make it,' he wrote, 'please take care of Nan and the boys [his wife and two sons].')[23]

Brian Montgomery, who was among the group of staff officers with Bill, was deeply impressed by the gentle and courteous way Bill talked to Scott, never losing his authority but never domineering and never revealing the turmoil he must have undergone when he was making a decision that could have ended in his friend's death at the hands of the enemy or, perhaps even worse, his capture. It indisputably required great moral strength on his part to conceal the anxiety he must clearly have been experiencing.

'I stepped out of the van feeling about as depressed as a man could,' Bill wrote later. 'There, standing in a little half-circle waiting for me, were a couple of my own staff, an officer or two from the Tank Brigade, Sun, and the Chinese liaison officers. They stood there silent and looked at me. All commanders know that look. They see it in the eyes of their staffs and their men when things are really bad, when even the most confident staff officer and the toughest soldier want holding up, and they turn where they should for support – to their commander. And sometimes he does not know what to say. He feels very much alone.

'"Well, gentlemen," I said, putting on what I hoped was a confident, cheerful expression, "it might be worse."

'One of the group, in a sepulchral voice, replied with a single word:

'"How?"

'I could have cheerfully murdered him, but instead I had to keep my temper.

'"Oh," I said, grinning, "it might be raining."

'Two hours later, it was – hard. As I crept under a truck for shelter I thought of that fellow and wished I *had* murdered him.'[24]

Bill faced crisis after crisis during his first two months in Burma, yet almost always seemed outwardly calm, confident and good-natured, frequently diffusing tension with his dry humour. With the exception of the moment he learned the RAF had departed from Burma, he rarely gave a hint to his staff or subordinate commanders that he was concerned about the turn of events.

That evening Bill received an urgent summons from Alexander to attend a conference next day at army HQ at Pyawbwe, more than 100 miles to the east, on the Mandalay road. He could have refused, explaining that the battle at Yenangyaung was at a critical stage, but he probably felt it was his duty to attend and he was also anxious to put forward a proposal he had been working on with Taffy Davies for a new offensive – being Bill, he still thought it might be possible to turn the tables on the Japanese, even at this late hour. That night Bill sat with other officers inside a circle of lagered tanks at 7th Armoured Brigade headquarters, listening to shells and mortar bombs falling on the men of Burma Division trapped in Yenangyaung, watching flashes from explosions lighting the night sky and wondering what was happening to his friend.

He left early next morning for Pyawbwe. The conference turned out to be about plans for an orderly withdrawal from Burma, should it become necessary. Wavell had indicated that if a withdrawal became imperative, it should be conducted in close cooperation with the Chinese, to prevent Chiang Kai-shek from later accusing the British of deserting him. As soon as discussions about a withdrawal had concluded, Bill stepped forward to present his plans for a major new offensive, explaining how and why it could work if he was given sufficient troops. The swift enemy advance up the Irrawaddy had left the Japanese 33rd Division at Yenangyaung dangerously exposed, he said. His plan was to set upon and destroy the 33rd Division, then cross to the Sittang valley to attack the enemy confronting the Chinese from the flank and rear. It was ambitious, he admitted, but attainable with significant help from the Chinese. Stilwell, whose instinctive inclination was, like Bill, to attack rather than defend, was enthusiastic and immediately offered another Chinese division to assist. Alexander also approved, but still refused to allow Bill to move Cowan's division from Taungdwingyi, much to Bill's irritation. Nevertheless, Bill still felt the plan could work with what forces he had available and he left the meeting more cheerful than he had been for some time.

His good mood vanished the moment he returned to his headquarters. The day had gone disastrously. The Chinese attack, which was due to launch shortly after first light, was delayed until 1230, then 1400, and did not eventually go in until 1500, by which time all communication had been cut and the Burma Division was making a desperate attempt to avoid capture and escape along a track that had been found and cleared by the tank squadron. Late in the afternoon, Scott finally led what remained of his division out of Yenangyaung. Haggard, red-eyed, filthy, reeking of smoke and oil, many men threw themselves face down into the water as soon as they reached the river. Bill was back in time to watch them as they staggered up the bank; they were a terrible sight, he thought, although he was encouraged by the fact that they were all still carrying their rifles.

Lieutenant Colonel Bill Amies, the principal administrative staff officer in the divisional HQ, organised hot meals to be ready and waiting as they returned. 'They were in a sorry state. General Bruce Scott was at full stretch from anxiety and responsibility. His first words when he alighted from an armoured car was "Amies, I have lost my Division." Poor man, he was so overwrought he was weeping. The heat and privation was too much for the general's fellow passenger, an elderly brigadier. He had to be hauled out of the carrier, but collapsed and died soon afterwards.'[25]

Later Scott explained what had happened: they had formed a column, with tanks and infantry in front, followed by the guns, ambulances with the wounded, and all the other vehicles that had survived the enemy shelling. For a short distance they made good progress, but the track petered out into soft sand and the ambulances got bogged down. With the column hopelessly stuck, Scott ordered as many wounded as possible should be loaded on to the tanks and told the troops to make their way out as best they could on foot.

That night, a young gunner officer volunteered to go back into Yenangyaung under cover of darkness to find out what had happened to the seriously wounded who had been left behind. He found the ambulances still bogged down on the track where they had been abandoned – inside, every man had either had his throat cut or had been bayoneted to death. The news did nothing to diminish Bill's hatred of the enemy. 'That our situation should have fallen to such a level that we had to abandon our wounded to the attentions of an enemy notorious for his savagery and brutality must mark that last day of the Yenangyaung battle … as one of the blackest days in the long history of British arms,' wrote Pat Carmichael, an officer in the 23rd Mountain Battery.[26]

Bill was still working with Davies on the details of his planned offensive several days later when a staff officer put his head round the door and announced that the Chinese were 'packing up'. The Japanese, employing their well-tried hooking tactics on the eastern front, had brushed all opposition aside and made such rapid progress that the Chinese army was in full flight and the route north to Lashio, the starting point of the Burma Road into China, was now wide open. The extra division that Stilwell had promised Bill for his operation was already on its way back to help deal with the crisis – Bill had heard the roar of their vehicles as they left during the night and wondered sleepily what was going on – and any further hopes Bill might have harboured for a counter-attack were dashed. From that moment on, it was not so much a question of if his corps would withdraw from Burma, but when and how.

There had been talk of the 7th Armoured Brigade and part of the 17th Division falling back into China, but Bill argued vociferously against it, firstly from a morale point of view and secondly because they would be moving into a famine-stricken area and would have little chance of being fed, not to mention the difficulties of eventually extracting them from China to join the remainder of the corps in India. When the idea was first floated at a meeting with Alexander, Taffy Davies could not restrain his fury. 'I am afraid that I was not as capable as Bill Slim of keeping my temper. I burst forth and said, "That's absolutely ridiculous. They're suffering from famine, if we send the army brigade there we can't send them anything and the troops will starve to death." And Alex said, "You may think that, old boy, but those are my orders." Afterwards I said to Bill Slim, "You can't agree with a thing like that." And he said, "I don't intend to do it, but you shouldn't get up and talk about it." Bill was always level-headed – he never lost his temper. One of his great gifts was that when he received orders from a superior with which he disagreed, he didn't argue about them on the spot, but quietly went away and did otherwise, or waited for things to fall into the pattern he himself wanted.'[27]

On 25 April, with the situation deteriorating fast, Alexander called another conference with Bill and Stilwell at Kyaukse, a small town on the main road 25 miles south of Mandalay. Stilwell gloomily reported that the Chinese were breaking up under constant and heavy enemy pressure; in the light of this Alexander decided the time had come for a general retirement of all troops across the Irrawaddy. With the Japanese about to seize Lashio, ending any hope of holding northern Burma, the objective now was to get out and save as much as could be saved to provide for the defence of India. Bill once again vented his strenuous objection to any part of his corps withdrawing into China and to his relief his argument was accepted. While the meeting was still going on, Japanese bombers attacked Kyaukse – all the officers dived for cover, except Alexander and Stilwell, who both stood quietly in the garden, Alexander under a tree and Stilwell leaning against a verandah railing chewing his cigarette holder until the aircraft had disappeared.

Bill noted that, paradoxically, the morale of the fighting troops improved as soon as the withdrawal was ordered, since they now had a clear objective – to get back to India alive. In the far north-west, work began immediately to improve the projected escape route into India and turn a rough jungle track more than 100 miles long into a road fit for motor transport. A stretch of 30 miles was without water of any kind; Bill agreed to hand over all Burcorps' non-fighting vehicles to help stock the route with dumps of rations, fuel and water.

Meanwhile, both Burcorps and the Chinese forces, constantly harried by the enemy, were converging on Mandalay, where the 16-span bridge at Ava, a few miles downriver, offered the only crossing point over the Irrawaddy. During the day and night of 29 April, Burcorps removed as many of its stores from the area as could be packed into what little transport they now had available, although a large dump of high-octane fuel scheduled for 7th Armoured Brigade was destroyed by mistake before the tanks could get there to fill up. Bill darkly blamed a 'senior staff officer' from Burma HQ for the cock-up. Captain Tony Mains of the 9th Gurkha Rifles was the officer ordered to carry out the demolition and he was, indeed, acting under the direct orders of General Alexander, who assumed that the Armoured Brigade had already taken what it needed.[28]

By then the fabled city of Mandalay, the last royal capital of Burma, had been reduced to a smoking ruin after burning for 27 days and nights. In the moat surrounding the old Royal Palace, corpses floated among the white lotus flowers and pink hyacinths; hundreds of bloated bodies, crawling with flies and picked over by crows, pigs and stray dogs, littered the deserted streets. George Rodger photographed the carved stone figures of two elephants, cracked from the heat and standing knee deep in ashes at the entrance to a temple which had burned down. 'Every temple had gone,' he reported, 'the bazaars and the shops had gone and the homes of 150,000 people; Mandalay itself had gone. What took a thousand years to build took but an hour to fall.'[29]

On 30 April the last troops crossed the Ava bridge under cover of darkness. There had been an anxious moment for Bill earlier when he found a line of Stuart tanks waiting on the south side of the bridge with the officers standing in a group in earnest discussion. He asked what was happening and one of the officers pointed to a sign at the side of the bridge indicating it had a weight limit of six tons – rather less than half the weight of a Stuart tank. But Bill saw the bridge had been built by a well-known British engineering firm and calculated that it would have a safety margin of at least 100 per cent, so he ordered the tanks to cross, one by one, although he confessed to a slight nervousness until the first one was safely over.

At 2359 hours, after it had been confirmed that all the Chinese and the whole of Burcorps had crossed to the north side and with the enemy advancing rapidly on Mandalay, the two centre spans of the Ava bridge were blown up and collapsed into the murky, swirling waters of the Irrawaddy. The noise of the explosion was, Bill thought sadly, 'a signal that we had lost Burma'.

10

A Hell of a Beating

After crossing the Irrawaddy, Bill moved his headquarters into an abandoned Buddhist monastery near Sagaing, one of many along a ridge dotted with monasteries and golden pagodas over-looking a sweeping bend in the river, a place that at any other time would have been a picture of tranquillity. There, he contemplated the formidable difficulties that lay ahead. He knew that with the Chinese in headlong retreat and the Japanese pushing rapidly north on the other side of the river he could not hold his position on the west side for very long. In any case, time was not on his side: the locals had warned him the monsoon rains could be expected to start in earnest on or around 20 May, after which much of their escape route would become impassable for wheeled vehicles. He had al-ready dispatched a reconnaissance party of engineers, with a column made up of one of each type of vehicle in the corps, to check the feasibility of the journey and the reports they were sending back were far from encouraging.

The planned route was along a driveable road heading north to Ye-u, where the road became a narrow track winding up and down through dense jungle for 120 miles to the Chindwin river – the last river barrier before India – at the village of Shwegyin. From Shwegyin, where the track ended, river steamers were to transport the troops six miles upstream to Kalewa to begin a long trek across the Kabaw valley, one of the most disease-ridden places on earth, where malaria, blackwater fever, typhus, dysentery and cholera were rife, to Tamu, close to the Indian border. Bill had been told that en-gineers from the Indian Army had started to drive a rough road over the 7,000-foot Shenam Pass to Tamu to facilitate the last leg of the retreat across the mountain range that marked the border.

While he was still at Sagaing he was visited by a deputation of local dignitaries, resplendent in morning coats, pin-striped trousers and solar topees. They presented him with a petition demanding that no military operations should take place in the Sagaing Hills as it was an important religious and monastic centre held in particular veneration by the Burmese people. They claimed that the Governor-General himself, Sir Reginald Dorman-Smith, had assured them that Sagaing's spiritual significance would be respected and as a result large numbers of officials had sought refuge in the area with their families.

Bill rather suspected that the dignitaries were probably more interested in protecting themselves and their families than the sanctity of the area, but he was, nevertheless, sympathetic. 'I was terribly sorry for these people,' he admitted. 'They were all high officials of the Burma Government, commissioners, secretaries, judges and the like; their world had tumbled about their ears.'[1] He told them that while he had no desire to undertake military activity in their area, he could make no such promise on behalf of the Japanese. The dignified nature of the deputation's mission was somewhat marred when, after it had departed, one of its members quietly returned a little later and asked if there was any chance of being given six months' pay in advance. Bill was obliged to explain he had neither the authority nor the funds to oblige.

Only a few days after he had set up in Sagaing, the speed of the Japanese advance forced Bill to move his headquarters again, this time to a copse in the grounds of another monastery several miles north of Monywa, a river port on the east bank of the Chindwin remarkable for a Buddhist temple with a huge stupa dating back to the fourteenth century containing more than 500,000 images of Buddha. At Monywa, Bill confessed to a major error of judgement: he allowed the brigade of Burma Division holding the town to set off towards Ye-u while the other two brigades were still 20 miles to the south, leaving the approaches to Monywa undefended.

In *Defeat Into Victory*, Bill made no attempt to gloss over his mistake. Indeed, he described in some detail the moment when he realised what he had done: 'We were sitting, after our rather meagre dinner, in the twilight under the trees – Davies, one or two others, and myself. We had just received a visiting staff officer from Army Headquarters, and I was behaving rather badly to him. I was, in fact, telling him what I thought about the "Blanket"[2] system of administration. I was being quite unjust, because Goddard, General Alexander's chief administration officer, had done an astounding job in circumstances of fantastic difficulty, and in any case the victim before me was not responsible. But tempers were frayed, and one or two things that day had annoyed me – more were going to. So, really enjoying myself, I was relating the administrative enormities that had been perpetrated against my long-suffering corps. At the end of each catalogue of crimes of commission and omission, I said, "And you can tell Army Headquarters *that*." My litany was still in full swing when looking up I saw, standing in the gloom, two or three white-faced officers whom I did not know.

'"And what do you want?" I asked, still in a bad temper.

'One of them stepped forward.

'"The Japs have taken Monywa," he said, "and if you listen you will hear them mortaring."

'A deathly pause fell on the gathering. Then, sure enough, softened by distance but unmistakeable, came the *wump*, *wump*, *wump* of Japanese mortars. The silence was broken by Taffy Davies.

'"And you can tell Army Headquarters *that*," he said.'

Bill's only excuse for leaving the town virtually unguarded was his concern that the Japanese would attempt to cut off their escape route to India in the north, but he candidly admitted he had made a foolish blunder. 'Threats were growing in many directions with competing claims on our slender resources ... I chose to meet the wrong one, and we paid heavily for my mistake.'[3]

Those who were present in the monastery garden when Bill got the news about Monywa remembered that he remained perfectly calm and apparently unconcerned. He simply called for a map and immediately began making plans to deal with the crisis. He ordered every available vehicle to be unloaded and reloaded with personnel, including the sick and wounded, and hurried along the track to Shwegyin. Despite his apparent composure, Bill confessed he spent a sleepless night on the hard wooden platform that had been the abbot's bed in an upper room of the monastery. He lay awake brooding and listening intently to distant explosions, the rattle of machine guns and the thump of mortars.

In fact the Japanese at that time had not yet occupied Monywa. What Bill could hear was a Japanese raiding party, which had landed on the west bank of the river, opposite Monywa, and was shelling and mortaring the small garrison defending the town. During the night, under the cover of darkness and machine-gun fire, the enemy set up a roadblock between Burma Division headquarters and the town. After a brief fight against overwhelming odds, Bruce Scott and his staff were forced to fall back, abandoning all their equipment but saving their ciphers and secret documents. On the morning of 1 May, six or seven hundred Japanese troops disembarked from naval launches on the east bank of the Chindwin, overwhelmed the garrison in Monywa and captured the town.

Bill dispatched the bulk of his headquarters north to Ye-u, but remained at the monastery with a small staff to be on hand to direct operations as Burma Division fought its way into Monywa, street by street, despite stiff opposition. Battles around the railway station were particularly bitter, with the area changing hands three times, but by 1500 hours much of the town was in its hands and an attempt by the Japanese to push more launches up the river had been thwarted. There then followed a farcical breakdown in communications when an order arrived, ostensibly relayed by the tanks of 7th Armoured Brigade, directing the entire division to pull out. After some confusion it was accepted as genuine and the division withdrew, leaving the town to the enemy. No such order had been issued. At first it was thought it had been put out by the Japanese, perhaps using codes captured when the divisional HQ was overrun, but Scott was insistent that nothing sensitive had been left behind; later it transpired it was probably a routine cock-up caused by the lamentable state of communications in Burma. In the end, it did not greatly matter – the battle at Monywa delayed the Japanese and bought sufficient time for the whole of Burcorps to concentrate at Ye-u.

Bill arrived in Ye-u on 3 May and immediately ordered a brigade of the 17th Division to set off in trucks along the sandy track to Shwegyin to occupy the principal towns along Burcorps' escape route – Shwegyin and Kalewa – and forestall any attempt by the Japanese to block their path into India. The retreat had become a race for Shwegyin, not just against the monsoon, but against the enemy: if the Japanese arrived there first, Burcorps was lost. That night, a Japanese 'jitter party' infiltrated the Allied lines and caused mayhem around Burcorps HQ. (During the hours of darkness the troops routinely tied tin cans containing a couple of pebbles to the barbed wire surrounding their camps to alert them if the wire was disturbed. The 'jitter party' was the Japanese response – two or three men would creep up to the wire, tie lengths of string to it, then retire to a safe distance, pull the string and start firing their weapons and throwing fireworks. 'We didn't get much sleep during jitter raids,' one Burma veteran recalled, 'but we did get the jitters.'[4]

The Burmese defence platoon that was supposed to protect the headquarters had deserted a couple of nights earlier, requiring the HQ staff to stand-to half the night. 'The proceedings were further enlivened,' Bill wrote, 'by an agitated British sergeant suddenly dashing into our midst, staggering up to Welchman … and gasping, "The battery's overrun. They're all dead and the guns lost." He then fainted gracefully but heavily into the brigadier's arms. Of course the battery was all right. The sergeant had been wakened from an exhausted sleep by a bang as someone threw a grenade or firework, and, still asleep, had panicked. Men's nerves were wearing thin.'[5]

On 5 May, the last units of Burcorps left Ye-u with the Japanese still in hot pursuit and the rearguard constantly in action to prevent the enemy outflanking and cutting off the retreating columns. Bill withdrew his HQ to Pyingaing – inevitably known to the men as 'Pink Gin' – about halfway between Ye-u and Shwegyin. The track from Ye-u was particularly difficult going. It was crossed by innumerable *chaungs*, dried-up river beds of soft sand in which wheeled vehicles quickly became bogged down. Where the track climbed into the hills *chaungs* were crossed by rickety bridges constructed of flimsy brushwood or bamboo. 'Anyone seeing this track for the first time,' General Alexander later reported, 'would find it difficult to imagine how a fully mechanised force could possibly move over it.'[6]

Adding to the misery were thousands of frightened refugees, men, women and children of all ages, clogging the road in a long dusty column, frequently harried by Japanese Zeros roaring out of the sky and strafing the track with machine-gun fire. Like the troops, they were trying to escape to India. More than a million Indians had made their homes in Burma before the war, either to serve as civil servants to the colonial administration or to set up small businesses. They were greatly resented by the Burmese and in considerable danger as public order collapsed and an epidemic of looting and arson swept the country. Many Indians felt they had no alternative but to leave. Travelling in bullock carts or on foot carrying their few pitiful possessions, close to starving, they walked until they dropped and many, particularly the elderly and the children, never found their feet again, but died at the side of the track from hunger, disease or simple exhaustion.

Bill was deeply moved by their plight and never forgot them. Years later, in a broadcast on the subject of courage, he paid tribute to his troops but added: 'Yet the outstanding impression of courage I carried away from that desperate campaign was from the Indian women refugees. Day after day, mile after mile, they plodded on through dust or mud, their babies in their arms, children clinging to their skirts, harried by ruthless enemies, strafed from the air, shelterless, caught between the lines in every battle, yet patient, uncomplaining, devoted, thinking only of their children – so very brave.'[7] (Not everyone was as sympathetic. The large number of refugees on the road greatly hampered the retreat. Lieutenant Colonel Bill Amies recalled being driven fast in a vehicle which hit 'an old Hindu who did not make the ditch in time ... [the driver, a fellow officer] bowled him over but drove on without stopping. I made no remark then or later.')[8]

There were also, in Ye-u and the nearby town of Shwebo, more than 2,000 wounded troops needing evacuation. Bill made available every vehicle he could spare, but there were very few ambulances left and most of the casualties were packed into poorly sprung trucks, which bounced and jerked along the rough track heading north in clouds of choking dust and furnace-like temperatures. Many of the most seriously wounded did not survive the journey.

Among the myriad problems Bill faced, it was becoming increasing difficult to supply the retreating troops now that Burcorps' lines of communication were so stretched. Setting up fuel and ration dumps, and water points, along the escape route involved moving stores long distances under the most difficult possible conditions. As a precaution, he ordered the men's rations – mainly bully beef and teeth-breaking biscuits fortified with 'vitamin W' (weevils) – to be cut to preserve stocks. His recurring nightmare was that the monsoon would arrive early, halt all movement and leave the men bogged down on impassable tracks with a terrible choice – either starve to death or be slaughtered by marauding enemy aircraft. 'Everyone realised,' Taffy Davies wrote, 'from the humblest private soldier [upwards], that within days of the initial heavy downpour the road to Assam, the lifeline of the Army, would disintegrate into an impossible morass. There was dreadful tension in the air. Would the weather hold?'[9]

Bad news flooded in every minute of the day. Major Charles MacFetridge, officer commanding 3rd Indian Light Anti-Aircraft Battery, carried out a recce of the road from 'Pink Gin' to Shwegyin and was appalled by what he found – he thought it was very unlikely that any of his guns would be able to get through. 'On my return from my recce, I told Brigadier Welchman at General Slim's HQ what I had seen. I was taken in to see General Slim. After listening to my description of the road and telling him that no guns of any kind could be got to Shwegyin, Slim summoned his CRE and G1 Ops. I cannot but think that Slim took swift action, because the road was vastly improved during the next few days.'[10]

In fact, engineers were working frantically widening and grading the road and laying tracks across the soft sand of the *chaungs*. Their success was such that Shwegyin rapidly became a bottleneck – the river steamers could not cope with the numbers of men and the amount of equipment that were arriving. When Bill realised that much equipment would have to be abandoned, he gave orders that only four-wheel-drive vehicles were to be shipped up the Chindwin to Kalewa. Lieutenant Colonel Amies described the scene when he arrived: 'Hereabouts army, corps, fighting troops and services of both divisions were discarding and destroying vehicles, weapons, equipment and baggage which either could not be ferried across the river, nor transported from the opposite bank up the dirt road under construction through the mountains into Assam. Abandoned cars, trucks, lorries and the impedimenta of thousands of refugees, European and Asiatic, Eurasian and Anglo-Burman, were mingled among the heaps of junk.'[11]

Shwegyin was in a horseshoe-shaped basin about 900 metres wide approached through a gorge and enclosed by steep cliffs, 60 metres high. A single ramshackle jetty, which had been rebuilt after it was submerged by a sudden rise in the level of the river, provided access to the six river steamers of the Irrawaddy Flotilla Company due to

transport Burcorps six miles upriver to Kalewa, where corps headquarters had been set up. The river was the only link between the
two small towns for moving guns and vehicles – there was not even
a cart track along either bank.

Each steamer could accommodate up to 600 men, packed in like
sardines, but no more than a single lorry, two or three guns and a
couple of jeeps. Loading them was a logistical nightmare. Space was
at a premium around the jetty as hundreds of civilian cars, abandoned by Indian refugees, had been dumped willy-nilly, obstructing
access and making it difficult to manoeuvre. Every vehicle had to
edge on to the jetty, then be manhandled along a gangplank on
to the ship – one slip could hold up the loading process for hours.
Once the vehicles and equipment were safely stowed, the troops
embarked. Every man filing on board was required to 'pay for his
passage' with a log cut from the jungle to provide fuel for the ship's
wood-burning boilers.

Bill was dismayed when he saw how long it took to load and
unload each steamer. In the meantime, he viewed the Shwegyin
basin, milling with soldiers, refugees, animals, vehicles, guns and
tanks, as a potential death trap. Although troops were deployed in
the jungle along the top of the escarpment and the banks of the
river, and a boom had been constructed across the Chindwin two
miles south of the town, Bill knew that a sustained attack, particularly from the air, could be calamitous. On 7 and 9 May, just as he
feared, Japanese aircraft bombed and strafed Shwegyin. A number
of vehicles were destroyed or damaged, but casualties were surprisingly light. The worst effect of the raids was that they unnerved the
Indian civilian seamen who crewed the steamers, many of whom
either deserted or refused to leave Kalewa, further slowing down
the evacuation. (Alexander, visiting the area from his headquarters
at Shwebo, was on board one of the steamers during a Japanese air
raid. He stood on the flying bridge throughout, chatting uncon-
cernedly to the chief engineer, William Hutcheon, and at the end of
the trip thanked him for 'a pleasant voyage'.)

On the morning of 10 May, Bill decided to see for himself what
was going on in Shwegyin. He left his jungle headquarters in Kalewa
in the early hours, accompanied by his ADC, and travelled downriver by launch, arriving at the jetty at around 0530, just as the first

pink light of dawn was creeping over the horizon. A steamer was moored at the jetty but loading had been held up while essential repairs were being carried out. Bill's launch tied up alongside the steamer. He climbed aboard and at the very moment he stepped on to the deck a stream of red tracer bullets whined over his head and a terrific fire fight broke out on the southern edge of the basin, with a deafening racket of rifle, machine-gun, mortar and artillery fire. 'It was,' he noted, 'the most unpleasant welcome I have ever had.'[12]

With as much dignity as he could muster and with bullets flying everywhere (although too high, he hoped, to cause him any trouble) he forced himself to walk up the track leading to brigade headquarters. He was aware he was being watched by soldiers under cover on all sides and was determined not to give them the pleasure of seeing their corps commander sprinting hell for leather to safety. At brigade headquarters there was anxiety but no panic. He was told that a large enemy force had moved up the river in naval craft during the night, landed about eight miles south of the town, trekked through the jungle and launched the attack which had coincided with his arrival. The outer defences had been breached, but the Indian battalion holding the escarpment at that point was resisting stoutly.

A second, heavier, assault came in further to the east while Bill was still at Shwegyin, but was beaten back when the Gurkhas climbed the steep face of the escarpment and counter-attacked. While the Gurkhas were engaged in confused and savage hand-to-hand fighting in the jungle at the top of the escarpment, the Japanese brought up mortars and a small artillery piece to pour fire into the basin and infiltrated snipers through Burcorps positions to 'make themselves a nuisance', as Bill put it.

When it became clear the Gurkha counter-attack had succeeded, at least for the time being, Bill returned to the jetty area where the repairs had been completed and 25-pounders of 7th Armoured Brigade were being loaded onto the steamer. The guns kept firing until literally the last moment before being manhandled on board. As they were being stowed on the deck, wounded soldiers who had been arriving in increasing numbers, some still walking but many on stretchers, were embarked.

Bill was aware of a group of about 100 Indian refugees cowering in the shelter of a mud bank and obviously hoping to escape on the steamer. Among them was a small boy, not much more than four years old, trying desperately to feed his mother with condensed milk from a tin that had been given to him by a British soldier, but she was beyond hope and died even as he pressed the milk into her mouth. Bill bribed an Indian family with the promise of a passage on the steamer if they would take the boy with them. When the steamer was fully loaded and about to depart, in an act of great humanity Bill allowed the remaining refugees to get on board if they could find space; they rushed the ship, filled every possible nook and cranny and even clung precariously to the rails as it cast off and chugged upriver to Kalewa and the road to India.

That steamer was the last to leave from the jetty at Shwegyin. Bill followed in his launch hoping to persuade the captains of other steamers lying upriver to return to Shwegyin to pick up more men and equipment. Most of the crews had deserted, but three skippers – two civilians from the Irrawaddy Flotilla Company and an officer in the Burma Naval Volunteer Reserve – courageously agreed to make the trip. The jetty had by then been made untenable by enemy mortar fire, but they were able to bring their ships close inshore under a cliff that provided shelter from the gunfire. They collected more wounded and administrative troops, but when they got back to Kalewa the crews had had enough – no inducements of any kind would persuade them to return.

By two o'clock all river embarkation had stopped. A single escape route remained for the rearguard troops left in Shwegyin – a rough path, very narrow and steep in places, just about traversable by men and mules, up the east bank of the Chindwin. An attempt by the Gurkhas to dislodge a strong enemy position on a hill overlooking the basin during the afternoon failed, after which orders were given to destroy all the residual equipment – guns, tanks and vehicles – to prevent it falling into enemy hands. Lorry engines were drained of oil, started up and set to run at full pelt until they seized. At eight o'clock that evening the gunners fired off all their remaining ammunition in twenty minutes – by far the heaviest artillery concentration put down throughout the campaign – and under cover of this barrage the remaining troops began filing up the path along the river, leaving Shwegyin lit by flames and explosions from burning equipment, acrid smoke mixing with the sickly stench of excrement and death which was everywhere.

By then much of Burcorps had left Kalewa and was trudging on a 70-mile slog under the burning sun across the malaria-infested Kabaw valley, which the soldiers grimly renamed, with their usual gallows humour, 'the Valley of Death'. April and May are the hottest months in Burma and the troops were entering the most arid region of the country. They were dead tired, filthy, dressed in rags, many without boots, surviving on very little food and water, their cheeks and eye-sockets hollowed out. Lack of vitamin C exacerbated suppurating jungle sores which spread rapidly and refused to heal. Men who themselves were hardly able to put one foot in front of another staggered along supporting sick and wounded comrades. Halts became fewer and fewer as officers found it was getting more and more difficult to get the men moving again. Most had stopped shaving and grown beards which made them look like a band of wild brigands. In solidarity Bill thought he would follow suit but was horrified when his stubble came through completely white. 'The probable effect on the troops of having a Corps Commander who looked like Father Christmas,' he noted, 'was such that I resumed shaving with the relic of a blade.'[13]

The Kabaw valley took a terrible toll on the refugees. 'There were hundreds of thousands of them,' Taffy Davies wrote. 'They died as they walked along this Via Dolorosa. They died of smallpox, of choleras, of weakness and starvation, or simply of old age – and where they died they lay. No one buried them, they were just pushed off the road into the verges of the encroaching forest, or down the steep banks on the lush ravines below. The stench was terrible. Never for one moment of that last horrible month was it absent from the nostrils of the troops.'[14] Some refugees found the ordeal too much to bear and hanged themselves from trees – grisly signposts to India for the following troops.

Bill's main concern was that the Japanese would move upriver in naval craft and strike out through the jungle to try and cut off the withdrawal. When apparently reliable information reached corps HQ that the Japanese had set up a roadblock and cut off Burcorps' rearguard, Bill jumped into one of the HQ's few remaining jeeps and drove south to where two battalions of the 1st Burma Division were bivouacked not far from the area. He knew the men would be in no real condition to fight, but even so he was dismayed by what he found. 'As I looked round the gaunt, ragged men, lying exhausted where they had dropped at the end of the day's march, my heart sank. I thought, "Nothing can rouse them. They have reached the end of their endurance." Yet, when their no less weary officers called on them, they struggled into their equipment, once more grasped their weapons, formed their pitifully thin ranks, and, turning their backs on safety, tramped doggedly off to another fight.'[15]

Luckily for them, there was no roadblock – a dog-tired staff officer, made jittery by a Japanese fighter strafing the road, had mistaken, from a distance, a Burcorps traffic control barrier for an enemy roadblock. The troops who had been sent off to deal with it stoically turned back, no doubt cursing, Bill thought, generals who disturbed them unnecessarily. Bill frankly admitted his nerves were probably quite as frayed as those of the officer who had made the mistake. He speculated around this time that if someone had brought him a bit of good news he would probably have burst into tears, adding drily that he was 'never put to the test'. (Ironically, the danger of being overrun by the pursuing Japanese army no longer existed. Although no one in Burcorps knew it at the time, the Japanese had halted their pursuit at Shwegyin, perhaps because they, too, were exhausted. Shwegyin turned out to be Burcorps' last battle.)

On 12 May, a week earlier than had been predicted, the monsoon burst with all its fury when the bulk of Burcorps was still nearly 200 miles from safety, greatly adding to the misery of the march. The only benefit of the monsoon was that the lowering clouds kept the Japanese air force on the ground, but men already pushed to the limit now had to struggle, soaked to the skin day and night, along tracks ankle deep in slippery mud. At nights there was no alternative but to bed down on the sodden ground under the dripping trees without even the cover of a blanket, while the rain beat down on them. A virulent disease called cerebral malaria carried off many men: it killed in a matter of hours once it took hold – a victim would start shivering in the evening and be dead by dawn.

Throughout the nightmare of the retreat, Bill ensured that the men knew he was with them. He constantly travelled up and down the length of the column in a jeep, speaking to as many soldiers as possible, man-to-man, asking the name of their unit, urging them on, doing what he could to lift their flagging spirits. Taffy Davies noticed that the men stiffened and tried to march as if they were on parade when they saw Bill was watching, this despite their pitiful condition, the fact that most of them had no boots and their uniforms were in rags. It was, he said, 'very moving'.

The officers, too, felt the benefit of his leadership. 'I cannot say what General Slim meant to his subordinate commanders during that arduous retreat,' said one battalion commander. 'He habitually visited formations, scattered all over the front, by jeep or car. He was always accessible and when he was in the offing and I was able to talk to him, I invariably returned full of confidence and pep.'[16]

Two days' march from the Indian border some relief arrived when the head of the column met an Indian Army mechanical transport company which had been sent along a roughly made road to assist the retreat. Bill wanted the trucks to continue south to pick up the sick and wounded, but the drivers, mainly new recruits, were so spooked by stories they had heard of Burmese dacoits attacking everything that moved that they refused. The problem was swiftly solved by putting an angry trooper from 7th Armoured Brigade into each cab to hold a gun on the driver. Faced with the choice of obeying orders or being shot on the spot, the drivers became considerably more cooperative and made a significant contribution ferrying into India those soldiers no longer able to walk.

The advance guard of Burcorps began crossing the Indian border, marked by an iron bridge over a fast-flowing mountain stream, on 15 May. It was not the end of their odyssey – they still had to climb a winding path across the 7,000-foot Shenam Pass, before reaching the rough road that led to the town of Imphal, their final destination. By 28 May almost all Burcorps troops had crossed into India.

On the last day of the retreat, Bill stood on a bank beside the road, watching the rearguard march into Imphal and felt a surge of pride. 'All of them, British, Indian, and Gurkha, were gaunt and ragged as scarecrows. Yet, as they trudged behind their surviving officers in groups pitifully small, they still carried their arms and kept their ranks, they were still recognisable as fighting units. They might look like scarecrows, but they looked like soldiers too.'[17]

Taffy Davies, who was with him, said later he thought Bill's eyes 'misted a bit' as he took the final salute.[18]

The 900-mile retreat from Burma in 1942, the longest ever carried out by a British army, was an epic unparalleled in British military history. There were those who said, after the event, that had they known what was involved they would never have made the attempt in the first place. The reality was that there were no alternatives. With the port of Rangoon in enemy hands, the army in Burma could not be supplied. The choice was to fight the Japanese and face almost certain annihilation, or escape to India.

It was, of course, a defeat, and an ignominious one at that, but that the withdrawal was accomplished at all was a miracle of organisation, management and leadership for which Bill Slim could have fairly claimed credit, but never did. The corps he commanded could so easily have been wiped out, but it was saved to fight another day largely because of his dogged determination to save it. His conduct of the retreat should have marked him out in the highest circles as a general of outstanding ability, yet it was Alexander who emerged as the hero of the hour, Alexander who answered reporters' questions at a press conference without once mentioning the name of Bill Slim, Alexander who was extolled by the BBC as 'a bold and resourceful commander [who] has fought one of the great defensive battles of the war'. (Long after the war, Bill privately admitted that he did not believe Alexander 'had the faintest clue what was going on'.)[19]

It did not matter in the least to Bill, who in any case abhorred personal publicity. He was satisfied with the knowledge that his indomitable spirit had been tested to the limit and not found wanting. He had also learned a lot about himself, that he could command an army under the most difficult circumstances imaginable, that he could keep his head in crisis after crisis and that he could retain the loyalty of his men in dreadful adversity.

There are no reliable figures to indicate how many people died during the retreat. It is thought that some 900,000 refugees set out on the trek to India and that between 100,000 and 200,000 probably never made it, dying of disease, exhaustion or at the hands of dacoits. Burcorps casualties amounted to some 1,500 dead and

12,000 wounded – more than half the strength of the corps – but those figures do not include the huge number of soldiers incapacitated by illness and disease. The corps also lost almost all its equipment. Japanese losses – 4,600 killed or wounded – were only about a third of those of Burcorps.

On 20 May, 59-year-old Vinegar Joe Stilwell arrived in Imphal at the head of a ragbag column of soldiers, civilians and nurses which he had force-marched 140 miles through the jungle in 14 days. Never a man to mince his words, a few days later at a press conference at the Imperial Hotel in Delhi he offered this pithy assessment of what had happened: 'In the first place, no military commander in history has ever made a voluntary retreat. And there's no such thing as a glorious retreat. All retreats are as ignominious as hell. I claim we got a hell of a beating. We got run out of Burma, and it's humiliating as hell. I think we ought to find out what caused it, go back, and re-take Burma.'

That is precisely what Bill Slim did.

11

The Arakan Debacle

D efeated, demoralised, racked by disease, exhausted beyond comprehension, their uniforms in tatters, the troops who hobbled out of Burma in May 1942 did not expect to be welcomed in India as heroes, but neither did they anticipate being treated with contempt and indifference, as if they had shirked their duty. That is what happened. The reception of 1st Burma Corps at Imphal was nothing short of a disgrace. They needed urgent medical attention, rest, secure shelter from the monsoon, food and water, dry clothes, new equipment . . . yet they were given virtually nothing. Men at the end of their physical and mental endurance, who had undergone almost unbelievable travails and who had managed to struggle on in the hope of welcome and relief awaiting them in India, found none.

It still rankled with Bill years later and his bitterness is evident in the pages of *Defeat Into Victory*. He compared the non-existent welcome his men received to that accorded to those who escaped from the beaches of Dunkirk, who were acclaimed as if they had won a great victory rather than suffered a catastrophic defeat, to the extent that 'Dunkirk spirit' became a symbol of fortitude and a byword for triumph in the face of adversity. Bill pointed out that his men had withstood a far longer and more terrible ordeal, with at least equal courage, and thus deserved an equal welcome. What they got, from officers who had never seen a Japanese let alone fought one, was abuse, sarcasm and censure for their lack of 'soldierly spirit', with the clear implication that they were incompetents at best and cowards at worst who should not have allowed Burma to have been overrun.

One of the problems was that the entire corps had been stigmatised by the early arrival in Imphal of cowed and demoralised noncombatants along with an undisciplined rabble of fugitives without officers, largely deserters who had fled at the first opportunity and

made their way to India, robbing, looting and even murdering en
route. They created an entirely false, and damaging, impression of
the fighting troops following behind, whose wretched condition
evoked no sympathy when they did finally arrive. Bill knew what his
men had been through and understood why they looked like emaciated, bearded savages – but to blimpish parade-ground officers accustomed to spit and polish, their appearance was an abomination.

It was clear from the outset that their welcome was going to be
anything but warm. Indian Army HQ had had plenty of notice that
1st Burma Corps was on its way to Imphal, but it seemed that no
preparations had been made for its reception. As each unit splashed
into Imphal through the driving rain, hoping for dry accommodation for the first time in weeks, it was directed to a random area
of jungle on a steep hillside and ordered to bivouac there as best it
could in the mud under the dripping trees. No tentage or shelter of
any kind was offered to the men, who had nothing but their weapons and the drenched, ragged uniforms they stood up in.

Philip Howe, the *teakwallah* who had hooked up with Burcorps
back in Prome, was still travelling with the 17th Indian Division
and accompanied Punch Cowan when he drove ahead into Imphal
to check on the accommodation for his men. A military police corporal met them, saluted smartly and escorted them to the campsite
allocated for the division. 'All of us were absolutely horrified when
we saw it,' Howe wrote later in his unpublished memoir. 'It was
the bare side of the lower slopes of a mountain. There was not a
tree to be seen. It had started to rain heavily again, and the water
was rushing around our feet ... "Punch" Cowan did not hesitate
for a second. He told the corporal in no uncertain terms that his
troops could not live in such a place and they must be put under
cover, especially as many of them were sick and desperately needed
medical attention. The corporal protested that this would be diso-
beying orders. General Cowan snapped back that he was going to
put his men under cover, orders or no orders.'[1] In the end he found a
number of uninhabited buildings which he turned into improvised
barrack blocks.

Bill, meanwhile, was trying to get leave for his men. He thought
his entire corps deserved to be sent on leave, although he recognised
that many of them would be spending it in hospital. He sought a

meeting with Lieutenant General Noel Irwin, the newly appointed commander of 4 Corps, who was responsible for the area, to press his case but Irwin immediately adopted a hectoring and sarcastic tone and indicated he had a very poor opinion of Burcorps and held Bill partly to blame for the loss of Burma. Bill was furious. He was *proud* of extricating Burcorps, not ashamed of it. He had not the slightest doubt that, had they chosen to stand and fight, with no possibility of reinforcements or resupply, the entire force would have been annihilated. To be lectured in this fashion by a brother officer was intolerable. When Irwin announced that leave was out of the question since reinforcements were slow to arrive and Burcorps was needed to defend Imphal against the possibility of a new Japanese attack, Bill lost his temper – an indication of how far he was being pushed. A very acrimonious exchange followed. Irwin was brusque, scornful and made it clear he did not feel Bill's men deserved any particular consideration. The meeting ended with Bill snapping: 'I never thought an officer whose command I was about to join could be so rude.' Irwin allegedly retorted, ludicrously: 'I can't be rude – I'm senior.'

Taffy Davies, who was present at the meeting, said Bill never forgave Irwin. 'To me, listening in, he [Irwin] seemed to be rather pleased that the useless, cowardly Burma Corps units would continue to live and fight in extreme discomfort and without any sort of sympathy or help.'[2]

(Irwin had had a very distinguished career and commanded a division at Dunkirk, but was a stubborn and difficult man, disliked by both his peers and subordinates. There may also have been an agenda in his hostility to Bill Slim. He was commissioned into the Essex Regiment – the regiment that had panicked and run away during the operation to capture Gallabat in the Sudan, two years earlier, an action Bill had led. Bill had sacked the commanding officer, who was a friend of Irwin.)

News of what happened at the meeting between Irwin and Bill somehow leaked out and soon spread around the men on the bush telegraph, further damaging morale. The Burma Corps men coined a dismissive term for their immaculately uniformed critics – 'the gabardine swine'. Bill estimated that 80 per cent of the fighting troops who had come out of Burma were suffering from malaria and was convinced that the treatment they received when they arrived in India contributed to the rising death toll: 'The effect of such a reception on tired men, keyed up by the expectation of something very different, can be imagined. Many lost the will to fight longer against the malaria, dysentery and exhaustion that attacked them.'[3]

In fairness to Irwin, he barely had enough equipment, rations and medical supplies for his own men, let alone the tattered horde that had descended on Imphal from Burma. On 18 May he sent an urgent (if belated) request to GHQ India in Delhi for '20,000 ground sheets, cooking pots for 5,000 and tarpaulins to accommodate 20,000 troops', but there was little expectation that his request would be dealt with speedily.

On 20 May, 1st Burma Corps was disbanded and Bill handed over command of his troops to 4 Corps. He toured as many units as he could to say goodbye, often with a lump in his throat, particularly when he was greeted with rousing cheers. It was one thing, he thought, to be acclaimed by an army he had led to victory, quite another to be cheered by an army he had led to defeat and withdrawal. It was an experience he found both moving and humbling. It was especially painful for him to bid farewell to his friends Bruce Scott and Punch Cowan; they had been through a lot together and he almost felt as if he was deserting them.

Bill was ordered to report to Ranchi, the summer capital of Bihar, where many of Burcorps' casualties were hospitalised. He had no transport, but his driver, an enterprising Scot in the Cameronians, managed to coax an abandoned civilian car into life, at least as far as Kohima in Nagaland, where the engine coughed, spluttered and finally died. Fortunately, from Kohima the road to the railhead at Dimapur was almost all downhill and so Bill and his driver coasted down the twists and turns of the mountain road until, still several miles from Dimapur, they were halted by an incline their car was unable to breast. They were obliged to hitch a ride on a passing lorry for the remainder of the journey.

At Dimapur, Bill discovered that the station had been bombed by the Japanese and most of the railway staff had fled. He was told there would be at least a day's wait for a military train. When a train arrived the following day he was able to observe a little cameo which caused him some amusement. The train halted at points outside the station while two engineer officers and a couple of senior railway officials gathered in the signal box to discuss which lever to pull to allow the train to enter the station. After considerable debate, a lever was identified and everyone watched with bated breath as one of the engineers grabbed it, squeezed the trigger and heaved it from one position to another with a resounding crunch. Nothing happened. It was then they discovered all wires to the signal box had been cut.

The train eventually got under way for Calcutta with every carriage packed with both soldiers and civilians. It was a very long journey – 400 miles to Calcutta and then another 250 miles to Ranchi – and took three days. Bill had to sit up all the way, but he managed to get some sleep. At Ranchi, a hill station surrounded by dense tropical forests, he discovered that most of his headquarters staff, including Taffy Davies, were in hospital suffering from malaria. Davies had been taken unconscious from the train at Ranchi stricken by malaria, amoebic dysentery, jungle sores and anaemia. He never fully recovered his health.

Although Bill had lost more than a stone in weight during the two months of the retreat, he counted himself very lucky that he had escaped malaria and he spent much of his time in Ranchi visiting the sick and injured in hospital. He was shocked by the conditions. No one had been prepared for the huge numbers of desperately ill troops coming out of Burma. There were insufficient beds, insufficient doctors and nurses, insufficient equipment and medicines. Schools and other public buildings had been requisitioned as temporary hospitals, but the facilities were grossly inadequate and Bill was distressed by the squalid conditions in which both officers and men were being treated, despite the heroic efforts of the medical staff, British and Indian, and hundreds of civilian volunteers who gave up their time and rallied round to help. Newspapers in Britain had been full of stories about the alleged indifference of the expatriate community in India to the suffering of the troops, but, as far as Bill could make out, the truth was rather different, at least where he was. He met dozens of European women working selflessly in the wards, canteens and kitchens and opening their homes for convalescing soldiers, and similarly large numbers of European men – tea planters, colonial civil servants, mine managers and the like – helping out at weekends or when they had finished work for the day.

Bill had departed from Burma with an abiding hatred for the Japanese – he routinely referred to 'the little yellow bastards' or 'yellow-bellies' in his letters home – and while he was in Ranchi he sat down and made a careful, unsparing and detailed analysis of what exactly had gone wrong and why Burcorps had been so soundly defeated. Like Stilwell, he made no bones about the fact that the Allies had taken a thorough beating and had been out-manoeuvred, outfought and outgeneralled by the enemy. Clearly the 'little yellow bastards' were going to have to be ejected at some stage in the future and if he was involved, which he certainly hoped would be the case, he wanted to avoid making the same mistakes again.

The list of blunders which he drew up was depressingly long – it filled seven pages in *Defeat Into Victory*. Fundamental to the disaster was a lack of preparation. No one had expected the Japanese to invade Burma and thus no one had properly planned the defence of the country. His two divisions were completely inadequate to meet the invasion. Even if the Chinese had played a greater role and been willing to obey Allied orders – which they were not – he doubted the outcome would have been any different.

The enemy formations had been specially trained and equipped to operate in the jungle, whereas his men viewed the jungle as a strange and frightening place. Training in jungle warfare – teaching men that the jungle could be their friend – would be essential in any future operations. Japanese outflanking tactics were nothing new, but they succeeded because the Allies had no warning. The best answer, Bill pointed out, was to 'do the same to the Japanese before they did it to us', but the absence of any intelligence made it impossible, probably their greatest single handicap.

Without mentioning any names, Bill was critical of the high command for not providing Burcorps with a clear objective, but he reserved the harshest criticism for himself, concluding with an excoriating – and characteristic – mea culpa. 'For myself, I had little to be proud of; I could not rate my generalship high. The only test of generalship is success, and I had succeeded in nothing I had attempted ... Defeat is bitter. Bitter to the common soldier, but trebly bitter to his general. The soldier may comfort himself with the thought that, whatever the result, he has done his duty faithfully and steadfastly, but the commander has failed in *his* duty if he has not won victory – for that *is* his duty.'

He was defeated, but not a defeatist. He knew that he would have to shake off the bad experience of the retreat, regain his confidence and learn from the mistakes that had been made if he was ever again to taste the joys of victory. Nevertheless, many of the people who met him around this time thought he was shaken by his experience in Burma. 'He looked tired and thinner than when I had last seen him in Burma,' said 'Mad Mike' Calvert, who visited Bill in Ranchi. 'For a commander the fruits of victory are sweeter than for those serving under him, but the converse of that is also true. Although Slim had taken over a hopeless situation when he came to Burma Corps it was obvious the bitter taste of defeat was still with him.'4

With little to do in Ranchi but brood and visit hospitals, Bill applied for leave to visit his family in Simla, where Aileen was now working as a volunteer nurse in the military hospital. (She would eventually be appointed Chief Visiting Officer for the Red Cross.) Twelve-year-old Una was with her, attending a local school, but John, who had every intention of following his father into the Indian Army, was at the Prince of Wales Royal Indian Military College in Dehra Dun.

Just as Bill was preparing to depart for Simla, he was informed he was to be given command of the newly formed 15th Indian Corps, part of the Eastern Army, based in Barrackpore, near Calcutta. He was obliged to cancel his travel plans and send a signal to Aileen to explain that would not, after all, be visiting. He hurried, instead, to Barrackpore to take over his new command and be briefed on his duties. In June 1942, the 15th Corps comprised two Indian divisions, the 14th and 26th, neither tested in battle nor trained in jungle warfare. The 14th Division, which had been training for service in the Middle East, was now charged with the defence of the southern sector of the Burma/India border while the 26th Division was to be responsible for assisting with internal security in the states of Bengal, Bihar and Orissa – a huge area of some 185,000 square miles – and the protection of 700 miles of Indian coastline along the Bay of Bengal. It was a mammoth task, but Bill was happy to be back in the saddle and was predictaby undaunted.

The first military cantonment of the East India Company,

Barrackpore was a charmless town which Bill came to loathe heartily, not least for its fetid slums – the worst he had seen anywhere in the world – and filthy streets thronged with mutilated beggars. He established his headquarters in Belvedere House, a handsome mansion in a park on the banks of the Hooghly river which had previously been used as a country residence by British Governor-Generals.

His first task was to weld his headquarters staff into a team, which he achieved in short order. Brigadier Tony O'Carroll Scott, his new chief of staff, remembered him with great affection: 'When he arrived, he was tired, thin and had been ill: but there was ever a light in his eye and his humour – a gruff, no-bloody-nonsense sort of humour that was particularly his own – had certainly not left him. The fact that we became a happy and efficient Corps HQ stemmed from the humanity of Slim himself. He was ready to speak personally to every man in the Corps from the divisional commander to junior clerk or soldier. Whether speaking in English, Gurkhali, Urdu or Pushtu it was always one man to another – never a great commander to his troops. He was human, but never soft – far from it. He did not suffer fools gladly but he was basically friendly and had the uncanny knack of creating a "happy show" around him. He inspired us all by his simplicity, his own rugged type of down to earth approach to men and events and his complete naturalness. He was a great leader, true; he was a great commander, true; but to us he was, above all, the well-loved friend of the family.'[5]

When Bill came to assess the tasks his corps had been given he felt reasonably confident in dismissing, temporarily at least, any chance that the Japanese would mount an overland attack on India while the monsoon was in full flood, but an assault from the sea was a different matter. In April the Fast Carrier Strike Force of the Imperial Japanese Navy had carried out a deadly attack on Allied shipping in the Bay of Bengal, sinking 28 ships, forcing the Royal Navy to retreat to East Africa and leaving the Japanese navy to rule the waves in the Indian Ocean. There was every reason to believe an attack on mainland India through the Bay of Bengal could be on the agenda, particularly through the Sunderbans, a vast and complex network of tidal waterways and mangrove forests at the delta of the Ganges and Brahmaputra rivers which coincidentally provided a home for Royal Bengal tigers.

The Sunderbans, Bill decided, positively 'invited' amphibious penetration and the defence of the entire area relied on a highly dubious warning system – a cadre of civilian coastal watchers who had been trained to report the appearance of hostile ships. Since there were very few telephones in the area they had to make their way, by boat or on foot, to the nearest telegraph office, from where a message was sent to Calcutta and then forwarded to 15 Corps headquarters in Barrackpore. Bill discovered that if a watcher tried to deliver a message to the telegraph office on Sunday and could not afford the extra fee involved it was not sent until the following day.

He recognised that a flotilla of light river craft would be needed to protect the Sunderbans and first approached the Royal Navy for help but was informed there were neither vessels nor men available. Adopting the 'make do and mend' attitude that was so much a part of his character, he simply raised his own private navy, acquiring vessels wherever and whenever he could, recruiting crew from the Indian Army's Inland Water Transport Service and an 'admiral' in the shape of a regular officer, a lieutenant colonel, who happened to have earned a coastal mate's certificate as an amateur sailor. The ships were to be deployed as light motor boats for reconnaissance, small heavily armed steamers for fighting and larger paddle steamers able to transport a brigade group. For armament he raided the arsenal in Calcutta, cannibalised 300 Maxim guns that had lain there untouched for more than half a century and put together 100 working weapons. Bill was obliged to admit that much of his second-hand fleet was not in prime condition (the boilers on the steamers had a tendency to blow up), nevertheless it was with some pride that he watched the flotilla's first exercise as it steamed through the winding waterways of the Sunderbans, its progress marked by thick black smoke billowing from every funnel. He thought the spirit of his private navy was embodied, later, by a young officer who sallied out in a rickety steamer armed with a single two-pounder anti-tank gun to engage a Japanese submarine which had been reported off the mouth of the Meghna river. Luckily for the young officer and his crew, the report turned out to be inaccurate.

In August, 15 Corps became embroiled in serious civil disturbances that erupted across the country following the arrest of leading members of the Congress Party, including Mahatma Gandhi and Pandit Nehru, after the party had passed a resolution demanding an immediate end to British rule in India. Ignoring Gandhi's call for non-violent demonstrations, an orgy of violence, arson, murder and sabotage ensued. There was rioting in major towns, government buildings were set on fire and looted, railway lines torn up and trains derailed. European passengers were pulled from the carriages and hacked to death. Thousands of people were arrested and hundreds killed in police and army shootings; some demonstrators were publicly flogged. Almost 60 infantry battalions were deployed before a tenuous order was restored six weeks later.

The army's role throughout was 'aid to the civil power', but the civil power was grievously ill equipped in every regard to deal with a major uprising. At one point, having observed the wretched state of the police uniforms, Bill arranged for hundreds of pairs of khaki shorts to be issued to them from army stores to raise their morale. A policeman with his backside showing through the seat of his trousers was, he observed drily, was at a distinct disadvantage in his attempts to uphold the majesty of the law. It was a typical Bill act – morale raising, considerate and sensible. At the same time, he did not hesitate to dispatch an entire battalion to deal with a police post in Bihar which had mutinied – his soldiers surrounded the post at midnight and surprised 100 sleeping mutineers without a single casualty. By dawn the recalcitrants were in prison 100 miles away.

While all this was going on his nemesis, General Noel Irwin, had been appointed commander of the Eastern Army and became Bill's direct boss. It was not to be a happy relationship. Irwin announced, soon after his arrival, that he intended to take direct command of Bill's two divisions. Bill was ordered to vacate Belvedere House at Barrackpore to make way for Eastern Army's HQ and move his own headquarters back to Ranchi, where he was to raise and train a new 15 Corps. Bill thought Irwin was making a grave mistake in attempting to run two divisions without a corps headquarters, along with all his other duties, but said nothing.

In truth, Bill was not sorry to leave Barrackpore; the temperate climate and the rolling green hills around Ranchi were a welcome relief after the burning heat of the Bengal plains. He moved his headquarters into the ground floor of Darbhanga House, a fine three-storey building with a large port cochère that had been built for a local maharajah. On the first floor was a large and airy apartment and when the troops were given permission for their families to join them, Aileen and Una travelled down from Simla with the family's wire-haired fox terrier, Judy, and moved in. Bill, of course, was delighted to be reunited with them; it was the first time the family had been together for two years. Una was enrolled at a nearby convent school and, largely unbothered by the war, she had very happy memories of her days in Ranchi. 'All the officers were in tents in the grounds of the house and I used to cycle round and visit them. At weekends I would bike off with other children for picnics in the lovely hills around Ranchi and in the evenings we often went to the cinema. I can remember lots of singing, fun and laughter in Ranchi.'[6]

It was a rare bonus for Bill to be able to enjoy, albeit only briefly, a semblance of family life. He also greatly appreciated the company of Nigel Bruce, his new ADC, who became a lifelong friend. Bruce was a volunteer soldier and old for a captain. Before the war he had been a hotelier in Cyprus, among other things; he was a keen amateur artist and yachtsman – he had sailed the Atlantic – and provided Bill with welcome opportunities for conversation on subjects other than the war. 'Slim was a rugged, fighting soldier with a fantastically developed degree of common sense; a totally evolved man, marvellous at personal relationships,' Bruce recalled. 'He was fascinating to be with, completely at ease, very natural. His enjoyment was conversation and he used to love talking to the junior officers. He had an ability to trust people and in so doing get the best out of them – trust begets trust and therefore everyone with whom he came into contact trusted him. He was a simple but profound man. His relaxation was walking and reading. He was interested in all sorts of topics – philosophy, mysticism, religion. He wasn't just a soldier, but a man of deep spiritual understanding. That was his strength; he used to say, "A soldier must serve a higher purpose than his own". But at the same time he loved *ITMA*[7] and would retire to his caravan to listen to it.'[8]

Bruce remembered a 'rat hunt' one mess night in Ranchi when all the officers were chasing a slipper across the polished floor with gumboots and Bruce managed to whack the corps commander across the head with his boot. Bill was completely unbothered. 'Another time he got locked in the lavatory in his caravan. He did not turn up for a rendezvous after breakfast and search parties were sent out. Eventually a Gurkha orderly found him locked in the lavatory. Of course there was general hilarity about this and he joined in.'

Bill was allocated the 70th British Division and 50th Armoured Brigade as the nucleus of a reconstituted 15 Corps. (Later they were joined by the 5th, 7th, and 20th Indian Divisions. All three commanders of the Indian divisions, Harold Briggs, Frank Messervy and Douglas Gracey, would later serve with Bill in Burma.) After his experiences during the retreat, he recognised that intensive training, particularly in jungle warfare, was going to be a prerequisite in defeating the Japanese and he drew up a training memorandum for the officers listing eight principles which embodied the lessons he had learned and provided the bedrock for his approach to jungle warfare:

1. The individual soldier must learn, by living, moving, and exercising in it, that the jungle is neither impenetrable nor unfriendly. When he has once learned to move and live in it, he can use it for concealment, covered movement, and surprise.

2. Patrolling is the master key to jungle fighting. All units, not only infantry battalions, must learn to patrol in the jungle, boldly, widely, cunningly, and offensively.

3. All units must get used to having Japanese parties in their rear, and, when this happens, regard not themselves, but the Japanese, as 'surrounded'.

4. In defence, no attempt should be made to hold long, continuous lines. Avenues of approach must be covered and enemy penetration between our posts dealt with at once by mobile local reserves who have completely reconnoitred the country.

5. There should rarely be frontal attacks and never frontal attacks on narrow fronts. Attacks should follow hooks and come from flank or rear, whilst pressure holds the enemy in front.

6. Tanks can be used in almost any country except swamp. In close country they must always have infantry with them to defend and reconnoitre for them. They should always be used in the maximum numbers available and capable of being deployed. Whenever possible penny packets must be avoided. 'The more you use, the fewer you lose'.

7. There are no non-combatants in jungle warfare. Every unit and sub-unit, including medical ones, is responsible for its own all-round protection, including patrolling, at all times.

8. If the Japanese are allowed to hold the initiative they are formidable. When we have it, they are confused and easy to kill. By mobility away from roads, surprise, and offensive action we must regain and keep the initiative.[9]

Bill was proud of the fact that he never felt the need to make any significant changes to this list for the duration of the war. Innovative, almost revolutionary, in 1942, these principles of jungle warfare would become totally accepted throughout the army by 1945 and, indeed, for decades to come.

From the start he introduced a relentless physical training regime for everyone in the corps, combatants and non-combatants alike, from the lowliest clerks and cooks to the most senior officers, including, of course, the corps commander, with daily route marches in full equipment which got progressively longer and tougher. Military training focused heavily on patrolling, digging fighting positions, concealment and night exercises. Everyone had to attend battle school, where live ammunition was used, and everyone had to qualify on a variety of weapons – pistol, rifle, bayonet, Bren gun, grenade and mortar. The message was constantly rammed home to the men that the jungle was their friend, not their enemy.

Headquarters staff were initially indignant that they should be expected to undergo the same training as the foot soldiers and one morning before a projected route march all the Indian clerks in one section reported sick. Bill was deeply sceptical when he heard the news and had a quiet word with the duty doctor suggesting he might administer something unpleasant that would make them really sick. Next morning they were all back on parade looking rather pale, and when Bill inquired if any of them would like to see the doctor again they all fervently assured him they were in no further need of medical attention and were quite ready for a route march.

In addition to physical and military training, headquarters staff were drilled to move at a moment's notice, to pack and set up quickly and efficiently. Bill applied a strict limit to the number of trucks available to each section to carry its equipment to force it to keep it to a bare minimum. Extraneous paperwork was destroyed every two weeks; Bill's motto was 'If in doubt, burn'. Everything had to be capable of being packed into *yakdans* – leather-covered boxes fitted with rings and chains that could be as easily stowed in a truck as slung on each side of a pack saddle. The drill for moving the headquarters was practised over and over again until the whole headquarters could be packed and ready to go in two hours and a fully camouflaged headquarters could be set up in the jungle in less time than that. 'Within three months we were a mobile and efficient fighting headquarters,' he noted, 'very different from the static and rather stodgy crowd who had left Barrackpore.'[10]

While the newly constituted 15 Corps was fully engaged with training, Irwin was making plans for a limited offensive in Arakan, the coastal strip facing the Bay of Bengal on the west of Burma, when the monsoon ended. A victory, even on a small scale, was badly needed to restore morale and General Wavell, the Commander-in-Chief, was under constant pressure from the Prime Minister in London; Churchill wanted action to begin the reconquest of Burma. Only weakly defended by the Japanese, Arakan (now Rakhine), was the most accessible part of the country to the Allies and offered the enticing possibility of regaining a toehold in Burma. The modest intention of the operation was to clear the enemy out of the Mayu peninsula and capture Akyab island, at its southernmost tip, where there was a port and airfield from which Allied bombers could reach most of central Burma, including, importantly, Rangoon. (It was also only 300 miles across the Bay of Bengal from Akyab to Calcutta and its capture would reduce the threat of an attack on the city by the Japanese air force.)

There were few worse places in the world to fight a war than Arakan. The Mayu peninsula was a thin finger of land, 90 miles long, with the Bay of Bengal on one side and the Mayu river on the other, with a series of razor-sharp mountain ridges, 2,000 feet high and covered in dense jungle, running like a spine down the centre of it. There were no metalled roads whatsoever, apart from a single lateral road that ran from the small port of Maungdaw in the west, to the village of Buthidaung on the Mayu river in the east through old railway tunnels that had been driven through the mountains. The narrow strips of flat ground on each side of the mountains were crossed by innumerable tidal waterways that ran inland for a considerable distance; mangrove swamps and rice paddies surrounded by bunds provided further obstacles. Malaria was endemic and the jungle was infested with blood-sucking leeches whose presence required that any habitation be raised off the ground. It was little wonder the troops came to loathe Arakan with a passion.

The start of the Arakan offensive was delayed for months by supply problems and the weather – heavy, unseasonal rains – and it was mid-December before Irwin finally ordered the 14th Indian Division, under Major General Wilfrid Lloyd, to advance into the Mayu peninsula and strike south on each side of the mountain ridge. (Before Irwin had taken over, operations in Arakan were to have been the responsibility of 15 Corps and Bill had taken some time to consider various military options. Among those he rejected as being too costly in lives was a straightforward frontal assault down the peninsula on each side of the mountain spine.)

The advance initially went well and by the end of the month the column on the west of the mountains had advanced to within ten miles of the tip of the peninsula and to the east it was 15 miles distant. Then everything went wrong. The Japanese had constructed a defensive line of massive bunkers made of heavy logs dug into the ground and covered by four or five feet of earth. Virtually impervious to artillery fire, they were cleverly concealed and mutually supporting. It was the first time British and Indian soldiers had seen anything like it and they initially assumed the bunkers had some kind of armour-plate protection. From within the bunkers a handful of men could hold off even the most determined attack and in the event that any attackers got close they simply called down artillery and mortar fire on their own position. Every attempt by the 14th Division to dislodge the Japanese from the bunkers failed.

On 10 January, Wavell and Irwin visited Lloyd's headquarters. Lloyd asked for tanks to deal with the bunkers and Irwin ordered Bill to send a troop of Valentine tanks from 50th Armoured Brigade to the front. Bill, supported by the brigade commander, protested that an entire regiment (50-plus tanks) should be deployed ('the more you use the fewer you lose') but he was overruled by Irwin who argued the front was too narrow and the delay in getting a regiment across the ground was unacceptable. More Allied reinforcements were brought up and on 1 February another attack was mounted with the support of eight Valentine tanks. This, too, failed – the tanks were knocked out almost at once. By this time Irwin had lost confidence in Lloyd and took over direct control of operations himself. On 18 February another attack went in and was again repulsed with very heavy losses – some gallant Punjabi troops penetrated close to the bunkers but were thrown back by a storm of enemy fire.

As one attack after another failed, Irwin had no hesitation in pinning the blame on the luckless Lloyd. He wrote to Wavell to express his 'disappointment' in Lloyd. 'He has not shown that determination of command which I had expected and is more prone to wait for suggestions or requests from his subordinate commanders than to impose his will on them ...'[11]

At the beginning of March, Bill was summoned to Barrackpore for a meeting with Irwin, who told him he wanted him to go to Arakan, assess the situation and report back. It was a strange request since Irwin had made many visits to the front himself and knew precisely what was going on; he had also made it pretty clear he did not hold Bill in particularly high esteem. Why would he value his opinion? (In the light of subsequent events some observers concluded that Irwin was setting Bill up to take the blame if, as then seemed likely, the Arakan offensive turned into a fiasco.) Bill asked Irwin if he should take his headquarters with him and assume operational control, but the army commander demurred. All he wanted was for Bill to 'look around' – an invidious instruction which left Bill greatly discomforted since he imagined Lloyd would think he was simply snooping on Irwin's behalf. (It remains a mystery why Irwin never called on 15 Corps when he was pouring troops into Arakan. 15 Corps was fighting fit and had been training hard for months in preparation for just the kind of operation that was taking place in Arakan. Yet for reasons best known to himself, Irwin chose to send in less well-trained formations.)

Bill arrived at 14th Division headquarters on 10 March and spent several days touring the forward areas. His conclusion was that the force – now nine brigades, three times the size of a normal division, with very long and difficult lines of communication – was far too big for a single divisional headquarters to control. He was unsurprised to find morale at rock bottom, with lots of jittery firing at night. While he was there a major firefight developed one night between two outposts of the same brigade. Next morning Lloyd's chief of staff joked: 'At least we won *that* battle.' Bill discussed the next phase of the operation in detail with Lloyd, who was planning another frontal attack with a fresh, newly arrived British brigade, improved artillery and air support. He seemed to be confident, this time, of success, but Bill was doubtful. He said he thought Lloyd was making the same mistake he himself had made in Burma in 1942 by considering the jungle to be impenetrable; his advice was that Lloyd should make an effort to insert a brigade along the spine of the ridge to strike at the enemy's flank. Lloyd replied that he had thought carefully about doing just that but had concluded it was just not possible.

Bill returned to Barrackpore, delivered his gloomy report to Irwin, much of it implicitly critical of the Eastern Army commander, and then went on leave – the leave he had postponed when he was given command of 15 Corps. He, Aileen and Una returned to Simla, stopping briefly at Delhi on the way so that Bill could attend a conference at General Headquarters. Back in the familiar surroundings of Simla, Bill took every opportunity to rest and forget about the problems in Arakan; he and Aileen met up with old friends and were able to enjoy the hill station's hectic social life, which was scarcely disturbed by the war.

On 5 April they were returning to Ranchi on an overnight sleeper train when they were woken at four o'clock in the morning during a halt at Gaya, the second largest city in Bihar, by someone banging on the door of their carriage. Bill put his head out of the window to find an agitated railway official standing on the platform. He was very sorry to trouble the Sahib, but the Sahib was wanted urgently on the telephone; Sahib was not to worry, the train would be held up for him. Still in his pyjamas and half asleep, Bill stepped down from the carriage and picked his way across the sleeping bodies on the platform (a feature, then as now, of all Indian railway stations). In the stationmaster's office he was handed a telephone. He announced himself in the way he always did: 'Bill speaking.' At the other end of the line, Tony Scott, his chief of staff, savouring the drama of the moment, announced: 'The woodcock are flighting.'

'Woodcock' was the code name for the move of 15 Corps

headquarters to Arakan. Bill's orders were to report to Irwin in Barrackpore as soon as possible; Scott, meanwhile, was leaving that morning to set up an operational headquarters in Chittagong, some 100 miles north of the Burma border. Scott knew that Aileen and Una were with Bill; he was to continue on the train to Calcutta and his wife and daughter were to alight at the junction station for Ranchi, where arrangements had been made for them to be picked up. Bill returned to the train and broke the news to Aileen, who was still awake. Ever the soldier's wife, she accepted it with her usual stoicism and immediately began packing a bag for Bill.

It was dawn when they said goodbye, with Bill waving from the train and Aileen and Una standing with their bags on the platform to await, hopefully, the train that was to take them back to Ranchi. 'We had had too many partings of this kind in the last twenty years,' Bill noted, 'but this was, I think she would agree, one of our most hurried and miserable.'[12]

Bill arrived in Calcutta in the late morning and went straight to Irwin's office, where he spent several hours being briefed on the latest situation in Arakan, which had worsened markedly while he was enjoying his break in Simla. Lloyd's final attack had gone in on 18 March; once again it was repulsed, once again with heavy casualties. Then the Japanese had mounted a counter-attack in force and began driving 14th Division back. Irwin had ordered the ground already taken to be held but when the 47th Indian Brigade became isolated, Lloyd ordered it to withdraw – against Irwin's explicit instructions. Irwin was furious, promptly dismissed Lloyd and took over personal command until the arrival of his replacement, Major General Cyril Lomax, commander of the 26th Indian Division.

Irwin told Bill he wanted him to leave for Chittagong immediately but that he was not to assume direct command until he had been ordered to do so. That night Bill dined with Wilfrid Lloyd at the venerable Bengal Club, which had been founded in 1827 for the 'society of Calcutta' and liked to compare itself with famous London clubs like the Athenaeum and the Reform. Bill wanted to hear Lloyd's side of the story and found him 'quite without bitterness'. Since both men had cause to dislike Irwin intensely, it is hard to imagine the dinner passed without them comparing notes and reaching possibly unflattering conclusions about the Eastern Army commander, but if they did so Bill forbore to mention it when he came to write *Defeat Into Victory* more than ten years later. (Lloyd was killed in an air crash in Egypt in January 1944, while he was commanding the 10th Indian Division in Persia.)

Bill left by air early next morning, picked up a fighter escort in Chittagong as a protection against marauding Japanese aircraft and landed on a forward airstrip close to the divisional headquarters, where he met Cyril Lomax for the first time and learned that things were even worse than he thought. The brigade covering the east side of the mountains had been virtually wiped out by a Japanese raiding force which had crossed the Mayu river under cover of darkness and the previous night, while Bill had been dining at the Bengal Club, the enemy had infiltrated through 'impenetrable' jungle on the mountain ridge, attacked the rear of a second brigade and captured the brigade headquarters. The situation, Bill noted, was 'fantastically bad'. He was, nevertheless, impressed by the calm confidence exhibited by Lomax and the way he was in process of regrouping and reorganising his forces. 'Never had a divisional commander, immediately on taking over a strange formation, in a new type of war, been confronted with a more desperate situation. I was filled with admiration for the way he took hold. Wherever he went he inspired confidence by his steadiness, decision, and obvious competence.'[13]

Bill stayed with Lomax for a few days, helping any way he could, but uncomfortably aware he had no operational role. ('I hope he did not find my presence a handicap,' he said.) When the front had stabilised he returned to Chittagong, where Tony Scott had set up the corps headquarters in an abandoned college. Chittagong, once a bustling port, had been subjected to frequent Japanese air raids and had become a ghost town, inhabited only by those too poor to leave. Those who remained in the town were already beginning to feel the effects of the famine that would sweep Bengal that year and cause the deaths of some two million people. The railway workshops, once the town's main industry, had been demolished to prevent them falling into enemy hands in the event of a Japanese invasion. Before the war, Chittagong's verdant hills, cooled by the fresh sea breezes, had been dotted by villas with gardens stocked with exotic shrubs and flowers; now there was an air of neglect and stagnation everywhere which Bill found terribly depressing.

On 14 April, Irwin finally transferred operational control of the Arakan offensive to Bill's 15 Corps rather too late, as in Burma, for him to rescue the campaign from disaster. He was very concerned about the morale and physical condition of the troops and warned Irwin, presciently, that there was a 'grave danger' that they would collapse in the face of a determined enemy attack. 'All Brigadiers ... are worried about the state of the troops. This is the most serious aspect of the whole show ... The British troops are tired and they are "browned off" with the operations in Arakan as a whole. Their health is deteriorating. The recent rain has added to the malaria and the three battalions and attached troops in 6 Brigade are now evacuating 50 men a day ... The Indian troops, except 4 Brigade, are tired too, but with them the fault is the inferior quality in physique training and spirit of the men ... I think the troops, both British and Indian, will fight on the whole well, for one more time, but won't go on much after that.'[14]

Commuting between his headquarters and the front in a Lysander light aircraft, he toured the operational area to get a clear picture of what was happening on the ground. At one point, looking for a forward brigade, the pilot put them down on an airstrip that had been abandoned by the Allies and was about to be occupied by the enemy. He turned the engine off before he realised his mistake and then could not get it started again. Bill waited in the observer's seat behind the pilot, expecting machine guns to open up from the jungle all around at any minute. Eventually the engine coughed into life and they got away safely before the Japanese showed up, to Bill's considerable relief.

Bill's prediction of a calamitous collapse quickly came to pass. Lomax was planning a counter-strike against the Japanese, hoping to lure the enemy into a trap. Troops were set up on three sides of a 'box' – north, west and east. The idea was to entice the Japanese into the box and then the 'lid' – a mobile force waiting in the south – would snap shut. Bill approved the plan, despite his worries that the troops were tired and demoralised after four months of defeat and frustration in a place they had come to hate.

Initially the plan went well. The Japanese, facing strong opposition on their flanks but little in front, moved into the box precisely as Lomax had intended. But just as he was about to give the order for the lid to be slammed, the bottom of the box collapsed. The two battalions holding the north side gave way and the Japanese poured through. In the confused fighting that followed the enemy managed to get astride the Maungdaw–Buthidaung road, cutting off the troops on the east side of the mountains. Most were able to escape on foot along jungle tracks but had to abandon almost all their transport.

With the collapse of the entrapment plan, Bill was convinced that the troops were 'fought out'. A liaison officer sent from his headquarters to visit the forward brigades confirmed his view in a devastating report: 'Outstanding was the fact that our troops were either exhausted, browned off or both, and that both Indian and British troops did not have their hearts in the campaign. The former were obviously scared of the Jap and generally demoralised by the nature of the campaign, i.e. the thick jungle and the subsequent blindness of movement, the multiple noises of the jungle at night, the terror stories of Jap brutality, the undermining influence of fever, and the mounting list of failures; the latter also fear the jungle, hate the country and see no object in fighting for it, and also have the strong feeling that they are taking part in a forgotten campaign in which no one in authority is taking any real interest ...'[15]

At a conference held at 15 Corps headquarters on 8 May, Bill asserted that the division had no alternative but to withdraw and set up a new defensive line around Cox's Bazar, the point from which the offensive had started, and sit out the monsoon. He argued that it would be better to stretch the enemy's lines of communication and that the open ground around Cox's Bazar would enable Allied tanks and artillery to be better deployed. Irwin initially demanded that the port of Maungdaw be held, perhaps because its evacuation would underscore the total failure of the entire operation, but Bill expressed his concern that the Japanese would lay siege to Maungdaw and cut the Allied lines of communication to Chittagong. After a sometimes heated discussion, Irwin grudgingly agreed to a general withdrawal, but to a line somewhat south of Cox's Bazar.

The withdrawal began on the following day. The Japanese quickly occupied Buthidaung and Maungdaw, but showed no inclination to chase the retiring Allied troops. Both sides settled down to sit out the monsoon. As far as the Allies were concerned, absolutely nothing had been achieved. In London Churchill was furious. 'This campaign goes from bad to worse,' he fumed, 'and we are being completely outfought and outmanoeuvred by the Japanese.'[16]

Irwin quickly sought to distance himself from responsibility for the debacle. 'We are about to be faced with the difficult problem of how to explain away the loss of Buthidaung and Maungdaw ...' he wrote in a letter to Wavell. 'Although the commanders are far from being much good, the cause unquestionably lies in the inability of troops to fight.'[17]

At a press conference the following day he criticised the equipment, training and motivation of the forces deployed in Arakan, yet refused to admit any blame attached to himself or his staff. It created widespread resentment.

On the morning of 26 May, Bill received two telegrams – one from Irwin severely criticising his handling of the Arakan campaign and indicating that he was going to be relieved of his command and another ordering him to report to Barrackpore immediately, which seemed to confirm Irwin's prediction. Nigel Bruce, who delivered both telegrams, reported that Bill did not seem particularly perturbed. 'He said he thought he'd write a book titled "From Corporal to General and Back Again". Then he said, "Wouldn't it be fun if Irwin was sacked too, and we found ourselves in the Home Guard together?"'

As they were strolling back to Bill's bungalow they could see a curious figure clad only in a towel leaping about on the verandah, waving a piece of paper and shouting 'God is good, God is good'. It was Tony Scott. Bruce thought the chief of staff had 'gone bats'. He had not. He had just received a message to say that Irwin was being replaced as commander of the Eastern Army. Bill's summons to Barrackpore was not to be sacked but to confer with the new commander, General George Giffard, the former C-in-C of West Africa Command.

Irwin received the news that he had been dismissed on the same day, while he was visiting 4 Corps in Imphal. He had the grace to accept his lot like a gentleman and is said to have dispatched another brief message to Bill, indicating a hitherto unnoticed humility. 'You're not sacked,' he wrote. 'I am.'[18]

In London, far removed from the steamy monsoon-drenched

jungles of Burma, general dismay had greeted the news of yet another defeat in the East. At the Trident conference in Washington,
DC, in May 1943, Winston Churchill made no secret of his disgust,
telling General Sir Alan Brooke, the Chief of the Imperial General
Staff, that he viewed the campaign as 'one of the most disappointing
and indeed discreditable which has occurred in this war. A complete
outfit of new commanders must be found ... The whole British
Army in India is being brought into disrepute by the thoroughly
bad conduct of these operations.'[19] (For some reason Churchill had
long distrusted the Indian Army and was always ready to believe the
worst of it; he once accused Wavell of 'creating a Frankenstein' by
putting modern weapons into the hands of sepoys.)

At the same conference Churchill and President Roosevelt decided that a fundamental restructuring of the command system in
India was required to defeat Japan and agreed to establish a South
East Asia Command (SEAC) later in the year to direct future operations – a decision that would have far-reaching implications for Bill
Slim's career. Wavell was removed as Commander-in-Chief and appointed the Viceroy of India; he was replaced by General Sir Claude
Auchinleck ('the Auk'), the former C-in-C Middle East Command
who had spent most of his military career in India. At the Quadrant
conference in Quebec in August, Churchill successfully argued for
the appointment of 43-year-old Louis Mountbatten, newly promoted to acting admiral, as Supreme Commander of SEAC, with
Vinegar Joe Stilwell as his deputy.

Bill, meanwhile, had been ordered to prepare for yet another offensive in Arakan. He had learned much about fighting the Japanese
from his brief and unhappy experience earlier in Arakan and, given
time to train the men and prepare detailed plans, he had no doubt
that the enemy could be beaten. The strategy he devised for this operation would develop into the ground rules adopted by the entire
Allied army for the recapture of Burma and the eventual defeat of
Japan.

To counter the Japanese encircling and infiltration tactics, units
surrounded by the enemy were to form what he called an 'administrative box', creating a well-stocked stronghold with a 360-degree
defensive perimeter which would stand firm until reinforcements
arrived. Bill liked to describe it as the 'anvil' against which the

enemy would be smashed by the 'hammer' of a relieving force. He knew from personal experience that while Japanese soldiers were fanatically brave, they were led by officers with little imagination perfectly willing to spend the lives of their men by throwing them mindlessly into the attack even when it was obvious it was futile.

Crucial to the success of the 'box' was the requirement for it to be supplied by air for as long as necessary. Bill demanded that officers inculcate in their men a sense of 'airmindedness', that an aircraft was just another vehicle and that being supplied by air was no more extraordinary than being supplied by road, rail or sea. To deal with the enemy's dreaded defensive bunkers, he proposed the simplest solution – go round the side or the back. Frontal assaults were costly and often fruitless. Capturing ground at the rear of the enemy, preferably across his lines of communication, forced him to counter-attack and left the bunkers vulnerable to being overwhelmed.

Bill recognised that none of these tactics would work without officers of a high calibre, able to hold their nerve, leading confident, highly motivated troops. Those who he felt were unable to cope with his new regime were replaced. He organised 'war games' at which groups of officers planned the campaign around a large-scale model of the terrain. 'Slim summed up at the close of each day,' recalled Anthony Brett-James, a young officer in the 5th Indian Division, 'and I was mightily impressed by his penetrating criticism and appreciation of the detailed tactics, and by his calm drive and humour; he showed insight into the Japanese mind and methods, and seemed to hold no illusions about what would face us in Arakan, yet he was able to look bravely and with certainty into the New Year, despite every past disaster in Burma. I sensed a nature as robust and tenacious as his own physique; in place of flash, superficiality, polish or elegance, waxed a purposeful, business like, imperturbable and seasoned personality.'[20]

Intensive jungle training continued through the monsoon with forward troops undertaking aggressive patrolling and frequent small-scale operations against Japanese positions. Meanwhile, Bill drew up detailed plans for the new offensive, for which he had been allocated three divisions. By the beginning of October, with his corps headquarters set up close to the front in the jungle near Bawli Bazar, Bill was poised to launch the attack in Arakan as soon as the monsoon eased. Then, out of the blue, he received a signal ordering him to report to Barrackpore and assume acting command of Eastern Army in place of General Giffard, who had been appointed commander of the 11th Army Group and army commander designate at SEAC. He was informed that Eastern Army was to be divided into two; with the old Eastern Command taking over rear area duties in Bihar, Orissa and most of Bengal, while a new formation, as yet undesignated, would become responsible for all land-based operations against the Japanese in Burma.

What Bill did not know was that the new formation would become the 14th Army and that his name had already been put forward to command it.

12

Army Commander

Admiral Lord Louis Mountbatten arrived in Delhi on 7 October 1943 to take up his appointment as Supreme Commander, SEAC, in a blaze of smoothly orchestrated publicity. Handsome, debonair, and a cousin of the King-Emperor, he emerged from his aircraft, tall, bronzed, smiling broadly and dressed, one perhaps sarcastic observer remarked, in a uniform of 'dazzling white and gold'.[1] Among the senior officers lined up to greet him there were undoubtedly some who felt they should have been given his job but their resentment 'melted in the glow of his personality ... no Hollywood star in an admiral's uniform could have looked more striking'.[2] The youngest supreme commander since Napoleon, there were those who questioned Mountbatten's experience and qualifications, at the age of 43, to handle such an important job, but none could question his charisma or his good looks.

The elevation to 'supreme command' of a man widely viewed as little more than an aristocratic playboy and socialite had been viewed with astonishment and disbelief in both London and Washington. Born His Serene Highness Prince Louis of Battenberg, a great-grandson of Queen Victoria, Mountbatten had shamelessly used his royal connections to advance his career. As Chief of Combined Operations he had presided over the disastrous Dieppe raid in August 1942, which resulted in 4,000 Allied casualties in a single day, yet Churchill's support for him never wavered and, once he had decided that 'Dickie' Mountbatten was the man to take over in South-East Asia, nothing could dissuade him. In his favour Mountbatten was energetic, full of ideas and ferociously ambitious, but he was also vain, highly strung, impetuous and prone to jealousy, with a predilection for shifting the blame when things went wrong.

Mountbatten stayed for the first five days with General Auchinleck before moving into Faridkot House, a gilded palace built for the Maharajah of Faridkot, which was to be his official residence. He could soon be found driving around Delhi in a new Cadillac sporting no fewer than four flags flying from the bonnet to signify his command of British, American, Dutch and Chinese troops. Soon after his arrival, his ADC telephoned Auchinleck's ADC to inquire where the C-in-C got his hair cut. Informed that 'the Auk' was perfectly happy with a local military barber, Mountbatten's ADC was aghast. 'Oh,' he said. 'The Supremo would not like his hair cut by a *native*.' A hairdresser from Trumper's, a fashionable barber in Jermyn Street, Mayfair, was promptly drafted into the RAF and flown out to India.[3]

During initial briefings with Auchinleck and SEAC's three service commanders-in-chief, Mountbatten was given precious little cause for optimism in Burma: the enemy had the upper hand everywhere, the attempted advance on the Arakan front had ended in disaster and the casualty figures were horrendous – for every man injured in battle, 120 were hospitalised because of disease.

One of the most pressing and critical matters on the agenda was to decide who would command future operations in Burma. 'The Auk', an old Indian Army hand who knew Bill well, had already put his name forward to the CIGS in London as the best man to to fight the Japanese but Mountbatten had never met Bill and, perfectly reasonably, did not want to make any decision until he had. (Before he left England, Mountbatten had talked to Noel Irwin who sourly told him that all the senior officers in Eastern Army, including Bill, were tainted and should be sacked, adding for good measure that morale was so bad there was nothing to stop the Japanese marching on Delhi if they so wished.)[4]

In Ranchi, Bill was still in the process of handing 15 Corps over to his friend, Major General Philip Christison (they were instructors together at Camberley), and was doing the rounds saying his farewells before taking over as acting commander of the Eastern Army. When the time came to leave, Air Commodore Alexander Gray, commander of 224 Group, Royal Air Force, with whom he had worked closely, insisted on personally flying him to Calcutta. He arrived early at Dum Dum airfield to discover, once again, that there was no one to meet him. Without his ADC (Nigel Bruce had broken his leg in Arakan), he was obliged to wander around the airport looking for driver willing to take him to Barrackpore. He eventually pulled rank and bullied an Indian driver waiting for a brigadier, but just outside the airfield he saw his own car approaching, with Steve Irwin,[5] his new chief of staff, in the back. He waved it down, changed cars and set off on the depressing stop and start drive to Barrackpore, crawling through chaotic streets jammed with trams, buses, taxis, rickshaws, bullock carts and army vehicles. He secretly confessed to a moment of vanity and pleasure that the pennant of an army commander – his pennant – was fluttering from the bonnet of the car, even though his appointment was only temporary.

At Belvedere House in Barrackpore he found himself sitting at the same desk, in the same office, that he had vacated to make way for General Irwin a little more than 12 months earlier when he was a corps commander. It was, he admitted, 'strange'. All that had changed was that the offices were more crowded with desks, there were more huts in the grounds and more dispatch riders coming and going. When he assembled his staff officers for a briefing he reassured them, no doubt to their relief, that he would not be replacing them with his own hand-picked officers but he made it clear he would not hesitate to sack those who fell short of the mark.

The day after Bill arrived in Barrackpore, Mountbatten left Delhi by air to confer with Chiang Kai-shek in Chungking. He took with him a memorandum drafted by George Giffard with details of Bill's career and Giffard's personal recommendation of his abilities as a candidate to take command of ground operations in Burma. On the return flight to Delhi on 22 October, his aircraft stopped for refuelling at an airstrip near Eastern Army HQ and Mountbatten took the opportunity to meet Bill. Warned in advance of his arrival, Bill and the RAF commander were waiting at the airstrip to greet him when his aircraft landed and after introductions Bill asked the Supremo if he would care to address the senior staff, some 80 of whom were gathered in the lecture hall at headquarters.

Mountbatten was surprised and unprepared, but he had already made some fundamental decisions about the future and considered there was no reason why he should not share them. What he had to say left his audience both profoundly shocked and deeply sceptical. He told them first he could see no reason why the battle stopped during the monsoon – heresy to men who had endured a Burmese monsoon. It was his opinion that fighting against the Japanese should continue uninterrupted through the year. Further, there were to be no more retreats – if lines of communication were cut and troops were surrounded they were to stand fast and would be supplied by air. In terms of welfare, he intended to set up a Medical Advisory Division which he expected would drastically reduce the numbers of men laid low by disease, particularly malaria. As to immediate operations, a planned land offensive in the north was now off and current thinking favoured an amphibious landing in the south. When Bill asked if sufficient naval forces and landing craft would be made available, Mountbatten jauntily replied: 'We're getting so many ships that the harbours of India and Ceylon won't be big enough to hold 'em.'

It was the kind of flippant remark that grated on officers who were always being promised more supplies and new equipment, promises that were never fulfilled. Everyone in the room knew that they were at the bottom of the pile in terms of priority – the men were already bitterly calling themselves 'the Forgotten Army' – and that Mountbatten's arrival was hardly likely to change that. The consensus was that the Supremo did not know what he was talking about and had no understanding of the realities of war in Burma. (When Giffard later heard about Mountbatten's remarks, he dismissed them as 'a piece of empty braggadocio', founded on ignorance.)

Mountbatten was aware from the silence and grim faces in the audience that his speech had not been well received. Afterwards, in Bill's office, he said, 'That didn't go down very well, did it?' Bill had to agree. 'They're not used to revolutionary ideas,' he explained, but added that personally he liked what Mountbatten had to say and would back him to the hilt.[6] Mountbatten, who was often uncomfortable with men older than himself, immediately warmed to Bill. 'Something happened at that first meeting,' Mountbatten later recalled, 'somehow we clicked.'[7] Bill was not being sycophantic – he had never been sycophantic in his life. He genuinely admired Mountbatten's ideas, not least because they aligned very closely with his own, particularly on the question of standing fast, air supply and fighting through the monsoon. They talked for some time about the need to raise morale. Bill suggested that the new formation should be given a different name since the Eastern Army was so stigmatised by defeat. He obviously had no thoughts that he might be offered the command because he was at pains to point out that he was only the acting commander of the Eastern Army. He described how Irwin had tried to sack him for the disaster in Arakan and confessed he was surprised to find himself where he was. Mountbatten was so impressed by Bill's character, candour, experience and theories that he decided, right then, to offer him command of the new army.

Bill was staggered. Typically he suggested that Mountbatten should wait until he had interviewed other candidates.

'No,' Mountbatten replied, 'my mind is made up. I want you. Will you take it?'[8]

In truth there was no job in the world Bill wanted more, but he still prevaricated, asking if Mountbatten should not clear his appointment first with General Giffard. Mountbatten was dismissive – he was the Supreme Commander, Giffard was his subordinate and would therefore do as he was told, and in any case Giffard had given him a favourable report on Bill and so it was unlikely he would create any difficulties.

There Mountbatten was wrong. Giffard was perfectly happy for Bill Slim to command the new army but he was deeply affronted not to have been consulted. The proper channel would have been for Mountbatten to confer with both Giffard and Auchinleck and then, if they were all agreed, for Giffard to formally offer the appointment to Bill. So it was that when Mountbatten casually informed Giffard what he had done, Giffard objected and said he would have to 'think it over'. Mountbatten, intensely irritated, suggested to Giffard that he should perhaps telegraph the CIGS in London to ask if he was required to obey orders or was permitted to protest. Giffard grudgingly yielded, but the relationship between the two men was irreparably damaged. 'I maintained my ascendancy over him from that moment,' Mountbatten noted, 'though I don't suppose he liked it.'[9] Mountbatten came to view his Army C-in-C as uninspired, too methodical and over-prudent.

Conversely Bill would get on well with Giffard, probably because they were kindred spirits and shared many characteristics in temperament and outlook. Both were no-nonsense fighting soldiers with great personal integrity, courtesy and humility; both were calm and self-assured in a crisis; both had the confidence to delegate authority; both were untrammelled by large egos. Bill liked to say of Giffard that he understood 'the simple fundamentals of war – that soldiers must be trained before they can fight, fed before they can march, and relieved before they are worn out'.[10]

The symbiotic relationship which developed between Bill and the Supreme Commander would become the most important dynamic of the Burma campaign and while Bill privately acknowledged Mountbatten's many irritating foibles – he claimed that 'the only way to get anything done is to see him [Mountbatten] last'[11] – he remained utterly loyal in public. Mountbatten, for his part, never wavered in his admiration of the 14th Army commander. 'I thought him absolutely splendid in every way and never changed my point of view from beginning to end,' he wrote after the war. 'I have reason to believe he liked me too from the beginning. Nothing could ever come between us. I saw Bill Slim whenever I possibly could and never missed a chance of seeing him on any visit to the front. We talked over everything with the utmost candour and he and I saw eye to eye all the way through.'[12]

On 13 November, GHQ India confirmed the appointment of Lieutenant General William Slim as commander of a new formation, to be called 14th Army, which would be charged with driving the Japanese out of Burma. The 14th Army would be made up of the 4th Corps, based in Assam, under the command of Lieutenant General Geoffrey Scoones, and the 15th Corps, in Chittagong, under the command of Lieutenant General 'Christie' Christison. Both were impressive professional soldiers with impeccable records from Indian Army families. Scoones was a Gurkha (more than enough to endear him to Bill). Small and wiry, he was shrewd, energetic, had a boundless capacity for hard work and shared Bill's concern for the welfare of the men. Christison, a genial Cameron

Highlander, was the son of a baronet who became Surgeon General in the Bengal Army – his father carried out the first successful operation under anaesthetic in the field outside Rangoon during the Second Burmese War in 1853 on a young ensign by the name of Garnet Wolseley. A linguist, athlete, musician, crack shot and keen angler, Christison was an authority on bird life and would somehow find time during the campaign to compile field notes on the birds of Arakan. His only son had been killed by enemy action in Burma the previous year.

Bill's new command would eventually become the biggest, and most ethnically diverse, army in the world, never better described than by John Masters, then a major in the 4th Prince of Wales's Own Gurkha Rifles: 'There were men from every caste and race – Sikhs, Dogras, Pathans, Madrassis, Mahrattas, Rajputs, Assamese, Kumaonis, Punjabis, Garhwalis, Naga headhunters – and, from Nepal, the Gurkhas in all their tribes and sub tribes of Limbu and Rai, Thakur and Chetri, Magar and Gurung. These men wore turbans, and steel helmets, and slouch hats, and berets, and tank helmets, and khaki shakos inherited from the eighteenth century. There were companies that averaged five feet one inch in height and companies that averaged six feet three inches. There were men as purple black as the West Africans and men as pale and gold-wheat of skin as a lightly sun-tanned blond. They worshipped God according to the rites of the Mahayana and Hinayana, of Sunni and of Shiah, of Rome and Canterbury and Geneva, of the Vedas and the sages and the Mahabharatas, of the ten Gurus, of the secret shrines of the jungle. There were vegetarians and meat-eaters and fish eaters, and men who only ate rice, and men who only ate wheat; and men who had four wives, men who shared one wife with four brothers, and men who openly practised sodomy. There were men who had never seen snow, and men who seldom saw anything else. And Brahmins and Untouchables, both with rifle and tommy gun.'[13]

Bill knuckled down quickly to whip this extraordinary mixed bag into a cohesive fighting force. He was, of course, already well known to the men of 15 Corps – 4 Corps would soon get to know him just as well. The strict training regimen he had introduced while he was commander of 15 Corps was now applied across the whole of 14th

Army, to all ranks with no exceptions. He constantly thrust home the message that training, underpinned by morale, good leadership and sound tactics, was the key to success for the 14th Army. 'What has a soldier got?' he asked. 'He has got his country, but that is far away. In battle, the soldier has only his sense of duty, and his sense of shame. These are the things which make men go on fighting even though terror grips their heart. Every soldier, therefore, must be instilled with pride in his unit and in himself, and to do this he must be treated with justice and respect.'

The fighting capacity of every unit, he said, was based on the faith of the men in their officers. He liked to quote the famous line ascribed to Napoleon: 'There are no bad soldiers, only bad officers.' To lay the myth of the Japanese as invincible super-soldiers and to acquaint the troops with real-life operations in the jungle, Bill instructed all front-line units to undertake aggressive patrolling, seeking confrontation with the enemy, setting ambushes and raiding on a small scale. Patrolling had to be done on foot, often hacking a path through dense vegetation while enduring the privations of the jungle – the ants, leeches and snakes, the leg sores and blisters, and the occasional rogue elephant charging out of the undergrowth. Slowly the men began to lose their fear of the jungle and began bringing back trophies plucked from the Japanese they had killed. News of these heartening mini-victories spread quickly and raised morale. Bill often told the story of a Gurkha patrol which returned with a large basket containing three Japanese heads which they proudly placed on their CO's desk before offering him a fish, from the same basket, they had caught while crossing a stream on the way back. It would make a fine dinner, they said, all it needed was a bit of a wash.

Supply continued to be a major headache. The 14th Army's area of operations stretched for 700 miles from the Chinese border to the Bay of Bengal and covered an area the size of Poland. It was the most difficult terrain in the world, much of it dense jungle and forbidding mountain ranges with no roads, only bullock cart tracks which became impassable in the monsoon. A railway built to serve the Assam tea plantations was only capable of shifting a fraction of what was needed, but 40,000 labourers employed by the Indian Tea Association were busy building the roads that would become absolutely vital as the war progressed. Rations and ammunition were in desperately short supply and Bill recruited his old friend, 'Grocer Alf' Snelling, whom he had last seen in a sandstorm in Mesopotamia, to be major general in charge of administration, work his magic and produce what was required. Even for Snelling, feeding the 14th Army in the best of circumstances was a very considerable challenge, not least because there were some 30 different ration scales to accommodate different religious and ethnic groups and famine was still ravaging India. The 14th Army logistics almost defied belief: 'Grocer Alf' had to feed 500,000 soldiers and 300,000 Indian labourers and porters every day, requiring 1,800 tons of food and water to be brought in by rail, road, sea and air and 50,000 trucks to transport rations to the forward areas. By the end of the campaign, Snelling had 18,000 acres of farmland under cultivation, growing vegetables and rearing ducks, pigs and goats. He even set up mobile breweries to provide beer for the troops.

Disease continued to be a major worry – Bill's army was being devastated by malaria and a host of other unpleasant tropical diseases, particularly in the forward areas. When quinine ran out in one battalion, the commanding officer informed his headquarters that there was no point in sending out patrols because within a week the 'men would be carrying one another'. Bill introduced Malaria Forward Treatment Units (MFTUs) – field hospitals set up in *bashas* (huts made of bamboo and woven leaves) a few miles behind the front – to offer prompt treatment for malaria, which dramatically cut down the time the man was away from his unit. When mepacrine became available to control the disease an unfortunate side effect was that it turned the skin yellow and a rumour swept through the ranks that it also caused impotence; as a consequence many men tried to avoid taking it. Bill had spot checks carried out on entire units: if it transpired that less than 95 per cent had taken their medication he sacked the commanding officer. He had to sack three before the message got across.

John Masters described the melancholy ritual of jungle medication: 'Pill taking continued. We drank shark liver oil, cheaper and easier to extract than cod liver oil, just as healthful and twice as foul-tasting. We took mepacrine. Our faces turned a dark, unhealthy yellow, also our urine. Rumours floated about. Mepacrine made a man impotent. Caused his hair to fall out. And his teeth. But it kept down malaria, and a man out of action with malaria was a man the Japanese had removed from the battlefield without any exertion or risk to themselves. No soldier got his food unless he had taken his mepacrine, under the eye of an officer.'[14]

Sickness was one factor – but only one – causing the low morale, which was far and away Bill's greatest concern. Desertions were increasing, some men were deliberately exposing themselves to malaria in the hope of being sent away from the front, and the 'Forgotten Army' epithet, which was now common currency throughout all ranks, encapsulated the misery felt by polyglot troops scattered over a huge area far from home. The heat and disease were bad enough, but worse was the suspicion that everyone else in the war was better supplied, better equipped and more highly regarded. The seemingly endless and humiliating defeats, the shortages of everything, the hardships of living in the jungle, the sense that no one at home knew or cared what they were doing, the dread of facing a barbaric, fanatical and fearless enemy whose ambition was to die for the Emperor on the field of battle ... Bill completely understood why morale was at a low ebb and he thought long and hard what he should do about it. He could do nothing about the past, and little about the daily hardships and shortages, but what he was able to do was lift spirits by simply spending time with the men.

There was little Bill enjoyed more than chatting to soldiers. At the end of the war he would estimate it was how he spent about a third of his time. For him it was not a chore – he enjoyed it, was genuinely interested in the men and they responded to his warm, natural, easy-going manner. His platform was usually the bonnet of his jeep with the men gathered round; he would quite often deliver three or four speeches in a single day, drawing on his singular ability to communicate high ideals in simple language. Sometimes, he said, he felt more like a parliamentary candidate than a general. And sometimes he got muddled up with the languages and would address Urdu speakers in Gurkhali, or vice versa. It did not matter. His intention was to make everyone, from the highest rank to the lowest, from front-line fighting soldier to the support troops, the clerks, the cooks and the cleaners, feel that they were an integral part of a great war machine working for a common cause against the incarnation of evil – the Japanese army. His constant refrain was that the primary mission of the 14th Army was not just to drive the Japanese forces out of Burma but to destroy them. Everything else, even the capture of ground, was to be subordinate to that aim.

Bill's searing honesty was very much a pillar of his character and he never hesitated to tell the troops that they would almost certainly be 'buggered about' every now and then. Whenever that happened, he said, they were not to blame their CO, or their brigade commander, or anyone else but himself. At the same time, he promised them he would never 'bugger them about' unless it was absolutely necessary. It was the kind of straight talking soldiers appreciated and it was around this time that Bill acquired the affectionate nickname that would spread throughout the 14th Army and stay with him for the rest of the war – 'Uncle Bill'. (General Giffard, who was five years older than Bill, was known as 'Pop'.)

'I learned,' he wrote, 'that one did not need to be an orator to be effective. Two things only were necessary: first to know what you were talking about, and, second and most important, to believe in yourself. I found that if one kept the bulk of one's talk to the material things the men were interested in – food, pay, leave, beer, mail, and the progress of operations – it was safe to end on a higher note – the spiritual foundations – and I always did.'[15]

Bill's thesis, now enshrined in the curriculum at the Royal Military Academy, was that morale, which enabled men to endure the brutality of combat, was founded on three factors: material, intellectual and spiritual. The material meant giving men a fair deal, providing them with the best possible living and working conditions in whatever circumstances they found themselves; the intellectual involved convincing soldiers that the task they had been set was attainable and the spiritual that its attainment was worthwhile, that the cause they were fighting for was just. 'We trusted him [Bill] not to embroil us in major botchery,' Patrick Davis, a young officer in the 4th/8th Gurkhas, explained. 'We accepted the possibility of death, and the certainty of danger, discomfort, fatigue and hunger, provided that our fighting was constructive and with a reasonable chance of success.'[16]

Wherever he went, Bill inspired trust and confidence in his leadership. Robert Rowland, a 22-year-old subaltern in the 7th/2nd Punjab Regiment, was at the Jungle Training and Reinforcement Camp in Chittagong when Bill paid a visit. 'I remember very vividly being impressed by what I can only describe as a mixture of informality coupled with a quality of steel and determination which was palpable. He was quietly spoken with a complete absence of rhetoric or pomposity ... The man was like no other commander I had met. Was he the only general in the war who commanded total respect from all ranks, despite the so-called handicaps of affection and amiability?'

Bill encouraged all his subordinate commanders to keep their men abreast of what was going on not just within their own units, but throughout the war. He wanted it pressed home that they were involved in a global conflict and that Germany had to be defeated first. When there were delays issuing equipment or shortages Bill required the men to be given explanations and to be told what was being done to remedy the situation. Information rooms were set up in every unit.

Mountbatten, too, played his part, tirelessly touring from one formation to another delivering what appeared to be an off-the-cuff speech but which, in fact, was carefully scripted. Every visit was stage-managed to give the impression of spontaneity and when he jumped up on to an ammunition box to address the troops he had an engaging opening line, actually filched from Bill, which he used over and over again: 'I know you think of yourselves as the forgotten army, but you're wrong ...' he would say, pausing for effect. 'You're not the forgotten army because no one has ever bloody heard of you.' It usually brought the house down. Youthful, charismatic and genuinely inspiring, Mountbatten was, Bill thought, 'a tonic'. The Indian troops and Gurkhas, in particular, considered it a signal honour to be led by a cousin of the King-Emperor; they called him 'Lord Mountainbattery'.

Mountbatten also established a war theatre newspaper, *SEAC*, which also played a major role in raising morale. The first time Bill met the editor, Second Lieutenant Frank Owen, he spent some time setting forth his views of how the newspaper should be run and lecturing him on what an editor's duties were. Owen listened politely, said he would do his best, saluted and left. Some time later Bill learned to his considerable embarrassment that 38-year-old Owen had been elected as a Liberal Member of Parliament at the age of 23, was the former editor of the *Evening Standard*, was considered to be one of the most brilliant editors in Fleet Street and was a co-author of *Guilty Men*, an important polemical work denouncing appeasement published in 1940.

SEAC, an eight-page broadsheet printed in Calcutta, was such an important morale booster for 14th Army that it was always included in the consignment when troops relied on being supplied by air. As well as reporting on the war in the Asian theatre, it kept the men abreast with what was happening in Europe, which became particularly important after D-Day, when an end was at last in sight to the struggle against Nazi Germany. The newspaper included a popular strip cartoon, Jane, and on the back page there was always a nostalgic photograph of some idyllic pastoral scene in England under the headline 'Home'.

To be closer to both his corps headquarters Bill moved 14th Army HQ out of Barrackpore, which he hated, to the city of Comilla (now in Bangladesh), 200 miles to the east. He found a house with a large garden planted with scented shrubs and shady trees and was pleased to find a pair of mongoose living underneath the house to keep the snakes away, but the city itself was as mildewed, dispiriting and filthy as every other town in India and was notable only for the large number of memorial plaques erected to commemorate civil servants and police officers murdered by Bengali terrorists. Bill's office in the Courts of Justice overlooked several of them on a wall opposite, a permanent reminder of Comilla's status as a hotbed of anti-British sentiment. (Comilla was home for many years to Bidrohi Kobi, the Bengali revolutionary poet and musician who led protests against the visit of the Prince of Wales to India in 1921.)

The Third Tactical Air Force HQ, under Air Marshal John Baldwin, and the joint USAAF/RAF Troop Carrier Command, under the American Brigadier General William D. Old, also moved to Comilla. At Bill's suggestion, all the senior officers shared the same mess, an arrangement which greatly facilitated mutual cooperation when air supply got under way. Bill claimed that they all got on so well together that the Americans acquired a taste for tea and the British even learned how to make a decent cup of coffee.

By the time of Bill's appointment to the 14th Army, many plans for the reconquest of Burma had been discussed and discarded. At the Casablanca conference in January 1943, Churchill and Roosevelt had approved extraordinarily ambitious proposals for a major offensive at the end of the monsoon involving a two-pronged assault on northern Burma from Assam and China combined with amphibious operations in Arakan aimed, ultimately, at seizing Rangoon. By May, reality had set in with the realisation that resources were simply not available for such an operation.

One of the difficulties for Allied planners was that Britain and the United States had very different strategic objectives in the area. President Roosevelt and Prime Minister Churchill had become effective warlords with power and influence that would never have been tolerated in peacetime. Both were deluded. Roosevelt held a hopelessly romantic view of a future China as another United States, democratic, liberal and peaceful, and an important ally. He believed this vision was attainable if the Nationalist forces of Chiang Kai-shek were given sufficient support. Before the Japanese invasion of Burma, the United States supplied the Nationalists through the port of Rangoon and the Burma Road. When Rangoon was lost, supplies were flown in from Assam over what American pilots called 'the Hump', the forbidding eastern end of the Himalayas. Unpredictably violent weather, heavy cargo loads, high mountain terrain and poorly equipped, frequently flooded airfields made it a difficult and dangerous assignment. It was also exorbitantly expensive and in December 1942 a start was made building a 500-mile road from Ledo in Assam across northern Burma to the Chinese frontier. Roosevelt's only real interest in Burma was to protect the supply route to Chiang Kai-shek. He certainly had no desire to help restore the British empire; indeed, he was more in tune with the cynics who suggested that SEAC stood for 'Saving England's Asian Cronies'.

(Vinegar Joe Stilwell claimed to an Australian journalist that he had once said to Wavell, whom he described as 'that Viceroy son-of-a-bitch in Delhi', 'How do you figure that Burma's a part of the

Goddam British empire? You took it by conquest from the Burmese and the Japs took it from you.')[17]

Churchill's grand vision was of a world atlas still coloured red around the globe. Despite the increasing clamour within India for independence, he clung to the fantasy that it would still be possible for Britain to control India after the war and that Burma would revert to its former status as part of the empire. He attached little importance to supplying China, dismissing Chiang's regime as hopelessly corrupt, and was doubtful the Chinese were likely to make any significant contribution to the war. (Bill's more pragmatic view was that the enormous resources devoted to building the Ledo Road would have been better spent on combat forces to destroy the Japanese and recapture Burma sooner, but no one in the higher echelons of global strategy sought his opinion.)

An added complication was that, as far as Churchill was concerned, just about the only man who knew how to fight the Japs was Brigadier Orde Wingate, whose widely publicised exploits behind enemy lines in Burma in 1943 had made him a national hero. Handsome, bearded, with heavy brows over piercing blue eyes, Wingate had the look and passion of a prophet. He was a great leader of men, but he was also an eccentric, insufferable, uncouth zealot who was chronically incapable of seeing any view other than his own and who inspired fervent loyalty and utter loathing in almost equal measure. A gunner officer, he had initially made his name in pre-war Palestine organising 'special night squads' of Jewish settlers to defend their *kibbutzim*; in the process he became a fanatical Zionist. When Italy entered the war in June 1940 Wingate was sent to the Sudan from where he helped foment rebellion in Abyssinia and restore Emperor Haile Selassie to the throne after his mixed 'Gideon Force' of some 3,000 regular troops and partisans defeated a well-equipped Italian army 36,000 strong. A photograph of Wingate, wearing shorts and a pith helmet, riding a white horse and leading Selassie in triumph into Addis Ababa, made the front page of newspapers around the world.

Bill had met Wingate in the Sudan and found him a 'strange, excitable, moody creature', but liked some of his ideas and admired his courage, passion and energy. In February 1942 Wingate arrived in Burma, brought in by Wavell, who wanted to experiment using irregular forces against the Japanese. He was given command of a brigade to train as a 'long-range penetration unit' operating behind enemy lines; his men would become known as 'Chindits', a corruption of *chinthe*, the mythical lion-like creature often seen guarding the entrances of pagodas and temples in Burma.

On 13 February 1943, Wingate led the first Chindit raid, code-named Operation Longcloth, into the Burmese jungle. Divided into seven infantry columns, the Chindits blew up bridges and railway lines, attacked outposts, set ambushes and caused general confusion among the enemy. Wingate drove his men mercilessly and insisted they kept constantly on the move in the curious belief it would help prevent malaria. Longcloth might have been an unmitigated success had not Wingate decided to move deeper into Burma, across the Irrawaddy. Arrangements for air supply became erratic as the Japanese deployed three infantry divisions to track down and destroy the Chindits. The operation rapidly turned into a nightmare as men succumbed to hunger, exhaustion and disease. Water was so scarce they sipped the meagre fluid contained in bamboo; mules were slaughtered for food. Unable to wash, the men were crawling with lice and tormented by leeches, ticks, mosquitoes and vicious red ants. There was no way to evacuate the sick and wounded; they were simply left to die. On 24 March, Wingate was ordered to withdraw before his entire brigade was wiped out. The Chindits broke up into small groups and infiltrated back through enemy lines. After three grim months in the jungle and trekking some 1,000 miles, the survivors finally got back to India. Around 800 of the 3,000 men who set out on the raid failed to make it home – some 450 had been killed in action and the remainder either went missing or were taken prisoner – and most of the expedition's field equipment was lost. Those who returned were in such debilitated physical condition that only around 600 were ever able to return to duty.

In real terms Operation Longcloth was costly and achieved little, apart from proving the feasibility of air supply: most of the damage inflicted during the raid was rapidly repaired and Japanese casualties were insignificant compared to the losses sustained by the Chindits. But the operation's panache and reckless audacity made it a psychological success in that it boosted morale and, after a series of disasters in Burma, the British public desperately needed some good news to come out of that far-flung theatre. The decision was taken in London that the operation, originally top secret, should be released to the media. It made headlines and was hailed as a bold and dramatic triumph – the first against the Japanese – an epic of courage and endurance which not only distracted public attention from the failures in Arakan but dented the myth of Japanese invincibility. 'This must surely rank,' Reuters proclaimed with breathless hyperbole, 'among the greatest guerilla operations ever undertaken.' Wingate was hailed in one newspaper as 'the Clive of Burma', no doubt to his considerable pleasure.

The Prime Minister was delighted by the reaction, eulogised Wingate as an officer of 'genius' and even suggested he was the man to command the army in Burma, a suggestion that stunned senior officers. Churchill was quickly dissuaded from such a move, but decided on the spur of the moment to invite Wingate to attend the Quadrant Conference in Quebec in August. On the voyage across the Atlantic in the *Queen Mary* Wingate frequently had the Prime Minister's ear to preach his conviction that Burma could be reconquered by Chindits units alone. If Churchill was impressed, his personal physician, Lord Moran, was less so, noting in his diary that Wingate 'seemed to me hardly sane'.[18] In Quebec, Wingate presented a grandiose plan for eight long-range penetration groups – some 26,500 men in all – to be inserted behind enemy lines during the forthcoming dry season. Despite vigorous protests about the resources such a plan would require, Wingate garnered a lot of support and returned to India with the rank of major general and the authority to contact the Prime Minister directly any time he felt the need, particularly if any senior officer had the temerity to try to thwart him.

Auchinleck was instructed to provide Wingate with everything he required but his bizarre personal habits – he frequently walked around stark naked with a miniature alarm clock strapped to his wrist and cleaned himself by rubbing his body with a rubber brush rather than taking a bath – did nothing to endear him to the C-in-C or his fellow officers. Many of them concluded he was mad and it was well known that he had attempted to commit suicide in Cairo in 1941. On one occasion Auchinleck arranged to visit Wingate at his training camp in the jungle. When he arrived he was informed by an embarrassed staff officer that the CO could not be disturbed. Auchinleck asked Alexander Greenwood, his ADC, to find out what was going on and Greenwood found Wingate in his tent, sitting half naked in a deckchair, reading a bible and chewing with relish on a large raw onion. The incident confirmed 'the Auk's' caustic opinion that the Chindit commander was 'a scatterbrain allowed power without any responsibility'.[19]

Bill, in fact, did not include himself in the legion of Wingate's many detractors. He had always been open to new ideas, was unbothered by the man's eccentricity and thought on balance the propaganda value of the first Chindit raid probably made it worthwhile, despite the horrendous cost in men and equipment. Where he differed, fundamentally, from Wingate was in future tactics. Bill thought long-range penetration operations should be integrated into the bigger picture, staged in cooperation with the front-line troops and supporting the overall strategy of the campaign, rather than as an independent striking force, which was what Wingate wanted. Wingate fervently believed that irregular operations could win the war; Bill just as fervently believed they could not.

In November, Bill attended the SEAC Conference in New Delhi convened to plan a major offensive in the new year. It was held in the splendid Secretariat Building, the same cream and red sandstone pile in which Bill had worked as a junior staff officer 15 years earlier. The conference was attended by large numbers of officers from India, Britain, the United States, China and Holland; Bill was forced to confess he found it 'a little bewildering' and most enjoyed talking to the young men wandering about the place hoping to interest someone in authority in various crackpot ideas for winning the war. Bill called them 'racketeers' trying to sell 'short cuts to victory'.

The conference agreed to mount a coordinated offensive across the whole Burma front in early 1944 designed to paralyse the enemy's four divisions occupying the country. American-trained and equipped Chinese forces would advance from Assam, Indian Army parachute regiments would drop behind enemy lines, Wingate's Long-Range Penetration Group would be widely deployed, the 14th Army would attack Arakan (again) and advance towards the Chindwin river from Imphal and there was also to be an amphibious operation to recapture the Andaman Islands in the Bay of Bengal.

The entire plan was dependent on large numbers of aircraft and ships being available but Supreme Headquarters seemed confident they would be forthcoming and Bill left the conference with 'the pleasant feeling that now we were really on the map in Whitehall and Washington'.

It was not a feeling that would last very long. Bill had barely got back to Comilla before the plans for the offensive began to unravel. Preparations for D-Day in Europe put paid to Mountbatten's impulsive promise that there would be so many ships available all 'the harbours of India and Ceylon won't be big enough to held 'em'. More than half the Allied amphibious resources in South-East Asia were ordered to return to Europe, obliging SEAC to cancel the Andaman Islands attack. Chiang Kai-shek then announced that, since his offer of sending troops from Assam was conditional on the Allies mounting a major amphibious operation, his offer was withdrawn as that operation had now been cancelled. Planning for an amphibious assault on Akyab island in Arakan went ahead in the hope that Chiang would accept it as a substitute for the Andaman Islands operation but, at the end of December, Mountbatten learned that the Generalissimo was implacable. The seaborne strike on Akyab was called off and all landing craft in the theatre were ordered to return to England or the Mediterranean.

Curiously, everything that remained of SEAC's grandiose plans would eventually come under the remit of the 14th Army. The Chinese troops of Northern Combat Area Command (NCAC), under the command of Vinegar Joe Stilwell, were still involved in the projected offensive, but Stilwell had taken an intense dislike to General Giffard, considering him, quite unjustly, to be incompetent and timid. At a heated meeting in Delhi on New Year's Eve, chaired by Mountbatten, Stilwell raised every kind of objection as to why he should not come under Giffard's command. He resisted every proposal put forward by the Supreme Commander and adopted an attitude, Bill thought, of 'surly obstinacy which showed him at his worst'. With Mountbatten becoming increasingly impatient and red in the face and Stilwell running out of arguments, the American suddenly announced that he would be perfectly willing to work with Bill, dismissing Bill's junior rank with the comment 'I would fight under a corporal if he would let me fight'. This risible compromise, which made a nonsense of the chain of command, was gratefully accepted by all present and Bill and Stilwell were left to sort out the details between them. (Bill always found Stilwell easier to deal with when there was no one else around; he was at his most cantankerous with an audience.) A farcical little charade at the end of the meeting defused tension: Stilwell saluted Bill and said, 'Sir, as 14th Army commander, do you have any orders for me?' 'No, sir,' Bill replied, 'and as deputy commander do you have any orders for me?' 'Not on your life,' Stilwell quipped with a grin.

By the New Year Bill had been given detailed instructions for what was expected of the 14th Army in the upcoming offensive: 15 Corps was to secure the Mayu peninsula in Arakan with the ultimate object of capturing the airfield on Akyab island and 4 Corps, with three divisions spread 250 miles along the central front, was to cross into Burma, dominate the area west of the Chindwin river and exploit across the river if the opportunity offered. Bill was also to coordinate plans, with Stilwell, for the Chinese advance in the north and the deployment of the Chindits under Wingate.

Air supply was crucial to the success of Bill's plans. He had been assured sufficient aircraft would be made available when they were needed, but it then emerged there was a critical shortage of parachutes. During one of the lone walks he was in the habit of taking before dinner in the comparative cool of the early evening, Bill had fallen to thinking about how the shortage could be overcome. Army issue parachutes were made of silk but the kind the 14th Army needed to drop supplies into the jungle did not have to be of such high quality – it would not be a disaster, for example, if one or two failed to open. He considered what other materials could be used to replace silk. Paper or jute, both readily available locally, offered possibilities – there were huge paper mills in Calcutta and most of the world's jute was grown in Bengal.

Next morning he called a meeting with Alf Snelling and other staff officers and set them to work to find supplies and experiment with designs. He was so enthused by the idea that he even had a go himself, which was why, when an old Indian Army friend, Maxwell 'Moti' Dyer, then commander of the 268th Indian Infantry Brigade, called at Bill's office he found the army commander on the floor on his hands and knees cutting up sacks with a large pair of scissors.

'Don't mind me for a moment or two, old boy,' Bill said, continuing to snip away. Dyer was mystified. 'If you don't mind me asking,' he inquired, 'what are you doing?' Bill explained patiently that he was cutting out a pattern for an experimental parachute, as if it was an entirely routine task for an army commander to undertake.

In less than a month, after a period of trial and error to find the best design and weave, local women were working day and night at sewing machines stitching canopies for parachutes made entirely of 'gunny' – the woven jute used to make sacks. Even the ropes were fashioned from jute. They were called 'parajutes', were 85 per cent as efficient as a conventional parachute and cost a little more than £1 each, as opposed to £20 for the silk version. 'Parajutes' saved the British taxpayer millions, Bill pointed out, adding wryly that the only thanks he got was a rebuke from the powers that be that he had not gone through the proper channels to acquire the supply of jute.

As the leading elements of the offensive began moving into the forward positions from which they would fly or march into Burma, Bill was acutely aware of how little he knew of the enemy's disposition and intentions, despite being privy to Ultra intercepts. Loyal tribesmen (and former headhunters) in the Naga Hills, straddling the India–Burma border, did their best to keep track of, and report, enemy movement, but the general intelligence available was disquietingly thin. What particularly worried Bill was that while he knew the name of his opposite number, Lieutenant General Kawabe Masakasu, commander of the Japanese Burma Area Army, he knew almost nothing of his character or how his mind worked.

Bill assumed that, like most Japanese generals, Kawabe would be a bold, confident and aggressive leader willing to fight to the last man. Years earlier, when Bill was studying for the Staff College examinations, he had researched the Russo-Japanese War of 1904–5 and had been very struck by the fact that the Japanese threw everything into the fray and sometimes only achieved victory with their very last reserves. It was, he had concluded, both a strength and a weakness in the Japanese tactics.

Someone had found for him a portrait photograph of Kawabe which he pinned to the wall of his office, opposite his desk. The general, with his shaven head, spectacles and protruding teeth, was like a cartoon caricature of a Japanese officer, apart from an enormous and utterly absurd 'handlebar' moustache, which looked as if it had been stuck on to his top lip to be twirled for a pantomime appearance as a villain.

Bill, who was the least vain of men, confessed to taking some comfort, when he needed cheering up, in the certain knowledge that he was better looking.

13

The Turning Point

On the morning of 4 February 1944, Bill left his headquarters in Comilla to visit a nearby reinforcement camp and watch a demonstration of a new flame-thrower. He was suffering from amoebic dysentery and feeling wretched, having just endured his ninth daily injection of emetine, a drug which caused vomiting as a side effect of the treatment. The previous day, despite the dysentery and the demands on his attention, he had found time to write a sweet letter to Una: 'I've got a lovely little kingfisher – blue with a yellow waistcoat – who sometimes sits in a bush outside my office window. He goes an awful "plop" into the water and doesn't always get a fish but he goes on trying … Lots of love my Poons, Daddy.'[1]

While the flame-thrower demonstration was taking place a dispatch rider roared up to Bill on a motorcycle and handed him a signal. It contained news that made him feel markedly worse: the Japanese had launched a massive attack in Arakan. The situation was still obscure, but it was clear the enemy was in considerable strength and had made alarming progress – some Japanese units were already reported to be five or six miles to the rear of one of 14th Army's divisions. Struggling with rising nausea, he raced back to his headquarters in a jeep to deal with the emergency.

Until that moment operations in Arakan had been going more or less to plan. The intention for the first phase was for Christison's 15 Corps to advance down the Mayu peninsula with two divisions, one on each side of the mountain spine, and capture the 16-mile road that ran from the port of Maungdaw on the west, through the old railway tunnels in the mountains, to Buthidaung in the east. A third division would be deployed and supplied by air further to the east to prevent the enemy attempting an outflanking counter-stroke. The objectives were more or less unchanged from the previous attacks which had failed so humiliatingly – what would be different this time were the new tactics Bill had devised, notably the extensive use of air supply and the concept of the 'admin box'. (After the war Mountbatten would claim credit for being the originator of the 'administrative box' but everyone in the 14th Army knew that it was Bill who was responsible; Mountbatten was the facilitator – endorsing Bill's strategy and making it possible by arranging sufficient resources, in particular aircraft.)

During November troop dispositions had been finalised. The 26th Indian Division, which had been holding the Arakan front through the monsoon, was withdrawn to Chittagong to be held in reserve. It was replaced by the 7th Indian Division under Major General Frank Messervy and the 5th Indian Division under Major General Harold Briggs – Bill knew both men well and had no doubts about their abilities as aggressive and energetic leaders. (Briggs had drawn up 'Five Commandments' which he insisted every man in his division learn by heart: the first was 'Be determined to kill every Jap you meet'.) A formation relatively new to the theatre, the 81st West African Division, largely made up of magnificent-looking warriors recruited from Nigeria, the Gambia, Sierra Leone and the Gold Coast, had been training hard in the jungle and was charged with guarding the flank.

The first task of the 81st West African Division was to build a 75-mile jeep track into their operating area and temporary airstrips along the river bank. Sappers, meanwhile, converted a narrow, winding footpath across the mountains at the Ngakyedauk Pass, five miles north of the Maungdaw–Buthidaung road, into a road capable of taking wheeled transport, tanks and medium artillery – a considerable engineering achievement – enabling supplies to be delivered to the 7th Division, on the east side of the mountains. Troops struggling to get their tongues around Ngakyedauk settled on calling it the 'Okey-doke Pass'.

Intelligence indicated the Japanese forces in Arakan amounted to little more than a division, mostly centred around the Maungdaw–Buthidaung road and further south protecting Akyab island. With three divisions committed and one in close reserve, Bill had great numerical superiority over the enemy, but that was how he wanted it. 'I had no intention, if I could avoid it,' he wrote, 'of pitting my army division for division against the Japanese on their own ground. I hoped that the Arakan campaign would be the first step towards building up a tradition of success, and I did not intend to take more risks than I had to at this early stage.'[2]

The main objective was a formidable jungle fortress that the Japanese had constructed during the monsoon in the hills around the tunnels on the Maungdaw–Buthidaung road and in two great natural buttresses, Razabil and Letwedet, on each side of the mountain range. They had burrowed deep underground to create living accommodation and store rooms with passages connecting innumerable machine-gun posts and strong points. They called it 'The Golden Fortress'. A captured Order of the Day signed by one of the Japanese commanders indicated its importance: 'The Mayu range is a fortress given to us by Heaven, to furnish us with defences, obstructions and concealments, with water, with quarters, with supplies of building materials unlimited. Indeed a thing of immense value. Its mountains and rivers will shortly become an unforgettable new battleground.'

Through December the 5th and 7th Divisions moved steadily south down the Mayu peninsula – the 5th on the coastal strip and the 7th on the east side of the mountains – and, by early January, Briggs' division had captured Maungdaw. Bill visited the town the day after it had been captured and was depressed by the decrepit state of the port. Apart from extensive damage caused by bombing and artillery, the dock equipment was rusting and in very poor condition and the whole place was overgrown with jungle vegetation. (There were loofah vines everywhere; enough, Bill noted, to provide 'these useful bathroom adjuncts' for years.) He initially doubted if the place was capable of restoration, particularly as it was blighted by mines and booby traps, but he underestimated the capability of the 5th Division engineers, who got the port open in a matter of days.

In mid-January, Bill made a tour of the Arakan front, flying from Comilla to a newly constructed forward airstrip in his personal twin-engined Avro Anson with an escort of four Hurricane fighters. A tragedy occurred shortly after he had landed. While the Hurricanes were still circling above, one of the pilots mistakenly let off a burst of machine-gun fire into the aircraft in front of him, which crashed, killing the pilot. The pilot who died was a best friend of the man who had caused his death. It was a tragic accident probably caused, Bill thought, by the strain that so many young pilots were under; it seemed the pilot had pressed the gun button in his cockpit instead of the camera button.

Bill was deeply impressed by the courage of the pilots at a time when huge formations of Japanese Zero fighters, sometimes up to 100 strong, were being regularly engaged by a handful of Spitfires. During his visit, Bill called in on a reconnaissance squadron of the Indian Air Force at the moment when it had been reported that a patrol of Hurricanes had just been been shot down. The squadron leader, a Sikh and an old friend of Bill's, immediately led the next patrol himself. Bill heard his friend had an unusual method of disciplining his pilots: if one of them made a bad landing, the squadron leader would take him behind a *basha* and beat him up. Bill did not know if it was true, but the squadron's morale was certainly unaffected.

During Bill's discussions with Christison and his commanders in Arakan, there was a consensus that the Japanese were moving reinforcements into the area in preparation for a counter-offensive. Captured documents indicated that a formation of the Indian National Army was close to the front on the east side of the mountains, possibly indicating the enemy's intention to advance into India. (The INA was a renegade force, led by Subhas Chandra Bose and made up of Indian expatriate volunteers and prisoners of war, which fought alongside the Japanese in the hope of overthrowing the British Raj. Encouraged by Bose, the Japanese believed that its presence in an invading force would encourage the local population to rise up against the British in the event of an invasion of India.) Bill thought that the counter-offensive would almost certainly begin with an outflanking attack to the east of the 7th Division and intelligence outposts were ordered to be alert to the possibility of enemy troop movements. On his way back to Comilla, Bill stopped at Chittagong to warn Major General Cyril Lomax, commander of the 26th Division, the reserve troops, that they were likely to be needed soon, probably in a hurry.

On 26 January, the battle for Arakan began in earnest when Christison ordered the 5th Division to launch a frontal attack on the intimidating defences of the Razabil buttress. Bill was not happy: it was precisely the strategy that he exhorted his commanders not to follow and which had signally failed a year earlier against the same position, although he chose not to interfere. He firmly believed his job as army commander was to identify the aims and objectives of the operation and then let his subordinate commanders work out how to achieve them, without him constantly looking over their shoulders. (If Bill was frustrated by Briggs' tactics, there is no indication of it in *Defeat Into Victory*; he merely says he expected the operation to be tough and 'it was'.)

The assault opened with a massive aerial pounding by American bombers and RAF dive bombers. As the field artillery opened up, M3 Lee tanks of the 25th Dragoons, which had been moved into Arakan in great secrecy, roared forward, followed by the infantry with fixed bayonets. As described by Bill in *Defeat Into Victory* it was an impressive and heroic sight, but it was also ultimately pointless. After five days of intense fighting, 5th Division casualties were rising alarmingly and little impression had been made on the massive log bunkers, within which the enemy appeared to be impregnable. 'Bunkers, wire, bamboo stakes and withering fire had brought our ambitious offensive to a halt,' the division's official historian noted despondently.[3]

Christison decided to switch the focus of his attack to the other side of the mountains and ordered the tanks, artillery and most of a brigade from the 5th Division to cross the Okey-doke Pass and join the 7th Division to assist in the capture on Buthidaung, as a prelude to the assault on Letwedet. Unlike Briggs, Messervy, the commander of 7th Division, was completely in accord with Bill's views about how to fight the Japanese. 'We want to be much more subtle and tricky,' he told his officers. 'We must be constantly "pulling a fast one" on the little yellow blighter – outwit him, out-think him, out fight him and lick him ... All experience in the Arakan has demonstrated the utter futility of a formal infantry attack supported by artillery concentrations or barrage against Japanese organised jungle positions ... The right answer to capturing these Japanese positions and killing Japanese in this type of country, and in these tactical circumstances, is quite simple. It is infiltration and encirclement ...'[4]

Messervy's plan for seizing Buthidaung involved both. He intended to deploy a brigade to cut the Maungdaw–Buthidaung road and create a corridor for a second brigade to attack the town, while a third brigade swept round to the east to cut off the garrison and prevent reinforcements being brought up. He never had the opportunity to test the strategy; his assault was due to begin on 7 February, by which time he was fully engaged beating back the Japanese counter-attack.

On 2 February, Bill had a long talk with General Giffard, who had stopped at Comilla on his way to visiting the front. They discussed the likelihood of an enemy counter-offensive. If Bill had to make use of his reserve division, Giffard promised to replace it with the 36th British Division, currently in Calcutta. After Giffard had left (he had a narrow escape when his convoy was shot up by Japanese Zeros as it was crossing Okey-doke Pass) Bill called a meeting of his senior staff officers to finalise the complicated plans for supplying a fighting division by air with everything it needed, from toilet paper to ammunition, from malaria pills to tins of bully beef. A pre-arranged packing programme was put into operation and the packers were ordered to stand by to be ready to work round the clock. By this time, a well-stocked 'administrative box', with supply depots, ammunition dumps, vehicle parks and a field hospital, had been established at the point where the Okey-doke Pass debouched into the valley on the east side of the mountains in an area of dried-up paddy fields about 1,200 yards square, surrounded by wooded hills.

Bill could have been forgiven for assuming he had made all the necessary preparations and so he was shocked when he returned to his headquarters on 4 February after the flame-thrower demonstration and learned that the Japanese had advanced secretly through the jungle, fallen on the rear of Messervy's division and were within two or three miles of the Okey-doke Pass and the 'admin box' before anyone knew they were on the move. He telephoned Christison to find out what was going on but Christison could tell him little other than that the situation was still confused and that the 7th Division was engaged in heavy fighting near Taung Bazar. Bill then called a meeting with his senior staff officers. He was, as always in a crisis, completely unflustered. He told them briefly what had happened and reminded them that things were rarely as bad, or as good, as they appeared when first reported.

Actually, things were quite as bad. The Japanese offensive in Arakan was code-named Operation Ha-Go ('headlong attack'). Its objective was to destroy 15 Corps and draw 14th Army reserves away from the central front, where the main offensive, Operation U-Go, was to be launched four weeks later with the aim of annihilating the remainder of the 14th Army. Thirty thousand troops, divided into three columns, were committed to Ha-Go. The main strike force of 7,000 men, under a Colonel Tanahashi, was to infiltrate between the flanks of the 7th Indian Division and the 81st West African Division and encircle the village of Taung Bazar, where a brigade of the 7th Division was based.

When Taung Bazar had been captured, Tanahashi's force was to drive south to attack the rear of 7th Division and the 'administrative box'. A second force was to cross the Mayu mountains and block the road to Maungdaw to isolate the 5th Division, while a third force attacked the 7th Division from the south.

Operation Ha-Go was expected to be successfully completed within ten days, but the Japanese fatally underestimated their enemy. They confidently expected both divisions, once surrounded, to withdraw in confusion in an attempt to protect their lines of communication. The last thing they expected was for their enemy to stand and fight, as Lieutenant General Sakurai Tokutaro, commander of the Arakan offensive, made clear in an order of the day: 'As they [the enemy] have previously suffered defeat, should a portion of them waver, the whole of them will get confused and victory is certain.'[5]

At 2300 on 3 February, 'Tanahashi Force' began advancing secretly through the jungle around Messervy's division. As dawn was breaking on the morning of 4 February, howling Japanese troops emerged through the swirling mist and fell on the unsuspecting 7th Division men dug in around Taung Bazar. At his headquarters in Comilla, Bill was kept abreast of developments almost minute by minute, although the situation remained confused. The only cheering news of the day, particularly as he knew that the enemy's supply arrangements were always problematic, was a report that a Japanese supply column had been discovered, its escort destroyed and large

quantities of ammunition and rice, along with a complete field ambulance, captured.

On 5 February, with intelligence indicating the Japanese were in
far greater strength than originally envisaged and fighting continuing on several fronts, Bill ordered the 26th Division into the fray.
Later that day General Giffard flew in from Delhi and joined Bill at
his headquarters. 'There were some commanders-in-chief I would
not have welcomed at such a moment,' Bill wrote, discreetly declin-
ing to mention any names, 'but General Giffard had the invaluable
knack of not interfering, yet making one feel that he was there,
calm, helpful, and understanding, if required.'[6]

Early next morning Bill flew to Chittagong in his Anson to watch
the last of the 26th Division move out to the front. They were, he
noted, 'workmanlike and cheerful'. When he returned to Comilla,
he learned that the Japanese had cut the lines of communication to
the 5th Division, the 7th Division headquarters had been overrun
and Frank Messervy had narrowly escaped with his life. Japanese
troops had launched attack after attack on the headquarters and
only been repulsed after savage hand-to-hand fighting around the
camouflaged tents and dug-outs. When the enemy brought up mortars Messervy judged his situation to be untenable and ordered his
staff to fight their way back through the Japanese lines to the 'administrative box'. After supervising the destruction of documents,
ciphers and equipment, Messervy, a grenade in one hand, led the
last group out along the bed of a *chaung*. (He must have had a
sense of déjà vu – in 1942, commanding the 7th Armoured Division
in North Africa, his headquarters had been overrun by the Afrika
Corps. That time he was taken prisoner but ripped off his insignia and escaped.) Although there had been heavy casualties in the
fighting, Messervy had his headquarters up and running again and
was in control of his division from within the box later that same
evening.

By 8 April the Japanese had driven a wedge between the 5th and
7th Divisions by cutting the Okey-doke Pass, effectively surround-
ing 7th Division. A day later, the 5th Division was also cut off. In
Tokyo the news was received with triumphant headlines: 'The
British Are Trapped', 'The British In Full Flight', 'New British
Army Destroyed In One Thrust'. Japanese radio stations confidently

informed their listeners that 'the March on Delhi' had begun and 'Tokyo Rose',[7] broadcasting in her silky voice to American servicemen in the Pacific, advised them to go home as 'the war in Burma is all over'.

Not only was it not over, it was only just beginning. Japanese commanders confidently anticipated the Allies would do what they had always done in such situations – yield their position, fight their way out and retreat. They were shocked to discover soon after Ha-Go was launched that the enemy was standing firm – and not only were they standing firm but they were fighting with a confidence and steely resolution which took the Japanese completely by surprise.

Bill had switched the whole of the 7th Division on to air supply two days previously. Ten days' rations for 40,000 men had already been pre-packed and waited at airstrips ready to go. When the first flight of heavily laden Dakotas of the joint USAAF/RAF Troop Carrier Command was forced to turn back by Japanese fighters, the commanding officer, Brigadier General William Old, a veteran of 'the Hump' airlift, personally took the pilot's seat to lead the next mission, which got through and dropped the first supplies to the beleaguered division. Old returned with his aircraft pitted by shell splinters. Thereafter operations continued day and night, by the light of flares, with ground crews reloading aircraft as soon as they touched down and air crews taking off again as soon as their Dakotas had been loaded and refuelled.

The first days of the airlift were marked by the biggest aerial dogfights yet seen in Burma as Japanese pilots pulled out all the stops to prevent supplies reaching their enemy. But the RAF's newly arrived Spitfires proved more than a match for the Zeros and Tojos of the Imperial Japanese Air Force: 65 Japanese fighters were shot down for the loss of 13 Spitfires and within days enemy fighters virtually disappeared from the sky. Now relatively unmolested, the Dakotas, flown by air crews from Britain, America, Australia, Canada, New Zealand, South Africa and India, got on with their work. Hundreds of tons of food, water, ammunition, weapons, fuel, uniforms, boots, cigarettes, beer and copies of the *SEAC* daily newspaper were heaved out of aircraft over the target areas by volunteer 'kickers-out' and floated down on 'parajutes' into the besieged boxes. More than

700 sorties would eventually carry some 1,600 tons of supplies into battle.

Bill claimed his single contribution to the effort was to gently suggest to Alf Snelling that it might be a good idea to include a case of rum in every fourth or fifth consignment to encourage the men to search for deliveries dropped in the jungle off target. Snelling apparently gave him the 'slightly pitying look professionals reserve for amateurs' and announced that he had *already* given orders for a case of rum to be included in *every* load. Thereafter, Bill let him get on with it, which he did.

On the day 'Tokyo Rose' boasted the war was over, Bill flew to 15 Corps headquarters to confer with Christison. The focus of the battle, and the most ferocious fighting, centred around the 'admin box', which the Japanese knew they had to capture, not least to re-supply their own troops. It was, in truth, a nightmare to defend. It had never been equipped to beat off an onslaught by thousands of troops, it was surrounded by hills occupied by the enemy and was crowded with fuel and ammunition dumps, hundreds of mules and trucks and administrative troops. The Japanese poured mortar and artillery shells into the box from the hills, yet the defenders held firm. Although the great majority of the garrison was made up of administrative troops, all of them had received basic weapon training at Bill's insistence and so every man within the 'box' became a fighting soldier – orderlies, cooks and clerks all grabbed weapons and fought like veteran infantry. Even personnel from the Officers' Shop and the Mule Company were pressed into service to man the perimeter.

The battle around the 'box' raged night and day for 20 days. Time and again the perimeter was breached and restored. Enemy shelling hit an ammunition dump which exploded and burned for three days, covering the area with thick black smoke. On one pitch-black night, several hundred Japanese soldiers infiltrated the 'box' and overran the main dressing station, where surgeons were operating on the wounded. Thirty-one helpless patients lying on stretchers were bayoneted to death and four doctors were lined up and shot. Such outrages, Bill noted, only served to stiffen the resolve of the men.

Elsewhere the 26th Division – the 'hammer' which was to smash the enemy against the 'anvil' of the 'admin box' – was making steady progress south, despite determined opposition. Elements of the 5th Division were fighting to open the Okey-doke Pass and 7th Division was sending out aggressive patrols to cut the enemy's lines of communication. All the while, the Japanese supply position was becoming more and more critical. Bill knew that time was not on the enemy's side – intelligence reports indicated that the enemy had only been supplied with sufficient rations and ammunition for ten days. By 13 February, he was quietly confident that the Japanese would be defeated – the first victory for the Allies in Burma and the first major test for the 14th Army. On the nights of 14 and 16 February the Japanese sent three battalions, yelling and screaming, into the attack. All were beaten back.

The enemy did succeed in capturing a height within the 'box' known as Company C Hill which overlooked the new location of the hospital, but a company of the West Yorkshire Regiment, supported by tanks from the 25th Dragoons, rapidly retook the position using bayonets to finish off the last of what Bill usually called 'the little yellow bastards'. By 21 February the strength of Tanahashi Force had been reduced to 400 men, most of them casualties.

Bill spent much of his time shuttling between Comilla and 15 Corps headquarters, and visiting the troops at the front. He was greatly heartened by the new fighting spirit that was evident everywhere. The long months of training in India had more than paid off: the men were stronger in body and soul, more cheerful and optimistic, confident in themselves and their comrades, no longer terrified of either the jungle or the enemy. He savoured one story of a pilot who had seen a hard-pressed artillery battery in the 'box' desperately loosing off rounds as the enemy closed to within 400 yards. A wireless signal was sent asking if they were OK. 'Fine', was the answer, 'but drop us a hundred bayonets.'

Organisation of the air supply was so sophisticated that recipients rarely had to wait more than a day or so for special orders to be delivered, whether it was a particular drug needed by the dressing station, or an extra large pair of boots, or spare parts for a weapon, or items as mundane as typewriter ribbons and replacement spectacles. When the 7th Division headquarters was obliged to withdraw into the 'box', most of the staff had to leave behind personal items like spare clothes, razors, toothbrushes and the like. Everything was replaced by air within 48 hours – and would have arrived sooner had not the first delivery been dropped to the Japanese by mistake. Frank Messervy lost his cap, with its distinctive red band, but it turned up several weeks later being worn by a Japanese soldier captured in an ambush and was duly returned to its rightful owner.

The Arakan campaign was the first time Messervy had held a command under Bill, although they had met earlier in the war in Eritrea. 'He was a most wonderful chap, such a warm person, always ready to help. Encouragement was his way of getting things done. He would never push. He wouldn't say, "Why the hell are you spread out like this?" He would say, "Look here, you seem to be very spread out." He wouldn't interfere, he would discuss things with you and make suggestions and then leave it up to you. It was the frankness of his approach that was so inspiring. I never saw him cross, never. I never saw him edgy. All the men loved him and they all had complete confidence in him. When he addressed the troops, whether they were Gurkha or Indian or British, his approach was just right. He spoke to them individually.'[8] Messervy never forgot an occasion when Bill answered the telephone at 7th Division head-quarters, instead of one of his staff officers, and someone at the other end of the line shouted: 'I've got a general here wants to talk to some bloody Chinaman I believe, name of Slim.' Bill was completely unbothered. 'Well, actually I'm that chap,' he replied calmly. 'And I'm the commander of the 14th Army.'

Bill's ability to remain calm, whether in the face of discourtesy or under intense stress in the heat of battle, was one of his great strengths. Throughout the Arakan battle he was juggling with the plans for three other overlapping campaigns, all of which would be conducted more or less simultaneously along a 700-mile front: Stilwell's drive into northern Burma with Chinese troops, the second Chindit expedition and the proposed offensive by 4 Corps on the central front. It meant frequent trips to visit Lieutenant General Geoffrey Scoones, commander of the 4th Corps, at his headquarters in Imphal, an hour's flight from Comilla in decent weather. The demands of overseeing all these operations tested Bill's capacity to the limit, but if he felt any strain from the weight of his many responsibilities he never showed it.

A constant concern was finding sufficient aircraft to meet the increasing supply requirements in Arakan and that concern became a full-blown crisis as the clock ticked down to the start of Wingate's second expedition, which was to operate behind Japanese lines in support of Stilwell's NCAC troops. Wingate needed the Dakotas of No. 1 Air Commando to tow the gliders which would carry the first airborne wave of Chindits into Burma – the same Dakotas that were already fully stretched maintaining the besieged troops in Arakan. By that stage air supply was critical to success or failure in Arakan – the whole of the 7th Division was being maintained by air, as was the 81st West African Division, most of the 26th Division and part of the 5th Division – in total around 180,000 troops. Without sufficient numbers of aircraft to maintain those troops, defeat was almost inevitable. At the same time, Wingate's expedition was an important component of the overall offensive and could not be postponed: one brigade had already entered Burma on foot on 5 February; three further brigades were due to fly in on gliders and join them on the nights of 5 and 6 March. It required the influence of the Supreme Commander to solve the problem: with some difficulty Mountbatten persuaded the Americans to release 25 C-46 Commandos from 'the Hump' for three weeks to enable the Dakotas to be made available for the Chindits.

After nearly three weeks of continuous fighting, during which none of 15 Corps positions had been captured and none had shown an inclination to retreat, the Japanese accepted defeat and withdrew, hotly pursued by the triumphant Allied troops, unaccustomed to the novel scent of victory in their nostrils. By then some 5,000 of the original Japanese invasion force had been killed or wounded; 500 bodies were counted around the perimeter of the 'box' alone and many more lay undiscovered in the jungle.

It was, unequivocally, a triumph for the 14th Army and Mountbatten offered his unstinting congratulations in an order of the day: 'You have given the Japanese a crack they will remember. They are learning that, just as wars cannot be won by sudden treacherous assaults, so, too, battles are not decided by surprise attacks.

'Three weeks ago the enemy sent a large and formidable force through the jungle to cut your lines of communication and attack you in the rear.

'They launched a major offensive in Arakan in the hope of defeating you and sweeping on into India.

'You have met the onslaught with courage, confidence and resolution.

'Many of you were cut off and encircled, dependent on supplies dropped from the air. But everyone stood firm, inspired and strengthened by the knowledge that powerful support was at hand from land, sea and air.

'Now, after bitter fighting in the jungle and the skies, the Japanese attack has been smashed.

'The enemy which infiltrated into your rear has been destroyed or scattered. The threatened passes are clear, the roads are open.

'You have gained a complete victory.'

Be that as it may, fighting continued for several more weeks. As soon as Okey-doke Pass had been reopened on 24 February, Christison gave orders for the offensive against Buthidaung to be resumed while the caves and crannies of the Mayu mountains were searched for enemy survivors. The advance was hampered by problems with air supply when the aircraft borrowed from 'the Hump' had to be returned, but Buthidaung fell on 11 March after a massive artillery bombardment – at one point 7,000 shells were fired in ten minutes – reduced the village to a smoking ruin. The enemy's last desperate throw of the dice came on 25 March, when a suicide force of some 400 men was infiltrated into the area of the 'administrative box'. None made it out alive.

By the end of March both Letwedet and Razabil – the bastions on each side of the mountain fortress – were in the 14th Army's hands and a savage battle was under way for the final redoubt – the tunnels. The western end was secured after a tank fired a shell directly into the mouth of the tunnel and blew up an ammunition dump, with spectacular effect. At the eastern end it took several assaults by a battalion of the Gloucestershire Regiment to shift the enemy but by 6 April they had succeeded. The Japanese made one last stand on a hill known as Point 551, overlooking the eastern end of the Maungdaw–Buthidaung road. It was finally captured by the 26th

Division, after three separate attempts and the most savage fighting of the whole battle, on 3 May.

Bill was pleased that the honour of the final strike fell to Cyril Lomax and his 26th Division, because it was in the the same area, almost exactly a year earlier, that his plans to ensnare the enemy in a 'box' had fallen apart. It was the first time a battle had been won in Burma on the same spot that it had previously been lost, although it was a phenomenon that would be repeated in the coming months. 'It always gave me especial satisfaction,' Bill noted. 'Revenge *is* sweet.'

The second Arakan campaign was not won without cost – 15 Corps casualties numbered 3,506 – but it was a turning point, an essential victory which boosted the morale of the whole 14th Army and proved beyond any doubt that the Japanese were far from invincible. For Bill it was a personal and tactical triumph: his training regimen had proved effective, as had his strategy for beating the enemy. His foresight in quickly setting in motion the air supply arrangements played a significant role, as did his ability to recover from the surprise of the initial Japanese onslaught by calling up his reserves without delay. Most importantly, as Mountbatten pointed out, a virtually new technique in warfare had been evolved, tested and vindicated.

Bill could not conceal his modest pride when he came to sum up the campaign in *Defeat Into Victory* many years later: 'This Arakan battle, judged by the size of the forces engaged, was not of great magnitude, but it was, nevertheless, one of the historic successes of British arms. It was the turning point of the Burma campaign. For the first time a British force had met, held, and decisively defeated a major Japanese attack, and followed this up by driving the enemy out of the strongest possible natural positions that they had been preparing for months and were determined to hold at all costs. British and Indian soldiers had proved themselves, man for man, the masters of the best the Japanese could bring against them. The R.A.F. had met and driven from the sky superior numbers of the Japanese Air Force equipped with their latest fighters. It was a victory, a victory about which there could be no argument, and its effect, not only on the troops engaged but on the whole Fourteenth Army, was immense. The legend of Japanese invincibility in the jungle, so long fostered by so many who should have known better, was smashed. I could not help feeling an especial pride that it had been my old 15 Corps that had done it.'⁹

After the victory a message was read to the troops from the Prime Minister to say that he was closely watching events on their front. 'All I can say,' an exasperated private soldier remarked, 'is that he ain't watching our perishin' rear close enough.'

14

The Chindits

If Lieutenant General Kawabe Masakazu, commander of the Burma Area Army, had hoped to convince Bill that the Arakan offensive was the main Japanese thrust and thus persuade him to reduce his defences on the front where Kawabe actually planned to strike, he was to be disappointed. It was true Bill committed five divisions to the Arakan battle, but he only did so to ensure victory: he had known since mid-January that the major Japanese offensive would be directed against 4 Corps in north-east India.

All the signs were there: increased enemy activity all along the front; intelligence reports indicating that strong reinforcements were being brought into the area; aerial reconnaissance reporting roads being built from central Burma towards the Chindwin river and large numbers of camouflaged rafts, for ferrying troops, had been spotted on the river bank; herds of cattle, presumably rations on the hoof, were being driven north; documents taken from a dead Japanese soldier killed in an ambush on 27 January indicated the presence of an entirely new division which had joined the two already facing 4 Corps. Bill was also able to read the enemy's radio traffic with the invaluable help of Ultra.[1] By the end of January it looked as if the strength of Kawabe's army had almost doubled. 'It would be unlike the Japanese,' Bill noted drily, 'to reinforce anywhere on that scale unless they intended seriously to attack.'[2]

Up until January, it had been Bill's intention that 4 Corps would seize the initiative, cross into Burma and engage the Japanese forces on the other side of the Chindwin. Since the end of the 1943 monsoon, two divisions of 4 Corps had been deployed along the India/Burma border with orders to mount aggressive patrols to expand the territory under Allied control on the Burmese side of the border. They had pushed forward to the Kabaw valley, the unloved burial ground of so many during the retreat, and to the Chin hills 150 miles south of Imphal, where the 17th Division, at the end of a long and precarious line of communication, had been fighting a bitter and bloody little private war, with each side setting ambushes, mounting raids, attacking and counter-attacking almost in turn. These two divisions, the 17th and the 20th, had been earmarked for the proposed offensive, but increasingly clear evidence of the enemy's intentions forced Bill to rethink his plans: an army being prepared for an offensive was in the worst position, both physically and psychologically, to mount a defence.

At a crucial meeting at 4 Corps headquarters in Imphal, Bill considered his options with Lieutenant General Scoones, the corps commander, and his intelligence staff. Scoones, like Bill, had a reputation for clear thinking and composure under pressure. It was thought the Japanese offensive was likely to be launched on 15 March with four divisions and the objective of capturing Imphal and 4 Corps' supply base at the Dimapur railhead, thus cutting the lifeline to the Chinese forces on the northern front, which were supplied through the base. Intelligence indicated that the relative strength of the opposing armies was about equal in terms of infantry, although the Japanese had a division in reserve which they could call upon. But 4 Corps had a distinct advantage in artillery and armour – its M3 Lee tanks outmatched anything the Japanese could bring up – and total air superiority. Seven RAF squadrons were available to 4 Corps and they had virtually swept enemy aircraft from the sky.

Bill considered he had three possible courses of action. He could forestall the expected offensive by crossing the Chindwin and attacking first, which neatly subscribed to his philosophy, learned in the Sudan, of always choosing the boldest alternative. But apart from undoubtedly being 'bold' it had little to recommend it: 4 Corps would be fighting superior numbers with its back to a great river and totally reliant on precarious lines of communication stretching back 120 miles across the worst terrain in the world. Bill thought that an attempt to beat the Japanese to the punch, even if successful, was unlikely to produce a decisive result, which was what he wanted.

The second option was to stand and fight, to concentrate the corps along the line of the Chindwin and attempt to destroy the Japanese as they crossed the river. But the problems of supply would remain and make his force vulnerable to the enemy's outflanking tactics.

The third course was to withdraw the forward divisions back to the Imphal plain and fight the battle on ground of his own choosing. The primary attraction was that the enemy's lines of communication, rather than his own, would be dangerously stretched, particularly since the calendar would put the Japanese under intense pressure – once the monsoon started their supply lines would become extremely unpredictable. The downside was that the operation would inevitably begin with a withdrawal and the abandonment of hard-won territory, with inevitable consequences for morale. And a commander who orders a withdrawal, even for the best of reasons, lays himself open to back-biting, both from his superiors and politicians far from the battlefield. (There were plenty of senior officers visiting 14th Army headquarters who advised Bill that the simplest way to beat the Japanese was to 'fling' a couple of divisions across the Chindwin.)

After a discussion with Scoones about the merits and demerits of the three alternative plans, both men independently came to the same conclusion – to fight the battle on the great plain surrounding Imphal, where the relatively flat ground would enable them to use tanks and aircraft to best effect. Bill admitted he was concerned about the effect on morale, but the prospect of being able to deal a crippling blow to the enemy before re-entering Burma was too tempting to pass up. The troops were generally in fine fighting spirit and he felt sure morale would soon recover once the battle was joined. He was confident, too, that if commanders explained to the men what was happening, they would understand why they were being asked to cede ground won at the cost of so much blood and toil. (In fact it did not become a problem because the men were confident in his judgement; they knew Uncle Bill well enough by then to recognise he would not ask them to cede territory without good reason.)

Bill also believed that the initial withdrawal would convince the Japanese that the Allies had no stomach for a fight and encourage them to press forward, regardless of the logistical risks, in the hope of a swift and easy victory. Arrangements were immediately put in hand to improve the defences of the hundreds of *basha* camps, ordnance depots, supply dumps, administrative units and hospitals that had sprung up across the 600 square miles of the plain in preparation for the 4 Corps offensive. Almost every unit was obliged to move, to be concentrated into fortified 'boxes' capable of all-round defence and stocked with sufficient ammunition and supplies to withstand a lengthy siege. Non-combatants and labour units were evacuated to reduce the ration scale and training for the remaining administrative troops was intensified.

Throughout this period of intense planning, Orde Wingate remained a major distraction for Bill. With the connivance of Mountbatten, who initially thought Wingate 'the cat's whiskers',[3] the Chindit leader had contrived to build the Long-Range Penetration Group (now called, for cover purposes, the 3rd Indian Division, or Special Force) into a formidable body with a strength of more than two divisions, complex command and control staff and his own 'private' air force – the American No. 1 Air Commando equipped with fighters, light bombers, transport aircraft, gliders and Sikorsky helicopters being deployed for the first time in anger. Bill was very displeased to discover, after the event, that Wingate had been 'given' 70th British Division, which had been part of his 15 Corps at Ranchi and was the only British formation trained in jungle warfare. Bill would have objected strongly had he been consulted, but he was not. His strong view was that the division's effectiveness was greatly weakened by being broken up and employed on Special Force operations.

When Bill invited Wingate to Comilla to discuss Operation Thursday – the code name for the planned Chindit incursion behind enemy lines in central Burma in coordination with the 4 Corps offensive – he was disconcerted to discover that Wingate's views had progressed considerably since the first Chindit expedition. It appeared he had abandoned the concept of small, lightly equipped columns harassing the enemy and cutting communications behind the lines in favour of a much larger penetrating force setting up strongholds and fighting pitched battles in the enemy's rear. He envisaged regaining control of Burma via a series of 'stepping stones', with the Chindits seizing one city after another and conventional forces following behind to consolidate the gains. Bill enjoyed talking strategy and tactics with Wingate, but thought he

was 'strangely naïve' when it came to fighting the Japanese. Bill did
not believe for a minute that the Japanese would be intimidated
into a withdrawal by Wingate's plan; in addition, the Chindits were
neither trained nor equipped for fighting set-piece battles and in
any case there were not enough aircraft to lift his existing force, let
alone a much larger one.

At a strained meeting in Bill's office on 3 December, Wingate was
impervious to any arguments against his plans and demanded he
be given another division – the 26th Indian. Bill refused to countenance the idea since the 26th Indian Division was his only reserve.
Wingate became threatening and said that, while he held a personal
loyalty towards Bill as his immediate commander, he had a higher
loyalty he was required to consider. Bill knew what he was talking
about – he had heard stories about Wingate having a direct line to
Churchill – but nevertheless he asked Wingate to whom he owed
this higher loyalty. 'To the Prime Minister of England,' Wingate
replied portentously, 'and to the President of the United States.' At
this, one of the staff officers present noted, 'everyone stared somewhat self-consciously into space'.[4] Wingate went on to warn Bill
that both had asked to be informed if any of his [Wingate's] superiors attempted to thwart his plans. He very much regretted that
this was one such occasion and thus he felt obliged to report the
fact to the Prime Minister, regardless of whatever unfortunate ramifications might fall on Bill's head as a result. Bill remained completely unruffled. He simply passed a signal pad across his desk and
told Wingate to go ahead and write whatever message he liked to
London. Wingate got up without another word and stalked out of
the room.

Bill neither knew if Wingate sent a message to the Prime Minister
(he didn't), nor did he care. The incident was not mentioned when
discussions resumed the following day and Wingate did not pursue
his demand for another division although he continued to make difficulties, now insisting he had not been allocated sufficient aircraft,
since only two of his brigades could be flown in and the third would
have to march. In vain did Bill insist that there were simply no more
aircraft available without cancelling other operations, which he was
not prepared to do. At the end of the day Wingate peremptorily
announced that he could not accept the orders Bill had drafted. It

was Bill's turn to threaten. He warned Wingate he had never had a subordinate commander refuse an order but if one did he knew what to do – clearly implying the prospect of a court martial. He advised Wingate to sleep on his decision and return to his office at ten o'clock. General Giffard was visiting 14th Army HQ at the time and, anticipating trouble with Wingate, Bill asked him to be present in his office when Wingate arrived next morning. As it happened, Giffard was not needed. A slightly subdued Wingate showed up on time, Bill passed his signed orders across the desk and Wingate accepted them without comment.

Between November 1943 and January 1944, Bill had no fewer than 14 meetings with the crotchety Wingate in an attempt to thrash out final plans for Operation Thursday, all this while there was a risk that Wingate would make good his threat to contact the Prime Minister directly to complain about the way he was being treated. The consequences could have been calamitous, as Lieutenant General Sir Henry Pownall, Chief of Staff to the Supreme Commander, noted in his diary on 18 January 1944: 'This will bring the P.M. straight down onto Giffard and Slim, for he has already expressed his doubts as to the quality of the military advice that Mountbatten has been receiving. He will jump at any chance of breaking another general or two and will then push very hard, and maybe successfully, to get Wingate installed as commander of 14th Army – which would be a most dangerous affair. Wingate may (or may not) be all right as a specialist but he simply hasn't the knowledge or the balance to be in high army command. The kinship of madness to genius might easily be disastrous and many good men would lose their lives on futile endeavours and harebrained schemes.'[5] (Pownall never anticipated his diaries being published and thus was remarkably candid about his colleagues: he described Wingate as a 'nasty bit of work' and 'quite a bit mad'.)

Wingate remained stubbornly insistent that special forces held the key to defeating the Japanese by recapturing Burma from within and nothing Bill, or anyone else, could say would dissuade him. On 19 January, Bill had another trying meeting with him, at Ranchi, at which he recalled Wingate became 'uncomfortably angry' when one of those present teased him about his new general's red hat. At this meeting Bill agreed in principle to release four battalions from

his reserve division to garrison the Chindit strongholds, but only if
the strategic circumstances allowed it. Wingate claimed he left the
meeting with the firm impression that the battalions were his to call
upon whenever he needed and when, a week later, he discovered
this was not the case, he fired off furious letters to both Giffard and
Mountbatten threatening to resign and accusing Bill, quite unfairly,
of a lack of commitment to the Chindit operation.

Giffard, ordered by Mountbatten to solve the problem, thought
he had agreed a compromise with the Chindit leader, but Wingate
continued to badger Bill to honour his 'promise', a promise Bill had
never made. That he continued to handle Wingate with tact and
courtesy throughout this period was a tribute to Bill's patience and
temperament. One half of his army was fighting desperate battles
in Arakan, the other half was preparing to receive a massive enemy
onslaught in Assam, yet Bill always made time to see Wingate, did
his best to accommodate and placate him, and never lost his temper.
Even when Wingate dispatched a memorandum to Mountbatten on
10 February in which he disdained the 14th Army, blithely suggesting it could 'hardly be expected ever to operate beyond the mountain barrier with its present establishment after the experience of the
past two years', Bill chose not to respond to the slight.

Partly as a result of Wingate making difficulties, detailed orders
for Operation Thursday were not issued until 28 February, more
than three weeks after the first Chindit brigade, with 4,000 men
and 50 mules, had entered Burma on foot with orders to set up
a stronghold behind the enemy lines. The plans were finalised,
General Christison observed acidly, only 'as far as any operation
involving Wingate could be'.[6] The Chindits were to be deployed
in northern Burma to support the advance of the Chinese NCAC
troops under Stilwell, who had been given orders by Mountbatten
to occupy a swathe of northern Burma to cover the building of the
new 'Burma Road' from Ledo in Assam. By February the NCAC
had made slow but steady progress, pushing the Japanese back with
a series of hooks and roadblocks around and behind the enemy. The
Chindits' orders were to assist the NCAC advance by cutting the
enemy's lines of communication and to 'inflict the greatest possible
damage and confusion on the enemy in North Burma'.[7]

On 3 March, Bill flew to NCAC headquarters at Taihpa Ga in

northern Burma to meet Stilwell and ensure all the arrangements were in place for Wingate's men, who were due to fly out within a few days. Stilwell was waiting to meet him at the airfield looking, as always, Bill thought, more like a duck hunter than a soldier in his windbreaker jacket devoid of badges of rank, campaign hat and leggings. Bill was always surprised, whenever he visited Vinegar Joe, by the unnecessarily primitive conditions in which he lived, sleeping on a cot with fly-blown blankets, using a packing crate for a desk, washing out of his helmet and eating from a mess tin. Bill assumed he wanted to convey the impression of being a tough, hard-bitten, fighting general, but, as that was exactly what he was, Bill wondered why he bothered.

The NCAC was due to launch its biggest attack against the Japanese 18th Division in the Hukawng valley the following day, supported by a recently arrived American special force unit which would become known as Merrill's Marauders, after its leader, Brigadier General Frank Merrill, a former military attaché in Tokyo before the war. Merrill had walked out of Burma with Stilwell in 1942 and actually owed his life to Bill, although he did not know it. During the retreat, Bill had restrained his Gurkha orderly from Tommy-gunning a group of soldiers in a jeep wearing unfamiliar helmets – they were Americans and Merrill was among them. Merrill's Marauders never numbered more than 3,000 men but they would eventually gain a reputation in Burma far out of proportion to their strength.

Stilwell seemed a little jumpy but Bill put it down to a commander's nerves on the eve of battle. When they got round to discussing Wingate's operation, the American reverted to his usual acerbic temperament. Stilwell didn't much care for Wingate, or his long-range penetration tactics. Since both men were eccentric, unconventional characters one might have expected them to be in sympathy with each other, but Stilwell was furious when the 1st Air Commando, an American unit, had initially been put under Wingate's command. He protested vigorously to Mountbatten that all American troops in the Burma theatre should be under his direct command; Mountbatten yielded but the damage had been done and Stilwell thereafter harboured a particular animus towards the Chindit leader.

After Bill had run through the plans, Stilwell started to express doubts about the value of Wingate's operation, but Bill cut him short by telling him to put himself in the position of the Japanese commander of the 18th Division. How happy would he be to find 10,000 enemy troops in his rear intent on cutting his communications? At last Stilwell grinned, looked over his steel-rimmed spectacles at Bill as he had done many times before, and said: 'That'll be fine if Wingate does it and stays there, if he goes in for real fighting and not shadow boxing like last time.'

Bill assured him there would be no 'shadow boxing' and promised that the enemy's lines of communication would be cut, and would remain cut, for some time. With that, Stilwell was satisfied and the two men parted amicably. Bill returned to Comilla and spent the following day at his headquarters. The next day, Sunday, 5 March, he flew to Lalaghat in Assam, where the first airborne wave of Wingate's Special Force was preparing to leave on what was at that time the biggest airborne operation of the war. (The brigade that had marched into Burma from Ledo was struggling through dense jungle with great difficulty but had by that date managed to cross the Chindwin with the help of inflatable boats brought in by gliders.)

As Bill's Anson circled the airstrip at Lalaghat he could see the gliders stretched out below with their Dakota tugs dispersed along the sides of the runway and a lot of activity around them as they were being loaded. He did not expect Wingate to be waiting to greet him as he landed and he wasn't, but Bill made his way to his temporary headquarters and found him in good heart. There had been no major problems with the preparations and the fly-in was due to begin shortly before dusk that evening, on time, with each Dakota towing two gliders in order to get the greatest number into the Chindits' operating area in the shortest possible time. The feasibility of a single aircraft towing two heavy-laden gliders had earlier been the subject of some debate, with opinion about equally divided, but after experiments both Wingate and Colonel Philip Cochran, the 33-year-old commander of 1st Air Commando, insisted it was perfectly possible. With this assurance, Bill and Air Marshal Jack Baldwin, commander of the 3rd Tactical Air Force, jointly approved the use of double tows, although Bill privately admitted to some misgivings.

With his nemesis, Oliver Leese (right) and Mountbatten at a conference in Delhi in May 1945. Leese tried to sack Bill; Mountbatten arranged the photo call to try to show they were still working together in harmony.

Senior officers of the Combined Headquarters at Comilla. Mountbatten is in the centre, front row, Bill is on his right. Between them, in a topi, is Bill's son, John.

At Rangoon in 1945 after the defeat of the Japanese. He is still carrying the carbine given to him by 'Vinegar Joe' Stilwell.

Sitting alongside Mountbatten in Singapore at the surrender of the Japanese in September 1945.

'Uncle Bill' as the troops remembered him.

Bill and Aileen relaxing in the garden of their home in Oxted after Bill
had been made CIGS.

In full dress uniform, as Governor-General of Australia, with Aileen at the
state opening of Parliament in Canberra.

Bill and Aileen at Government House in Canberra during the visit of the
Queen Mother to Australia in 1958.

With their new dog,
Suzie, on the steps of
Yarralumla House.

A portrait of the
Governor-General by
the Australian artist
Ivor Hele.

Bill at the investiture of the Victoria Cross in 1966 to Lance-Corporal Rambahadur Limbu for his courage rescuing wounded comrades under heavy fire in Sarawak. Limbu is showing his medal to his five-year-old son, Bhakta Bahadur, who recently retired as a major in the Gurkhas.

'We did it together.' Bill and Mountbatten at a Remembrance Day service in Whitehall.

Four sites widely dispersed in a circle around the town of Indaw, on the Mandalay–Myitkyina railway, had been selected as assembly areas. Given the code names Aberdeen, Piccadilly, Broadway and Chowringhee, they were chosen because they were in uninhabited areas far from roads, they offered flat, clear ground suitable for the landing of gliders and for building temporary airstrips, and there was water available nearby. Aberdeen was to be the assembly point for the brigade marching into Burma; Chowringhee was allocated to III Brigade, Broadway and Piccadilly were divided between 77 Brigade, under the command of Brigadier Mike Calvert. Immediately after landing, work would begin constructing crude airstrips for following Dakotas to bring in the remaining Chindits.

'Mad Mike' Calvert, a former army boxing champion, belonged to that curious breed of Englishmen who viewed war as a great game, made even more enjoyable by the fact that it was so dangerous. Born in India in 1913, he was sent to a minor public school in England, where he set out deliberately to break every rule in the book and as a result was beaten frequently. After being commissioned in the Royal Engineers he trained as a commando and at the time of the Japanese invasion he was running the Bush Warfare School in Burma and carrying out what he described as a 'little freelance raiding'. One night during the retreat Calvert took the opportunity to cool off with a swim in the Chindwin and encountered, in the water, a Japanese officer with the same idea. They fought silently in the inky waters of the river for several minutes until Calvert got the upper hand and was able to grasp his slippery adversary and hold him under the surface until he stopped struggling. As Calvert swam back to the shore he could see the body drifting away downstream. A natural recruit for the Chindits, he was awarded the DSO during the first expedition and was never happier than when he was blowing something up, setting ambushes or creeping through the jungle to attack an enemy outpost. In his memoirs he recalled leading a bayonet charge against a Japanese position and described the vicious fighting that followed as 'everyone shooting, bayoneting, kicking at everyone else, rather like an officers' mess guest night'.[8]

During the afternoon at Lalaghat Bill watched the feverish preparations, taking care to keep clear of the mules, which lashed out in all directions as they were coaxed into bamboo stalls inside the gliders. He listened in, impressed, as Cochran, a cheerful ex-fighter pilot with abundant chutzpah, delivered a heroic final briefing to his pilots which might have been scripted in Hollywood. 'Anything you boys have done in the past can be forgotten,' he told them. 'Tonight you are going to find your souls. Tonight you are going to take these troops in and put them down *just right*. If there is any trouble with the first few gliders a red flare will be fired. But the man who has that flare has just told me it's in a mighty deep pocket and will take a lot of finding. In other words, those boys are going to do a tough job and we are going to all do our bit to help.'[9]

'As the afternoon wore on,' Bill wrote, 'the atmosphere of excitement and suspense at Lalaghat grew – the old familiar feeling of waiting to go over the top, intensified by the strangeness and magnitude of this operation. Everyone, even the mules, moved about calmly, quietly and purposefully. Except for those patient beasts, it was, all the same, obvious that everyone realised that what was … the biggest and most hazardous airborne operation of the war was about to begin.'[10]

As dusk approached, Bill, Jack Baldwin, Wingate and a handful of other senior officers – among them Lieutenant General George Stratemeyer, the American chief of Eastern Air Command and Brigadier General Old of Troop Carrier Command – were waiting on the airstrip for zero hour and the first of the Dakotas to take off. Suddenly a jeep roared up and two American airmen jumped out with a photograph still wet from the darkroom. It was a picture of the Piccadilly landing site, taken two hours earlier by a hand camera, which clearly showed it had been obstructed with dozens of huge tree trunks – landing a single glider there would be impossible. Everyone looked at it, and then at each other, with dismay.

Wingate's first reaction was to fly into a fury that his orders had been disobeyed. He had decreed that there should be no overflying of the landing zones during the previous week to avoid alerting the enemy and he began shouting, demanding to know who had defied him. What happened next would the subject of bitter dispute.[11] Wingate claimed in his report,[12] written on 17 March, that, despite the evidence that Piccadilly had been blocked, he was anxious for the operation to continue and his only concern was sending others on a dangerous job when he was not going himself. Once Calvert had made it clear he was still ready to go, Wingate maintained that Bill left the final decision to him: 'I consulted at once with the Army Commander who agreed with my arguments and left me to decide, so far as I myself was concerned ...'[13]

Bill's recollection, as recounted in *Defeat Into Victory*, was very different. He contended that Wingate virtually went to pieces when the photographs arrived, descending into despair and concluding that as the whole operation had obviously been betrayed, probably by the Chinese, it clearly had to be abandoned. While Wingate was working himself up into a highly excitable and emotional state, Bill quietly asked the airmen who had brought the picture if the other two landing sites had been photographed. They confirmed that they had and that they were clear.

Bill described how he drew Wingate to one side to calm him down and speak to him privately. He explained to him that the Chinese could not have betrayed the operation because, as far as he knew, they had no knowledge of it; certainly they would not have known the location of the landing grounds. When Wingate continued to insist that he had been betrayed and that the operation should be cancelled, Bill tried another tack. Piccadilly had been the landing site Wingate had used in 1943 and a picture of it had appeared in an American magazine. We know the Japanese are blocking potential landing strips throughout north Burma, he said. What would be more natural for them than to block a site they knew had already been used?[14] Wingate remained unconvinced. Even if Broadway and Chowringhee were not obstructed, who was to say the Japanese were not hiding in the jungle, waiting to ambush and destroy each glider as it arrived? Sending them in now, he said to Bill with great emphasis, would be tantamount to 'murder'. Bill continued to argue that if the other two landing sites had been compromised they would certainly have been blocked like Piccadilly. Wingate slowly began to calm down. If the operation went ahead, he said, the risks would be considerable. Bill could not but agree. In the end Wingate turned to Bill, looked him straight in the eyes, and said: 'The responsibility is yours.'

Bill did not need to be reminded of his responsibilities. 'Not for the first time,' he wrote, 'I felt the weight of decision crushing in on me with an almost physical pressure. The gliders, if they were to take off that night, must do so within the hour. There was no time for prolonged inquiry or discussion. On my answer would depend not only the possibility of a disaster with wide implications on the whole Burma campaign and beyond, but the lives of these splendid men, tense and waiting in and around the aircraft. At that moment I would have given a great deal if Wingate or anybody else could have relieved me of the duty of decision.'[15]

He was acutely aware that if he gave the go-ahead and Wingate was right in thinking the operation had been compromised, it would be a catastrophe: many lives would be lost, Stilwell's activities would be put in jeopardy and the imminent Japanese offensive on the central front would not have the distraction of the Chindits causing 'damage and confusion' behind their lines. If he postponed the operation it would have a calamitous effect on morale. The men were keyed up and ready to go; they would never get to the same pitch again and there was also the risk that the enemy would discover all the aircraft crowded on to the Lalaghat airstrip, with disastrous consequences.

After deliberating for no more than a few minutes, Bill made his decision. 'The operation will go on,' he said. Among those present was Derek Tulloch, Wingate's chief of staff. 'I admired Slim tremendously on that occasion,' Tulloch wrote after the war. 'He had, of course, a poker face – useful for any commander – which enabled him to appear completely unruffled, indeed almost unconcerned. Yet the final decision to go on with the operation rested squarely on his shoulders and in the event of a disaster he would carry the major share of the blame. Watching him closely, at this moment of crisis, I gained the impression, which has always remained, that he had the utmost confidence in both Wingate and in the success of the operation.'[16]

Bill claimed that Wingate accepted his judgement without a word; Bill had the feeling he was relieved. Philip Cochran went off to warn the Piccadilly pilots about the change of plan and Bill followed him, intrigued to see how the American would break the news without causing consternation. It was simple. Cochran gathered together the Dakota pilots and glider pilots destined for Piccadilly, jumped up on to the bonnet of a jeep and announced: 'Say, fellers, we've got a better place to go to.'[17] Bill was impressed.

Shortly after six o'clock, only 70 minutes behind schedule, the first Dakota roared down the runway with its two gliders in tow. Bill watched with his heart in his mouth as the gliders lurched up off the strip and the aircraft lumbered into the air at the last minute and began the slow, circular climb to gain height and cross the surrounding hills. As soon as it was clear, the next Dakota began its run and then the next and the next. Several times it seemed to Bill that an aircraft would overrun the strip before it became airborne, but in the end all 31 aircraft got away safely into the darkening sky.

Bill decided to wait for news in the control tent at the end of the runway with Wingate's staff officers, all of them sustained by Tulloch's batman bringing in mugs of scalding hot, sweet tea. Wingate himself paced in and out restlessly, speaking to no one, vigorously combing his beard with his fingers. Bill remembered it as a bright, moonlit night; the interior of the tent was lit by hurricane lanterns and a single electric bulb, but it was brighter outside than in. All the Dakotas were in radio contact with an airfield at Hailakandi, 20 miles away, which in turn was in telephone contact with the control tent at Lalaghat. The first messages to come through were not encouraging and spoke of gliders breaking loose or being cast off by their towing aircraft.

At one point there was a report of red flares only a few miles away, indicating that a tow was in distress, and when Bill stepped outside for some air he thought he saw a red Very light soar into the air in the far distance, but there was still no firm news. A garbled call over a field telephone from another airfield said that one of the Dakota pilots had seen firing on the Broadway strip. Then, shortly after 2.30, a signal arrived from Calvert. It simply said 'Soya link'. With mordant humour an artificial sausage, the most detested item in the ration scale, had been chosen as the code word to indicate the failure of the operation. Bill was stunned. He immediately assumed that Wingate had been right and he was wrong: the Japanese must have been waiting to ambush the gliders as they arrived. Wingate, too, obviously made the same assumption, gave Bill a long, bitter, withering look and stalked off without a word. Aircraft still en route to Broadway were recalled.

In fact, as the picture became clearer over the next few hours,

Bill thankfully realised he had jumped to the wrong conclusion. There was no enemy at Broadway. What went wrong could be ascribed to a catalogue of human and mechanical errors. First, the doubting Thomases who had said that a Dakota could not tow two gliders had been partially correct, certainly in the turbulent air conditions over the mountains in Burma. The drag on the tow lines was too much as was the strain on the Dakota engines, causing them to overheat. A number of gliders had to be cut free and were forced to crash-land before reaching their objective – nine ended up in Japanese-held territory. The glider carrying essential ground-control equipment was among those missing, making it impossible to coordinate the landings. When one of the leading gliders crashed at Broadway, some of those following hurtled into the wreckage; others smashed into surrounding jungle. Only 35 of the 61 gliders that set off reached their destination; 23 Chindits were killed and many injured, but more than 400 arrived safely, including Mike Calvert. Every man was immediately set to work to clear the site and construct a crude airstrip for the Dakotas which were due to fly in the following day with reinforcements. At 6.30 a.m. a second signal – 'pork sausage' – was received from Broadway indicating success and that flights could begin that evening.

It was after dawn when Bill left the control tent at Lalaghat. Although the reports coming in were still sketchy, he felt a great sense of relief that the Chindits had not been ambushed; provided they were not discovered by the Japanese during the next 12 hours, he felt confident the airstrips would be ready to receive troop-carrying transports by nightfall. They were. Less than 24 hours after the first gliders had left Lalaghat, the first troop-carrier transport plane landed at Broadway piloted by the redoubtable Brigadier General Old. Between 5 March and 10 March the Dakotas of No. 1 Air Commando flew almost 600 sorties transporting around 9,000 men, 1,350 animals, mostly mules, 250 tons of stores and two artillery batteries into the heart of the jungle. By 16 March, the brigade that had entered Burma on foot under Bernard Fergusson had reached its assembly point, Aberdeen, after marching 360 miles across extraordinarily difficult country in just over six weeks – a remarkable feat. On the following day Bill had the satisfaction of telling Stilwell that he had kept his promise – the Chindits had cut both the main road and rail supply lines to the Japanese forces on the northern front.

On 13 March Wingate issued a grandiloquent, almost Shakespearian, Order of the Day to congratulate his men: 'Our first task is fulfilled. We have inflicted a complete surprise upon the enemy. All our Columns are inside the enemy's guts. The time has come to reap the fruit of the advantage we have gained. The enemy will react with violence. We will oppose him with the resolve to reconquer our territory of Northern Burma. Let us thank God for the great success He has vouchsafed for us, and press forward with our sword in the enemy's ribs to expel him from our territory. This is not a moment when such an advantage has been gained to count the cost. This is a moment to live in history. It is an enterprise in which every man who takes part may feel proud one day to say, "I WAS THERE".'[18]

There followed an ignominious wrangle at headquarters about whether or not the Chindit operations should be made public. Bill was all for keeping quiet and letting the Japanese find out for themselves what had happened, but the thirst for good news prevailed and a press release was prepared mentioning only 'troops of the 14th Army' and not, significantly, mentioning Wingate at all. He was furious. 'To Wingate,' Bill noted, 'this was *Hamlet* without the Prince of Denmark.' Wingate argued forcefully that all the battalions involved, and the commanders, including himself, should be named to boost morale. Bill subsequently agreed, but only because he felt that if the enemy thought it was a repeat of Wingate's ineffective expedition the previous year they would not take it too seriously. He did not, needless to say, share this view with Wingate.

A few days after the fly-in, Bill returned to Lalaghat airfield to congratulate the pilots and ground crew on the success of the operation. He walked around with Tulloch chatting to the men and at one point casually mentioned that he might need to use two of Wingate's reserve brigades in an emergency to bolster defences in Imphal. He suggested that Tulloch should not mention it to Wingate as it would 'only worry him'; Tulloch got the strong impression that Bill wanted to gauge what Wingate's reaction would be. But Tulloch's first loyalty was to Wingate and so he told him what Bill had said as soon as he returned from a visit to Broadway. Wingate, predictably, exploded and flew to Comilla next day, threatening again to hand in his resignation. Bill was obliged to explain, with his usual exemplary patience, that as both brigades were not due to be deployed with the Chindits for at least two months – they had been earmarked to go in on the second wave – it would be foolish not make use of them immediately if they were needed and that they would be released when Wingate needed them.

Wingate was mollified – temporarily. But there was another bust-up within days when Wingate suggested using a brigade of Special Force to disrupt enemy communications on the Assam front and asked Bill for more transport aircraft to fly the brigade in more quickly. Bill refused, firstly because all available aircraft were already committed and secondly because he did not want the Chindits to be distracted from assisting Stilwell's Chinese forces. Wingate clearly believed that Bill was obstructing him from winning the war. He sent a telegram to SEAC HQ with instructions that it should be forwarded 'verbatim, repeat verbatim' to the Prime Minister, claiming that only lack of transport was preventing Special Force from a historic victory: 'Get Special Force four transport squadrons now and you have all Burma north of 24th parallel plus a decisive Japanese defeat.' He added, with breathtaking disregard for the truth: 'General Slim gives me his full backing.'[19]

On 22 March, Wingate visited Bill at Comilla for what would be the last time. Bill had learned earlier that day, or possibly the previous evening, that Wingate had 'taken his name in vain' in his signal to the Prime Minister and so, inevitably, there was a row – nothing new to Wingate, who would do anything to get his own way. But the meeting ended curiously. As Wingate was leaving he suddenly turned to look at Bill intently from under his pith helmet and said, completely out of the blue: 'You are the only senior officer in South-East Asia who doesn't wish me dead.'[20] With that, he went out of the door without another word.

Bill did not know what to make of it, but the incident came back to haunt him when, three days later, a signal arrived at his Comilla headquarters reporting Wingate as missing. He waited anxiously for further news, genuinely concerned at the implications of possibly losing the Chindit leader. They were not friends, but were certainly close colleagues and Bill had never been numbered among the many senior officers who professed a loathing for the man. On the following day the wreckage of the B-52 Mitchell bomber in which Wingate had been returning to Lalaghat from Imphal was discovered in jungle-covered hills near Bishenpur. All ten men on board, including two British war correspondents, were killed instantly.

Mountbatten addressed a special Order of the Day to the Chindits which paid a glowing tribute to their lost leader: 'General Wingate has been killed in the hour of his triumph. The Allies have lost one of the most forceful and dynamic personalities that this war has produced. You have lost the finest and most inspiring leader a force could have wished for, and I have lost a personal friend and faithful supporter. He has lit the torch. Together we must grasp it and carry it forward. Out of your gallant and hazardous expedition into the heart of Japanese-held territory will grow the final re-conquest of Burma and the ultimate defeat of the Japanese. He was so proud of you. I know you will live up to his expectations.'

They were sentiments with which Bill agreed, while avoiding the Supremo's soaring rhetoric. 'There could be no question of the seriousness of our loss,' he wrote. 'Without his presence to animate it, Special Force would no longer be the same to others or to itself. He had created, inspired, defended it, and given it confidence; it was the offspring of his vivid imagination and ruthless energy. It had no other parent. Now it was orphaned.'[21]

Even had he been so inclined, Bill had no time to grieve. By then the long-awaited Japanese offensive on the central front was well under way.

15

An Attack on the Raj

After watching the departure of the Chindits at Lalaghat, Bill had flown to 4 Corps headquarters in Imphal on 7 March to review Geoffrey Scoones' plans for meeting the Japanese offensive, Operation U-Go. Throughout this period Bill suffered from constant pain as a result of his earlier war wounds, undoubtedly exacerbated by the need to spend so much time in his uncomfortable Anson flying between various headquarters. He did not enjoy flying at the best of times, but bucking and yawing in the turbulent air over Burmese mountain ranges made it a thousand times worse. When the Anson landed at the airstrip in Imphal, Bill clambered out with some difficulty and found Scoones waiting to meet him with a jeep.

They drove directly to the headquarters where the methodical Scoones ran through a lengthy and detailed appreciation listing all the options open to the enemy and the strategy he intended to adopt to meet each of them. U-Go was still expected to be launched on 15 March. Astonishingly, neither man was aware, as they talked that afternoon, that large columns of enemy troops were already moving through the jungle towards Allied positions. It was a shocking failure in intelligence which would set 4 Corps on the back foot from the start.

Scoones had two divisions deployed in forward positions across the Indian border almost as far as the Chindwin river and a third, the 23rd, in reserve at Imphal. The 20th Indian Infantry Division, under Major General Douglas Gracey, occupied the town of Tamu at the head of the Kabaw valley; the division had been raised in April 1942 and was untried, but well trained. More than 80 miles to the south, around Tiddim in the Chin hills, linked to Imphal by a dirt track and separated from 20th Division by a wilderness of jungle-clad mountain ridges, was Punch Cowan's experienced

17th Indian Division, known as 'the Black Cats' for their divisional sign, which had been almost continually in action since December 1941. Opposing them was the Japanese 15th Army – 65,000 fanatical, highly trained Imperial troops under the command of 56-year-old Lieutenant General Mutaguchi Renya – which was believed to be massing along the Chindwin river. Mutaguchi was known to be ambitious and headstrong and a strict adherent to the samurai code of Bushido – the 'way of the warrior'.

Scoones anticipated that the Japanese would attempt to cut off and destroy both his forward divisions before launching an attack on Imphal. At the first sign of the start of the offensive, therefore, the bulk of 17th Division would be ordered to withdraw immediately to the Imphal plain, leaving a brigade 40 miles south of Imphal to block the Japanese advance. The 20th Division would retreat from its forward positions in the Kabaw valley and fall back to the Shenam Saddle, a complex of hills on the road from Tamu to Imphal, which it would hold at all costs. Once the Japanese were committed to battle on the Imphal plain, a combined strike force made up of 17th and the 23rd Divisions would mount a massive counter-attack supported by armour, artillery and aircraft.

Bill was happy with the plan. He hoped that Mutaguchi, who probably had little regard for the fighting calibre of the Allies, would imagine that both 14th Army divisions were simply falling back in the face on the Japanese thrust, rather than luring him into a trap where he would be required to fight at the end of impossibly long and difficult lines of communication. Bill knew, better than most, what it was like to fight a battle with poor lines of communication. 'I was tired of fighting the Japanese when they had a good line of communication behind them and I had an execrable one,' he wrote. 'This time I would reverse the procedure.'[1] The calendar also exerted considerable additional pressure on the enemy – Imphal had to be captured before the monsoon began in May or the Japanese supply routes would become impassable and the troops would starve.

The great battles of Imphal and Kohima which followed would be the sternest test yet of Bill's qualities as a general. Crucial to the future of the whole Burma campaign, fast-moving, highly complex strategically and logistically, they would demand cool thinking, resilience, a willingness to take risks, composure in a crisis and a profound understanding of what could be expected of the troops. They were not epic army against army set pieces of the kind that had been seen in North Africa and Europe, but vicious, confused, bloody, personal clashes, often hand-to-hand, over sometimes apparently meaningless patches of ground. Bill described them as swaying 'across great stretches of wild country; one day its focal point was a hill named on no map, the next a miserable, unpronounceable village a hundred miles away. Columns, brigades, divisions marched and counter-marched, met in bloody clashes, and reeled apart, weaving a confused pattern hard to unravel ... At no time and in no place was the situation, either to commanders or troops [clear]. Into Scoones' headquarters, from every point of the compass, day and night, streamed signals, messages, and reports, announcing successes, setbacks, appealing for reinforcements, demanding more ammunition, asking urgently for wounded to be evacuated, begging for air support.'[2]

By this time Bill was 52 years old, approaching an age at which many men think about slowing down. But as commander of the 14th Army, his responsibilities, both physical and moral, were not just daunting but escalating. He had to keep track of events and control of the hostilities on four different and widely dispersed battlefields spread over a front 700 miles long – in Assam at Kohima and Imphal, in Arakan, in northern Burma where Stilwell's Chinese forces were in action and in the jungles behind enemy lines, where the Chindits were operating. He had to be ready to respond to changing circumstances and adapt his plans again and again when things started to go wrong, as they almost always did. Above all, he needed the moral courage to accept the burden of high command, the knowledge that thousands of lives were in his hands and the certainty that whatever happened he could not avoid sending men to their deaths.

He was under no illusions about what might happen if Imphal and Kohima were lost: 'Victory in Assam [for the Japanese] would resound far beyond that remote jungle land. It might, indeed, as they proclaimed in exhortations to their troops, change the whole course of the world war ... If it succeeded, the destruction of the British forces in Burma would be the least of its results. China, completely isolated, would be driven into a separate peace; India, ripe as they thought for revolt against the British, would fall, a glittering prize, into their hands.'³

A lesser man might have buckled under the burden, but those close to him never failed to be impressed by his resilience. 'He never showed any anxiety or strain,' said his friend Ouvry Roberts, commander of the 23rd Indian Division. 'He'd drive up in his jeep with a smile on his face, jump out and say, "Hello Ouvry, how's things?" Then he'd ask me to introduce him to the officers who were waiting to meet him – many of whom he'd know – and he'd chat to them, ask them questions, assess morale for himself and in this way he would really know what the situation was.'⁴

After Bill had returned to Comilla from the 7 March meeting with Scoones, reports began arriving at 4 Corps headquarters of unusual enemy movements. On 9 March, a two-man patrol from the 1st/10th Gurkhas observed some 2,000 Japanese troops, accompanied by mules and light artillery, crossing the Manipur river south of Tiddim and heading in the direction of the 17th Division, but no action was taken as the report was uncorroborated. (Aerial reconnaissance was difficult because of the density of the jungle.) Two days later news reached 4 Corps HQ that approximately 3,000 enemy troops had been seen moving north round the right flank of Cowan's division. Cowan, clearly aware from patrols and intelligence reports that something was up, expressed his concern to Scoones that the enemy was on its way to set up blocks on the road from Tiddim to Imphal and that if his division was to withdraw without a fight it should get on the move without delay. Scoones disagreed; he still doggedly believed the Japanese offensive would not begin until 15 March and was reluctant to order the withdrawal.

But by 13 March the accumulated evidence of major enemy troop movements could no longer be denied and Scoones belatedly accepted that the offensive had, indeed, begun. He telephoned Cowan and ordered him to start pulling back and, as a precaution, he sent a brigade from his reserve division in Imphal to help extricate the 17th Division if it was needed. (Cowan was subsequently blamed, in the *Official History*, for being too slow in getting his division on the move; in fact, he was so worried by the delay that earlier in the day on 13 March he had deliberately disobeyed his orders and instructed his division to start withdrawing before receiving the go-ahead from corps headquarters.)

By 1700 hours on the following day the entire division – 16,000 men, 2,500 vehicles and 3,500 mules – was heading north along the narrow, winding road through the hills that led to Imphal, leaving Tiddim behind in flames. All the men marched – the transport was kept for equipment, supplies, the sick and the wounded. On the first day they covered 20 miles, blowing up bridges behind them and planting mines and booby traps for the pursuing Japanese, but within days the enemy was swarming over the Tiddim road and what should have been an orderly retreat quickly turned into a desperate battle for survival as the division found itself fighting through one roadblock after another.

Scoones telephoned Bill in Comilla to tell him what was going on, but by then Bill had another major crisis on his hands. With reserves already being committed to extricate 17th Division, there were simply not enough troops to protect the massive Dimapur supply base and railhead at the base of the mountains. Its loss would be catastrophic, not just for 4 Corps; supplies for China and for Stilwell's Chinese forces fighting in north Burma were all shipped through Dimapur on the Bengal–Assam railway and then flown to China over 'the Hump' from airstrips along the Brahmaputra valley.

The crisis could only be solved by immediate reinforcements and time was desperately short. Bill could see no other solution than flying in more troops, but all available transport aircraft were committed to 'the Hump'. On the last occasion Bill had 'borrowed' aircraft from 'the Hump' it had required the permission of the American Chiefs of Staff in Washington and it had taken several days for approval to come through. When Mountbatten stopped off at Comilla on the morning of 14 March on his way back to Delhi from a meeting with Stilwell, Bill and Jack Baldwin met him at the airport and explained the grave situation they were facing. Bill told the Supreme Commander, quite bluntly, that unless he could get reinforcements on to the battlefield urgently the Imphal–Kohima battle might well be lost, in which case 'the Hump' route would be shut down. It would be 'madness', he said, not to divert the aircraft that the 14th Army needed.

Mountbatten promised to do what he could. He could hardly

be blamed if he was not at his best that day – his head was heavily bandaged and he was in considerable pain from an eye injury. A few days earlier, during a visit to Stilwell's forward headquarters, he was driving a jeep along a jungle track when a stem of bamboo, pushed aside by the front wheel, sprang back violently and hit him in the left eye. He was taken to a hospital in Ledo where it was thought he might lose the eye; when he had discharged himself from the hospital against medical advice earlier that day he was warned that leaving prematurely might well cost him his eye. (In fact he made a full recovery.)

On the day of Bill's meeting with Mountbatten, Japanese tanks and infantry launched attacks on 20th Division positions and under cover of darkness the following night a great mass of enemy troops began crossing the Chindwin, braced for action by a stirring order of the day issued by General Mutaguchi: 'The Army has now reached the stage of invincibility and the day when the Rising Sun shall proclaim our definite victory in India is not far off. This operation will engage the attention of the whole world and is eagerly awaited by 100,000,000 of our countrymen. By its very decisive nature, its success will have a profound effect upon the course of the war and may even lead to its conclusion. Our mission is thus of the greatest importance and we must expend every energy and talent in the achievement of our goal ... Conscious of their great responsibilities and of their duty to our heroic ancestors, both officers and men must fight to the death for their country and accept the burden of duties which are the lot of the soldier of Japan. The will of the Emperor and our countrymen must be fulfilled.'[5]

Tokyo Radio spoke of troops marching 'joyfully' across the frontier 'with tears streaming down their tawny cheeks'. Meanwhile, the situation with 17th Division was becoming ever more dangerous. On a visit to 4 Corps headquarters, Bill learned that Scoones had been obliged to commit another brigade from his reserve division to help extricate 'the Black Cats'. While it left Imphal dangerously exposed, Scoones had no choice in the matter – if the 17th Division failed to make it back to Imphal all the plans for meeting and defeating the enemy offensive would collapse. It must have seemed to Bill that Allied plans were unravelling even before the battle had properly begun.

He, of course, blamed himself, particularly for leaving the timing of the withdrawal to Scoones. The reality was that Scoones had made a mess of it and ordered the withdrawal far too late, a delay which meant the carefully prepared plans agreed with Bill for an orderly withdrawal were in jeopardy almost before the first shots had been fired. But Bill felt he was better placed to make the decision himself and should probably have set a date before the offensive started. What held him back was the fact that there was no certainty that an attack was imminent. If he ordered the forward divisions to pull back and the offensive did not happen, much hard-won territory would have been unnecessarily given up, his own plans for an offensive would be compromised, the Chinese advance in the north would be imperilled and morale would suffer. He would also, he privately admitted, look extremely foolish. 'As I contemplated the chain of disasters that I had invited, my heart sank. However, I have always believed that a motto for generals must be "No regrets", no crying over spilt milk. The vital need now was to bring in reinforcements, not only to replace the vanished reserve in Imphal but, above all, to ensure that Dimapur was held. To achieve this I bent all my energies.'[6]

Faced now with a desperate need for more troops, Bill sent a signal to Mountbatten setting out the rapidly deteriorating situation. He could wait no longer for the aircraft; he needed 25 to 30 Dakotas to be made available *at once* to move the 5th Division by air from Arakan to the front. Mountbatten had an excellent working relationship with Bill and knew he would not make such a request unless it was absolutely necessary: he decided to act first and seek permission afterwards. Risking the wrath of Washington (President Roosevelt had warned him not to ask for more aircraft from the Americans), he ordered 30 aircraft to be diverted to the 14th Army immediately on his own authority.

All this time Allied commanders were still unaware that Mutaguchi had inserted a very considerable force to the north of the main thrust which was hacking its way through the jungle towards Kohima, the vital little town in the Naga Hills that straddled the road between Imphal and Dimapur. Bill recognised that the 138-mile Dimapur–Imphal road was 4 Corps' Achilles heel. Single-track for much of its length, from Dimapur it snaked up into the Naga Hills, with a sheer precipice on one side and a mountain wall on the other, to Kohima, from where it ran more or less parallel with the front, and not far behind it, to Imphal, making it exceptionally vulnerable to attack.

Before the war Kohima, the administrative centre of Nagaland, was likened to a kind of Shangri-la – a hill station perched 5,000 feet above sea level in the lush green Naga Hills, where wild orchids and rhododendrons bloomed in profusion. The British Deputy Commissioner, Charles Pawsey, lived in a bungalow overlooking a terraced garden and tennis court with sweeping views of the surrounding hills. (A current tourist brochure describes Nagaland as 'the Switzerland of the East; the exquisitely picturesque landscapes, the vibrantly colourful sunrise and sunset, lush and verdant flora – this is a land that represents unimaginable beauty ...')

Bill took a rather different view, referring to the Naga Hills as 'those hellish jungle mountains'. He had every reason. Sixty-four days of savage fighting would transform Kohima from a sleepy little hill town into a charnel house, a wasteland of ruins more reminiscent of the Somme than Switzerland; no building survived unscathed, the streets were cratered by shells, every tree was smashed and stripped of its leaves and the stench of death, from decaying unburied corpses, crawling with maggots and covered with flies, was everywhere.

Blocking the Japanese advance on Kohima was the hill village of Sangshak where two battalions of the 50th Indian Parachute Brigade, under the command of 32-year-old Brigadier Maxwell Hope-Thompson, had recently arrived having been diverted from jungle warfare training. The Japanese attacked Sangshak on the night of 22 March without waiting for artillery support and were beaten back, suffering heavy casualties, after savage close-quarter fighting. For four days the 50th Brigade held out heroically at Sangshak against repeated Japanese attacks, despite being desperately short of ammunition, supplies and water. Attempts to supply the beleaguered troops by air were very difficult because they held such a small area of ground – many of their air-dropped provisions fell straight into the hands of the enemy. When, at 1800 hours on 26 March, Hope-Thompson was ordered to withdraw, the brigade had virtually been destroyed. Japanese troops entered the village and found mutilated bodies and discarded weapons scattered everywhere around the smoking ruins of a missionary church. Arriving in Imphal, Hope-Thompson was admitted to hospital with a nervous breakdown but his brigade had inflicted more than 600 casualties on the Japanese and held up the advance on Kohima by a week, buying vital time for 4 Corps to reorganise.

By this time Bill recognised that the threat to Kohima was as grave as that to Imphal, with numerous reports of strong enemy columns climbing the Naga Hills towards the town. He had assumed that because of the forbidding terrain, it would be impossible for the Japanese to maintain any force larger than a regimental group, but it was rapidly becoming clear that virtually an entire division was making for Kohima at astonishing speed. He had greatly under-estimated the enemy's ability to move through 'impenetrable' jungle and willingness to advance with the most tenuous lines of communication. It was, Bill said, 'the second great mistake I made in the Imphal battle'.

Meanwhile, Mutaguchi was closing in on Imphal. The fly-in of 5th Division to defend Imphal had begun on 19 March and by 27 March two complete brigades were on the ground, along with the divisional headquarters. It was the first time in history that an entire division had been transported by air from one battlefield to another. Every aircraft arriving with troops departed packed with non-combatants to avoid catastrophically overloading the Imphal ration strength. By the end of the airlift the situation had become so critical, with leading Japanese units not much more than 30 miles from the airstrip, that some 5th Division troops were sent straight into action the moment they landed. One battalion commander was astonished to discover that two of his companies were already on their way to the front before he had arrived.

In the meantime, Bill had asked General Giffard for 33 Corps, under Lieutenant General Montagu Stopford, to be moved to Dimapur by road and rail from the reserve in southern and central India. An uncommitted Chindit brigade was sent by rail to Jorhat, 50 miles north of Dimapur, to threaten the flank of any attack on the base. Bill was concerned about maintaining all these reinforcements, particularly if there was heavy fighting, but the indomitable 'Grocer Alf' Snelling assured him they could cope. The 14th Army would soon have a ration strength of around 750,000 – the population of a considerable city – scattered over an area stretching from the foothills of the Himalayas to the Bay of Bengal.

On 28 March, Bill flew to Dimapur for a conference with his commanders at which it was agreed to block the Japanese advance at Kohima. The only troops available to send to assist Kohima was the 161st Indian Brigade of the 5th Division, which Bill had presciently diverted to Dimapur, pending the arrival of 33 Corps. After the conference Bill took Freddy Warren, the young brigade commander, aside to brief him in more detail on the formidable task that lay ahead. They walked up and down outside the office where the conference had been held as Bill explained that the Japanese were likely to reach Kohima by 3 April and if they tried to by pass the town they could be ready to attack Dimapur by 10 April. The garrison at Kohima was only manned by 1,500 soldiers and another 1,000 non-combatants. Further reinforcements were on their way but they could not be expected to arrive before the enemy attacked in strength. Bill warned Warren that his brigade was going have to hold Kohima until then, whatever it took.

While he was in Dimapur, Bill toured the area to inspect the preparations being made to defend the base. The base commander told him that his ration strength was around 45,000 but when Bill asked him how many of them were soldiers, he replied with a shrug that he might be able to scrape together 500 men who knew how to fire a rifle. It was hardly good news. Bill watched non-combatant labour digging bunkers and rifle pits under the direction of storemen and clerks. 'As I looked into the faces of the willing but untried garrison,' he wrote, 'I could only hope that I imparted more confidence than I felt.'[7]

Warren's brigade set off for Kohima on the day after the 28 March conference but a classic military muddle ensued in the tradition of the Grand Old Duke of York ('He marched his men to the top of the hill and he marched them down again …'). Warren had barely begun to prepare the defence of the town when he was ordered to return to Dimapur after reports that an enemy strike force was outflanking Kohima and heading for the base. Almost as soon as the brigade arrived back in Dimapur the reports turned out to be false and so it turned round once again and headed back to Kohima, by which time it was virtually too late. As the brigade approached

Kohima up the winding road from Dimapur (a road with which it had become all too familiar), the leading vehicles were almost engulfed in a tsunami of panic-stricken refugees, men, women and children, fleeing the town. The Japanese, having marched 160 miles in 20 days across 'impassable' terrain, had begun their attack. Only one battalion, the 4th Queen's Own Royal West Kent Regiment, managed to get into the town before the enemy cut the road.

On the following day Japanese forces broke through to the Imphal–Dimapur road 30 miles north of Imphal, blew up a bridge and set up a powerful roadblock, effectively cutting off Imphal from its land-based supply line – thereafter 4 Corps' only link with the outside world was by air. Everything now depended, Bill wrote, 'on the steadfastness of the troops already meeting the first impetus of the attack. If they could hold until help arrived, all would be well; if not, we were near disaster.'

The good news was that Cowan's 17th Division managed to reach Imphal from the south still full of fight, despite the mauling it had received as it struggled out of the unwelcome embrace of the enemy. 'We are the better troops,' the pugnacious Punch Cowan announced on his arrival, 'and every man in this division knows it.'[8] Around 1,200 casualties had to be flown out to hospitals elsewhere in India, but the division had inflicted far heavier losses on the enemy than it had sustained itself. Bill visited the division at its camp on the outskirts of Imphal a few days later and was pleased to see that their morale was still high, their spirits unbroken. He was also amused to observe that Ouvry Roberts' 23rd Division was pretty cock-a-hoop, too, asserting that it 'rescued' the doughty 17th on its first taste of action.

With Imphal cut off, Kohima surrounded and Dimapur under threat, Stilwell, on the northern front, was becoming increasingly worried that his line of communication – the railway which ran through thorny scrub, bamboo and elephant grass from Dimapur to Assam, along the Brahmaputra valley – would be cut. His Chinese troops, with the help of Merrill's Marauders, had been driving south from Ledo, relentlessly pushing the Japanese back, since the end of 1943. On 19 March, his 61st birthday, they had broken into the Mogaung valley, within striking distance of the strategically important town of Myitkyina, on the west bank of the Irrawaddy, which was to be a vital link on the Ledo road. But if his line of communication was cut off before Myitkyina had been captured, he would have no alternative but to retreat back to China. Stilwell was so concerned he contacted Bill and offered to provide one of his divisions to help out at Imphal, even though it would inevitably hold up his own advance.

On 3 April, Bill flew to 33 Corps headquarters at Jorhat for a conference with Mountbatten and all the land and air commanders on the northern and central fronts. When he arrived he was greeted by a posse of photographers who asked if they could take his picture. He agreed and then, on the spur of the moment, said he wanted to be photographed shaking hands with an American private. It was a bit of mischief; he had always been tickled by the fact that privates seemed to be thin on the ground in the American forces. So they went off in search of a private and, sure enough, could not find one. The lowest rank they could light upon was a corporal. Bill stomped off to the officers' mess with a spring in his step, greatly cheered. That he could indulge in such whimsy at such a moment was very much a part of his character; his sense of humour rarely deserted him, even at the worst of times. (A few weeks earlier he had arrived late to address a conference of 4 Corps officers at Imphal, having been misdirected by MPs. He delighted the audience with his opening remark: 'I know you think the Military Police are bloody awful. Now I know why.')[9]

Stilwell had already arrived in Jorhat. Bill thought the American looked old and tired, which was perhaps hardly surprising – dealing with the duplicitous Chinese generals, and the Generalissimo in particular, would have been infuriating even to a man with great patience and tact, qualities Stilwell notably lacked. Standing outside the mess where they could be sure no one was eavesdropping, Stilwell repeated his offer to loan a Chinese division to 4 Corps. Bill was touched by Vinegar Joe's willingness to help, knowing what it would cost him. Stilwell's goal was to capture Myitkyina before the monsoon – if he was obliged to withdraw an entire division from his strike force he could forget that.

Bill thanked him but refused the offer. He explained that reinforcements were arriving at Imphal, the troops were fighting well and even though it was going to be a hard battle he was confident of a successful outcome. He thought it was better for Stilwell's force to push on for Myitkyina as hard as possible. Stilwell asked if Bill could guarantee that his line of communication would not be cut. Bill replied that he could not be sure that some Japanese units would not get down into the Brahmaputra valley and disrupt his communications, but he promised it would not last for more than ten days. Before they returned to the mess, Stilwell treated Bill to a rare wintry smile and confessed that he had hoped Bill was going to say just that.

After lunch Mountbatten arrived for the conference in the company of a number of senior staff officers. Bill took the floor to explain why he had refused Stilwell's offer and reiterated his conviction that the enemy would be defeated at Imphal. 'His calm air of confidence dominated the whole conference,' one of the officers present later reported.[10] He outlined the situation at Dimapur and Kohima and said that Kohima would be reinforced once it could be accomplished without endangering the safety of Dimapur. Kohima was going to be held since it would be hard to recapture and its loss, he added, would 'undermine Naga loyalty'.

(Bill never underestimated the contribution made by the Nagas, Chins and other hill tribes, most of whom remained fiercely loyal to the British. They gave the enemy false details about 14th Army troop movements and numbers, guided British and Indian troops through the jungle to point out Japanese positions and provided local information for Allied air strikes without any thought of reward. As the Japanese considered all hill tribesmen to be illiterate primitives, they were allowed to wander freely around Japanese camps. On his desk at his Comilla headquarters Bill had a copy of a Japanese operational map which had helped enormously in the planning of the defence of Imphal and Kohima. It had been stolen from a Japanese commander's tent by two Naga tribesmen. To make it look like an ordinary theft the Nagas had made off with clothing and equipment as well as the map; the victim of the theft probably did not for a minute consider that the thieves had understood the importance of what they had stolen and was thus unconcerned it might find its way into enemy hands.)

By 6 April the tiny garrison defending Kohima was in desperate straits; the town was completely surrounded by more than 6,000 crack troops of the Japanese 31st Division under the command of Major General Sato Kotoku, who had warned his officers that they must be 'prepared for death by starvation in these mountain fastnesses'.[11]

The gruesome horror of the battle for the hills along Kohima ridge that ensued would never be forgotten by those who survived it. For 14 terrible days and nights the garrison held out, its perimeter shrinking inexorably under pressure from wave after wave of attacks, always preceded at night by nerve-shattering howls and screams. One hill after another fell to the Japanese until at last the defenders were concentrated around what was known as Garrison Hill, where the fighting centred around the legendary tennis court of the deputy commissioner's bungalow, with opposing sides so close they were able to lob grenades at each other instead of balls. (Kohima war cemetery now occupies what used to be the deputy commissioner's terraced garden and the site of the tennis court is marked with white concrete lines.)

Conditions on Garrison Hill were as bad as anything endured by the troops on the Western Front in the First World War. The men were filthy, exhausted, their nostrils filled with the sickening stench of dead bodies that lay everywhere. None of the wounded could be evacuated and many were forced to lie in the open, where they were often wounded again by flying splinters from mortars and artillery. Throughout, the beleaguered garrison was entirely dependent on air supply. It was a tricky and dangerous operation and the men watched in dismay as the first delivery of precious supplies, *their* supplies, was dropped straight into the hands of the enemy, but thereafter the aircrews became more expert and kept the garrison supplied with ammunition, rations and, most vital of all, water. American C-47 pilots boasted they could drop supplies within a 100-yard circle almost without fail.

Just when hope was fading, Allied reinforcements arrived at last. On 15 April a brigade of the 2nd Division broke through enemy roadblocks to reach Garrison Hill and three days later, after heavy fighting, the siege of Kohima was partially lifted when the 1st Battalion of the Punjab Regiment drove a wedge through the Japanese positions and got into the town, which by then had been more or less destroyed. Almost every building had been reduced to ashes and rubble, the dead still lay unburied, parachutes festooned what remained of the trees and there were bomb craters everywhere. 'If Garrison Hill was indescribable for its filth and horror and smell,' Major David Wilson, one of the relieving troops recalled, 'the sight of its defenders was almost worse. They looked like aged, blood-stained scarecrows, dropping with fatigue; the only clean thing about them was their weapons, and they smelt of blood, sweat and death.'[12]

Casualties began to be evacuated under the cover of darkness that night, but the battle continued with undiminished ferocity as more 14th Army troops moved in for a counter-attack. The Japanese took heavy casualties but nothing – neither bombs, shells, flame-throwers, mortars nor grenades – seemed to be able to shift them from their strongly fortified bunkers. Major Bushell of the 1st Royal Berkshires described the action: 'To begin with I took over an area overlooking the tennis court … The lie of the land made it impos-sible to move by day because of Japanese snipers. We were in Kohima for three weeks. We were attacked every single night … They came in waves, it was like a pigeon shoot. Most nights they over-ran part of the battalion position, so we had to mount counter attacks … Water was very short and restricted to about one pint per man per day. So we stopped shaving. Air supply was the key, but the steep terrain and narrow ridges meant that some of the drops went to the Japs. My company went into Kohima over 100 strong and came out at about 60.'[13]

Following events from his headquarters at Comilla, Bill could not understand why Sato did not simply bypass Kohima and head straight for Dimapur, which would surely have fallen to a division-strength assault. He discovered later that the unenterprising Sato's orders were to capture Kohima and dig in – and that is what he intended to do, no matter the cost. It apparently did not occur to him that he could have left a small force to contain Kohima and inflict terrible damage on the Allies by going for the supply base at Dimapur. Bill recalled ruefully that he would have been saved a great deal of anxiety had he known that at the time. Later he joked that he had stopped an RAF raid on Sato's headquarters because the Japanese general was so 'helpful'.

The 14th Army commander had no business at the front but Bill was unable to resist an urge to visit Kohima after the siege had been lifted. David Wilson, known as 'Chuckles' because of his sunny disposition, was brigade major of 161st Brigade at Kohima and well remembered Bill's visit: 'One day the Royal Berkshires were faced with a nasty little action at Viswema, just north of Mao Songsang, the highest part of the road. The wireless sets started crackling. The High Command was on us in a big way. Bill Slim himself, with John Grover [commander of 2nd Division] in tow to see what was going on. We were on one spur with the Japanese on the next, and The Royal Berkshires trying to dislodge them. The mountainside was very steep, but somehow we had to get above and behind the Japanese. It was not easy, and we were well and truly held up.

'Bill Slim seemed to know everyone in his army. He got hold of Leonard Tetley, commanding 99th Field Regiment, and suggested that he called forward his battery of eight 3.7-inch mountain guns, deployed them on the ridge we were on, and shot up the Japanese over virtually open sights at about 3,000 yards' range. Soon eight marvellous little guns were on the ridge, happily blattering away at the Japanese to excellent effect, but they were followed by a very angry senior officer, the corps commander Royal Artillery – "Hair Trigger" Stevens himself – who wished to know in no uncertain terms: "What fucking fool ordered these guns forward without telling me?"

'He had not noticed Bill Slim was standing quietly with the rest of us. Bill quietly came up behind him and said: "I really am terribly sorry, Brigadier, I am afraid it was me." With the help of the guns the Japanese positions collapsed and the Berkshires were able to move forward. While this was going on, Bill Slim turned his attention to me. Somehow he knew that I had been … in Malaya and he started talking about how things had changed since then, particularly our position in the air, which made air supply possible: that in its turn had made us less dependent on the road, so that we could now get behind the Japanese and cut them off. Our old doctrine of "fighting for the road from the road" was finished.

'I must have been mad … for I had the temerity to reply, "Sir, if the road does no longer matter, why are we being so pressed to open this road to Imphal?"

'A wonderful grin spread across Bill Slim's face. "Young officers should not argue with their Army commanders in the face of the enemy", he said and roared with laughter.'[14]

At the beginning of May, Stopford's 33 Corps was ordered to launch a counter-attack to clear the Japanese from Kohima and drive south down the Imphal road to link with 4 Corps. For the next four weeks, dozens of separate, desperate mini-battles were fought in and around Kohima, with each side gaining, then losing, then regaining ground. There could be no overall command or control: exhausted Allied soldiers faced exhausted Japanese soldiers and fought to the death, hand-to-hand, by moonlight as well as by day. The village of Kungpi changed hands no less than five times. Several battalions lost so many men they had to be amalgamated with other units.

Meanwhile, in Imphal, Mutaguchi was steadily being lured into the trap which Bill had set for him. Before war came to the Imphal plain it was, like Kohima, a tranquil Elysium, rich in flora and fauna. Wild marigolds, primulas, jasmine and lilac bloomed in the forests of bamboo and teak where tiger, leopard and elephant roamed and brightly coloured parrots flitted through the trees; the lakes and rivers teemed with fish and were home to snipe, duck, geese and heron. The town itself, in a green bowl circled by blue hills, boasted the oldest polo ground in the world, the ruins of a royal palace surrounded by a moat and the Ima Keithel, a colourful bazaar run entirely by *imas* (mothers) which, amazingly, continued to function throughout the fighting.

Bill faced the battle at Imphal with a lot more confidence than he had had at Kohima. Scoones had at his command the bulk of four divisions, well dug in and covering all the main avenues of approach to the plain, which was 30 miles long and 20 miles wide and greatly favoured the deployment of armour and artillery; he also enjoyed superiority in combat aircraft and there were a number of airstrips through which the corps could be supplied. Bill's intention from the outset was not simply to win this battle but to destroy Mutaguchi's army completely and render it utterly impotent as a fighting force before sending the 14th Army over the Indian border to recapture Burma.

He never wavered from this objective, to which everything else, including the capture of ground, became subordinate. When he talked to the troops, his constant refrain was that their duty was to kill the enemy, whom he compared to insects. 'The Jap is not an animal,' he liked to say, 'there is nothing splendid in him. He is part of an insect horde with all its power and horror.' (Although he privately admired the courage and tenacity of Japanese soldiers, he was contemptuous of their commanders' willingness to needlessly sacrifice their lives.)

On 29 March, two Japanese divisions had launched the assault on Imphal – the 15th Division attacked from the east and the north, the 33rd from the west and south. Thereafter the fighting, continuous, muddled and ferocious, focused on the perimeter with the line moving backwards and forwards as one side or another gained an advantage. The Japanese had confidently expected the defenders of Imphal to retreat, as had happened before, and were taken aback to be met by defiant resistance from well-trained and well-supplied troops backed by armour, artillery and air support: throughout the battle RAF and USAAF fighters and bombers denied the air to the enemy and flew sortie after sortie to hammer the Japanese positions and their lines of communication right back to Burma. 'The Jap assaults crashed like waves in a heavy sea against the fortress walls of Imphal,' the *SEAC* newspaper reported, 'but it was the waves that broke.'

After Tokyo Radio falsely claimed that Imphal had fallen, General Auchinleck addressed an anxious Assembly in Delhi to deny the report and emphasise his complete confidence in the commanders and troops defending the frontiers of India. Reporting on the position 'as made known to me by Lord Louis Mountbatten who is responsible for operations on this front', General Auchinleck said, 'Imphal is still in our hands and is strongly held. Penetrations by small parties of the enemy are always possible, but are not likely to be of major importance. Our commanders do not intend to let Imphal fall into enemy hands.'[15]

In fact the security of Imphal was only seriously threatened when, after heavy fighting, the Japanese managed to seize the twin peaks of Nungshigum, a prominent hill which towered over the northeast corner of the plain, overlooked 4 Corps' most important airstrip and was only six miles from the corps HQ. The permanent loss of Nungshigum could have been a major problem, but on 13 April it was regained in an intrepid operation, involving air, armour, artillery and infantry, which typified the new aggressive spirit of the 14th Army. Bill described the action:: 'While Hurribombers, their guns blazing, dived almost into the tree-tops, and tanks, winched up incredible slopes, fired point-blank into bunker loop-holes, our infantry stormed both peaks – and held them. The Japanese grimly defended their positions until the last men still fighting were bombed or bayoneted in their foxholes.'[16] Nungshigum would be the closest the enemy got to Imphal.

Bill was horrified by the way the Japanese continued with their attacks at Imphal even when their position was hopeless. (After the war he discovered that the commander of the 33rd Division, Major General Tanaka, had issued an order warning his men that the division should expect to be annihilated.) So many of the enemy were killed in utterly suicidal assaults that bulldozers were used to bury their bodies. Bill often told the story of Gurkhas checking over the bodies on a battlefield and discovering a man still alive. One of the Gurkhas was about to finish him off with his kukri when a passing British officer intervened and told him not to kill him. 'But sahib,' he protested not unreasonably, 'we can't bury him alive.'

Meanwhile, yet another logistical crisis loomed. Operation Stamina, the code name for the air supply operation, was absolutely vital to the success or failure of the Allied plans and so Bill was stunned when he was informed on 4 May that 79 of his transport aircraft on loan from the Middle East were needed for other operations elsewhere and must be returned by 8 May. The timing was particularly ironic, because Scoones had just warned him that insufficient supplies were getting through to 4 Corps by air and unless the main supply route along the Dimapur–Imphal route was opened by mid-June the situation would become critical. Without more rations he would have to start flying combatants out of the area: already the men were suffering from severe food shortages as the ration scales had been cut by a third – in the outlying posts high in the surrounding hills some unfortunates were having to subsist on hard biscuits and jam. Bill signalled Giffard, laying out the disastrous consequences that would result from losing the aircraft and Giffard went straight to Mountbatten who once again, on his own authority, ordered the aircraft to remain. The Supremo received unqualified support for his decision from the Prime Minister a few hours later, who signalled: 'Let nothing go from the battle you need for victory. I will not accept denial of this from any quarter, and will back you to the full.'[17]

(Operation Stamina would become the greatest air supply undertaking in the history of the war. Between 18 April and 30 June, more than 12,500 reinforcements and almost 19,000 tons of critical supplies were flown into the area while 13,000 casualties and 43,000 non-combatants were evacuated.)

By the middle of May, Bill's worst anxieties were over. 'At Kohima the Japanese had been thrown definitely on the defensive: on the Imphal–Kohima road the advance had begun; around Imphal, Scoones could feel assured that, unless the enemy were greatly reinforced, danger from the north and east was unlikely. The Japanese 15th Division had been well hammered and was losing cohesion ... Our command of the air over the whole battlefield was virtually unchallenged and, thanks to this and to the daring of our patrols, the enemy supply system was falling into confusion. Most significant, too, the monsoon was almost upon us. The more satisfactory turn that events had taken did not pass unnoticed in other circles than the 14th Army. The number of visitors at my headquarters notably increased. In the opening stages of the battle most of my visitors had been rather gloomy, a state of mind perhaps understandable, as India was full of rumours of disaster. Now ... they tended to optimism.'[18]

Bill even allowed himself to take a break from the war to attend a concert at the town hall in Comilla performed by the 'Forces Sweetheart', 27-year-old Vera Lynn. Vera arrived in Chittagong in early May, having travelled from Britain by flying boat (her first ever flight) with her pianist and a piano, to entertain the 14th Army troops in Arakan. Wearing an ENSA uniform, she sang at dozens of open-air concerts, often in torrential rain, on improvised stages constructed from aero-engine crates. The men loved her and called for encore after encore. Bill sent his car to collect her so she could perform in Comilla and after the concert she had her photograph taken with him. 'He was a very impressive man, a real soldier,' she recalled. 'I got the impression that he was a very strong character, but you could tell by the way the boys talked about him that they thought the world of him.'[19]

What Vera mainly remembered about the Comilla concert was the fact that it was the one occasion during her tour on which she was able to wear the only dress, in pink chiffon, that she had brought with her. When she was not performing, she spent most of her time visiting the troops in hospital and answering the question that almost every one of them invariably asked: 'How are things at home?' She also stayed with Aileen in the Slims' bungalow in the hills of Shillong for some 'R & R' away from the heat. She thought Aileen, who was working as a volunteer in the local hospital, was 'a lovely lady'. (Noël Coward, a friend, predictably, of Mountbatten, also performed for the 14th Army in Burma around this time, but with considerably less success.)

Along the Kohima ridge the last stronghold to be captured was the Deputy Comissioner's garden and tennis court. After several failed attempts to outflank or storm the position, Allied engineers bulldozed a track to a point above the garden. A Lee tank was winched up the track then crashed down on to the tennis court and destroyed the Japanese trenches and bunkers. The 2nd Battalion, The Dorsetshire Regiment, followed up and finally cleared the enemy off the ridge, which had become a 'vision of hell', with innumerable half-buried human remains churned up in the mud.

By then General Sato had become convinced that the battle could not be won. His men were not only worn out, they were starving. The division had begun the assault on Kohima with only three weeks' supply of food, expecting to resupply from captured Allied stocks. They had now been in action for more than six weeks, had captured very little in the way of supplies and were making do with what they could forage from increasingly hostile local villages. Sato, in despair, asked permission to withdraw to resupply and save further casualties. Mutaguchi refused and threatened him with a court martial if he disobeyed his orders. Sato had reached the stage where he was no longer prepared for his soldiers' lives to be further sacrificed. On 31 May, disregarding his own future, he formally ordered his troops to withdraw. 'We fought for two months with the utmost courage and have reached the limits of human fortitude ...' he wrote. 'Shedding bitter tears I now leave Kohima.'[20]

Although fighting continued in the area as Allied troops pursued the retreating Japanese, Sato's decision formally ended the battle for Kohima. It was a costly victory for the Allies – 4,000 soldiers killed, missing or wounded. But the Japanese losses were significantly greater – 5,764 battle casualties and many more unaccounted for.

News of the D-Day landings in Normandy on 6 June boosted morale throughout the South East Asia Command and raised the hope that a swift victory in Europe would bring an end to their 'Cinderella' status. The men of the 14th Army were sick and tired of 'make do and mend', of fighting with obsolete equipment, of being told that everyone's first priority was the defeat of Nazi Germany in Europe. Nazi Germany seemed to be a very long way away to a filthy, exhausted soldier sitting in a trench in the jungle, drenched by the monsoon, plagued by every kind of insect, beset by previously unimaginable tropical diseases and facing an enemy considerably more barbaric than any 'bloody Kraut'.

No one knew better than Bill the strain the troops were under. There was so much for them to bear – the jungle, the monsoon, the poor rations, the disease, the dangers, being so far away from home and the psychological stress of constantly losing, one way or another, close friends. But at the same time it was clearly evident to Bill that his army was very different from the dejected force which had trooped out of Burma two years earlier. There was a new fighting spirit, new confidence and steadiness, new pride.

Bill succumbed to an attack of malaria at about this time and was hospitalised in Shillong for several days, to his intense frustration. It was not just that he was being kept from the heart of the action at a critical time; it was that he had broken his own rules. He had decreed that to contract malaria was a breach of discipline and had forbidden all troops to bathe after sunset, when malarial mosquitoes were most prevalent. But returning from the front one day, tired and very muddy, he had stripped off, washed in the open and landed himself in a hospital bed. It was going to be difficult, he thought, in future to repeat his exhortations to the men about the dangers of washing in the open at night. He did not, however, allow himself to be cut off from what was going on and established a small tactical headquarters at his bedside. He also passed the time playing chess with a fellow patient, a young Australian gunner officer by the name of Robert Crichton-Brown, whom he would meet again

when he was Governor-General of Australia and Sir Robert was a
prominent businessman.

While Bill was in hospital, Mountbatten chided him, in a letter,
to take better care of himself: 'I do beg of you to take proper care
of your health because to have a bad go of malaria on top of all you
have been through is a serious matter and as much of our future
operations depend on you retaining your health and strength, please
look after yourself.'[21]

Mountbatten was certainly following his own advice. He had decided, in April, to move SEAC headquarters from the torpid atmosphere of Delhi to the more agreeable environs of Kandy, the last
capital of the ancient kingdom of Kandy, in Ceylon, 1,600 miles
to the south. It was a bizarre decision that many interpreted as the
product of a man who could not stand the heat deciding to vacate
the kitchen. Mountbatten took over as his residence the splendid
King's Pavilion, a miniature white palace with a nine-hole golf
course and an orchid garden patrolled by white peacocks. The headquarters staff occupied huts among lily ponds, palms and hibiscus
trees in the former botanical gardens. SEAC HQ at Kandy would
soon become a byword for luxury and elegance, of balls and parties,
both figuratively and literally far removed from the squalid lives of
the fighting troops, the nearest of whom were at least 1,400 miles
away across the Bay of Bengal in Arakan.

Around the time of the D-Day landings Bill's considerable diplomatic skills were called upon when a serious problem arose with
the Chindits. On 17 May he had passed operational control of the
Chindits to Stilwell in order to tighten the command and control
structure on the northern front, where the Chinese had captured the
airfield at Myitkyina and had embarked on a long drawn-out siege of
the town. Stilwell almost immediately fell out with Major General
Walter Lentaigne, a brigade commander on the first Chindit expedition whom Bill had chosen to replace Wingate. (Wingate, characteristically, had separately promised three, possibly four, of his subordinates – none of them Lentaigne – that they would succeed him
in the event of his death.) When the monsoon began to make air
supply problematic for the Chindits, Lentaigne ordered the evacuation of the bases around Indaw and set up a new stronghold further
to the north, near the Indawgyi Lake, from where he was able to

evacuate his casualties with the help of two RAF Sunderland flying boats. Stilwell complained that the Chindits were not following his orders and by shifting north had allowed the Japanese to move reinforcements into Myitkyina. An exasperated Lentaigne protested that Stilwell was demanding the impossible from his exhausted men and was not giving him enough time to reorganise. The row culminated in Stilwell reporting to Mountbatten that Lentaigne had disobeyed orders to carry out an operation and asking for the Chindits to be detached from his command and replaced with a British parachute formation.

Mountbatten ordered Bill to go up to the northern front to sort it out. He might have thought that the commander of the 14th Army had quite enough his plate already, with battles raging in Kohima and Imphal, but Bill was probably the best choice as he was one of the very few Limeys – perhaps the only Limey – Stilwell respected. Between 6 June and 12 June, Bill was obliged to shuttle between his own headquarters and those of Stilwell and Lentaigne, patiently listening to the concerns and grievances of both men.

'I found Stilwell bitter and Lentaigne indignant, both obviously and very understandably suffering from prolonged strain,' Bill recalled. One of the major problems was that Stilwell, in his current belligerent mood, was simply refusing to talk to Lentaigne. It took some time for Bill to make him see reason, but in the end he looked at Bill over the top of his spectacles and asked, 'What do you want me to do?' Bill said he wanted him to meet with Lentaigne, talk things over with him, give him a chance to reorganise and get his casualties evacuated, and keep the Chindits under his command until Myitkyina had fallen. Stilwell agreed. (Myitkyina eventually fell on 3 August after a siege lasting two and a half months; the Japanese garrison commander ordered his remaining troops to break out as best they could, then committed suicide.)

Throughout the battle Bill should have enjoyed the matchless asset of a stream of intelligence fed to him from the MI6 Special Liaison Unit in Delhi, courtesy of Ultra, but a shortage of Japanese-speaking interpreters caused critical delays in the information reaching him. However, Ultra did provide him with enemy operational and movement orders, location of different formations and strength returns. 'Some of the most interesting signals had been

those showing the [enemy's] shortages of rations and equipment,'
Frederick Winterbotham, the MI6 officer in charge of the unit,
recalled after the war. 'General Slim told me that the intelligence
from Ultra about Japanese forces had been invaluable throughout
the campaign, but the real triumph had been the information that
led up to the final attack by the Japanese at Kohima and Imphal. It
had become very evident from Ultra that the Japanese supply position was desperate and that their attack was being planned in order
to capture the 14th Army supply depots so as to keep the Japanese
army in business. Ultra also showed that the Japanese air force in
the area had dwindled so as to be practically useless. It was these
two factors which determined the plan to allow the Japanese attack
to spend itself while the 14th Army formed a defensive box around
their bases at Imphal and Kohima.'[22]

More heavy fighting was required, almost always in torrential rain,
before the enemy was cleared from the Kohima–Imphal road, but at
1030 on 22 June leading troops and tanks of the British 2nd Division,
driving south, linked up with the 5th Indian Infantry Division, advancing north from Imphal, at Milestone 109, 30 miles from Kohima,
finally ending the siege of both garrisons. That evening the first
supply convoy, lights blazing, rumbled into Imphal from Dimapur.
The opening of the Kohima–Imphal road effectively signalled the
collapse of Operation U-Go and end of the Japanese offensive in
India. Although the fighting continued for another two weeks, there
was no realistic hope of the Japanese achieving their initial objectives
and, on 8 July, Mutaguchi reluctantly accepted defeat and ordered
his starving, battered troops to begin withdrawing. It was a bitter pill
for the Japanese general to swallow. U-Go was to have been his personal triumph, the pinnacle of his career: it was Mutaguchi who had
persuaded the General Staff to expand U-Go from a spoiling attack
against 4 Corps into an invasion of India and perhaps the overthrow
of the British Raj. His dreams of glory in the service of the Emperor
crushed, Mutaguchi was relieved of his command, recalled to Tokyo
and forced into retirement at the end of the year, his mind unhinged.
Sato was similarly removed from command but demanded a court
martial to clear his name and air his complaints about Mutaguchi;
he was effectively gagged by doctors who decided he had suffered a
mental breakdown and was unfit to stand trial.

On 2 July, Bill and Jack Baldwin, commander of the 3rd Tactical Air Force, met Mountbatten to discuss the next phase of the campaign. A month earlier the Chiefs of Staff in London had issued an initial directive which decreed the priority for South East Asia Command should be to 'develop, broaden and protect the air link to China', presumably, Bill thought, as a result of pressure from the Americans. His strong view was that the best and quickest way to secure the lifeline to China was to kick the Japanese out of Burma entirely and recapture the port of Rangoon. At the 2 July meeting he argued that the Chiefs of Staff proposals were far too modest, that neither London nor Washington had understood the extent of the Japanese defeat at Imphal and Kohima and had thus not appreciated the opportunity it presented for a decisive victory. He claimed that his army would be ready to launch a full-scale invasion of Burma as early as November and that it would require no more manpower than would be needed to maintain a defensive line in the north.

Bill knew that Mountbatten would have to get approval for an offensive but he had no intention of waiting for the Chiefs of Staff to make up their minds. After the 2 July meeting he moved his forward headquarters to Imphal and ordered his staff to begin planning operations for the capture of Mandalay, to be followed immediately by an advance on Rangoon. Bill's chief of staff, Brigadier John 'Tubby' Lethbridge, christened Bill's unofficial plans Operation Sob – 'Sea or Bust'. Bill's tenuous authority for all this was an addendum to the Chiefs of Staff directive which spoke of pressing 'advantages against the enemy by exerting maximum effort ... and in pressing such advantages to be prepared to exploit the development of overland communications to China'. As far as Bill was concerned, that meant recapturing Burma.

On 23 July, Mountbatten submitted two plans to London for approval. The first, Operation Capital, involved the 14th Army and Chinese troops under Stilwell occupying all the territory between the Chindwin and the Irrawaddy rivers and seizing Mandalay. The second, Operation Dracula, envisaged an amphibious landing in early 1945 to capture Rangoon and an advance north to Mandalay. To Bill's disappointment the initial reaction from London was to limit the 14th Army to holding operations until Dracula had been launched; indeed, at one point there was even a suggestion that the 14th Army should withdraw to Imphal to be rested prior to being moved south to provide sufficient resources to ensure the success of the amphibious operation, although it was quickly dropped. Bill privately thought it was pretty unlikely that Dracula would ever come to pass, particularly since the early optimism about the imminent collapse of Nazi Germany was proving to be ill founded and had scotched hopes for Burma to be given greater priority in terms of resources.

In August Mountbatten, concerned that events in Europe and the Pacific were overshadowing the achievements of the 14th Army, briefed a press conference to set the record straight. 'I go round and talk to the men in the Command,' he said, 'and what worries them is that their wives, their mothers, their daughters their sweethearts and their sisters don't seem to know that the war they are fighting is important and worth while, which it most assuredly is ... In point of numbers engaged this must have been one of the greatest land battles fought between the Japanese and British forces and I am glad to say the Japanese have now been flung out of India.' The Allied forces, he continued, had suffered 10,000 killed, 2,000 missing and 27,000 wounded, but these had been 'amply avenged' by the killing of no fewer than 50,000 Japanese. In addition to human losses, the enemy was forced to abandon the majority of its tanks and artillery on the battlefield. Two of the three enemy divisions that crossed the Chindwin had been rendered combat ineffective by the end of the battle. It was, Mountbatten emphasised, the greatest defeat the Imperial Japanese Army had ever suffered on land.

'We are still pushing on in spite of the Jap, and, what is holding us up more is the weather,' Bill wrote to his friend Gibbos, then at the Gurkha Recruiting Depot, on 15 August. 'I have no doubt we have got a lot of difficulties to meet and the yellow belly will come back at us again, but there is no doubt that the old Fourteenth Army has given him the biggest defeat he has ever had in his whole history. I rather think he knows it.'[23]

Under Bill's command, in the space of less than a year the 14th Army had been forged into a formidable fighting machine with a new-born esprit de corps second to none, curiously exemplified in the bush hats that everyone, including Bill, wore. 'The 14th Army's distinguishing feature was the bush hat,' George MacDonald Fraser of The Border Regiment explained, 'that magnificent Australian headgear with the rakish broad brim which shielded against rain and sun and was ideal for scooping water out of wells. In some ways it was a freak, in the steel helmeted 20th century, and it may have cost some lives under shell fire, but we wouldn't have swapped it. It looked good, it felt good … everyone carried a razor blade tucked into the band in case you were captured, in which event you might, presumably, cut your bonds, or decapitate your jailer by stages, or if the worst … We were the 14th Army, the final echo of Kipling's world, the very last soldiers in the old imperial tradition. I don't say we were happy to be in Burma, because we weren't, but we knew that Slim was right when he said, "Some day you'll be proud to say I was there".'[24]

The combined operations of the 14th Army in Arakan, Kohima and Imphal and behind enemy lines on the northern front had virtually destroyed five enemy divisions, shattered for ever the tattered myth of Japanese invincibility on the battlefield and severely degraded the capability of the Imperial Japanese Army to defend Burma – just as Bill had hoped and predicted.

16

The Pursuit

With the rout of the Japanese 15th Army at Imphal and Kohima, Bill was more than ever convinced that the best way to drive the enemy out of Burma was by an overland advance from India. There were many voices, in Kandy, Delhi, London and Washington, which continued to argue that it was folly, that the terrain presented an impenetrable barrier, but Bill was on the spot, was sure it could be done and was frustrated that outside Burma no one seemed to be aware of the scale of the Japanese defeat, evidence of which was mounting daily in losses of manpower, armour, artillery and equipment.

The view in Washington was that Burma was something of a sideshow and would not ultimately contribute to the final conquest of Japan. The United States poured its considerable resources into the campaign in the Pacific, as the springboard from which war could be won. By 1944 the United States Navy had established its dominance in the area and its submarines were enforcing a stranglehold blockade on Japan, a country wholly dependent on imported fuel and raw materials, ultimately sinking 1,300 enemy ships. In July, US Marines had captured the Marianas, a string of volcanic islands with airfields that brought Japanese cities within the range of B-29 bombers.

As far as Bill was concerned, the war in the Pacific was utterly divorced from his war in Burma. He understood that forcing the Japanese out of Burma was unlikely to result in the defeat of Japan, but it still had to be done. He knew that General Kawabe, commander of the Burma Area Army, would need time to reorganise and resupply his troops, presenting the Allies with a perfect opportunity for a decisive strike. He believed there was little prospect of mounting an amphibious operation in the south due to a shortage of landing craft, but, if the enemy could be driven back across the Chindwin by the end of the monsoon, the 14th Army would then be poised for a final battle on the plains of Burma in front of Mandalay, prior to sweeping down to Rangoon. It was to this end that he applied himself, even while the Chiefs of Staff were still dithering about what to do.

First the enemy had to be cleared out of India, no easy task in the dreadful conditions created by the monsoon, which had started in mid-June. Low clouds shrouded the tops of the hills and rain poured down in unceasing torrents, sweeping away already precarious mountain tracks connecting one position with another, turning the ground into a quagmire and transforming jungle streams into boiling cataracts difficult to cross. Men were soaked to the skin day and night, covered in mud, slipping and sliding in ankle-deep sludge; grabbing the tail of a mule and getting pulled along was sometimes the only way to climb a steep slope. Uniforms rotted; fingers and toes became white and wrinkled. Exhausted troops no longer bothered with blankets at night but lay down to sleep in the mud in their sodden uniforms and frequently woke covered in leeches. Sickness and disease, particularly malaria and scrub typhus, took an increasing toll. Dysentery was the great scourge; those men unable to eat existed on a diet of rum and tinned milk. Evacuating casualties was a nightmare – unit war diaries spoke of half a company taking ten hours to carry two stretchers for four miles – although many men succumbed to exhaustion and disease and died in the jungle.

While the Japanese had been decisively beaten, they continued to fight tenacious rearguard actions. Bill did his best to visit all the front-line units, travelling by jeep or on foot, and was encouraged by their undiminished fighting spirit, despite what they were suffering. Full of admiration, he watched bedraggled men struggling up steep slopes, through mud with the 'consistency of porridge' halfway up to their knees, in pursuit of the enemy. 'It was campaigning at its hardest,' he noted, 'but everyone was cheerful.' (Cheerful? It is possible Bill put a bit of a gloss on things when he came to write *Defeat Into Victory*.) He spoke to casualties who had endured long, jolting journeys in the wet and cold and was assured by them 'in their various languages' that they were fine when it was patently obvious that they were not; some were quite evidently dying. It was a humbling experience for a man of considerable sensitivity. 'I asked for the impossible,' he admitted, 'and got it.'

Visiting the wounded in hospital one day, Bill came across a young Gurkha with an extraordinary tale to tell. Nineteen-year-old Rifleman Ganju Lama of 1st/7th Gurkhas was with his company near Bishenpur when enemy tanks broke through their forward position. Leaving cover, he crawled over open ground towards the tanks with his Piat anti-tank gun. Despite being shot in the hand, shoulder and leg, he dragged himself to within 30 yards, knocked out two tanks then moved further forward and killed or wounded every member of the enemy tank crews as they attempted to escape. When Bill asked him why he had moved so close to the Japanese tanks he replied simply: 'Well, sir, I'd been trained not to fire the Piat until I was certain of hitting and I knew I could hit them at 30 yards so I went 30 yards.' Rifleman Ganju Lama was later awarded the Victoria Cross, one of the eight VCs that would be awarded to the Gurkhas in Burma in 1944.

When the 11th East African Division, largely made up of troops from Kenya, Uganda, Nyasaland, Tanganyika and Rhodesia, arrived at Palel Plain in India to join 33 Corps, Bill paid them an early visit to give the officers and NCOs a pep talk. Frank Owen was present and reported on the occasion for an issue of *Phoenix*, the South East Asia Command magazine. Owen described Bill as resembling a 'well-to-do West Country farmer', with his weatherbeaten complexion, broad nose, jutting jaw, twinkling hazel eyes and evident common sense.

'The General stood on an ammunition box. Facing him in a green amphitheatre of the low hills that ring Palel Plain, sat or squatted the British officers and sergeants of the 11th East African Division. They were then new to the Burma Front and were moving into the line the next day. The General removed his battered slouch hat, which the Gurkhas wear and which has become the headgear of the 14th Army. "Take a good look at my mug," he advised. "Not that I consider it to be an oil painting. But I am the Army Commander and you had better be able to recognise me, if only to say, 'Look out, the old bastard is coming round' ... I have commanded every kind of formation from a section to this army, which happens to be the largest single one in the world. I tell you this simply that you should realise I know what I am talking about. I understand the British soldier because I have been one, and I have learned about the Japanese soldier because I have been beaten by him. I have been kicked by this enemy in the place where it hurts, and all the way from Rangoon to India where I had to dust off my pants. Now, gentlemen, we are kicking our Japanese neighbours back to Rangoon."

'The General, who has been fighting the Japanese for more than three years, tells this young division what the enemy soldier is like, and how to beat him. He dissects the anatomy of the Japanese Army, its strategy, tactics and supply. He explains its strength and puts a sure finger on its weaknesses … Then Slim relates at one critical point in the retreat in a jungle clearing he came across a unit which was in a bad way. "I took one look at them and thought My God, they're worse than I supposed. Then I saw why. I walked round the corner of that clearing and I saw officers making themselves a bivouac. They were just as exhausted as their men, but that isn't my point. Officers are there to lead. I tell you, therefore, as officers, that you will neither eat, nor drink, nor sleep, nor smoke, nor even sit down until you have personally seen that your men have done these things. If you will do this for them, they will follow you to the end of the world. And if you do not, I will break you."' Owen reported that as Bill stepped down from the ammunition box and replaced his hat, the division rose as one man and cheered him.

Towards the end of July, Bill's plan for an overland advance into Burma – Operation Capital – was given a tentative green light by the Chiefs of Staff. Bill was instructed to be ready to launch Operation Capital in December in the event that it was eventually approved. (Actually his plans were already well advanced since Operation Capital was not so very different from the first stages of his private enterprise, Operation Sob, 'Sea or Bust', and he was looking to start operations in November.)

It meant extensive retraining for his army to fight and manoeuvre in the open country of the central Burma plain, terrain very different from that to which they had become accustomed. 'For two years our formations had fought in jungles and amongst hills,' he explained. 'They were now about to break out into open country with unobstructed views and freedom of movement away from tracks. Not only would the laborious tactics of the jungle have to be replaced by speed, mechanisation and mobility, but also commanders and troops would have to adjust their mentality to the changed conditions. This was especially so in the case of armour and artillery. Instead of one or two tanks, surrounded by infantry, carefully nosing forward along a narrow jungle track, we might hope to use powerful, rapidly moving, armoured formations on extended fronts.'[1]

Not all Bill's senior officers agreed that it was feasible for the 14th Army to capture Rangoon overland and a number voiced their opinions at a conference Bill convened in Dehra Dun in the north of India (where his son, John, was studying at the Royal Indian Military College). Among those taking part was Brigadier Bernard Fergusson, recently returned from the second Chindit expedition. Fergusson was appalled by what he considered defeatist talk. 'I remember but will not reveal the identity of a divisional commander who said – and not without support from others – that to prevent the Japanese cutting the road behind one a force of at least a brigade would be needed every X miles; there were only Y brigades in the 14th Army; it was Z hundred miles to Rangoon – ergo, it would be impossible to capture Rangoon overland.'[2]

What most angered him about such negative arguments was that they completely ignored the proven potential of air supply. It was too much for Fergusson, who owed his life, and that of his men, to provisions dropping from the sky. 'Something like a brainstorm broke over me; I got to my feet and I gave them an earful ... in the hush that followed a tall, languid, fair-haired Brigadier whom I had never seen before got up on one of the terraces opposite ... "I don't quite know who the last speaker was," he drawled, "but obviously he was talking sense. I mean, it's obvious isn't it? I mean it's obvious to anyone who uses his brains" ... We might well have gone on like this, but for a dry interruption from Slim at his table. "Brigadiers West[3] and Fergusson having left us in no doubt as to their views, they will now kindly keep their mouths shut for the rest of the conference". But it was nicely and jocularly said ...'[4]

While Bill never shirked the responsibility of making decisions, he was always ready to consider contrary views; meetings of his senior staff were conducted in an open, democratic fashion, with everyone being allowed to have their say. His chief engineer, Brigadier William Hasted, remembered lively discussions in the senior officers' mess: 'The senior mess ... was extremely close-knit, with absolutely no rivalries. In it "Uncle Bill" was just what his affectionate nickname implied. We all spoke freely what was on our minds. We had no secrets from one another, and Uncle Bill joined wholeheartedly in the conversation on whatever subject. His presence commanded a natural respect born of our knowledge of the greatness of the man himself, but there was no ghastly hush as so often happens in senior messes when the commander enters. His quick witted and pene-trating mind was more than a match for anyone round the table, and woe betide the speaker who knew little of his subject or facts. He was a great judge of character and very quickly put his finger on weaknesses. I think this enabled him to get the best out of everyone who served under him; although he didn't suffer fools gladly, he accepted those posted or serving under him and knew whether to ride on a curb, or snaffle, or when to use the whip, which was in fact seldom necessary.'[5]

On 6 August, Bill's 53rd birthday, he issued formal orders to Monty Stopford, commander of 33 Corps, to continue the relentless pursuit of the enemy and, if the opportunity offered, prepare to es-tablish bridgeheads across the Chindwin. Both 33 Corps' advancing columns needed to be supplied by air, with RAF and USAAF pilots flying through storms, mist and cloud in conditions that would have grounded everything before the war. Progress was painfully slow and difficult; disease and the monsoon were as formidable an enemy as the Japanese. (In the space of just 26 days a single brigade of the 5th Division lost 94 men killed or wounded in action and 507 from sickness.) Much of the pursuit was against the grain of the country and entailed climbing one razor-backed ridge after an-other. Even in the valleys things were little better: with the *chaungs* in full spate bridges needed to be built before the advance could be resumed; jeeps bogged down again and again in the mud; gun teams stripped to the waist manhandled their weapons forward when the tracks became impossible for towing vehicles. As leading patrols pushed the enemy rearguard back through the dripping jungle their path was littered by the gruesome relics of an army in retreat – abandoned equipment and muddy, decaying corpses, sometimes lying singly by the track, or sitting grotesquely in wrecked vehicles, or propped against trees or huddled together in rudimentary bashas. One 14th Army driver decorated his jeep with a skull, but when Bill saw it he told him to remove it. 'It might be one of ours,' he said gently, 'killed on the retreat.'

Vengeance dive bombers and Mitchell bombers repeatedly blasted the retreating Japanese columns, forcing the enemy to take refuge in the hills where hundreds died of exhaustion or starvation. At Tamu, once a thriving centre for smuggling goods into India, advance patrols from the 11th East African Division found 550 enemy corpses unburied in the streets, many of them huddled at the feet of a miraculously undamaged stone Buddha in the centre of the town. Among the dead were those still clinging precariously to life, lying in indescribable filth and dying of wounds, disease or starvation. Fourteenth Army doctors discovered that many captured enemy troops were suffering from acute beriberi, caused by a lack of vitamin B in their diets.

Bill was naturally more concerned about the condition of his own men, many of whom were severely malnourished after being ravaged by dysentery and existing for months on a monotonous diet almost entirely devoid of fresh meat and vegetables. By the beginning of August he had sufficient breathing space to send the most stressed front-line units back to India for rest and recuperation. Among the few sources of entertainment available for the troops in rear areas was an ENSA unit called the India Repertory Company, commanded by Jack Hawkins, who became one of Britain's most popular film actors after the war. One of the company's productions was *Love in a Mist*, a play about two young couples stranded on Exmoor in fog. Hawkins had planned to send his actors on leave before they reached Imphal until he received what he described as an 'unnerving' telegram from Bill insisting that the show should go on. 'There was no way Jack could refuse such an order,' recalled Doreen Lawrence, one of the actresses involved and Hawkins' future wife. 'We opened the following night and the event was made more special by General Slim himself attending. He was wildly popular with his men, who would do anything for him ... After the show he came backstage to greet and thank us, saying how delighted he was we had finally arrived in Imphal. He invited us to take tea with him in his tent.'[6]

By 25 August the only Japanese troops left in India were prisoners. As the enemy was remorselessly pushed back and one little mountain settlement after another fell to the advancing 14th Army, Bill felt a tinge of regret that his men were not rewarded with flag-waving locals cheering their arrival. They marched instead, in torrential rain, through smoking ruins on constant alert for snipers and booby traps, watched by a few frightened villagers, dressed in rags, sheltering in the remains of a pagoda or temple. The Japanese had long outstayed their welcome, but the Burmese could hardly be blamed for concluding that soldiers of any nation brought with them little but death and destruction. As far as they were concerned, the arrival of another army was not a cause for celebration.

At the beginning of September, after much hard fighting, the East African Division occupied Sittaung, which was found to be another Tamu, with hundreds of unburied bodies lying in the streets. A few days later a small bridgehead was established on the east bank of the Chindwin river, setting the stage for the next phase of the battle – to drive the enemy back to Mandalay.

On 16 September, to his great satisfaction, Bill was finally given official authority to capture the whole of Burma (which he was planning to do anyway). At the Octagon Conference in Quebec, Mountbatten had secured the agreement of the combined Chiefs of Staff to extend the mandate they had tentatively approved in July. The directive began, 'Your object is the destruction and expulsion of all Japanese forces in Burma at the earliest possible date.' Bill told Giffard that he would be ready to launch an offensive on 15 November.

By then Bill's men could no longer realistically claim to be 'the Forgotten Army'. The Prime Minister had paid generous tribute to the fighting troops in Burma in the House of Commons and newspapers were at last taking an interest in what was going on in South-East Asia. 'The triumphs of his 14th Army in the weeping forests of Burma have brought him into the headlines,' the *Observer* reported in an affectionate profile of Bill published on 10 September. 'As the world turns more of its attention from the Western war to the destruction of our Japanese foes he will receive the wide renown that his deeds deserve but he himself would keep at bay.' Bill was quoted as telling journalists gruffly, 'I'm afraid you can't make a Monty out of me', which the *Observer* attributed to his lack of desire for self-publicity rather than a dig at Montgomery's love of it.

Bill's basic human decency shone through the *Observer* profile and was an attribute that was evident to everyone who crossed his path. Alexander Greenwood, Auchinleck's ADC, was often sorely tried by visitors to Flagstaff House, the C-in-C's official residence in Delhi: on one memorable occasion he reported that Noël Coward, Cecil Beaton and the painter Simon Elwes were all staying 'in a cloud of exotic aromas' and infuriated staff by being unpunctual for meals and requiring special attention at all hours. Bill was different. 'He arrived carrying a briefcase and his luggage consisted of one suitcase. I noticed the first thing he did when he arrived was to unpack photographs of his wife, Aileen, and his two children, which he then arranged by his bed at the side of his alarm clock. There was no nonsense about Slim and he had no allergies. He was very approachable, kind and tolerant and he had that strange, difficult to describe, charisma of great leadership.'[7]

Towards the end of September came the news that the King had conferred honours on the 14th Army commanders 'in recognition of the valour of the men fighting under them'. It made the front page of the Friday, 29 September edition of *SEAC* under the head-line: 'KNIGHTHOODS FOR GEN. SLIM AND 3 CORPS COMMANDERS'. The story began: 'London, Thursday – The King has recognised in traditional fashion the signal victory won by the Fourteenth Army over the Japanese by conferring knighthoods on the Army commander and all his Corps Commanders.' Bill was awarded a KCB and KBEs went to Scoones, Christison and Stopford. Mountbatten was quoted as saying it was the first time, as far as he knew, that a British army had been honoured by having its commander and three corps commanders knighted simultaneously in the field.

'Lieutenant-General Slim was faced with a series of situations many of great gravity,' Bill's citation read. 'He faced all these with calm courage and determination. As the situation developed he saw clearly that the Japanese Forces had reached a position which would give him the opportunity to defeat them ... and he said from the beginning of the operations that he would do so decisively. He made his plans to this end and allowed nothing to divert him. He has in consequence inflicted a major defeat on the Japanese Forces which are now retiring in complete disorder, leaving dead and dying men, guns, tanks and great quantities of equipment behind them.'

The newspaper, perhaps tactfully, did not make the point that Bill came from very different stock from his corps commanders. Scoones was born into a military family and was educated at Wellington and Sandhurst; Christison was the son of a baronet and Stopford was the great-grandson of an earl. *SEAC* drew a discreet veil over Bill's far humbler origins as the son of a commercial traveller, not that Bill himself would have cared. He was not the kind of man to present himself as anything other than what he was.

Soon after news of the knighthoods had been released, Bill drafted a Special Order of the Day which paid generous tribute to the men who had done the fighting: 'In my last Order of the Day I told you that you had defeated the Japanese Armies opposing you and that it remained to destroy them. The extent to which you have done that is shown by the 50,000 Japanese left dead on the soil of India and Northern Burma, the great quantities of guns and equipment you have captured, the prisoners you have taken, the advances you have made and the flight of the remnants you are still pursuing.

'To the 15 Corps in Arakan fell the unique honour of being the first British-Indian formation to hold, break and decisively hurl back a major Japanese offensive. Theirs was an example of tenacity and courage which inspired the whole Army. 4 Corps met the main weight of the Japanese Assam offensive and, in one of the hardest fought and longest battles of the war, shattered it. 33 Corps in their brilliant offensive from the north not only drove a large Japanese force from what could have been an impregnable position but destroyed it. Together the 4th and 33rd Corps have swept the enemy out of India ...

'To the officers and men of every formation and unit that served or serve the Fourteenth Army I send my congratulations. You have inflicted on the Japanese the greatest defeat his Army has as yet suffered. He is busily trying to build up again and reinforce his broken divisions. He will fight again and viciously, but we have paid him something of what we owe. There still remains the interest. He will get it.'

Elsewhere in the war, confident predictions that Germany would be defeated before the end of the year looked increasingly optimistic, but in the Pacific US troops had landed in the Philippines after the biggest naval battle in history and photographs of General Douglas MacArthur wading ashore and fulfilling his promise that he would return[8] made the front pages across America. Although the Japanese were still fighting hard throughout the Pacific theatre, they were being forced back everywhere.

At the end of October, Bill embarked on a tour of all the 14th Army positions, covering 1,000 miles in nine days, 400 by road and 600 by air. His programme included everything from a full-dress inspection of an entire division, to going round the rear areas where extensive retraining was taking place for the upcoming offensive, to visiting the most forward airstrip only a few miles from the front, to stopping his car on the road to chat with three oil-smeared engineers in a mobile workshop at Kohima. Bill was always at his best talking informally, man-to-man, with ordinary soldiers, listening to their concerns with a sympathetic ear, sharing a joke and bolstering their morale.

Patrick Burgoyne, a 20-year-old Lance Bombardier in 3023 (East Africa) Field Regiment, remembered an inspection by the army commander. 'We were drawn up in a road above a paddy field in Dimapur. I was standing next to my friend Dixie Dean, a bombardier who had served in North Africa, then returned to the UK where he expected to stay. Much to his annoyance he had been posted again to the Far East. Slim saw his medals and asked him where he had served and who with and when Dixie explained Slim said "OK, fair enough." Then Dixie piped up, "No, sir, I don't think it is fair at all." Slim laughed and said, "What are you talking about? You have nothing to worry about – I've been serving overseas for eleven years."'[9]

Bill returned from his tour in time to meet Lieutenant General Sir Oliver Leese, who had arrived in India to replace George Giffard and take over as commander of the newly formed Allied

Land Forces, South East Asia (ALFSEA). Mountbatten had sacked Giffard back in April. The two men had never got on: Mountbatten thought Giffard was too old for the job, too set in his ways and too complacent, while Giffard held himself aloof, openly opposed many of Mountbatten's initiatives and made no secret of the fact that he resented being subordinate to a younger naval officer. Mountbatten first tried to persuade Giffard to retire on medical grounds and, when that failed, he felt he had no alternative but to tell him that he had lost confidence him. The gentlemanly Giffard accepted the news with reasonable grace and agreed to stay on in the job until a replacement could be found. Bill made no bones about the fact that he was sorry to see Giffard go after they had been working harmoniously together for more than 15 months. 'He had seen us through our efforts to become an army and through our first and most desperate battles. Fourteenth Army owed much to his integrity, his judgement, his sound administration, his support in our darkest hours, and to the universal confidence he inspired among us. We saw him go with grief.'[10]

Leese, the son of a baronet, an Old Etonian and Coldstream Guardsman, had won a DSO in France in the Great War and had recently commanded the Eighth Army in the final battle at Cassino. He also had a reputation as a dandy and was said to be the last senior officer to wear plus-fours and stockings in preference to battledress trousers and gaiters. His introduction to South East Asia Command was memorable, not to say bizarre. He reported at Kandy in November and was immediately invited to Mountbatten's birthday party at the officers' club the following night. (The party was rather late, since Mountbatten was born in June.) The Supremo offered to drive Leese to the club in his small Austin car and as they arrived the band struck up 'Happy Birthday' and a very pretty Wren walked across the ballroom floor and kissed Mountbatten on the lips with some enthusiasm. Leese was shocked not just by that incident but by the numbers of equally pretty girls who seemed to spend most of the evening draped over the arms of Mountbatten's chair. He was not entirely surprised to discover later that Indian Army officers referred to Kandy as Wimbledon – because it was all 'balls and rackets'.

The creation of ALFSEA led to some reorganisation in the

theatre. Bill was relieved of responsibility for 15 Corps operations
in Arakan and a separate Lines of Communication Command
was established to control administrative and logistical functions,
leaving him free to concentrate on the upcoming battle commanding two corps – the 4th, now under Frank Messervy (Scoones had
been promoted and returned to India), and the 33rd, still under
Monty Stopford, each with two divisions and a tank brigade. Bill
was a good delegator and could never be accused of breathing down
his subordinates' necks, but at the same time he had a remarkable
ability to assess the strengths and weaknesses of the men under his
command. Messervy was an old friend and a dynamic battlefield
commander but had a tendency to be impetuous and take risks and
so Bill personally appointed his chief of staff, Brigadier Eddie Cobb,
to keep an eye on him and restrain his ardour. Messervy protested at
this slight, complained he knew nothing of Cobb and did not want
him as chief of staff. Bill's response was terse: 'No Cobb, no corps.'
Messervy capitulated.

On 14 November, Leese flew from Kandy to his own headquarters at Flagstaff House in Barrackpore, where he had asked Bill
and Philip Christison to meet him the following day. Both arrived 'rather indignant' about being called away from the front.
Leese apologised, assured them he would never call them back
to Barrackpore in the future and had only done so to save time.
Leese had met Bill briefly some years earlier when he (Leese) was
chief instructor at Quetta. 'I got a good impression of Slim,' Leese
wrote later to his wife, Margaret, 'though I think he bellyaches.
He was slightly defensive about the Indian Army, the difficulties
of Burma and the need to understand how to fight the Japs. I said
how glad I was to come to his great 14th Army. He showed no signs
of wanting to see me but I feel somehow that all will be well. He is
very proud of his Army and well he may be. I think he is sound in
his tactics.'[11]

Leese corresponded regularly with his wife and thereafter made
frequent references to how much he liked Bill and how well they
were getting on, but the reality was rather different. Giffard had
given Bill a more or less free hand in the field and restricted himself
to coordinating operations with GHQ India and Stilwell's Chinese
forces in the north. Leese, who had arrived with a retinue of staff

officers he had brought with him from the Eighth Army (a practice of which Bill disapproved), soon stirred up resentment by his more forceful and dynamic involvement in 14th Army affairs. 'His staff,' Bill noted pointedly, '... had a good deal of desert sand in its shoes and was rather inclined to thrust Eighth Army down our throats.' Bill responded in kind. When Leese's liaison officer was chatting to Bill soon after his arrival he was taken aback when Bill asked, 'Well, what do you think of the Fourteenth Army?' Before he could reply, Bill barked, 'I think it's a damn good army.' Relations between Bill and Leese never approached the warmth and mutual regard that marked his dealings with Giffard; eventually Leese would make an abortive and suicidal attempt to remove Bill from his command, and in the process would more or less destroy his own career.

On 18 November, Bill returned to Kohima to undertake the sombre duty of unveiling a memorial to the men of the 2nd Division who had lost their lives there earlier in the year. It was a stone monolith, cut from the hills by local Naga tribesmen, erected in the grounds of the District Commissioner's demolished bungalow, where some of the fiercest fighting had taken place, and engraved with the now famous inscription:

> *When you go home*
> *Tell them of us and say*
> *For your tomorrow*
> *We gave our today.*

In a short speech, Bill said the memorial, which had been paid for by subscription within the division, was a tribute to a proud formation who showed 'what first-class British troops can do at their very best'. Pipers from Scottish regiments played a Lament and a bugler sounded 'The Last Post', while local people joined the men of the 2nd Division in a minute's silence. (The memorial now forms part of the Kohima War Cemetery, immaculately maintained by the Commonwealth War Graves Commission. It contains 1,387 graves, and a second memorial at the highest point of the cemetery commemorates 917 Hindu and Sikh soldiers who were cremated. The youngest soldier buried at Kohima was just 16 years old when he died – Ghulan Muhammad of the 2nd Punjab Regiment.)

During the second week of December engineers from the 14th Army managed to complete a floating Bailey bridge across the Chindwin near Kalewa (at 1,154 feet, it was at that time the longest in the world) and the 11th East African Division poured across the river. Three days later the Japanese had been cleared out of Shwegyin – the scene of carnage and chaos during the retreat in 1942 – and by the middle of the month a bridgehead eight miles by twelve had been established on the east bank of the river.

Shortly after Shwegyin had been recaptured, Bill drove into the town and walked among the burned-out, rusting tanks and vehicles that had been destroyed and abandoned two and a half years earlier. It was a symbolic moment which he relished with considerable pleasure. 'As I walked among them, resavouring in imagination the bitter taste of defeat, I could raise my head. Much had happened since then. Some of what we owed we had paid back. Now we were going to pay back the rest – with interest.'[12]

On 15 December a significant event, which Bill did not feel worth mentioning in *Defeat Into Victory*, took place on a makeshift parade ground in Imphal – the first occasion in military history that an army commander and his three corps commanders had been knighted together on the field of battle. To Bill's great pleasure, Aileen, Una and John flew in to Imphal to watch the ceremony. Uncharacteristically, Bill confessed beforehand that he was nervous. When his chief engineer, who had borrowed a couple of scrapers from an airstrip construction company to create a suitable parade ground, asked him if it was satisfactory, he grunted, 'There's more than enough room for me to make a fool of myself.' One of his staff officers told a group of war correspondents who were covering the event that Bill was worried about a gammy knee and had been practising kneeling in the privacy of his *basha*.

In the shadow of the mountains where so recently the Japanese had looked down on Imphal plain, the prize they were destined never to capture, and with artillery still rumbling far to the south, the parade formed up and the various dignitaries arrived – Mountbatten in his admiral's uniform, Wavell, the Viceroy, in his field marshal's uniform, and the Maharajah of Manipur, heavily bejewelled, in a long coat of pale blue silk, a turban of green and gold, and white jodhpurs, attended by a large retinue of servants in similar turbans. A descendant of the ruling dynasty of the former kingdom of Manipur, the Maharajah clearly enjoyed his food. An irreverent Australian correspondent, Ron McKie, estimated the Maharajah weighed at least 20 stone, noted rather rudely that he walked 'like a blancmange nudged by a spoon' and described him as 'a blend of Titania and Fatty Arbuckle'.

The Viceroy, representing the King, inspected a guard of honour symbolising the cosmopolitan make-up of the 14th Army – there were Gurkhas and Punjabis, East Africans, RAF aircraftmen in blue berets and Scots in tam-o'-shanters. A servant from the Viceroy's House in New Delhi, in a gold and azure turban and buckled shoes, stepped forward with the gilt and red plush kneeling stool, salaamed in front of the Viceroy, placed the kneeling stool at his feet, salaamed again and withdrew. Then Bill issued an order almost certainly never previously heard on any parade ground: 'Lieutenant Generals, by the right, quick march.' The four generals marched forward, line abreast, and halted a short distance from the Viceroy. Bill was the first to step forward, limping slightly. He saluted, knelt cautiously, was tapped lightly on each shoulder with a sword and presented with the insignia of a Knight Commander of the Order of the Bath. Following the ceremony there was a brief drinks party and a curry lunch, after which everyone returned to the war.

'When they [the men of the 14th Army] watched the Viceroy honour their General the other day,' the *News Review* reported, 'they saw the dawn of their own victory over the Land of the Rising Sun ... Under the leadership of this blunt, hard-working soldier, three-quarters of a million men – British, Indian, African, Gurkha – had learned to fight in a way no other army has fought before. They learned to fight without a supply line behind them, to live with nothing beyond what they could carry, to perform extensive operations in isolated groups hundreds of miles from their base. They had fought not only the Japs but the jungle too. By opening the gate to central Burma, killing 40,000 Japanese crack jungle demons, Slim's men are setting the seal of doom on Japan's forces in the East.'

By the end of the year, with bridgeheads across the Chindwin growing in strength daily, Bill had every reason to be satisfied with the 14th Army's achievements. An area of Burma more than twice the size of Ireland had been liberated and the enemy had sustained some 90,000 battle casualties. Against any other enemy, Bill would have expected prisoners to be numbered in thousands, but only about 600 were captured and almost all of them were either seriously wounded or in the final stages of utter exhaustion. It was an indication, he said, of the fanatical nature of Japanese resistance. Fourteenth Army casualties were not insignificant – 40,000 men killed or wounded, although many recovered from their injuries to fight again.

When Bill came to review the year he was at pains, once again, to point out the mistakes he had made and his belief that he was only saved by the fighting qualities of his troops: 'If you are a general, whether your army has won a great battle or lost it, it is hard not to slur over your own mistakes, to blame others for theirs; to say, if you lost, what bad luck you had, and, if you won, how little luck had to do with it. My army had indubitably won this battle and I look back now on its conduct with considerable personal satisfaction, allowing myself, in the warm glow of success, a good deal more credit, no doubt, than I deserved. Yet the plan of the Imphal battle had been sound and we had adhered to it. Basically, it had been to meet the Japanese on ground of our own choosing, with a better line of communication behind us than behind them, to concentrate against them superior forces drawn from the Arakan and India, to wear them down, and, when they were exhausted, to turn and destroy them. All this we had done in spite of my mistakes in mistiming the withdrawal of the 17th Division from Tiddim and underestimating the strength of the Japanese thrust at Kohima ...

'Our estimate of the Japanese mentality and generalship had also proved right. Kawabe and his subordinates showed the over-boldness, the rigidity, and the disregard of administrative risks that I had expected and which gave me my opportunity. We had learned how to kill Japanese; how to use tanks in any country that was not a swamp; how to build roads and airfields with little equipment and strange materials. Our troops had shown themselves steadier, more offensive, and better trained than ever before. They did not now accept any country as impassable, either for the enemy or themselves. They refused to be jittered by encirclement; they were as ready as the enemy to strike out into the jungle and to infiltrate. We had by degrees become better in the jungle than the Japanese. Most important of all, every British, Indian, African and Chinese division that had served under Fourteenth Army had met picked Japanese troops in straight, bitter fighting and had beaten them. Our troops had proved themselves in battle the superiors of the Japanese; they had seen them run. This was the real and decisive results of these battles. They had smashed for ever the legend of the invincibility of the Japanese Army. Neither our men, nor the Japanese soldier himself, believed in it any longer.'[13]

Thus was the stage set for the next crucial phase of the battle – Operation Capital, the advance on Mandalay.

17

The Master Plan

Bill was a 'list' man. He found it useful to make a list of the options available to him as an army commander at war and further lists of the advantages and disadvantages of each. It helped him think and was an aid to the decision-making process when he was faced, as he was in the second half of 1944, with myriad problems of supply, transportation, air support, medical provision, engineering, communications, reinforcements, reorganisation and training in preparation for the final struggle to oust the Japanese from Burma.

The list with which he was most preoccupied during planning for Operation Capital contained just three questions:

1. How and where could the 14th Army best bring the enemy to do battle with the greatest advantage to itself?
2. What was the greatest strength of the army that could be maintained east of the Chindwin to face the Japanese?
3. What would be the strength of the enemy?

His first choice of battlefield was the Shwebo plain, a vast, gently undulating savannah between the Chindwin and the Irrawaddy, to the north-west of Mandalay, which would enable the 14th Army to use its superiority in armour and in the air to the best advantage. The plain, largely cultivated and interspersed with scrub, was in the dry belt of central Burma with scattered villages and few trees, crisscrossed by cart tracks, bounded on the west by the Chindwin and on the south and east by the Irrawaddy.

Paradoxically Bill also believed, from what he knew of Japanese tactics, that Shwebo plain would be the enemy's choice, too. He had learned in October that General Kawabe had been recalled to Tokyo in disgrace after the Imphal disaster and replaced by Lieutenant General Kimura Hyotaro, about whom he knew little except that he was well regarded. Kimura's chief of staff, Lieutenant General

Tanaka Shinichi, was responsible for day-to-day operations and had a reputation for steely determination.

Bill was sure the Japanese would act true to form, be aggressive, overconfident, inflexible, extremely unwilling to lose face by ceding territory and psychologically incapable of accepting defeat. His judgement, confirmed by intelligence reports, was that the enemy would want to hold on to Mandalay at all costs and choose to cross the Irrawaddy and fight on the Shwebo plain in the hope of driving the 14th Army back to the Chindwin by the time of the next monsoon. As Bill put it: 'He [the enemy] would see the Chindwin behind us; not the Irrawaddy behind him.'

In fact he was entirely wrong. Kimura was a more pragmatic, wily tactician than most Japanese generals and recognised that his depleted forces stood no chance against the mighty 14th Army on open ground. All his divisions were grossly under strength after the catastrophic losses at Kohima and Imphal and were only being made up with drafts of poorly trained conscripts; in a pitched battle he would be obliged to deploy his field artillery on the front line to confront the massed Allied armour and would therefore not be able to offer fire support to the infantry. He had few tanks, few anti-tank weapons, and only a handful of aircraft to face the 1,200 available to the Allies. Kimura thus decided the best option to protect Mandalay was to withdraw the bulk of his army behind the Irrawaddy and hope the Allies would become overstretched and exhausted trying to batter across the formidable barrier of the river.

Bill and his staff meanwhile continued to plan for the battle on Shwebo plain. The logistics were extraordinarily complex, but he had the support of a hand-picked team of staff officers led by Tubby Lethbridge, his outstanding chief of staff, Billy Hasted, his indefatigable chief engineer, and his old friend 'Grocer Alf' Snelling, his chief quartermaster, who had been pulling rabbits out of a hat for Bill for years. By then the 14th Army had established three bridgeheads across the Chindwin and so crossing the river was no longer a problem, but transporting and supplying the troops on a battlefield more than 200 miles from the nearest airfield and 400 miles from a railhead was a major headache. Bill calculated that the absolute maximum force that could be maintained in battle east of the Chindwin was four complete divisions, plus two further infantry brigades and two tank brigades. It was known that the Japanese had ten infantry divisions in Burma along with other formations, but two were fighting a rearguard action against the Chinese on the northern front, at least one division was deployed in Arakan and the threat of an amphibious landing in the south tied up at least one more.

Bill's intelligence staff concluded that the 14th Army advancing across the Shwebo plain would probably face five and one-third enemy divisions, one independent mixed brigade, one tank regiment, 30–40,000 line-of-communication troops who were trained to fight if required and two divisions of the renegade Indian National Army. Bill candidly admitted that they were 'not the odds that I should have liked' and only a year before he would not have considered them. Malaria was still reducing the fighting strength of all units and reinforcements were not arriving quickly enough to replace those men who had finished their service and were being sent home. Despite this, what gave Bill the confidence to go ahead was not just his crushing superiority in tanks and aircraft, but the fighting spirit of his men. His was an army with its tail up facing an enemy army with its tail between its legs – an exact reversal of the situation during the retreat two and a half years earlier.

Despite all his careful preparations the whole operation was put in jeopardy when, on 10 December, three squadrons of USAAF Dakotas – 75 aircraft in all – he was relying on to maintain the spearhead troops, were suddenly diverted to China. The first he knew of it was being woken at dawn in his headquarters at Imphal by the roar of aircraft taking off, one after another, from a nearby airstrip. He assumed they were making an early start on deliveries to the 14th Army and was dismayed to learn later that morning that they had been withdrawn to help defend American airfields in the north that were in danger of being overrun by the Japanese. Some had already been loaded with supplies for the 14th Army, which had been dumped at the side of the runway before they took off. Bill was furious that no one had had the courtesy to warn him that he was going to lose so many aircraft – he barely had enough to meet the needs of his army as it was. For the next few days his staff, already stretched to the limit, were fully occupied, day and night, reworking the details of the airlift for the advance. It was perhaps small wonder that some officers reported Bill looked tired and drawn at the investiture ceremony on 15 December, by which time he was facing yet another major crisis.

As leading elements of the 14th Army poured across the Chindwin in early December, Bill expected the first major battles to take place in the Zibyu Taungdans, a ridge of hills, 2,000 to 2,500 feet high, which ran roughly from north to south across the path of their advance about 25 miles east of the river. He assumed the Japanese would cover the passes and concentrate troops to the east to destroy any invaders who made it through the hills. What happened came as a complete surprise. The 19th Indian Division, under the command of Major General Pete Rees, known to his men as 'the Pocket Napoleon' because of his diminutive stature, swept through the Zibyu Taungdan range with very little opposition, having reported that the enemy's defensive positions in the defiles seemed to be designed for delay rather than prolonged resistance. This could have been because the enemy was surprised by the strength and speed with which the 14th Army had advanced inland, but it could also mean, Bill accepted with a sinking heart, that the Japanese had no interest in holding the Zibyu Taungdan range, which could only further mean they were not preparing to make a stand on the Shwebo plain.

When intelligence sources and aerial reconnaissance began reporting that the general drift of enemy troop movements was back across the Irrawaddy, not forward, Bill knew he had made a major mistake and realised that Kimura was planning to make a stand behind the river, not in front of it. 'It looked,' he noted with heroic understatement, 'as if this battle, like so many of mine, was not going to start quite as I intended ... The fact that the first foundation on which I had built my plan had collapsed was, to say the least, disconcerting.'

Actually, one of Bill's great strengths was his refusal to be disconcerted, no matter how bad the news. He was always preaching to his subordinates the need to be flexible, to fight the battle not the plan, and never were those qualities needed more than at that moment. It was clear the advance could not continue as originally planned and that there was no point in attempting frontal assaults across the huge expanse of the Irrawaddy against a well-organised, entrenched enemy. There was also no time to lose since the entire 14th Army would soon be on the move following orders that were now obsolete.

Bill, as usual completely unflustered, sent a signal to ALFSEA on 16 December (the day after the knighthood ceremony) scrapping the plans for Operation Capital. On the same day he sat down with his staff and calmly considered the options in the light of this new and unexpected situation. A frontal attack across the Irrawaddy would have been suicidal, but the majority of 4 Corps had yet to cross the Chindwin, which offered an opportunity to adapt a plan which had earlier been discarded when it was thought every available man would need to be concentrated on the Shwebo plain. The new plan, which was dubbed Operation Extended Capital, was difficult, audacious and risky but would later be hailed by military historians as a masterstroke. In its essence, it was simple enough – the Japanese were to be persuaded that the whole of the 14th Army was deployed to attack Mandalay while 4 Corps secretly veered away from the main advance, crossed the Irrawaddy far to the south and struck at the enemy's rear. Making it work was another matter.

On 18 December, Bill flew to 4 Corps headquarters at Tamu to brief both corps commanders. With a map spread on a table outside Messervy's caravan, he outlined what he wanted them to do. Messervy's 4 Corps would move secretly down the Gangaw valley alongside the Chindwin, following the route Bill had taken in the opposite direction in 1942, then proceed overland to Pakokku, 70 miles south of Mandalay, where they would cross the Irrawaddy. While Stopford's 33 Corps distracted the enemy by attempting forced crossings of the river around Mandalay, 4 Corps would emerge in the enemy's rear and strike at Meiktila, the Japanese nerve centre and nodal point of road, rail and air communications, where there were supply and ammunition dumps. A threat to Meiktila would force the Japanese to counter-attack: thus would Kimura be caught in Bill's favourite 'hammer and anvil' strategy, with 4 Corps providing the anvil at Meiktila while 33 Corps in the north was the hammer – with the enemy in between.

Bill made it clear that the forthcoming battles at Mandalay and

Meiktila were but a prelude to the dash for Rangoon – Operation Sob ('Sea or Bust') – which he wanted to capture before the start of the next monsoon. All the men standing round the table that morning recognised that the ultimate, and up to that moment elusive, goal – the final defeat of the Japanese in Burma – was at last within their grasp. Bill did not acquaint his immediate superior, Oliver Leese, with the details of Operation Extended Capital until December 20 – after he had issued orders to his corps commanders – neither did he ask for ALFSEA's sanction for what he was planning to do. Leese was not pleased.

Operation Extended Capital would be hailed as Bill's masterpiece, the apogee of his career as a fighting general, the moment at which he was required to control the gamut of military arts – deception, surprise, speed, flexibility, leadership, logistics, et cetera – with skill and complete assurance. 'I am confident,' he wrote in a signal to ALFSEA, 'that ... there is every prospect of attaining the object. The enemy is still disheartened and disorganised and provided that we can maintain the pressure, we may well inflict a major defeat on him. If, however, he is given time to recover, we may be forced to employ considerably greater forces after the 1945 monsoon to achieve the same object. I believe that the prize before us is of value quite out of proportion to the few extra resources required to achieve it ...'[1]

Fundamental to the success of Operation Extended Capital was the need to keep the Japanese guessing and to prevent them discovering what was going on. The 19th Division was transferred from 4 Corps to 33 Corps to persuade the Japanese that both corps were making for Mandalay. After 4 Corps had moved out and begun its trek south on 19 January, a dummy headquarters was set up at Tamu, using the same radio channels, with messages passed back and forth indicating the corps was moving on to the Shwebo plain and confirmed by 'indiscreet' conversations in clear by staff officers and doctored news broadcasts. In the meantime, the real 4 Corps maintained strict radio silence as it moved slowly south into the Gangaw valley. Roads and airstrips had to be built to maintain the great army as it progressed. When Bill wanted to visit a forward airstrip he found it was so busy that his Anson was obliged to circle for half an hour before it could land – every time it began an approach an American DC3 loaded with supplies nipped in in front.

The stretch of the Chindwin then in Allied hands was used to move supplies on crude rafts built from teak logs. Bill never forgot an exchange with William Hasted, his chief engineer, at the beginning of the advance. Standing on the river bank upstream from Kalewa, Bill pointed to dense forests nearby and said: 'Billy, there's the river and there are the trees. In two months I want 500 tons of supplies a day down that river.' Hasted looked thoughtfully at the river, then at the trees, then grinned at Bill. 'The difficult we do at once,' he replied, 'the impossible will take a little longer and for miracles we need a month's notice.' 'You're lucky,' Bill retorted. 'You've got two.'

Three logs lashed together formed a raft that would carry a Sherman tank or ten tons of supplies. The logs were dragged from the forest by elephants under the direction of 'Elephant Bill', a near legendary figure in the 14th Army. James Williams was an Englishman employed as a forest assistant with the Bombay Burma Trading Corporation between the wars, running 70 elephants to extract timber from the teak forests in upper Burma. He was evacuated with his wife and children during the retreat but later joined the 14th Army as commanding officer of the No. 1 Elephant Company. 'They [elephants] built hundreds of bridges for us,' Bill wrote in an introduction to Williams' autobiography after the war, 'and launched more ships for us than Helen ever did for Greece.'

Sunken boats were raised from the river bed, repaired and added to the 14th Army's fleet. Bill was particularly proud of two wooden 'warships' that were built at a shipyard in Kalewa. Punt-like vessels with a lightly armoured bridge and armed with a Bofors gun, two Oerlikons and two Browning light automatics for anti-aircraft fire, they were capable of 12 knots. Bill presided over the launching ceremony and christened one *Pamela*, after Mountbatten's youngest daughter, and the other *Una*, after his own. It was perhaps just as well he left for his headquarters shortly after the ceremony because both vessels sank overnight due to leaking nail holes in the timber.

However, they were soon refloated and patrolling the Chindwin.

Bill claimed to be the only general who had 'designed, built, christened, launched and commissioned warships for the Royal Navy' although he later received a pained note from the Admiralty informing him that only 'their Lordships' (of the Admiralty) were authorised to suggest names for His Majesty's ships of war.

Reports from the 19th Division indicated that it had advanced 200 miles in 20 days towards Shwebo, an extraordinary feat since it was fighting much of the way and had to cut a track through the jungle for the trucks and artillery. Bill took off in a light aircraft to watch its progress from the air and was mightily impressed. 'Through the gaps in the treetops that screened the hills below, I could see on every rough track files of men marching hard with a purposefulness that could be recognised from 500 feet. Behind them gangs, stripped to the waist, were felling trees and hauling them to make rough bridges across numberless streams and gullies that cut the route, while guns waited to move on again the moment the last log was in position. Dust rose in reddish clouds as whole companies with pick and spade dug into banks to widen the road and let the lorries pass. These men hacking out a road, dragging vehicles, pushing on with such fierce energy to get to grips with the enemy, were a heartening sight.'[2]

As Stopford's 33 Corps continued clearing the Japanese from the Shwebo plain, 4 Corps was making slow but steady progress on its 300-mile trek to the Irrawaddy at Pakokku, some 20 miles southwest of its confluence with the Chindwin. Messervy's troops were following a rough fairweather track that wound through the hills and was never intended to take heavy transport. The three tonners found it difficult enough, but negotiating 50-ton tank transporters round narrow bends in the road with a precipice on one side required great skill and considerable courage. At some points the gradient and the road conditions were so difficult that tanks had to tow their own transporters.

Bill knew that a single Japanese reconnaissance aircraft flying over the Gangaw valley would give the game away. He relied on RAF fighters to maintain a screen through the hours of daylight and to shoot down any enemy aircraft approaching the area. Both at the time and later, he paid generous tribute to the help the 14th Army received from the RAF and the USAAF. 'The air forces, British and

American, were magnificent. The transport planes that remained with us flew incredible hours. They identified themselves completely with the army. It was as much a point of honour with them as with the soldiers that, not only the troops, but all the thousands of tons of supplies and gear required, should get through in time.'

As always with the 14th Army, the equipment needed to cross the Irrawaddy was in desperately short supply – there were not enough boats, pontoons or rafts and only a few power craft with horribly unreliable outboard engines. Bill had told both corps commanders that he knew he was asking them to make the crossing on 'a couple of bamboos and a bootlace', but neither demurred. 'They realised no more was available; what was lacking in material they made up in ingenuity, skill, organisation and determination. The only equipment my army had in full supply was, as ever, brains, hardihood and courage.'[3]

Bill's big tactical dilemma was to decide on the timing of the crossings. There was merit in holding 4 Corps back until two divisions of 33 Corps had got across north of Mandalay to convince Kimura that it was the main Allied thrust. Bill wanted him to believe that 4 Corps was still waiting in the wings in support of Stopford on the left of the advance. On the other hand, the longer 4 Corps was kept waiting at Pakokku the greater the risk of discovery and the consequent unravelling of his plans. After much deliberation, Bill decided the risk was too great: he ordered Messervy to be ready to begin crossing the river more or less simultaneously with 33 Corps. The detail of where and how the divisions were to get across the river he left to the corps commanders.

Bill candidly admitted he was not immune to morbid fears, to lying awake at night worrying if he had done the right thing. He called it 'the burden of anxiety all commanders must carry'. He brooded about whether he was asking too much of the men, acutely conscious of the fact that no army in any other theatre would have been launched on such a venture with so little equipment. He tormented himself with images of a Japanese pilot breaking through and reporting 4 Corps' location, or an enemy agent crouching in the jungle and counting the Allied tanks as they rumbled along a track, or a prisoner being tortured until he talked and Kimura switching his focus to the south to destroy 4 Corps before it could get a foothold on the east bank of the river. 'Imagination is a necessity for a general,' he wrote, 'but it must be a controlled imagination. At times I regained control of mine only by an effort of will.'

He drew most comfort by visiting the men, both those at the front and those in the rear areas labouring heroically to provide the fighting troops with the great tonnages of supplies, ammunition and equipment they needed. During a visit to 20th Division, Bill joined an audience of about 200 men for an ENSA show which was being staged not far from the river, almost within artillery range of the enemy. He enjoyed it and was sorry he had to leave early, but just as he was about to get up from his seat someone whispered to him that a Japanese raiding party was blocking the road to the airstrip, so he simply stayed and watched the rest of the performance, by which time the enemy had been driven away.

By then Bill had moved his tactical headquarters from Imphal, first to a location in the jungle near Kalewa and then to Monywa, only some 20 miles behind the front, where his staff occupied the least battered houses on the outskirts of the town once the booby traps left by the departing Japanese had been cleared. The RAF headquarters under Air Vice-Marshal Stanley Vincent moved with him and from then onwards the two headquarters lived side by side and worked and moved as one, a vital element in 14th Army's ultimate success.

Junior officers not frequently in contact with Bill were often surprised by how relaxed he appeared. Lieutenant Colonel Frederick Erroll, a Territorial officer in the County of London Yeomanry who would become a Tory MP immediately after the war, had occasion to visit the 14th Army commander in Monywa: 'He was seated at a table in a tent and when I entered I noticed he had some papers in his hand. Looking up, he said, "Well, Erroll, how are you?" and putting the papers aside, added, "I am just correcting some proofs of an article I am writing for the *Birmingham Post*." Considerably astonished, I said, "But really, sir, I can hardly believe it. Surely the big battle going on must be causing you a great deal of anxiety." Pausing for a moment and then looking straight at me with his determined jaw stuck out, General Slim replied: "There is nothing more I can do. I have done all I can and must now sit back and let everybody get on with their part. Of course, I would love to be out there with them and to know exactly how things are going, but that's not my job – so I might just as well get on with this while I am waiting".'[4]

(During the heat of the campaign Bill also wrote a long paper, which was submitted to the CIGS, forcibly arguing for improved status and pay for the infantry – 'the arm which endures most, is always in the forefront of battle and therefore worthy of special honour'.)

Bill recalled the accommodation at Monywa as being 'very comfortable', despite the snakes that inhabited the piles of rubble everywhere. It was his habit to visit the War Room every night to check on the situation map before going to bed and one night he nearly stepped on a krait, one of the deadliest of all small snakes – its bite can kill within minutes. Thereafter Bill made his way rather cautiously to the War Room after dark, using a torch, considering the risk of a snake bite was greater than that of the beam of his torch giving his position away to a patrolling enemy aircraft. He liked to recount a story of visiting the War Room late one evening and listening in, unobserved, to an exchange between the duty officer and a younger, recently arrived, colleague. As he lifted the blanket which served as a door, he saw the older man tap the situation map with his index finger. 'Uncle Bill,' he announced with great authority, 'will fight a battle here.' 'Why?' asked the mystified younger man. 'Because,' was the answer, 'he always fights a battle going in where he took a licking coming out.'

By the beginning of February, six weeks after Bill had briefed Stopford and Messervy at Tamu, 200 miles to the west, both corps had either reached the banks of the Irrawaddy or were within sight of the river, along a front stretching for 200 miles opposite Mandalay. At the northern end of the front, 19th Division had already established a bridgehead and patrols were being pushed across the river to harass and confuse the enemy. At one point, after a particularly fierce firefight on the banks of the river, during which a number of the enemy were killed, a patrol of 20th Division watched in astonishment as the remaining Japanese, rather than be captured, simply marched into the river, in close formation and with full equipment, and were swept to their deaths in the fast-flowing waters.

As always, no matter how hectic and burdensome the demands on him, Bill's thoughts were never far from his family. 'We have started a very big battle,' he wrote to Una on 13 February, 'and there will be a lot of fighting for some time now. However, we got our first troops over the Irrawaddy last night and so that's a good beginning. I shall be busy for the next few weeks, so won't be able to write a lot, but I <u>would</u> like to hear from you … I hope you are behaving like a little lady, but I doubt it. Lots and lots of love my Poons, Daddy.'

As far as Bill knew, Kimura was still unaware of the danger developing in his rear and still expected the entire might of the 14th Army to strike at Mandalay. (After the war it was revealed that Kimura knew of Allied movement on his southern flank but regarded it as no more than a demonstration designed to draw his forces south.) Messervy's 4 Corps, concentrating at Pakokku, 50 miles to the southwest, had had a difficult march – in one three-mile stretch through the hills, several hundred trees had been felled to block the track and elephants were needed to clear them. The heat and the dust grew worse as the men laboured to improve the track sufficiently for it to be able to take tanks and the transporters carrying boats. Bill visited the column as it closed on Pakokku. 'Their jungle-green uniforms and their faces were red from the dust,' he noted 'and the jungle itself on each side of the track was red too, every leaf thick in dust.'

At four o'clock on the morning of Monday, 12 February, leading elements of 33 Corps began crossing the mighty Irrawaddy, the longest river crossing in the history of the Second World War. Two crossing points were chosen, seven miles apart, where reconnaissance had indicated there were no enemy troops permanently posted on the opposite bank, but in both places the river was more than 1,500 yards wide and partially obstructed by submerged sandbanks which created dangerous and unpredictable currents. Although the night was dark, a freshening wind caused more problems for the heavily laden and underpowered boats. Several ran aground and were only refloated with great difficulty and many of the outboard engines proved to be unreliable.

All this notwithstanding, by dawn bridgeheads had been established at both crossing points with little opposition. Ferrying stopped during daylight hours and resumed again at dusk. The Japanese were uncharacteristically slow to react and by the time they launched a counter-attack substantial numbers of 33 Corps troops were across the river and the two bridgeheads had joined up. For the next two weeks the fighting was ferocious, with the enemy launching wave after wave of suicide attacks supported by tanks. Losses on both sides were heavy, but the bridgehead held.

Meanwhile, Messervy's plans had not, initially, gone well. The main crossing at Nyaungu, south of Pakokku, was scheduled to be launched 24 hours after 33 Corps began crossing near Mandalay. The first boats, with a company of the South Lancashires, set out at 0345 and paddled silently across the river despite the strong wind and a nasty chop on the water. By five o'clock, they had splashed ashore on the opposite bank, scrambled up the cliffs bordering the river without encountering any enemy and set up a defensive position while the boats returned to collect the remainder of the battalion.

Thereafter, everything went wrong. As dawn rose there was confusion and delay trying to embark the second wave, which was to cross on boats using outboards. Some of the engines would not start; some of the boats leaked badly. Eventually the reserve company, which should have been last, set out first, but instead of heading directly for the east bank it decided to circle and wait to take its proper place. The strong wind and current was too much for its feeble engine and it began to drift downstream and the remaining boats, not realising what was happening, turned to follow it. At that moment, rifle and machine-gun fire broke out from the east bank – two company commanders were killed and several boats, including that carrying the commanding officer, sank. Under cover of fire from Allied guns and tanks, the remaining boats returned. The crossing had failed, leaving the single company that had got ashore in great peril.

Six miles to the south, a subsidiary crossing at Pagan had also failed. A Sikh battalion attempted to cross the river in captured native boats with Burmese crews but when they came under fire the crews panicked and turned back. (Pagan, now called Bagan, was the capital of several ancient kingdoms in Burma and is one of the country's most sacred and beautiful cities with more than

2,000 pagodas and temples, built between the eleventh and thirteenth centuries, scattered across the surrounding plain. To watch the sun rise over Bagan from the west bank of the river is one of the world's great natural spectacles.) The beauty of the scene was unlikely to have made much impression on the officers contemplating the failure of the crossing that morning, but there was cheering news a little later when a small boat set out from the opposite shore with two figures waving a white flag. When they came ashore they turned out to be officers in the Indian National Army. The Japanese, they explained, had marched out of Pagan in a great hurry, heading north, leaving the INA to garrison the town. The INA, they said, had no greater wish than to surrender. A British officer and platoon of Sikhs went across the river to investigate and discovered it was true – the Japanese had left and the INA troops remaining were only too happy to lay down their arms. 'This incident,' Bill observed drily, 'was, I think, the chief contribution the Indian National Army made to either side in the Burma War.'[5]

Back at Nyaungu a seond attempt to cross the river, this time supported by heavy covering fire, succeeded and by nightfall three battalions had joined the company of South Lancashires on the east bank. They stood to all night, expecting an attack, but nothing happened. The following day, more or less unmolested by the enemy, men, mules, guns, tanks and supplies poured across the river. The only enemy encountered were driven into caves near the village of Nyaungu and when they refused to surrender the entrance to the cave was blown in and they were left to suffocate inside. By 16 February a bridgehead had been firmly established and linked to the Sikhs now occupying Pagan downstream.

Between 18 and 21 February the remainder of Punch Cowan's division was ferried across the river and the advance on Meiktila began while the last units were still crossing. As 'the Black Cats', supported by tanks, moved rapidly on a wide front towards Meiktila, fighting all the way (one encounter, eight miles from the town, resulted, Bill mentioned nonchalantly, in 'a good killing') disaster threatened from quite another, and completely unexpected, front.

On 23 February, Bill learned that Chiang Kai-shek was demanding the immediate return of all the US and Chinese forces fighting with the NCAC because they were needed, he claimed, for a projected offensive against the Japanese in China. What was worse, as far as Bill was concerned, was the proposal to use US transport aircraft allotted to the 14th Army to fly them out. Bill warned Mountbatten that the loss of the aircraft would be fatal to Allied operations in central Burma. Mountbatten flew to Chungking to reason with the Generalissimo, to no avail. Chiang insisted the troops had to be withdrawn and advised Mountbatten to halt the 14th Army at Mandalay.

'Throughout the next crucial days the threat of this disaster hung over me,' Bill confessed. 'I could not if I wished – and I had no intention of doing so – now call off the battle; I could only more urgently force it to a conclusion. Yet I confess that, while this uncertainty lasted, I was hard put to it to maintain before my own staff, commanders, and troops that appearance of freedom from anxiety so essential in an army commander.'[6]

The crisis was partially resolved when Mountbatten persuaded the US Chiefs of Staff of the vital necessity of the aircraft to the 14th Army. They agreed the aircraft could remain until 1 June, or until Rangoon was captured, whichever was the earlier. With that Bill had to be content. The Generalissimo's orders to withdraw on the NCAC front remained, putting additional pressure on Bill to capture Mandalay without delay.

Cowan, now poised outside Meiktila for the final assault, had received intelligence that the town was more heavily defended than had first been thought. Two large lakes on the west of the town made an attack on that side difficult and so his plans were to set up roadblocks on the main approaches, then swing round with infantry, tanks and artillery and air support to strike from the north and east. The battle was very quickly joined and Meiktila, in peacetime a tranquil city of lakes, pagodas and elegant red-brick colonial buildings, surrounded by rice paddies, was turned into a war zone with billowing smoke, explosions, the roar of aircraft and tanks and the rattle of small-arms fire in the streets.

Bill spent that day, 28 February, with the 19th Division on the Mandalay front. When he returned to his headquarters at Monywa and studied the reports from Meiktila he decided to fly there the following day. In *Defeat Into Victory* he explained that he got the impression from the reports that the attack was being held up. As he did not want to 'risk a second Myitkyina' (where the initial assault by Stilwell's troops had degenerated into a drawn-out siege) he decided his presence was required to oversee operations. This is clearly nonsense. Bill knew better than anyone that an army commander's duty was to direct operations from the rear, not the front line. Furthermore, he had absolute confidence in Punch Cowan, who was a close friend, someone he had known for years and whom he greatly respected as a fighting general. The only conclusion that can be drawn from Bill's decision was that he simply could not bear to be away from the action.

The first problem was that the RAF refused, politely but emphatically, to fly him to Meiktila. He was informed, to his great irritation, that it was far too dangerous: the airstrips around the city had not been properly repaired, were frequently under fire and Japanese fighters were reported to be operating in the area. An unidentified but clearly courageous RAF officer made it clear to the army commander that the RAF was happy to fly his staff anywhere at any time, but not him, not to Meiktila and certainly not tomorrow.

Bill was about to take up the matter with Stan Vincent when he remembered that an American general visiting his headquarters had arrived in his own Mitchell bomber. In the senior officers' mess that night he slyly asked the American if he would care to accompany him in the morning to see something of the battle at Meiktila. The American said he would and immediately suggested making the trip in his Mitchell. Problem solved.

They left early next morning, with Bill feeling like a schoolboy playing truant. They stopped at 4 Corps headquarters on the river bank opposite Pagan to collect Frank Messervy, then continued to an airstrip within earshot of the battle, although the only evidence of the fighting was a few Japanese bodies sprawled on the edge of the field. They were offered a second breakfast – biscuits and tinned food from a captured enemy store. Bill ate it only for the satisfaction of eating enemy supplies. It was his first meal supplied by the enemy and it was not, he reported, very good.

Cowan sent a couple of jeeps to meet them and they 'bounced merrily' along the road to his battle headquarters just outside the town. Cowan may not have been too thrilled by a visit from the army commander, corps commander and an American general at the height of the battle, but he gave them a detailed briefing about what was going on and the progress that was being made, against a backdrop of explosions and gunfire. Tanks and infantry were slowly fighting their way into the town street by street, but the resistance was fanatical and there were snipers everywhere.

Bill was impressed by his friend's command of the situation and became quite lyrical in his praise. 'He was very short of sleep and remained so for several days. Yet throughout he was alert to every change in the situation on any sector, and swung his air and artillery support to meet and take advantage of it. His firm grip on his own formations and on the enemy never faltered. To watch a highly skilled, experienced and resolute commander controlling a hard-fought battle is to see, not only a man triumphing over the highest mental and physical stresses, but an artist producing his effects in the most complicated and difficult of all the arts.'[7]

Cowan should probably have tried to dissuade Bill from getting any closer to the battle, but apparently he did not, for the visitors took off again in a jeep to the north of the town and then proceeded, cautiously, on foot, into the heat of the battle where a brigade was 'cracking a particularly tough nut'. Bill, of course, talked to various subordinate commanders on the way, 'all very busy with their own battles and all in great heart'. What they felt to find the army commander suddenly in their midst is not on record, but perhaps may be imagined.

Advised that the best place to observe the action was from a huge pagoda on a rise overlooking a lake, they crept along a path screened from the enemy by bushes, crossed the pagoda's wide terrace and crouched behind a wall where a party of Indian signallers was already sheltering. Peering carefully over the wall, Bill could see in the far distance burning houses bordering the main road leading into the town, but right in front of him a mini-battle was taking place. Twenty or thirty Gurkhas were lying on the ground behind whatever cover they could find, under enemy fire. From a small spinney on the left more Gurkhas were firing Bren-gun bursts and in between was a Sherman tank in a hollow, concealed from the enemy. Suddenly the tank revved up its engine, lurched forward, fired a couple of shots and quickly withdrew.

Bill could hear enemy machine guns firing but at first could not see where they were firing from. He raked the ground with his field glasses and eventually located three low grassy hummocks with loopholes – classic Japanese bunkers sited for all-round defence and impervious to any but the heaviest shells. The Sherman lobbed two or three smoke grenades on to the ground in front of the bunkers and under the cover of the smokescreen the Gurkhas raced forward 100 yards or so closer to the bunkers. By the time the smokescreen cleared they were all under cover again. Another smokescreen was laid and once again they dashed forward.

Bill noticed the tank had disappeared. To get a better view they moved forward and crouched behind a thick cactus hedge. Suddenly the tank appeared at the rear of the enemy bunkers and Bill and his companions realised they were directly in its line of fire if it over-shot, which it promptly did. They threw themselves to the ground as shells screamed over their heads. The only casualty was a young American airman who had attached himself to the group and threw himself, rather foolishly, into the cactus hedge and emerged, Bill reported, like a 'blood-stained pin cushion'. To everyone's relief, the tank moved again to a flank and they were able to watch the de-nouement of the action as the firing swelled to a crescendo and the Gurkhas charged, thrusting Tommy guns through the loopholes. From behind the bunkers half a dozen khaki-clad figures emerged and ran for it, zig-zagging like mad to avoid the bullets whistling around them. They were all cut down.

It was closest Bill had been to real fighting since he had been ap-pointed an army commander and he clearly enjoyed every minute. As a rear party appeared to deal with the casualties and strip the enemy dead of papers and identity tags, they made their way back to Cowan's headquarters where they learned that 17th Division troops were well advanced into the town but the enemy resistance showed no sign of breaking. That night there was savage hand-to-hand fighting as survivors emerged from cellars and other hiding places to renew the battle. Fanatically courageous as always, they died where they fought.

By six o'clock on the evening 3 March, after some of the most ferocious close-quarter fighting yet seen in Burma, Meiktila had been taken. In one small area of the town, measuring no more than 200 yards by 100, 876 enemy bodies were counted; the last defenders chose to jump into the lake and drown. 'The capture of Meiktila in four days and the annihilation of its garrison – for, as the Japanese themselves admitted, hardly a man escaped – was a magnificent feat of arms,' Bill wrote proudly in *Defeat Into Victory*. 'It sealed the fate of the Japanese army in Burma.'

When Kimura realised what was happening in his rear he began diverting reinforcements destined for Mandalay to Meiktila but it was too late – the 17th Division was too firmly entrenched to be dislodged. While he was directing the battle to clear the surrounding area, Punch Cowan received the tragic news that his son, an officer in his and Bill's old regiment, the 1st/6th Gurkhas, had died of wounds received during the assault on Mandalay.

Mandalay is dominated by Mandalay Hill, 760 feet high, which rises abruptly from the surrounding plain, overlooks the entire city and is one of the most sacred places of the Buddhist faith. According to legend, Buddha climbed the hill with his faithful disciple Ananda and prophesied that a great city would be founded below the hill in the 2,400th year of his faith – 1857, the year the capital moved from Amarapura. The steep sides of Mandalay Hill are still covered with shrines, pagodas and temples and on the crest is an enormous standing buddha pointing with an outstretched hand towards the city. In a shrine nearby is a marble plaque dedicated to the memory of the men of the 4th/4th Prince of Wales's Own Gurkha Rifles, who died during the 'gallant and fierce assault' that led to the capture of the hill in 1945.

As 19th Division troops closed on Mandalay in early March 1945, Mandalay Hill was clearly visible and every one of them knew it represented a formidable defensive position, fortified by concrete emplacements and honeycombed with bunkers and machine-gun nests. The 4th/4th Gurkhas began their attack on the night of 8 March, storming the bunkers on the lower slopes of the hill and gradually clawing their way up towards the giant buddha at the summit. Next day they were joined by two companies of The Royal Berkshires. The Japanese held out with their usual fearless determination for three days and nights but, by 11 March, Mandalay Hill was in Allied hands. The last defenders, holed up in tunnels and cellars under the pagodas, were killed when drums of petrol were rolled into their hideouts and ignited with tracer bullets.

Bill visited Mandalay Hill shortly after its capture. 'The blackened marks of fire and the sights and stench of carnage were only too obvious, while distant bumps and bangs and the nearer rattle of machine-guns showed that the clearing of the city was still going on. Through all this noise and the clatter ... came a strange sound – singing. I followed it. There was General Rees, his uniform sweat-soaked and dirty, his distinguishing red scarf rumpled round his neck, his bush hat at a jaunty angle, his arm beating time, surrounded by a group of Assamese soldiers whom he was vigorously leading in the singing of Welsh missionary hymns. The fact that he sang in Welsh and they in Khasi only added to the harmony. I looked on admiringly.'[8]

Once Mandalay Hill had been taken, the division tackled the city's final redoubt, Fort Dufferin, which guarded the former palace of the last Burmese king. It reminded Bill very much of the toy fort he used to play with as a boy in Bristol. Surrounded by a moat 230 feet wide, each of the fort's four crenellated walls were more than a mile long and 26 feet high, backed by earth embankments 70 feet thick at the base. Within the compound were government offices, a barracks, park, polo ground and the splendid Royal Palace, built of teak, intricately carved and decorated with crimson and gold. Sadly, the Palace would not survive Allied bombing (although it has since been partially rebuilt).

By 16 March the fort was completely surrounded but there was no expectation the Japanese troops within would surrender. Bill likened what followed to a scene from the siege of Delhi during the Indian Mutiny. As medium guns were brought up, rafts and scaling ladders were prepared, but all attempts to cross the moat failed, driven back by heavy machine-gun fire. Neither artillery nor RAF bombers could make much impression on the walls of the fort and several attacks with 'bouncing bombs' (similar to those used by the Dam Busters in Germany) only succeeded in blasting a small breach 15 feet wide in one wall, suicidally narrow for a successful infantry assault.

Bill had agreed with Pete Rees not to waste any more time attempting to capture Fort Dufferin but to simply starve the defenders into submission when, on the morning of 20 March, a small group of men appeared at one of the gates waving white flags. They turned out to be Anglo-Burmese prisoners and they reported that the Japanese garrison had fled during the night through drains leading into the southern part of the city. The enemy had left behind a large dump of stores and ammunition, along with a number of booby traps. Rees passed through the fort gates more with a sense of nostalgia than triumph – before the war he had served as Military Secretary in Government House, within the walls of Fort Dufferin.

On 21 March, Air Vice-Marshal Vincent personally flew Bill to Mandalay in an L-5 Sentinel aircraft. They landed on the racecourse and drove into the town in a jeep through lines of cheering troops. At Fort Dufferin, Bill hoisted a Union flag from a hastily constructed saluting base, called for three cheers for the King-Emperor and made a short speech before driving back to the racecourse. It was an event that caused some irritation in the higher echelons of the command – both Mountbatten and Leese were said to be 'hurt' that they were not present for the triumphal entry into Mandalay. 'It was apparently resented,' Vincent noted sarcastically, 'that those who were actually responsible had taken the credit.'[9]

Elsewhere on the 14th Army front, the enemy, now greatly confused and disorganised, was being steadily driven back. By the end of the month the Japanese forces in central Burma had lost most of their armour, a large number of their guns and suffered horrendous casualties, numbering in the thousands. Evidence of Japan's increasing desperation was a significant increase in kamikaze attacks on the US fleet in the Pacific. B-29 bombers were now mounting massive raids on the Japanese mainland – on 9 March 325 US aircraft attacked Tokyo with incendiaries and reduced 10,000 acres of the city to ashes; 100,000 people were killed. By the end of the month the iconic island of Iwo Jima, less than 700 miles south of Japan, had been captured after one of the bloodiest battles of the war in the Pacific. Okinawa fell a few months later.

Bill, meanwhile, was planning the next phase of operations in Burma – the dash to take Rangoon before the monsoon, expected in mid-May. He often described the enemy as ants and extended the analogy in *Defeat Into Victory*: 'We had kicked over the ant hill; the ants were running about in confusion. Now was the time to stamp on them.'

On 2 April, Bill flew to 4 Corps headquarters, then established in Meiktila, to confer with his senior commanders. The plan was for a two-pronged advance on Rangoon – 4 Corps would move down the Mandalay–Rangoon railway to the east, while 33 Corps would approach via the Irrawaddy valley to the west. Both routes were still infested with the enemy, both were more than 300 miles long and both entailed considerable risks. If Rangoon was not taken before the monsoon broke, there was a danger that almost the entire 14th Army could find itself marooned without supplies in south Burma and forced into a disastrous withdrawal, while the enemy would be provided with breathing space to bring in reinforcements from Thailand. Bill knew the penalties for failure, but was, typically, ready to accept them.

In fact, the race was not just against the monsoon. Operation Dracula, the amphibious and airborne landing south of Rangoon planned to coincide with the overland advance from the north, which had earlier been cancelled, was suddenly reinstated and scheduled to be launched during the first five days of May. It became a point of honour with every man of the 14th Army that they should take Rangoon first. (Bill had urged the reinstatement of Dracula as 'insurance' at a meeting with Leese at Monywa on 19 March, although he fervently hoped the 14th Army would be waiting on the shore in Rangoon when Dracula was launched.)

While Bill was in Meiktila he spent time, as always, talking to the troops with the usual galvanising effect, admiringly recalled by George MacDonald Fraser of the 9th Battalion, The Border Regiment, who may have been a private soldier or a lance corporal (he was busted on three occasions, once for losing a tea urn) at the time. 'The biggest boost to morale was the burly man who came to talk to the assembled battalion by the lake shore – I'm not sure when, but it was unforgettable. Slim was like that: the only man I've ever seen who had a force come out of him, a strength of personality I have puzzled over since, for there was no apparent reason for it, unless it was the time and place and my own state of mind. Yet others felt it too, and they were not impressionable men. His appearance was plain enough: large, heavily built, grim-faced with that hard mouth and bulldog chin; the rakish Gurkha hat was at odds with the slung carbine and untidy trouser bottoms; he might have been a yard foreman who had become managing director, or a prosperous farmer who had boxed in his youth ...

'[He] emerged from under the trees by the lake shore, there was no nonsense of "gather round" or jumping up on boxes; he just stood there with his thumb hooked in his carbine sling and talked about how we had caught Jap off-balance and were going to annihilate him in the open; there was no exhortation or ringing clichés, no jokes or self-conscious use of barrack room slang – when he called the Japs "bastards" it was casual and without heat. He was telling us informally what would be, in the reflective way of intimate conversation. And we believed every word – and it all came true ... I think it was that sense of being close to us, as though he were chatting off-hand to an understanding nephew (not for nothing was he "Uncle Bill") that was his great gift ... He thought, he knew, at our level; it was that, and the sheer certainty that was built into every line of him, that gave Fourteenth Army its overwhelming confidence; what he promised, that he would surely do. And afterwards, when it was over and he spoke of what his army had done, it was always "you", not even "we" and never "I".'[10]

On 8 April, Bill issued a Special Order of the Day to his victorious troops which glowed with pride: 'You have won the battle for Central Burma. It has been no easy triumph. You have won it against the obstacles of nature, and against a numerous, well-equipped and vicious enemy. You have earned Victory by skill, boldness and resolution ... and by your refusal to let difficulties overcome you, by your grim endurance, your unquenchable fighting spirit and by your magnificent audacity ... We have advanced far towards a final victory in Burma, but we have one more stage before it is achieved. We have heard a lot about the Road to Mandalay; now we are on the road from Mandalay. The Japanese are mustering their whole remaining strength in Burma to bar our path. When we meet them again, let us do to them what we have done before, and this time even more thoroughly.'

Shortly after dawn on 11 April, Bill stood by the roadside at Pyawbwe with Frank Messervy and watched as men of the 5th Indian Infantry Division, the division with which he had started the war as a brigade commander, surged past the start point on the drive to take Rangoon. Among the group of officers standing with Bill was Lieutenant Colonel Jack Masters, the GSO1 of Rees' 19th

Division. Masters had not seen Bill close up since they had served together in Persia three and half years earlier, but the moment Bill spotted him he grinned and said cheerily: 'How's it going, Jack? Pete driving you mad?'

For Masters, the sight of an entire division moving off to do battle was a moving moment: 'The dust thickened under the trees lining the road until the column was motoring into a thunderous yellow tunnel, first the tanks, infantry all over them, then trucks filled with men, then more tanks, going fast, nose to tail, guns, more trucks, more guns – British, Sikhs, Gurkhas, Madrassis, Pathans ... All these men knew their commanders and as the vehicles crashed past most of the soldiers were on their feet, cheering and yelling ... Only a fool would grudge us the excitement and the sense of glory, for no one on that plain had wanted war, and all of us had known enough horror to last several lifetimes.'[11]

The division immediately ran into stiff resistance near Pyawbwe – it took nine days to fight through the area – but thereafter the advance inexorably gathered momentum. An irresistible urge to be in the thick of the action still afflicted the commander of the 14th Army and still provoked him into perhaps unwise expeditions to the front, even at this late stage in the battle. When reports reached his headquarters in Meiktila that a Japanese counter-attack was threatening 19th Division's lines of communication and that the main road to Rangoon was under fire, he flew to the divisional headquarters at Toungoo the following day to see what was going on. Driving from the airstrip into Toungoo, he quickly discovered for himself that the road was indeed under enemy fire, but he made it safely and found Pete Rees perfectly cheerful and confident the counter-attack would be beaten back.

Bill took the opportunity to tour some of the front-line positions. He stopped to watch a gunner, stripped to the waist and glistening with sweat, slamming shells into the breach of a 25-pounder firing into the hills where the Japanese were reportedly concentrating for another attack. During a lull in the barrage Bill stepped into the gunpit and apologised to the men for demanding so much from them on half rations. (Supplies of food had had to be cut back to ensure sufficient fuel and ammunition reached the front.) 'Don't you worry about that, sir,' one of the gunners replied. 'Put us on quarter

rations, but give us the ammo and we'll get you to Rangoon.'[12] It
was a remark, Bill thought, that exemplified the spirit of his army.

Next day, 1 May, Bill decided to view the fighting from the air.
Accompanied by Frank Messervy and a number of staff officers, including an American major, Robert Fullerton, the party took off
from Toungoo and headed south at about 2,000 feet. Bill was sitting
in the cockpit, next to the pilot, and could see columns of smoke
rising from Rangoon, some 50 miles distant. It seems no one on
board realised they had crossed into enemy-held territory until there
was a sudden explosion. They had been hit by cannon fire from
the ground and Fullerton, who had been standing looking out of
a window midway down the cabin had taken the full blast in his
legs. The pilot put the aircraft into a steep dive and turned back for
home without waiting for orders. Landing safely at an airstrip just
behind the front, emergency surgery saved Fullerton's life, but he
lost a leg. Bill felt very guilty about what had happened, particularly
as he knew that Fullerton was one of the top four polo players in
the United States.

That afternoon the heavens opened, announcing the arrival of
the monsoon, and its concomitant misery, two weeks early. Cowan's
division, poised only 30 miles from Rangoon for the final strike,
suddenly found itself bogged down in continuous drenching rain,
ending all hopes of capturing the town before the arrival of the
troops who were due to land by sea and air in Operation Dracula
the following day.

In the end, the fall of Rangoon was something of an anti-climax.
As the first landing craft made their way cautiously up the river
towards the port of Rangoon, they were surprised to be hailed by
an RAF officer in a sampan who cheerfully informed them that the
Japanese had evacuated the city several days earlier. Allied prisoners
of war had tried to alert the RAF by painting 'JAPS GONE' on
the roof of their jail in big white letters and, when this provoked no
response, they added 'EXTRACT DIGIT'.[13] Wing Commander
A. E. Saunders, on patrol in a Mosquito, decided to investigate but
promptly burst a tyre as he attempted to land on a bomb-cratered
airstrip nearby. Fortunately he and his navigator were unhurt and
when they learned from the emaciated prisoners that the enemy
had indeed departed, they made their way to the docks and, with

considerable sang-froid, commandeered the sampan and set out downriver to meet troops who had landed in Operation Dracula.

Bill was delighted when he heard of Wing Commander Saunders' escapade. Saunders was a member of 221 Group which, as far as Bill was concerned, was a part of 14th Army in all but name. 'If we could not get to Rangoon first ourselves,' he explained, 'the next best thing was for someone from 221 Group ... to do it.' At 1630 hours on 6 May, the 1st/7th Gurkhas of the 48th Indian Infantry Brigade, advancing south through the monsoon 27 miles from Rangoon, linked up with the 1st Lincolns, who had landed in the city during Operation Dracula and were marching north to meet the 14th Army.

Two days later, on 8 May 1945, the Allies in Europe accepted the unconditional surrender of Nazi Germany and all over the world millions of people took to the streets to celebrate victory in Europe. Celebrations in Burma were rather less frenetic, judging from the memoirs of Signalman Dennis Newland in Meiktila: 'First there was a football match which we did not think was very good. Then General Slim gave an address in which he hoped our own victory would be not too long coming. We went back to the main unit for some food and returned for an open-air film show. After this finished we missed the truck back to the wireless village and thumbed a lift ... in a staff car, which turned out to be General Slim's own car. His driver told us he was instructed by the General to give lifts to soldiers when the car was running empty. It was now raining and the driver took us back to the wireless village which was beyond his destination – Uncle Bill was very highly thought of.'[14]

Although there was much mopping up still to do, the capture of Rangoon essentially marked the end of the battle for Burma; on 14 May, a victory parade marched through the streets of the ravaged city. In nine months of continuous fighting, Bill had coaxed his polyglot army – three-quarters of them Indians, all volunteers – across nearly 1,000 miles of the most difficult and forbidding terrain in the world, annihilated five enemy divisions (305,000 Japanese soldiers fought in Burma; 60 per cent died of wounds, starvation or malnutrition) and inflicted the worst defeat on the Imperial Japanese Army in its history. With the most meagre of resources he had met every challenge and risen above it and proved himself to be both an administrative genius and master of warfare. The reconquest of Burma was, Mountbatten claimed, nothing less than a tour de force and 'a classic in the art of generalship'. Bill's strategy would eventually provide a template for the modern doctrine of 'manoeuvre warfare', defined as 'the means of concentrating force to achieve surprise, psychological shock, physical momentum and moral dominance'.

Perhaps no man on earth at that time was better qualified than Lieutenant General William Slim to expect the unexpected and to cope with sudden and dramatic changes of circumstance. But not even Bill could have ever anticipated that at this moment of personal triumph he would be relieved of his command.

18

Sacked

There is a possibility that Oliver Leese considered he was acting in Bill's best interests when he tried, at the beginning of May 1945, to remove him from the command of his beloved 14th Army. Most observers, however, thought baser instincts – pique, jealousy, frustration – were at play. Whatever Leese's motives, his attempt to sack Bill Slim a few days before the victory parade in Rangoon was a colossal misjudgement that sent shock waves through the 14th Army.

Leese's appointment to ALFSEA in November 1944 had not been a happy one. He arrived to find that Bill and Mountbatten had established a close working relationship based on mutual trust and regard and frequently found himself excluded from the decision-making process. Any hope of him stamping his authority on operations or keeping Bill on a tighter rein seemed unattainable. Although Leese's dealings with Bill were superficially cordial, he tended to be condescending about him in letters to his wife, describing him as 'an extraordinary devil' who 'can never stop crabbing about something'. Later he complained that 'Slim and most of the others are really strangers and we have very little in common'.[1] He also developed a singular loathing for Mountbatten, whom he described as 'crooked as a corkscrew' and whom he resented for undermining his authority by dealing directly with Bill.

Sandwiched at a command level between the glamorous Supremo and the highly popular commander of the 14th Army, Leese unquestionably felt overshadowed and bitterly complained to Frank Owen, editor of *SEAC*, about the lack of publicity he was getting. Owen instructed a clerk to go through all the back issues published since Leese's arrival and count the number of times his name was mentioned and the column inches devoted to his activities. He reported back to Leese that more space had been devoted to him than both the two previous Commanders-in-Chief together, but Leese was still aggrieved. His grudge, it transpired significantly, was that Bill featured more frequently in *SEAC* than he did.

There were many in the 14th Army who speculated about the nature of the relationship between the two men, since they were so obviously very different personalities. Major John Hill, a company commander in the Royal Berkshire Regiment recalled a visit from Leese while the battalion was in Meiktila: 'Although an eminent soldier, he seemed to me, probably unintentionally, to be slightly supercilious and haughty. His parade-ground smartness, with Sam Browne belt and service dress cap, made him seem very far removed from the realities of our life in this no-holds-barred war. He was so very different in approach and dress from the down-to-earth, dour, tough Slim – a soldier's general every step of the way.'[2]

The background to Leese's attempt to sack Bill is contained in a file lodged in the Liddell Hart Centre for Military Archives at King's College London and marked 'The information in this file is only to be made available to reputable historians who are not directly connected with the press'. It was compiled by Major General S. W. Kirby, the official historian of the Burma campaign, not for publication so much as for posterity. Kirby asked for the file to remain closed until after the deaths of Mountbatten, Leese and Bill.

On 3 May, the day after Allied troops entered Rangoon, Leese flew to Kandy for a meeting with Mountbatten. Among other matters discussed, Leese raised the issue of future senior appointments within South East Asia Command and offered the view that Bill was 'extremely tired' after three years of continuous fighting in Burma. At that time planning for the recapture of Malaya by the 14th Army was well advanced and Leese said he was concerned that Bill was not 'up-to-date' with the amphibious operations that would be required. The solution, he suggested, was for Bill to be given command of the 12th Army (also called the Burma Army), a new formation which was to remain in Burma and administer the country, and that Philip Christison should take over the 14th Army.

At the time of this meeting Mountbatten was recovering from a bout of amoebic dysentery and felt far from well, but he recalled telling Leese he would not countenance any changes which might carry the 'slightest indication' that Bill was being removed from his command. He authorised Leese to discuss the matter with Bill 'on a friendly basis', but warned him to handle it extremely carefully, adding that he had the highest opinion of Bill, complete confidence in him, and would not consider any action which might affect his future, operations in the theatre or the morale of the 14th Army. Finally, he ordered Leese to report back before making any approach to Sir Alan Brooke, the CIGS, in London.

Leese, conversely, apparently left the meeting with the clear impression that Mountbatten approved his proposals, so much so that he unwisely resolved to offer command of the 14th Army to his friend Christison (they were students at Staff College together) even before he had talked to Bill, or, indeed, cleared the appointment with London. Christison was still in command of 15 Corps, which had steadily pushed the Japanese back in Arakan, captured vital airfields and provided the assault force for Operation Dracula, the success of which had convinced Leese that Christison was the man to command future operations in Malaya. Leese dispatched a signal to Christison, who was then in Rangoon, saying he would like to see him at Akyab on 6 May.

On 5 May, Leese telegraphed the CIGS, with a copy to Mountbatten, outlining his plans for changes in the command structure at ALFSEA and proposing Christison for command of the 14th Army as 'he had immense experience of amphibious operations and the 14th Army's next operation would be predominantly amphibious'. He added that he had discussed his proposals with the Supreme Commander *and that he had agreed* [author's italics]. In a letter written to Brooke on the same day, Leese explained his thinking: 'Slim has been in continuous active service since 1941 and has been in Burma without a break since the finish of Field Marshal Alexander's operations in 1942 [actually he was in India for much of that time]. He has stood up to the strain well, but I do not think he has it in him to start off on another vigorous campaign with a completely new conception, without a rest. I have, therefore, asked you to allow me to transfer him from the 14th Army to the new Burma Army, which I intend to set up to control the operations and administration in Burma ... I feel that if our propaganda is good, Slim can be built up as the conqueror of Burma, and is the right man to set Burma on a sound footing for the future.'[3]

Christison, who was mystified at being summoned back to his headquarters to meet Leese, had a difficult journey from Rangoon to make the meeting in Akyab. All the nearby airfields had been closed because of the intensity of the monsoon, but he was able to get a lift on a destroyer, which sailed into a typhoon and very nearly foundered en route. He arrived at his headquarters at four o'clock on the morning of 6 May looking, he said, 'like a piece of chewed string'. When Leese, accompanied by a number of staff officers, arrived, Christison's first words to him were: 'Oliver, what's all this in aid of?'

In his unpublished memoirs, Christison tried to set down what he remembered of their subsequent conversation word for word. If his memory was correct, Leese seemed to have taken leave of his senses, or at least his grasp on truth. 'After breakfast Oliver took me aside and said: "Christie, Dickie has felt for some time that Slim has become a very tired man and I must say I agree. Now Dickie has suggested to me that I send Slim on indefinite leave [this was a lie], and I have done so. [This was another lie.] He has already left 14th Army [another lie] … You, with your many combined operations successes behind you, are to take over the 14th Army. You may have five days' leave and then proceed to GHQ Delhi where you will prepare the plans for the invasion of Malaya. When you are ready, Dickie and I will come to Delhi to hear and approve your plans."'

Christison, flabbergasted by this unexpected news, asked if Bill had been sacked. No, Leese replied, but 'both Dickie and I felt he needed a rest'. It was all very tricky, he added. He had wanted Dickie to see Slim and give him the bad news, but Dickie had refused and said it was his [Leese's] job as Bill's immediate superior. Christison not unnaturally assumed his appointment had been cleared through all the usual channels and Leese gave him no indication it was confidential so he had no hesitation spreading the good news among his staff officers. That evening an impromptu farewell dinner was organised in his honour in the mess as a celebration of his promotion.

On 7 May, Leese continued on to 14th Army headquarters at Meiktila for what would be a sticky interview with Bill. He was hoping that Bill would accept the new command arrangements without causing too much trouble. Bill was not, after all, being demoted, he would still be an army commander. What Leese did not appreciate, and perhaps did not understand, was Bill's visceral connection to the 14th Army. It was *his* army, the troops were *his* troops. He loved them as much as they loved him. He had not the slightest desire to command any other army.

Bill had intended to visit Rangoon that day, but, hearing Leese was on his way to see him, he waited at his headquarters. He had no idea what Leese wanted to talk to him about. Leese arrived at three o'clock in the afternoon in the company of his chief of staff, but went in alone to talk to Bill. After congratulating Bill on the success of the 14th Army, he announced without preamble that he was making changes in the command structure. 'Before we talk of anything else,' he said, 'I must tell you that I have decided to give Christison command of the 14th Army and to ask you to stay on in command of the troops that will be left in Burma. I do not consider you capable of planning a large-scale amphibious operation like Zipper [the code name for the recapture of Malaya] or of commanding the 14th Army in such an operation, so I do not think it would be fair either to the 14th Army or to yourself to leave you in command of it.'[4]

Bill was utterly stunned. He thought, he would later tell Mountbatten, that he had 'not done too badly, not so badly anyway to be sacked in such ungracious terms'. When he had recovered his composure he asked when he would be replaced. 'As soon as possible,' Leese replied. Bill agreed that the sooner Christison took over the better, but indignantly rejected Leese's suggestion that he should take command of the Burma Army. (Privately, he viewed it as an insulting offer.) As it was obvious that Leese had lost confidence in him it was better for all concerned for him to go altogether, he said. If you do that, Leese warned, it will mean the end of your military career. I am aware of that, Bill replied, but I still think it is much better that I should go. Nothing, he said, could possibly make him change his mind.

Drawing on his natural dignity, Bill did not question Leese's decision. He had always claimed the right to remove subordinate commanders when he thought it necessary and so he could hardly deny Leese the same right. He told Leese that as far as he was concerned there would be no fuss either in or outside the 14th Army; he would make no protest nor embarrass him in any way. As soon as his successor had arrived he would return to India and ask to be retired. Leese seemed surprised by Bill's resolve, pressed him to think seriously about what he was doing and suggested he should take a couple of days' leave to discuss it with his wife. Bill replied that that would be helpful for him to arrange his affairs, but that he would not change his mind. Despite this, Leese claimed he still hoped that Bill would come round and later that afternoon he telephoned Mountbatten's chief of staff in Kandy to tell him that, while Slim was thinking it over, he had been most understanding and had accepted the plan as being the best for the operation. Leese believed he would accept the changes and was 'at heart happy'. He was clearly unaware that Bill made a single angry entry in his diary that night: 'Sacked.'

Bill asked Tubby Lethbridge, his chief of staff, to get the senior officers together so that he could warn them of what had transpired. 'The most incredible thing has happened,' Lethbridge wrote in a hasty note to his wife that night, 'Bill has been sacked just at the moment when this masterpiece of his was being finished ... There has been, I suppose a clash of personalities. Bill is, I think, the finest man I have ever met, and every one of us would quite literally die for him – he is that sort of chap. The whole thing has sickened me and shaken my faith in fellow man. He of course took it magnificently, being the magnificent gentleman he is. I don't know what he will do – I think he will retire. The thing doesn't make sense ...'[5]

The unfolding drama in the higher echelons of ALFSEA was overshadowed the following day by news of the Armistice in Europe – the long-awaited VE Day and the unconditional surrender of the armed forces of Nazi Germany. Bill spent the day in Rangoon discussing logistics with senior commanders. He gave no hint of what had happened. 'Throughout the long day Bill Slim was his normal, cheerful and ruggedly delightful self,' recalled Colonel Jim Godwin, one of his staff officers, who was with him. 'Never once did I sense, even alone in the Beechcraft during the flight, that there was anything out of the ordinary on his mind or worrying him unduly.'

When Godwin got back to Meiktila late that evening he was sent for by Lethbridge, who 'straight away blurted out through a mixture of emotion, anger and Scotch "Uncle Bill has been sacked. He wants to see all senior staff at 1000 tomorrow morning."' Godwin was speechless and wondered if, for a moment, Tubby had 'gone round the bend'.[6]

Promptly at ten o'clock next morning Bill strode into a conference room where about 230 officers were gathered in sombre silence. He went straight to the point: 'I have a very painful announcement to make to you, gentlemen. Two days ago the Commander-in-Chief visited our headquarters, as you know, and told me I was unsuitable for the coming operations and could not command 14th Army further. I can't tell you what a painful announcement this is for me to make to you when, as you will guess, I have only one ambition and that is to go on commanding the 14th Army, of which I am extremely proud, until the Jap is beaten flat. But that is not to be.

'I have been offered command of the 12th Army, the static army to be left behind to mop up the mess we have left the Japs in. I have refused. I have been asked to reconsider my decision and I am doing so now to the extent that I am going off now to talk things over with my wife. I am not a rich man. I am telling you chaps now – I owe it to you, who have helped me through so many tough spots before. I want no mention of this outside these four walls and I want no adverse criticism of it and no action on anyone's part in sympathy for me. There are higher loyalties you owe than just to me as your immediate commander. You have your loyalties to the Commander-in-Chief and to the King and country. That is all, gentlemen.'

He turned on his heel and walked out in silence, leaving the entire room in shock and several officers discreetly wiping their eyes. The consensus was that a monumental act of folly was being committed. Jim Godwin spoke for many when he suggested that Leese and Mountbatten must be 'out of their minds, stark, staring mad', adding, 'I never trusted that affected, silk handkerchief-waving Guardsman [Leese].' A number of officers began talking about resigning and there were nervous predictions about what would happen when the troops discovered their beloved Uncle Bill had been sacked.

When Leese heard about Bill's speech he was furious and insisted that the 14th Army commander had not been 'sacked'. Bill, meanwhile, flew to Shillong where Aileen was working in a military hospital as a VAD helper. In truth, Aileen was not entirely unhappy with his news; actually, she was delighted. She was, of course, furious at the injustice of his dismissal, but at the same time the prospect of retirement, having a husband safe at home, getting away from the war and returning to England after so long away, was a blissful prospect. 'I watched her loyal indignation submerged by relief,' he noted, 'that after so many years I would be out of the war.'

Back on duty at Meiktila, Bill wrote to both Auchinleck and Leese saying he could not continue to serve under someone who did not have the fullest confidence in his capabilities and confirming his intention to retire. Meanwhile he tried to carry on as if nothing had happened while waiting for Christison to arrive and take over from him. Jim Godwin reported that the days following the news of Bill's dismissal were dreadful. 'The cheerful atmosphere at HQ evaporated, morale was at rock bottom, vicious anger was the predominant emotion.' At one point Godwin thought the whole headquarters would go on strike or mutiny and, despite Bill's demand that there should be no 'quixotic nonsense', a number of divisional and brigade commanders wrote to him to apply for a transfer because they no longer wanted to serve under Leese. Bill told them not to be stupid and tore up their letters.

'Outwardly he was his usual imperturbable rugged self, through which humour and pleasure could still shine vividly,' Godwin noted. 'At night, however, it was a different story. He always drank sparingly and never lingered in the mess overlong, preferring to read or write alone. Now, for hours on end, his footsteps could be heard pacing slowly up and down the creaking floor of his upstairs room, the only one in a rather shattered house standing alone by the lake in Meiktila.'[7]

Mountbatten clearly still had complete faith in Bill's judgement. On 16 May, at Mountbatten's request, Bill interviewed General Aung San, the young leader of the 11,000-strong Burma National Army which had originally fought on the Japanese side in the hope that Japan would free Burma from colonial rule, but now wanted to transfer its allegiance to the Allies. Aung San, who had been branded a 'traitor rebel leader' by Churchill, had been promised safe conduct to and from 14th Army headquarters; nevertheless, the arrival of a Burmese national wearing the full uniform of a Japanese major general and carrying a sword understandably raised many eyebrows.

Bill's task was to assess the possible contribution the BNA could make to clearing the Japanese out of Burma and the extent to which it could be trusted. The negotiations did not start well when Aung San presented himself as representing the army of the 'Provisional Government' of Burma. Bill would have none of it: there was only one government of Burma, he said, and that was the British government. He did not recognise any 'provisional' government and if the BNA were to join the Allies he (Aung San) would have to accept Bill's orders as a subordinate commander.

When Aung San continued to protest, Bill warned him that there were many influential voices calling for his arrest to face well-substantiated murder charges. 'I have been urged to place you on trial,' he continued. 'You have nothing in writing, only a verbal promise at second-hand that I would return you to your friends. Don't you think you are taking a considerable risk in coming here and adopting this attitude?'

'No,' Aung San replied.

'Why not?'

'Because you are a British officer.'

Bill could not stop himself from laughing at this response. They continued their discussions in much better humour with Bill chiding Aung San at one point that he had only approached the Allies because he could see they were winning. 'It wouldn't be much good coming to you if you weren't, would it?' Aung San retorted, making Bill laugh again. Aung San's evident honesty and courage impressed Bill; he seemed to be much more of a genuine patriot than the unscrupulous revolutionary Bill had expected. Bill reported to Mountbatten that he could 'do business' with Aung San and recommended that the Burma National Army should be incorporated in the Allied command to assist in mopping-up operations. (After the war Aung San played a prominent role in securing independence for Burma but he was assassinated in 1947 when a gang of armed paramilitaries financed by rival politicians broke into the Secretariat Building in Rangoon and shot and killed seven Cabinet ministers, including Aung San. His youngest daughter, Aung San Suu Kyi, was just two years old at the time.)

Although he had plenty to occupy him, it was impossible for Bill not to brood about the future and on the evening of the day he

interviewed Aung San he wrote a gloomy letter to his friend Reginald
Savory, who was then the Indian Army's Director of Infantry in
Delhi: 'I received a very nasty shock last week when Oliver Leese
sent for me and informed me that he was removing me from command of the Army. He gave as his reason his opinion that I was not
capable of planning or carrying out the forthcoming operations of
the Army. I have always said that commanders should have a very
considerable right of selecting their own subordinates, and if that is
how he feels his action in removing me is perfectly proper. All the
same, you will realise how I feel about leaving the Fourteenth Army,
which has been my baby and has always treated me so exceedingly
well ... Leese offered me command of the Burma Army ... but I did
not feel in the circumstances that there would be enough confidence
between us to justify my accepting the offer, I have therefore written to the C-in-C suggesting that I go on leave pending retirement
... Aileen is indignant but delighted. Whether she will be quite so
delighted when we are living on what remains of a pension after
Income Tax has been deducted I am not so sure, but we have got
to start some sort of new life, and the sooner we begin the better.'[8]

Savory, who had known Leese for years, declared himself to be
'absolutely at a loss' to understand why he had done such an extraordinary thing. The only explanation, Savory concluded, was 'a
swollen head coupled with extreme jealousy' of Bill.

By then rumours that Uncle Bill had been sacked had swept all
ranks of the 14th Army and been greeted with disbelief and fury.
In Whitehall and Delhi, it transpired, there was similar disbelief.
Auchinleck, the Commander-in-Chief Indian Army, happened to
be in London and when, over lunch with Brooke, he was asked his
opinion on Leese's proposal he replied without equivocation that in
his opinion the removal of Slim would be disastrous for the morale
of the Indian Army and the success of future operations and urged
emphatically that it should not happen. That night Brooke noted in
his diary: 'Leese is going quite wild and doing mad things. Prepared
a fair rap on the knuckles for him.' On the following day he sent
a signal to Mountbatten expressing his 'surprise and displeasure' at
Leese's misplaced initiative. 'I have every confidence in Slim,' Brooke
added, 'whose record has been outstandingly successful and unless
very strong arguments can be adduced I have no intention – repeat,

no intention – of agreeing to his supersession by Christison.'⁹

Leese continued to insist that there had been a 'misunderstanding' and that there was never any question of Bill being sacked. In a desperate attempt to save the situation, he dispatched his chief of staff, Major General George Walsh, to Meiktila to make another stab at persuading Bill to take the Burma Army job and dissuade him from the notion that he had been sacked. Walsh assured Bill that Leese had not lost confidence in him and that he would retain the status of army commander. Bill replied that as it was the intention to reduce the troops in Burma to three or even two divisions, it would hardly be an army command. While he appreciated the efforts being made to save his face, he repeated that it would be better for everyone if he went, assured Walsh he had no intention of making difficulties for anyone and asked once again for his successor to be sent to 14th Army headquarters without further delay.

On the issue of his sacking, Bill was unyielding. 'He was quite adamant that he had been sacked and nothing I could say could persuade him otherwise,' Walsh reported. 'He said to me, "What would Monty have said if, after the completion of the campaign in Africa, someone else had taken over his command?" I replied, amongst other things, that Monty at that time was comparatively fresh whereas he, Slim, had borne the heat and burden of the whole war ... I took him once again through Leese's plans ... but I realised at the conclusion of my talk with General Slim that nothing would change the attitude he was adopting.'¹⁰

Bill continued making the rounds of his front-line units – the battle to clear the last pockets of Japanese out of Burma was continuing – to say goodbye to his commanders and the troops. Senior officers at 14th Army headquarters laid on a farewell dinner for him, which he morbidly described as tantamount to 'attending my own funeral'.

But, like Mark Twain, reports of his death had been greatly exaggerated. On 20 May, Leese received a furious signal from the CIGS, an ominous harbinger of his own fate: 'I wish to make it quite plain that I consider the manner in which you have attempted to carry out changes in the highest appointments under your command has been most unsatisfactory and irregular ... I find it hard to understand how you can spare the services of General Slim at this juncture. He has been considerably successful in all the operations he has run and had proved himself to be one of the ablest leaders.'[11]

When Mountbatten was shown a copy he summoned Leese to Kandy and bluntly told him that if Slim wished to retain command of the 14th Army he (Mountbatten) could not agree to his supersession. Mountbatten made an oblique reference to their meeting in his private diary: 'Oliver Leese had flown down specially to report to me over a certain matter and I gave him dinner. He then went to his bungalow to think over what I had told him and on Tuesday morning [22 May] came back to see me. This particular problem, a knotty and difficult one, has now been settled.'[12]

The 'knotty and difficult problem' was solved very simply by Leese grudgingly conceding. After sleeping on it overnight, he decided to recommend that Monty Stopford, the senior corps commander in Burma, be appointed to command the Burma Army, allowing Slim to remain with the 14th Army and entrusted with the forthcoming operations in Malaya. A telegram to this effect, drafted by Mountbatten but signed by Leese, was immediately dispatched to 14th Army headquarters.

Jim Godwin was sitting in the early morning sun with another staff officer on the verandah steps of the mess at Meiktila 'grumbling about the situation as usual' when a jeep pulled up with Michael Oldman, Bill's assistant military secretary, at the wheel. Oldman asked where the army commander was and Godwin jerked a thumb towards Bill's room on the first floor. He raced up the rickety stairs and knocked on the door which Bill opened. 'I have a signal for you sir,' Oldman said, 'which I think might interest you.' A moment later Godwin heard a deep chuckle and then laughter; he ran up the stairs and one look at Bill's face told him all he wanted to know. It was a reprieve, but for Bill a major problem remained – how could he continue to work under someone who had tried to sack him?

While waiting for formal approval of Stopford's appointment from London, Mountbatten obviously felt he should write to Brooke explaining in detail the background to what had happened. He perhaps wanted to extricate himself from any responsibility for the debacle; certainly he placed the blame squarely on Leese. 'I can assure you I would not dream of allowing an officer who had done as well as Slim has to be superseded against his will ...' he wrote.

'Oliver freely admits he has made a blunder in simultaneously tele-graphing you and, without waiting for your view, seeing Slim. He is very contrite about the unnecessary trouble he has caused through this and I am sorry that I did not realise sooner that the question was being mishandled.'[13]

On 24 May, Bill flew to Calcutta for a meeting with Leese at ALFSEA headquarters in Barrackpore at which Leese made it clear how anxious he now was for Bill to command 14th Army oper-ations in Malaya. Bill, however, was not so easily won over. He recognised that Mountbatten was behind Leese's change of heart, said he did not see how he could serve under someone who had no confidence in him and obstinately refused to reconsider his de-cision to retire. Either Mountbatten or Leese, or both, had antici-pated this eventuality and Leese produced a letter to Bill from the Supreme Commander with a personal appeal for him to stay on. It gave Bill the face-saving excuse he needed to accede, to avoid put-ting Mountbatten into the 'invidious position' of having to choose between himself and Leese. The reality was, of course, that Bill des-perately wanted to stay with the 14th Army. Leese, doubtless, was re-lieved since further opprobrium from London would undoubtedly fall on his head if Bill insisted on going. Bill returned to Burma for a couple of days then flew to Delhi to study plans for the Malayan operation.

On one matter Leese was certainly correct – Bill was tired and badly needed a rest. On 1 June, Mountbatten asked the CIGS for permission to send Bill to England for a month's leave, pointing out that he had been in Burma for a long time and 'thoroughly de-served' a short period of rest. 'I have gone into this carefully in the last few days,' Mountbatten added, 'and with the present stage of planning there is no doubt that he can be spared for a month with-out detriment to future operations and his appearance in England would fit in extremely well with our deception plans.' Brooke un-hesitatingly agreed.

Leese, perhaps trying to make amends, did everything he could to facilitate Bill's trip, booking rooms for him and Aileen at the Dorchester, arranging for an ADC and writing to his wife to enlist her assistance. 'Would you please do everything you possibly can to help them? Neither of them have been at home for many years, and therefore they are completely out of touch with people and with conditions in England in wartime ... I am awfully anxious that after his past record everything possible should be done to help General Slim have the best possible leave.' It is possible all this was intended for the public record, since he qualified his sentiments in another letter two days later in which he complained that Bill was 'almost a megalomaniac' and 'the world's bellyacher' who had 'resented my coming out here at all and has made things difficult all along for me and my staff'.[14]

Mountbatten was still concerned about long-term damage to the relationship between the two men and a few days later, during a conference in Delhi, he met Bill alone in his bedroom at the Viceroy's House and asked him candidly if, under the circumstances, he was prepared to serve loyally under Leese. Bill's reply hardly filled Mountbatten with much optimism. He said yes, of course, he would serve under Leese with the utmost loyalty, but it would be without any confidence; he admitted it would be awkward serving under someone who had tried to sack him and he did not see how mutual trust could ever be re-established. He also added that neither he, nor his senior commanders, trusted Leese's military judgement and gave several examples of Leese refusing advice and then being forced by events to change his mind. It was not exactly a ringing endorsement. Auchinleck's chief of staff had already told Mountbatten that the attempted sacking of Slim had had a 'disastrous effect' in the feeling of GHQ towards Leese.

On 3 June a photograph of Mountbatten, Leese and Slim standing shoulder to shoulder at the Delhi conference was published in the *SEAC* newspaper. It was a photocall that had been specifically arranged by Mountbatten in an effort to quell the rumours that were still seething through 14th Army – a popular version of events was that Leese wanted to sack Uncle Bill so that he could claim the glory of recapturing Malaya – and promote the notion that all three were working together in harmony.

Two days later, Bill and Aileen flew to Britain on leave – their first trip home for nearly seven years – in the personal aircraft of Lieutenant General Richard 'Windy' Gale, then commanding the 1st Airborne Corps, who had been in India discussing airborne aspects of Operation Zipper. While Mountbatten's chief of staff,

Lieutenant General Frederick 'Boy' Browning, expressed disappointment that, for security reasons, Bill would not get the 'great ovation' he deserved on his return to Britain, Bill himself probably thought quite enough fuss was made. There was a reception at the Mansion House, a Lord Mayor's luncheon in Birmingham, visits to his old schools – King Edward's and St Philip's, where he had a reunion with the deputy head, Frank Leighton – a trip to Germany to pay his respects to Montgomery only a few weeks after he had accepted the surrender of Germany on Lüneburg Heath, meetings with the War Cabinet and the Chiefs of Staff in Whitehall and an invitation to lunch with the Prime Minister at Chequers, during which Churchill held forth confidently on his prospects for the upcoming General Election. When Mrs Churchill pointed out to her husband that the Forces' vote was uncertain, Bill chipped in 'Well, Prime Minister, I know one thing. My army won't be voting for you.' (Clement Attlee, the Labour leader, had promised to bring the troops home earlier from foreign climes: it was a vote winner – Labour won by a landslide a few days later.)

In the midst of their hectic schedule, Bill and Aileen managed a week of blissful peace in a rented cottage in the Cotswolds and visits to the family – his mother, aged 93, was still living in Bournemouth and his brother, Charles, was still practising as a GP near Wolverhampton. Back in London towards the end of his leave, Bill returned from a visit to Whitehall looking so bemused that Aileen asked him if something was wrong. No, he said, but something surprising had happened. 'They've made me Commander-in-Chief,' he said.

Two days after Bill had left India on leave, Mountbatten drafted a letter to the CIGS seeking advice about Leese's future. Leese had admitted he had made a thorough mess of things and was doing his best to sort matters out, Mountbatten wrote, but the question was whether it was in his power to remedy the situation completely. It was extremely difficult to do the right thing in a straightforward and honourable way, he pointed out, when so much mistrust and suspicion had already been sown by actions outside his control. If he decided to sack Leese he was worried about repercussions in the newspapers, sacking two commanders-in-chief in less than twelve months. 'Fortunately I like Oliver Leese,' he added, 'in the sense that I enjoy his company, but since my row with him and my over-ruling of Slim's appointment he is a changed man ... Personally I believe that if he stays in Kandy where I can keep an eye on him we shall have no more difficulties.'

Brooke was unconvinced and replied on 19 June in unequivocal terms: 'To my mind Oliver Leese has lost the confidence of most of his senior commanders and has placed himself in a difficult position which is going to render it difficult for Slim to serve under him ... I should feel there was no alternative but to replace Leese at the earliest possible moment ... I should not feel satisfied to continue with a commander who had so completely lost the confidence of his subordinates through his own actions.' Brooke recommended replacing Leese with the man he had tried to sack – Bill. Mountbatten promptly abandoned his support for Leese and unhesitatingly accepted Brooke's suggestion, noting that such a move would suit him 'admirably'.

Mountbatten first tried to pass the buck and persuade 'the Auk' to take responsibility for sacking Leese, who was at that moment taking a short holiday in Srinagar as guest of the Maharajah of Kashmir, but Auchinleck would have none of it. On 1 July, Mountbatten sent Leese a handwritten note in Kashmir to say that he was 'unable to retain his services'. 'Dear Oliver,' it began, 'I am afraid I have an extremely painful duty to perform and one that I had hoped, on purely personal grounds, I might be spared ...'

Bill's promotion to full general and confirmation of his appointment as C-in-C ALFSEA, in place of General Oliver Leese, was confirmed on the same day.

Writing to his wife two days later, Leese admitted he had made a 'silly error of judgement' but claimed that Mountbatten wanted to get rid of him anyway. 'I am very glad to leave here,' he added petulantly. 'It has been a horrid party with Mountbatten and Slim.'[15]

On his return from Kashmir, Leese called Christison to his quarters to fill him in on the background. Christison found the former C-in-C in his bath, drinking a large whisky. 'Christie, I've been sacked,' he said. 'I'm for home. Brookie [Alan Brooke, the CIGS] went to Churchill and told him the Indian Army wouldn't fight without Slim. When Churchill asked, "Who sacked Slim?" Brooke answered, "Leese" to which Churchill replied, "Well sack Leese". I gather I'm carrying the can for Dickie over this.'[16] The following day Leese was formally relieved of his command and recalled to London, his career blighted for ever. (Brooke told Mountbatten he intended to reprimand Leese in the 'strongest possible terms for his inexcusable behaviour' but he was forestalled when Leese burst into his office in London and boomed '*Peccavi*' (I have sinned).) Leese was appointed GOC Eastern Command, but was said to spend most of his time preparing for retirement, supervising the refurbishment of his house in Shropshire and setting up a business selling mushrooms and cacti.

When Bill came to write *Defeat Into Victory* he put together a summary of the events that led up to his abortive sacking but in the end decided not to use it to avoid embarrassing Leese. His only mention of the affair was a bland reference to 'considerable reorganisation of the higher army command in South East Asia' which led to him being chosen to succeed General Leese.

To his credit Leese bore no grudges. In a report on operations in Burma during his period at ALFSEA he described the campaign as a 'personal triumph' for Bill. 'Throughout the campaign he led his Army magnificently. His is the credit for the planning and execution of the battle for central Burma which finally defeated the Japanese Armies. Having seized the initiative, he forced General Kimura to conform to his strategy until he was driven out of Rangoon. He made an excellent plan and pushed it resolutely through.'[17]

Actually Bill's tenure as commander of ALFSEA would be even shorter than that of his predecessor. On 6 August the first atomic bomb was dropped on Hiroshima, killing at least 70,000 people. Bill heard the news in Rome, where he and Aileen had stopped briefly on their way back to India. Three days later, fulfilling Stalin's promise to act 90 days after the war ended in Europe, one million battle-hardened Soviet troops, transferred from Europe and supported by 5,500 tanks and self-propelled guns, launched a massive attack on Japanese forces in Manchuria. On the same day a second nuclear bomb was dropped on Nagasaki, killing 30,000. At noon on 15 August, Emperor Hirohito announced the surrender of Japan in a recorded radio address to the nation. 'Should we continue to fight,' he told his stunned subjects, most of whom were hearing his voice for the first time, 'not only would it result in an ultimate collapse and obliteration of the Japanese nation, but also it would lead to the total extinction of human civilisation.'

When Bill returned to duty he was fully occupied organising the re-occupation of territory captured by the Japanese and repatriation of thousands of prisoners of war, many of whom were in a pitiful condition, not much more than walking skeletons dressed in rags. Bill would never forgive the Japanese for their bestial treatment of Allied prisoners of war. 'There can be no excuse for a nation,' he wrote, 'which as a matter of policy treats its prisoners of war in this way, and no honour for an army, however brave, which willingly makes itself the instrument of such inhumanity to the helpless.'[18]

General MacArthur, then the US Supreme Commander in the Pacific, had been entrusted with overall control of the surrender and decreed that the 'archaic' practice of ceremonially forcing Japanese officers to hand over their swords should not be enforced. Bill chose to ignore this edict. In fact he had already issued orders, with Mountbatten's approval, requiring all senior Japanese officers to surrender their swords in front of parades of their own troops and he had no intention of rescinding them. When he was warned that a Japanese officer's honour was so bound up with his samurai sword that he might continue fighting, or commit suicide, rather than surrender it, Bill's response was unsympathetic. If they wanted to go on fighting, he said, he was ready for them and if they chose suicide they would be given 'every facility' to succeed. (Bill took possession of General Kimura's sword, which he kept prominently displayed as a trophy wherever he was living for the rest of his life.)

At eleven o'clock on the morning of 12 September 1945, Admiral Mountbatten and General Itagaki Seishirō, commander of the Japanese Seventh Army, signed the documents marking the un-conditional surrender of all Japanese forces in South-East Asia at a ceremony in the council chamber of the Municipal Buildings in Singapore. Afterwards, as the Japanese officers were marched away to the jeers of the crowd, Mountbatten read the text of his Order of the Day from the steps of the building, in which he warned that the Japanese were finding the humiliation of defeat very hard to accept and 'may try to behave arrogantly. You will have my support in taking the firmest measures against any Japanese obstinacy, impudence, or non co-operation.'

Bill sat on Mountbatten's left throughout the ceremony. 'I looked at the dull impassive masks that were the faces of the Japanese generals and admirals seated opposite. Their plight moved me not at all. For them, I had none of the sympathy of soldier for soldier, that I had felt for Germans, Turks, Italian, or Frenchmen that by the fortune of war I had seen surrender. I knew too well what these men and those under their orders had done to their prisoners. They sat there apart from the rest of humanity. If I had no feeling for them, they, it seemed, had no feeling of any sort, until Itagaki[19] leant forward to affix his seal to the surrender document. As he pressed heavily on the paper, a spasm of rage and despair twisted his face. Then it was gone and his mask was as expressionless as the rest. Outside, the same Union flag that had been hauled down in surrender in 1942 flew again at the masthead.'[20]

19

From Railwayman to Field Marshal

Three days after the surrender ceremony in Singapore a 'Victory Dinner' was hosted by leading Burmese politicians at the venerable Orient Club in Rangoon to celebrate the end of the Japanese occupation of their country. The club, overlooking the Royal Lake, had miraculously survived the bombing of the city unscathed, but the building had been vandalised and looted during the war and was in a sorry state. In the days before the event an army of workmen had been brought in to clean the place up and by the night of the dinner the Orient Club had regained some of its lost glamour, with potted plants everywhere and searchlights illuminating the flower-decked entrance as guests arrived in a motley cavalcade of vehicles – jeeps, staff cars, rickety taxis and the occasional pre-war limousine which had been successfully hidden from the Japanese.

Mountbatten was the guest of honour accompanied by his senior commanders – Bill, of course, along with Christison (to whom no blame had been attached for Bill's attempted sacking), Stopford, Messervy and their naval and air force equivalents. 'I can't remember what was on the menu,' one of the other guests recalled, 'as I was so over-awed by the sight of so many red tabs, gold braid and medal ribbons.'[1]

After coffee, the speeches began. The former finance minister offered everyone a warm welcome, followed by other members of the pre-war Burmese government anxious to praise the Allied forces for their achievement in freeing Burma from the tyranny of the Japanese. Then Mountbatten rose to his feet, paid eloquent tribute to everyone who had taken part in the campaign, expressed his sympathy for the bereaved families of all those who would never return, complimented the old government for its fortitude during the years of occupation and wished the Burmese people a happy and prosperous future. His speech, which was rewarded with lengthy applause, was supposed to signify the end of the formal proceedings, but as the musicians struck up and traditional Burmese dancers in native costumes prepared to take to the floor to put on a show there was a loud thumping on a table and a small figure clad in jungle green stood up. It was Bill's new friend, General Aung San.

At first it seemed as if he would follow the general tone of the previous speakers, but he quickly changed his tune into a rant against colonial rule. The British, he said, had pillaged his country, robbed it of its natural resources, its rice, its teak, its oil, its precious gems. They had reduced the Burmese people to poverty; it was high time for Britain to get out and allow Burma to govern itself ... There was an embarrassed silence when Aung San finally sat down.

Mountbatten, stony-faced, pushed back his chair, rose slowly to his feet and walked out without a word, closely followed by all the other Allied officers, to the consternation of their Burmese hosts. (It was a foretaste of what was to come as pressure for Burmese independence, which had been fomenting long before the Second World War, was whipped up again with the promise of peace. In January 1947 the British government succumbed to that pressure and agreed to grant Burma independence. As Bill put it so succinctly, 'We cleaned up the mess, handed over the keys to the original tenants, and went home.')

Despite Aung San spoiling the party, Bill was still savouring the perquisites of victory. On 26 September he wrote to Tubby Lethbridge, who by then had been promoted to major general and was serving at the headquarters of the Control Commission in Germany: 'I could not help thinking at the surrender at Singapore how much you would have enjoyed it. To see those seven apes – and they really did look like apes – come waddling in, with a chap with a pistol behind each one, to sign and seal on the dotted line could have made up to you for all those nights when you were being roused, while I hogged it in my caravan. Actually the surrender ceremony was very impressive and the Supremo is at his best on occasions of this kind. I have just come back from a tour of my area, considerably extended even since you and I found it large enough. Everything is going quite well. The Jap is quite docile – the little brute is rather fawning on us hoping to get away with it. In most places he is obeying our disarmament orders quite nicely and I have got a sword for you which I will pack and send ... Welcher, Billy Hasted and Dan Munro, the only members of the old gang I have with me, send their love. Yours, Bill.'²

As C-in-C ALFSEA, Bill had acquired exotic personal transport which the likes of Al Capone would have greatly envied – two Cadillac armoured saloon cars. Twenty-one feet long, weighing three tons and costing a staggering £23,000 each, they were prototypes manufactured by General Motors in the United States as an experiment and sent to South-East Asia for trials along with two technicians to maintain them. These monsters had plenty of room for other passengers and Bill would often tell his regular driver, Bill Richardson, to stop and offer a lift to any soldiers marching in the same direction. Richardson recalled that at the end of a long day it was always Uncle Bill, never an ADC or subordinate, who would go off and rouse the cooks to ensure his driver had a meal.

Even though he was no longer part of 14th Army (he had been succeeded by Lieutenant General Miles Dempsey), Bill was determined to keep its spirit alive. Whenever he was touring his area and had the opportunity to talk to 14th Army men he liked to share with them a favourite prophesy: 'You may not think much of yourself as you walk down Chowringhee [one of the main streets in Calcutta] in your battered bush hat and jungle battledress, enjoying a delicious "V" cigarette.³ There may be smarter gents in town who'll have annexed the available girls but one day, soldier, back in Blighty, someone will say to you, "If you were in the Fourteenth Army, you must have been a pretty good chap; come and have a drink on me".'

Unfortunately Bill's last months in Burma were marred by problems with his health. He was travelling a great deal and was frequently in pain, both from old wounds and from haemorrhoids, which at one point became so troublesome he was admitted to hospital for an operation. Aileen, who had returned to Simla to close down their flat and settle their affairs, also had a spell in hospital, but when she recovered she collected 15-year-old Una from her school in Shillong and they joined Bill in Kandy, moving into what Una remembers as a 'very hot tin hut' in a cocoa plantation close to the headquarters.

Una spent her days exploring on her bicycle and occasionally playing Monopoly in the evenings with one of her father's ADCs, a young Coldstream Guards officer by the name of John Brabourne, who would become a well-known film producer after the war. Brabourne was originally appointed ADC to Oliver Leese more or less at the moment Leese was sacked and he was astonished when he learned that Bill was perfectly prepared to take him on. Only 21 years old, he quickly became a friend of the family and when Aileen hosted a tea party for the Mountbattens she dragooned Brabourne, much against his will, to attend and help entertain her guests, among them the Mountbattens' eldest daughter, Patricia. Aileen was not deliberately match-making, but she could not help but be pleased when Brabourne and Patricia instantly fell in love; they would marry the following year in Romsey Abbey, close to Broadlands, the Mountbatten family home in Hampshire.

Bill's health was not helped by worries about his future. He did not know how long his appointment as commander ALFSEA was likely to last and, being Bill, he had little expectation of being offered another senior military post. In the immediate post-war years there would be, he thought, too many generals chasing too few jobs. The days of the Raj were drawing to a close and India, which had been his home for so long, was unlikely to offer him employment. If he was obliged to return to England, he had no idea what he would do, only that he would need to find a job, as he had few savings and could not imagine him and Aileen living out their days on his army pension.

The problem was solved in October when Mountbatten received a signal from Whitehall with the news that the Chiefs of Staff intended to reopen the Imperial Defence College in London early in the new year. They wanted the first commandant to be a respected commander who would give the college the prestige it deserved and they had all agreed General Slim would be the ideal choice. General Auchinleck, who had been copied in, warmly welcomed the idea.

The Imperial Defence College was founded in 1927 to provide high-flying senior officers from all three services, as well as diplomats, colonial officials and police officers, with an understanding of imperial defence needs; it had closed on the outbreak of the Second World War, 18 months after Bill had finished his course there. Bill's first reaction was to turn down the job because he did not want to desert Mountbatten at a time when South-East Asia was still in turmoil and so much remained to be done. It was Mountbatten who persuaded him he must accept. Aileen, too, undoubtedly exerted some influence – the prospect of being able to live as a family in peacetime Britain for the first time in her married life was not one she would readily sacrifice. Privately, both of them were also worried about Bill's health.

Bill's doctor recommended that the family should return home by sea to give Bill a chance to recuperate: passages for Bill, Aileen and Una were booked on the RMS *Georgic*, a former White Star transatlantic liner that had been converted into a troopship at the beginning of the war, departing from Bombay at the beginning of December with nearly 5,000 jubilant troops returning home from the war. John Slim did not travel with them – he had been commissioned into his father's old regiment, the 1st/6th Gurkhas, and was serving as ADC to Punch Cowan, who had been appointed commander of the British-Indian Division of the Allied Occupation Force in Japan. On the day before they embarked, in a simple ceremony in Bombay, Bill was presented with the regalia of Chief Commander of the American Legion of Merit, awarded by President Roosevelt for 'exceptionally meritorious conduct'. That evening Punch Cowan, his wife and daughter, who were also in Bombay, joined the Slims at a combined celebration and farewell dinner in the Taj Hotel. Next morning John Slim and the Cowans were on the quayside to wave goodbye when the *Georgic* slipped her moorings.

The *Georgic* docked at Liverpool on Christmas Day 1945, proudly flying the battle flag of the 14th Army from her foremast. She was greeted by military bands playing carols – and pouring rain – but Bill knew the men would all want to get home as quickly as possible and vetoed any long-winded welcoming ceremony. A car was waiting to drive them to his brother, Charlie's, home at Bilston in the West Midlands where the family, including his 93-year-old mother, had gathered for a happy reunion.

Although Bill was awarded a GBE in the New Year's Honours List, no triumphant victory parades were laid on to celebrate his return; indeed, to the intense irritation of the men of the 14th Army he remained largely unknown and unrecognised by the great British public. Mountbatten, Montgomery and Alexander were the heroes of the hour, feted everywhere, partly because they all actively enjoyed the limelight, whereas Bill very definitely did not. The first book on the Burma campaign, Alfred Wagg's *A Million Died*, published in 1943, portrayed Alexander as the protagonist of the retreat and barely bothered to mention Bill. *Burma Victory*, an hour-long documentary film sponsored by the Ministry of Information and released towards the end of 1945, also sidelined Bill's contribution. There was footage of Mountbatten stoking morale with rousing speeches to the troops, Wingate leading the Chindits on jungle raids behind the lines, Stilwell building the Ledo road and Leese planning the final offensive. Bill does not get a mention until the last few minutes: he is shown at a Burmese festival looking very self-conscious with victory garlands around his neck while the narrator belatedly explains who he is.

Burma Victory certainly reflected Churchill's view of the campaign. Although he had met Bill over lunch at Chequers while Bill was on leave during the previous summer, Churchill clung to the view that he was only a bit player, that it was Alexander who had safely brought the army out in 1942, that Wingate was the man who had shown the Japanese could be beaten and that Dickie Mountbatten and Oliver Leese together were largely responsible for the ultimate victory. Bill would only get three perfunctory mentions in Churchill's war memoirs and no mention at all in the six volumes of Churchill's biography written by Martin Gilbert.

There is no evidence that Bill was bothered by this in the slightest and in any case he had plenty to keep him busy. First, he and Aileen had to find somewhere to live. After a short spell in a hotel in London they located a small Victorian house in Trevor Place, Knightsbridge, round the corner from Harrods, which was available at a rent they could just about afford. (Actually, Bill grumbled that they could *not* afford it.) Una was packed off to boarding school and Aileen was obliged to rekindle her skill as a cook after years in India being looked after by servants. Bill, meanwhile, was searching for premises for the Imperial Defence College, the lease on its original building in Buckingham Gate having expired. He settled on the magnificent Seaford House in Belgrave Square, the former home of Lord Howard de Walden, which had been requisitioned by the government in 1940 as the headquarters of the Assistance Board and was later occupied by the Air Ministry. (The college, now renamed

The Royal College of Defence Studies, continues to occupy Seaford House; lectures are still held in the rococo splendour of Lord de Walden's panelled dining room.)

Bill's priority for the first post-war course at the college was to generate a relaxed, collegiate environment for the students. He recognised that men who had been fighting a war needed time to reflect on their experiences, time to analyse their actions and those of others, time to consider the future of warfare in a rapidly changing world with nuclear weapons to be factored into every equation and an 'Iron Curtain' lowering across Europe. Under Bill's direction the course became both an extended post-mortem on the war, a study of the lessons learned and an examination of how those lessons could be applied to future conflicts.

There were a few familiar faces at the start – the senior naval instructor was Guy Russell, by then a rear admiral, who was a fellow student with Bill in 1937 and among the students was Walter Lentaigne, whom Bill had promoted to lead the Chindits after Wingate's death, and Edric Bastyan, a staff officer at ALFSEA who would go on to be the Governor of South Australia. Another student on the first course, Brigadier William Oliver, described the relaxed regime Bill forged: 'He created an atmosphere not unlike that at university, with the students as post-graduates who could make as much or as little of it as they wished. The day would start at a reasonable hour and there was a pleasant lack of formality. There was a lecture or discussion most mornings. In the afternoon there was a syndicate discussion, or one could read in the library – or just go home. The tone was set by the Commandant, who played us with a very loose rein. It was the stature of the man himself that impressed us. Here was a great commander who obviously thought the course worth while. So we got on with it.'[4]

Bill recruited expert lecturers to address students on a wide range of subjects, not necessarily directly connected with the military. It was typical of Bill that he would include among them Arthur Horner, the fire-eating general secretary of the National Union of Mineworkers, one of the most prominent and influential Communists in British public life and a conscientious objector in the First World War. It is unlikely his views held much sway with an audience of war veterans rather more inclined to vote Conservative than Communist, but he was listened to with courtesy and respect as a visitor. As a dyed-in-the wool hardline Marxist, Horner was obviously unimpressed by the privilege he sensed in the room and the opulence of the surroundings. When Bill and Guy Russell were showing him out after his lecture he turned to them and said: 'Well, there's one thing. When the revolution comes you'll be the first to be strung up to the lamp-posts.' It was as much as they could do not to laugh.

Away from the college, Bill discovered a natural talent as a broadcaster. In the bitterly cold winter of 1946, when food and fuel shortages severely damaged public morale, Bill was asked by the BBC if he would be interested in giving a series of talks for the Home Service, perhaps with the aim of lifting the spirits of the nation, just as he had lifted the spirits of the men in the 14th Army. His first talk, entitled 'What Is Courage?', broadcast on the Home Service on 24 November 1946, at 0915 and again at 1500, drew a clear distinction between moral and physical courage and concluded that the moral version was a 'higher and rarer virtue'.

Bill's homely, fireside-chat manner, was an instant success on the radio. Just as he was able to communicate and inspire when he was talking to troops in the jungle, so was he similarly able to do so when sitting in front of a microphone. It was not an effortless facility – he worked hard on his scripts, drafting and redrafting his written words suitable for the spoken word – but the result was a warm, thought-provoking conversation piece, larded with anecdotes and humour that captivated audiences across the country. The author Ronald Lewin, who joined the Talks Department at the BBC at about the time of Bill's first broadcast, clearly remembered how within the department his talk on 'Courage' was held up as a model of how it should be done.[5]

He loved to tell stories in the vernacular. One of his favourites was about a company of British infantry drawn up in front of the Red Fort in Delhi to deal with a disturbance in the town, where shops were being burned and looted and there was fighting in the streets between Muslims and Hindus. The company commander warned his men that they must remain strictly neutral. Before they set off into the town a young soldier asked his sergeant: 'What did 'e mean by nootral, sarge?' 'Nootral, me lad,' the sergeant replied, 'means that when you go down into that adjectival bazaar, you're just as likely to be 'it by a Mo'amadan brick as by an 'Indoo brick.'

Bill's appointment as commandant of the IDC was for two years and by the spring of 1947 he was starting, once again, to fret about his future. Discreet inquiries about another army appointment drew a blank. On 13 May he received a blunt letter from the War Office saying that, in view of his seniority and the claims of other senior British officers, the War Office would be unable to offer him employment when his contract at the IDC ended. A month later GHQ India similarly regretted that it would not be possible to offer him another appointment in the Indian Army: 'In the circumstances the commander-in-chief will have no option but to recommend ... your retirement from the service on the grounds of no further employment being available for you.'[6]

He did, however, have two offers that would have sorely tempted a man with fewer moral scruples. In the summer of 1947 Mountbatten, by then Viceroy of India, pushed through plans for the disastrous partition of India on the basis of religious demographics – one homeland for the Hindus and another for the Muslims – which would release an orgy of violence unlike anything ever seen on the Indian sub-continent, resulting in at least 12 million people becoming homeless and creating an atmosphere of mutual hostility and suspicion between India and Pakistan that endures to this day. In July, a month before partition, Jawaharlal Nehru, who would be the first prime minister of an independent India, suggested to Mountbatten that Bill should be commander-in-chief of the Indian Army. Remarkably, on the following day Muhammad Ali Jinnah, governor-general designate of Pakistan, approached the Viceroy with a proposal that Bill should be appointed governor of East Bengal. Mountbatten forwarded both offers to Bill but he unhesitatingly turned both down.

In a personal letter to Mountbatten dated 17 July, he explained that he did not feel he could serve two masters – the British and the Indian or Pakistan governments – since their policies were bound to differ. 'I should thus have to choose either to be loyal to my employers and disregard British policy or to support it against the intentions of the Government that paid me.' He added, significantly, that he was by no means an ardent believer in the desirability of keeping the two Indian dominions within the Empire. 'I think there is, from one point of view, a lot to be said for keeping them out. As I understand one of the chief reasons for HMG wanting me to go to India is to do what I could to keep India in the Empire, I don't think I should be a good choice for their purpose ... I give up command of the IDC in December and then, as far as I know, go on leave pending retirement. Whether I shall get any job in civil life or elsewhere after that I do not know – probably not if I go on refusing ones I am offered like this.'[7]

Actually, Bill got a job in civilian life very soon. The post-war Labour government under Clement Attlee embarked on a major programme of nationalisation and set up the British Transport Commission to oversee all rail, road and canal transport. Attlee was an old soldier himself, having fought at Gallipoli as a captain in the South Lancashire Regiment in the Great War not far from where Bill's regiment was in action, and instantly approved when Bill's name was put forward to join the BTC's Railway Executive, which was to run the newly formed British Railways from 1 January 1948. It was widely agreed that the down-to-earth man-management skills of the former commander of the 14th Army would make a significant contribution to reorganising Britain's outdated railway system.

Bill himself was not so sure. When he was asked by Attlee to take the job he immediately expressed his doubts. 'I told the Prime Minister that I knew little of railways, was not sure of the effect of nationalisation, and anyway was not a Socialist. I added that I had only voted twice in my life and both times for Churchill. He laughed and said I would find plenty of colleagues who knew all about railways; I was wanted for other qualities. As far as nationalisation was concerned, he thought an open mind would show me its necessity and it was not a political appointment. If I took the job he would rely on me to do my best to make a success of it.'[8]

Bill allowed himself to be persuaded and by the time Lord Hurcomb, chairman of the Commission, invited Bill 'with some trepidation' to the Commission's headquarters in the old Marylebone Hotel to discuss the job he was positively enthusiastic: 'He did not beat about the bush but in his simple and direct way said that he was anxious for employment, would greatly prefer a public appointment and was attracted by the prospect of working in a large organisation which had many problems ahead of it and a vast staff with which he could make contact.'⁹ Hurcomb did not recall Bill asking about remuneration, which was surprising as it would have been an important factor to a man constantly short of money; perhaps Bill had already discovered that the post paid £5,000 a year.

Before he started his new career as a 'railwayman' (Bill's description) he and Aileen were delighted to find themselves among the 2,000 guests invited to Westminster Abbey on 20 November 1947 for the wedding of Princess Elizabeth to the Duke of Edinburgh. (Although Bill remained less well known to the British public than those generals who enjoyed the limelight, his stature was recognised where it mattered.) The royal wedding, which was recorded and broadcast by the BBC to an estimated audience of 200 million people around the world, briefly brightened the post-war years of austerity when food rationing, shortages and power cuts still dominated domestic life.

Around the time Bill started work at the Railway Executive in January 1948, he and Aileen moved out of London to an Edwardian house with a garden, Greentops, in the Surrey village of Limpsfield Common, near Oxted, from where he commuted to his office every day, by train of course. (He liked the idea of having a garden because he had taken up croquet with some enthusiasm.) He discovered the railways were not so very different from the army in the pride and loyalty the old railway companies generated in their employees, from the general manager downwards. Each company had its own distinctive methods, cherished traditions, its own livery and fierce esprit de corps. The challenge was to weld these disparate companies into a single entity without destroying that spirit. He compared it with attempting to amalgamate a kilted regiment with one that wore trews.

Paradoxically, Bill found that being an outsider, free from ingrained partisan loyalties, was a positive advantage. 'I could bring an unprejudiced and, I hoped, reasonably common sense judgement to bear on some of the many, often not over-important, differences that delayed progress.' He left the technical stuff about running a railway to the experts and concentrated on raising the morale of the staff, constantly touring 'the front line', talking to the men (and women), listening to their problems and discovering for himself how the railways operated at the ground roots. His experience of industrial relations was strictly limited to his brief employment at Stewarts & Lloyds, more than 30 years earlier, and the unions at first reacted with hostility to a 'general who knew sweet Fanny Adams about the railways', but Bill's effortless charm and the force of his personality soon won them over. Such was his success that he was elected deputy chairman of the Executive after only a few months.

It was perhaps to be expected that those employees in uniform responded most warmly to the Deputy Chairman. 'His personal leadership was perhaps most felt among the Railway Police,' Lord Hurcomb recalled after his retirement in 1953, 'where General Slim is well remembered. By the Civil Engineering Department he was well known all down the line and at functions of the senior technical staff his appearance, often accompanied by Lady Slim, was always welcomed with enthusiasm. But of course it was in the approach to wider aspects of development and policy that [his] untrammelled judgement and wise outlook were most evident ... and his influence was all the greater by reason of the respect and liking with which he was universally regarded.'[10]

During his time at the Railway Executive, Bill established a rapport with the Prime Minister – among more pressing matters, they could also share reminiscences of their service at Gallipoli. Attlee took a close personal interest in industrial relations in the nationalised industries and discussed with Bill possible ways in which the relationship between officers and men in the army could be applied to civilian life. In a memorandum circulated under the title 'Management and Men in Socialised Industries', Attlee referred to his talks with Bill and emphasised 'from his great and my limited experience' the importance of officers knowing their men off parade adding, 'General Slim had stressed the danger in industry of divorcing the management from the workers.' Attlee went on to suggest that there was need in the nationalised industries for 'the kind of spirit and leadership which obtained in a good regiment'.

There was discussion in the Cabinet about Bill being asked to broadcast a series of talks on the subject of leadership which could then be published as a pamphlet and circulated around the nationalised industries, but the idea was finally rejected lest it gave the impression that 'the Government thought that the military spirit should be introduced into industry'.[11] (Ironically, that is obviously exactly what Attlee thought should happen.)

In fact, Bill's spell with British Railways was to last less than a year. In September 1948, the recently ennobled Viscount Montgomery of Alamein, who had succeeded Viscount Alanbrooke[12] as Chief of the Imperial General Staff two years earlier, accepted the post, in Fontainebleau, of chairman of the Commanders-in-Chief Committee of the Western European Union. Montgomery wanted his successor to be Lieutenant General Sir John Crocker, who had commanded 1 Corps on D-Day. What Montgomery fervently did not want was to be succeeded by Bill. When he heard Bill's name was in the frame, he contended that no officer with an Indian Army background would be acceptable as CIGS, that Bill was out of touch with events in Europe and that in any case he had retired from the army and was therefore no longer eligible to be considered.

But Bill had powerful support in the form of his influential friend Dickie Mountbatten, who, on a brief return visit to the UK, had an audience with the Prime Minister and argued strongly that Slim was the obvious choice as Montgomery's replacement. Attlee hesitated, cited Montgomery's strong opposition as a possible problem and pointed out that Montgomery was right in one regard – that Slim had retired from the army. Mountbatten refused to listen. Slim, he insisted, was the best man for the job: Attlee could solve the retirement objection by arranging for him to be returned to the active list as a field marshal, then he should simply summon Montgomery and tell him, whether he liked it or not, that he was to be replaced by Slim. Attlee finally agreed.

Montgomery was incensed when he was called to Downing Street and informed of the Prime Minister's decision. He repeated, once again, all the reasons why he thought Slim should not be the CIGS, finally overstepping the mark by saying that appointing Slim was out of the question anyway as he had already told Crocker that he was going to get the job. For the Prime Minister this was the last straw. 'Then,' Attlee is said to have snapped, 'you must untell him.'[13]

Bill claimed, perhaps a little ingenuously, that the offer to take over as CIGS came as a shock. 'One day in my railway office at Marylebone, the telephone rang. It was the Prime Minister's secretary saying that Mr Attlee would like to see me at Chequers. I asked what it was about but the discreet secretary said he thought the Prime Minister would prefer to tell me himself. So I went down to Chequers where Mr Attlee in his usual clear and business-like way without preliminaries told me he proposed to recommend me to the King as CIGS ... Next day, to most people's surprise, certainly not least my own, I was announced as the next CIGS.'[14]

Bill's 22-year-old son, John, who had transferred from the Gurkhas to the Argyll and Sutherland Highlanders after the partition of India, was on a course at the School of Infantry in Warminster when his father's appointment to the highest position in the British Army was reported by BBC Radio. He recalled that the whole mess erupted into spontaneous applause.

'Thrilled as I was,' Bill wrote in his unpublished memoir, 'I was in an odd position. The war had given me a good deal of experience in command; between 1937 and 1945 I had gone from substantive major to general, from command of a battalion to an army group. Quick, but it had needed a great war and lots of luck in the game of snakes and ladders. My two years as commandant of the Imperial Defence College had kept me up to date until a year ago with major strategic problems, but the CIGS had a dual personality. He was one of the three Chiefs of Staff who held joint responsibility for all three fighting services and for combined advice on defence matters to the Cabinet but he was, in addition, the professional head of his own service, the Army. I was not so nervous about the first, but for the second I had certain obvious handicaps.

'I was an Indian Army officer and a retired one at that. No Indian Army officer had ever been CIGS, nor indeed had any retired officer. This could hardly, I thought, commend itself to many. It was 30 years since I had served, as a junior officer, in the British Army; my service since then, including the last war, had almost all been in the East. Many of the prominent British and Allied commanders who had gained their laurels in Europe and North Africa I had hardly met. I had never worked in the War Office, could count on the fingers of one hand the times I had been inside it; I was in every

way out of touch with day to day army affairs and even more so with
the Whitehall politics, policies and personalities, civil and military,
among which I was now to be so suddenly plunged.'

First, though, there was a tricky obstacle to overcome – money.
Montgomery's military assistant, Lieutenant Colonel Richard
Craddock, visited Bill at his office to discuss logistical arrangements
for the handover and when Bill inquired about an expense allowance Craddock was obliged to admit that it was miserly for all three
Chiefs of Staff – £1. 10s. a day. Bill was indignant. Not only was
he taking a drop in salary, from £5,000 a year to £4,575, but his
expenses at the Railway Executive were considerably more generous
– £600 a year – and he would also have to relinquish directorships
worth another £2,000 a year (although he was able to keep his
Indian Army pension of £1,665 p.a.). In his position as CIGS he
was obviously going to have to entertain regularly, particularly as
he knew very few senior officers in the British Army, he had no
money of his own and 30 shillings a day was woefully inadequate.
The unfortunate Craddock was sent off 'to do something about it'
and was said to have found an ex-14th Army man at the Treasury
who was sympathetic: the CIGS's expense allowance was increased
to £250 for six months with the sly proviso that the other two Chiefs
of Staff should remain in ignorance of the arrangement, described
by Treasury mandarins as 'highly unorthodox'.

Bill started work as CIGS on 1 November 1948 (his promotion
to field marshal was confirmed two months later). No one could
describe his first day at the War Office better than the man himself:
'One chilly morning in 1948, in black overcoat and homburg hat, I
walked up the main steps of the War Office to be confronted by the
tall frock-coated Head Porter in his gold-banded top hat. He looked
down on me and I looked up at him; there could be no question
which of us was the more impressive figure. He asked me, civilly
but without cordiality, what was my business, and was about to
direct me to the side entrance for unimportant callers, when I rather
hesitantly said, "As a matter of fact, I'm the new CIGS." A look of
amazed incredulity passed over his face but he made a stout effort
at recovery. He apologised, explained he had not been warned what
time I would be arriving and said he would warn Vice-CIGS of
my arrival.' (Actually, the Vice-CIGS, Lieutenant General Gerald

Templer, had a clear memory of sending an ADC to meet Bill,[15] but why spoil a good story?)

Bill continued his account with a description of his new office. 'I looked curiously round the room. On the walls, so close as to be almost touching, hung oil paintings of 18th and 19th century Commanders in Chief of the British Army, bewigged, be-ribboned and be-horsed. They looked down on me, the interloper, with haughty and unanimous disapproval. Uncomfortable under their scrutiny, I swivelled my chair round and looked behind me. Here a long row of framed photographs recorded my more recent predecessors. The line ended in an unmistakeable double-badged beret; after that no space was left for another likeness. I hoped this had not for me too ominous a significance.

'Swinging round once more, I noticed opposite my desk, high on the only wall not covered by pictures, a pelmet-like affair obviously housing rolled maps. On either side from it dangled long cords, each with a label; presumably if a string were pulled the appropriate map would appear. I walked across and studied the names on the labels – India, Africa, Asia, Europe. I felt rather more ignorant of modern Europe than, say, Asia, so I gave Europe a manful tug. With a startling rattle and a crash, a huge map came hurtling down. With it, also, came a miniature dust storm, while corpses of long dead moths pattered about my head. When I dared open my eyes, I found myself, at a few inches range, staring at a part of the map. Across it, printed in the boldest letters, I read "Austro-Hungarian Empire".'[16]

Bill liked to tell another story about his first day which he swore was true. In the Fire Instructions posted above a light switch was the recommendation that the first thing to do in the event of a fire was to shout 'FIRE'. Bill decided to test the system so he opened the door and shouted 'Fire'. Nothing happened. He shouted again, rather louder. 'FIRE.' This time a figure emerged at the end of the corridor and came running towards him. It was his messenger, a man called Marshall. 'Coming, sir,' he panted and as he drew closer Bill could see he was carrying a bucket containing paper, coal and firewood.

After this introduction, worthy of a Gilbert & Sullivan opera, Bill was immediately pitched into a crisis. Templer knocked on his door, introduced himself – they had not previously met – and dropped a bombshell. 'I am very sorry to tell you,' he said, 'that I offered your resignation, on your behalf, last night.' Bill remained apparently unperturbed. 'I see,' he replied. 'You had better tell me about it.' The issue was National Service, the mandatory conscription of young men between the ages of 17 and 21 into the Armed Forces which was due become law in January 1949. There was no argument that conscription was needed – the blockade of Berlin had begun in June, divisions between North and South Korea were hardening, the reoccupation of Malaya, Singapore and Hong Kong was stretching resources and tension was fomenting in Egypt – but the politicians and the military fundamentally disagreed on the time young men should be required to serve. The politicians, as always with an eye to public popularity, insisted one year was sufficient; the military asserted a minimum of 18 months was essential, particularly for the army and particularly for those troops destined for the Far East. After training and transport had been taken into consideration, no National Service posting to the Far East was liable to last beyond five months if conscription was limited to 12 months. It meant that by the time a conscript had learned enough to become effective, he would virtually be on his way home, a ridiculous waste of manpower and money.

As CIGS, Montgomery initially argued for two years on the implicit understanding he would be prepared to settle, albeit unwillingly, for 18 months. But then, shortly before he was due to hand over to his successor, he stunned his colleagues at a meeting in the War Office by announcing that he had agreed with the Minister of Defence that National Service should be for a term of 12 months only, after receiving an assurance that British military commitments in the Far East would be scaled back. (The Minister, A. V. Alexander, later denied he had ever given such an assurance.)

On the night before Bill took office there was a meeting of the Army Council at which Templer told Alexander that if the government forced through National Service for one year only all the military members of the Council would resign. Templer added that although he had never met the new CIGS he believed he knew enough about him to say that he would assuredly resign with them.

Bill was not thrilled to have his resignation offered before he had started and privately confessed to ignoble personal anxieties about the prospect of having to return to civilian life and look for another job (his post at the railways had already been filled). He toyed with excuses to sidestep the issue: that it was not his sole responsibility, that perhaps the damaging effects of 12 months' conscription were exaggerated, or that there were factors of which he was as yet unaware. In the end, of course, he did what he knew in his heart was right. The force of the 18-month argument was undeniable and, since it was primarily an army issue, Bill accepted that it was his responsibility to force a change of heart on the government. He also accepted that he had to be ready to resign if he failed.

He sought an urgent interview with the Prime Minister which went better than he could have hoped. He presented the case in his usual lucid, straightforward manner and Attlee listened with 'alert attention, showing a well-founded appreciation of the defence considerations involved'. After asking a few questions, the PM told Bill he would consider what he had had to say and get back to him. Bill did not perhaps fully appreciate the strength of his hand. The last thing Attlee wanted was for the head of the army to resign only a few days after being brought back from civilian life to take on the job, and the possible risk of him being followed out the door by the Chiefs of Staff of the RAF and the Royal Navy. The political fallout would be considerable. A few days after Bill's meeting, it was announced that the term for National Service would be 18 months.[17]

After this tricky baptism, Bill did his best to settle into his new job, but he was never entirely comfortable dealing with politicians and civil servants or the guileful machinations of Westminster and Whitehall. He remained, first of all, a soldier, happiest in the company of other soldiers, and got away from his desk at the War Office as often as he could for, as he put it, 'a little fresh air' – usually visits to army units around the country. When he arrived at the Guards Training Depot in Caterham with Major General John Marriott, an old friend from Eritrea days, the guard turned out and presented arms. Bill acknowledged the formality with a salute but Marriott mischievously informed him that the courtesy was not for him at all – the guard only turned out for members of the royal family or the commander of the Household Troops, namely himself. Bill did not have to wait long to get his own back. After inspecting the Depot the commanding officer asked Bill for his opinion. 'Splendid,' he replied and then, with a sly look at Marriott, added: 'I haven't seen anything so good since the last time I inspected an Indian training battalion.' As they were getting into a staff car to return to London, Marriott murmured, 'Fifteen all, I think.'

During his first full year as CIGS, Bill travelled extensively, touring the Middle East in April, returning to Benghazi and Tripoli in Libya in June, visiting India, Pakistan and the Far East in October and November and setting off for Canada and the United States just two weeks after returning from the Far East. The schedules of his foreign tours are all filed in the National Archives and indicate the extraordinarily hard-working days he endured, usually starting between 8.30 and 9.00 in the morning and continuing without respite through the day, often ending with a formal dinner in the evening.

In Cairo, Bill and his military assistant Richard Craddock, stayed with the Commander-in-Chief, who happened to be General Sir John Crocker, the officer who had been promised Bill's job by Montgomery. The luckless Craddock later reported that Lady Crocker had given him 'half an hour's hell' about Bill's appointment. Why was it, she demanded, that a man who had been out of the army for ten months had been brought back to do her husband's job?[18] Craddock could perhaps have been forgiven for thinking that she should perhaps ask the question of his boss, rather than him. Bill was highly amused when he heard about it, but he soon charmed Lady Crocker and peace was restored to the household.

On a bleak December morning in 1949, Bill was the reviewing officer at the Sovereign's Parade – the passing out ceremony – at the Royal Military Academy, Sandhurst, the college that had been denied to him so many years earlier. Before the event, anxious to strike the right tone, he worked on his speech, about the essentials of soldiering and true leadership, with the same diligence he applied to his broadcasts. He spoke of courage, initiative, willpower and knowledge, but identified another essential attribute: 'When a man's heart sinks into his empty belly with fear, when the ammunition doesn't come through; when there are no rations and your air force is being shot out of the sky; when the enemy is beating the living daylights out of you – then you will want one other quality, and unless you have got it you will not be a leader. That quality is self-sacrifice and as far as you are concerned it means simply this: that you will put first the honour and interest of your King and Country, that next you will put the safety, well-being and the security of the men under your command, and that last, and last all the time, you will put your own interest, your own safety, and your own comfort. Then you will be a good officer.'

Some time later, watching an exercise on a training ground in Germany, he came across a platoon commander who had graduated at the same parade. Bill asked him out of curiosity what he remembered of his speech. Unexpectedly encountering a field marshal, no matter how good-natured, was clearly an unnerving experience for the young officer. After an extended pause, during which he was obviously racking his brains, he suddenly brightened and blurted out: 'Well, sir, all I remember is you said the Japanese were a lot of little yellow bastards.' Bill thought it was hilarious and repeated the story with relish when he returned to London.

In the summer of 1950, against the advice of his doctor, Bill set off on an extended tour of the Far East, Australia and New Zealand that was to last six weeks. By then his back was giving him serious problems and he required medical treatment at almost every stop, but he soldiered on, driven as always by his acute sense of duty. In Australia his object was to convince the government of Robert Menzies of the primacy of the Middle East in global strategy. Menzies, who would become the longest serving Prime Minister in Australian history, took an instant liking to Bill. They had similar family backgrounds – Menzies' father was a storekeeper and the son of Scottish crofters who had emigrated to Australia in the mid-1850s. With his straight-talking manner, utterly devoid of obfuscation or, even worse, airs and graces, Menzies thought that Bill was more like an Australian than an Englishman and his enduring regard would have profound consequences for Bill in two years' time. One incident particularly impressed the Australian Prime Minister: when Bill was confronted by an anti-British demonstration he ignored the aides who were trying to hustle him out of the way and walked across the street in his field marshal's uniform to talk to the demonstrators, much to their amazement.

Bill noted in his diary on 20 June 1950 that Menzies was 'right on our side', but five days later everything changed when Communist forces in North Korea invaded the south, launching the first significant armed conflict of the Cold War. On 27 June the Security Council passed a resolution confirming that members of the United Nations would 'furnish such assistance to the Republic of Korea as may be necessary to repel the armed attack and to restore international peace and security in the area.' The outbreak of the Korean War turned Australia's attention firmly towards matters closer to home and Bill returned to Britain in July without any commitment from Menzies in support of the UK's Middle East strategy.

By the autumn of 1950 the Korean War was dominating the strategic agenda on both sides of the Atlantic. After China's intervention there were alarming reports at the end of November that the United States was considering deploying nuclear weapons. Attlee flew to Washington for an urgent meeting with President Truman to discuss concerns about atomic warfare and seek closer consultation, closely followed by Bill and Air Marshal Sir Arthur Tedder, Chief of the Air Staff. Bill spent an entire day in talks with General Omar Bradley, the US Chief of Staff. Bradley was a professional soldier, like Bill, and the two men got on well. The worry in Europe was that escalation of the Korean War might create a geopolitical imbalance, rendering NATO defenceless against an attack by Russia while the US was fully engaged fighting China. In the event the crisis wound down quickly and European concerns were assuaged by the appointment, in December, of General Dwight D. Eisenhower as the Supreme Commander at NATO, indicating America's firm commitment to the defence of Europe.

Many of the British troops sent to fight in Korea were National Servicemen, who by 1951 made up about half the strength of the army. Bill was generally impressed by them, although surprised at the number who were illiterate. While there were misfits and troublemakers among their ranks – in a BBC broadcast he pointed out that it was unfair to blame the army for failing to teach young men in 18 months what their families had signally failed to teach them in 18 years – most knuckled down to military life. What most impressed him was their eagerness to see active service. Bill persuaded the Ministry of Defence to introduce a voluntary one-year extension of service to enable National Servicemen to stay with their battalion if it was scheduled for active service overseas. He also encouraged

National Servicemen to join the Territorial Army after they had been demobbed, declaring that anyone who volunteered for the TA was 'twice a citizen'.

Burma and the 14th Army remained resolutely lodged in his memory and often claimed priority for his attention, sometimes to the irritation of his colleagues. He would be invited to a demonstration of a new weapon, for example, and could rarely resist pointing out that they had managed perfectly well without such a weapon in Burma and recalling at some length what they had achieved with 'a couple of bits of string'. He was on his way to the Prime Minister's office at the House of Commons one afternoon for a meeting when he ran across a couple of 14th Army veterans and became so absorbed in reminiscing with them that he entirely forgot about the meeting. When, next morning, he was asked if he had had to apologise to the Prime Minister he agreed that he had but said the PM was 'very nice' to him.

In February 1951 the Burma Star Association was founded to promote comradeship among Burma veterans and raise money for a welfare fund for members and widows in need. Membership was confined to those men and women who had been awarded the Burma Campaign Star. Lord Louis Mounbatten was its first patron; Uncle Bill was proud to be the first president and remained in that office until his death (his son, the 2nd Viscount Slim, also a distinguished soldier, took over from his father and is the president to this day). Apart from when he was out of the country, Bill attended every annual reunion, usually held at the Royal Albert Hall. No one who was present at the first one will ever forget the moment when Bill made an appearance on the stage; the entire auditorium burst into cheers and wild applause, which went on for several minutes, for the return into their midst of their hero. 'I've never heard anything like it,' one veteran recalled. 'It was quite moving.'

Winston Churchill was returned to Downing Street after the October 1951 General Election and renewed his formerly rather brief acquaintanceship with his CIGS, who was by then chairman of the Chiefs of Staff Committee by virtue of seniority – Tedder had been replaced by Sir John Slessor as Chief of the Air Staff and Admiral Rhoderick McGrigor was about to take over as Chief of the Naval Staff. Bill was not in the least overawed by the new Prime Minister.

During a meeting at Downing Street about 'standardisation', then very much in vogue in the armed services, Churchill wandered away from the subject after a few minutes and began reminiscing about his experiences with the 21st Lancers at the Battle of Omdurman. 'When I was at Omdurman,' he said, 'I rode with a sabre in one hand and a revolver in the other ...' Bill immediately chipped in: 'Not much standardisation there, Prime Minister.'

All three Chiefs of Staff were required to join the Prime Minister's party on the *Queen Mary* which sailed for New York on 29 December; Churchill wanted to meet senior members of the Truman administration and resurrect the 'special relationship' that had existed between the two countries during the war. Most of the topics scheduled for discussion came under the remit of the Chiefs of Staff – defence policy, American bases in Britain, the French proposal to set up a European Defence Community and the practical implementation of the North Atlantic Treaty. Bill had already formed a good relationship with Omar Bradley, the US Chief of Staff, but there was a row when the question of appointing an American admiral to be Allied Commander in the Atlantic, which had been informally agreed by the Attlee government, cropped up. Churchill lost his temper but for some reason he attached all the blame to the unfortunate McGrigor whom he witheringly dismissed as 'a man who cannot distinguish a great event from a small event'. Slim, he added, was quite different – 'I can work with him'.

In April, Bill returned to the United States on a private visit after being invited to deliver the annual Kermit Roosevelt lecture at the US Army Command and General Staff College at Fort Leavenworth in Kansas. (The lecture was named in memory of the second son of President Theodore Roosevelt, an explorer, writer and soldier who committed suicide in 1943.) On this occasion he was accompanied by Aileen, although the logistics were challenging, as he explained in a letter to his friend Major General William Dimoline, who had commanded the 11th (East Africa) Division in Burma and who was then the UK representative on the Military Staff Committee at the United Nations in New York:

My dear Dimoline, Aileen left in the Media *on Saturday from Liverpool and is due in NY late on Saturday 29 March and may*

disembark then or more probably on Sunday morning. As you know
I don't arrive until April 3. This means that Aileen will have to stay
with Mrs Kermit Roosevelt at 3 Sutton Place NYC for four days before
I get there. As this is rather an imposition on Mrs Roosevelt would you
and your wife be angels and take Aileen off her hands for a few hours
on one of those days. It would be terribly kind of you, I had quite a lot
of difficulty in persuading the PM to let me go at all. He can be very
obstinate in these matters.[19]

In fact Churchill refused to allow Bill to leave the country for more
than two weeks, obliging him to cancel a visit he wanted to make
to Canada. On Sunday, 6 April, he gave a talk on the subject of
'Freedom and Discipline' on the CBS radio network in New York
and two days later he was at the college in Fort Leavenworth to
deliver his lecture on 'Higher Command in War'. He defined command as 'a mixture of example, persuasion and compulsion by
which you get men to do what you want them to, even if they don't
want to do it themselves. If you ask me to really define it, I should
say "Command is the projection of personality – and like all true
art, and it is an art, it is exercised by each man in his own way".'

His personal motto, he explained, was 'no details, no paper and
no regrets'. 'Don't keep dogs and bark yourself,' he said. 'Don't get
involved in details more properly handled by subordinates; talk to
people and get them to talk to you rather than commit everything
to paper. When I say "no regrets" that is important. You do the best
you can. You may have got it wrong, you may have lost the battle,
you may even have lost a good many of your men's lives, which hurts
even more ... Don't have regrets, don't sit in the corner and say, "Oh
if only I had gone left instead of right", or "Oh if only I had fought
in front of the river instead of behind it". You have done the best
you could, it hasn't come off. All right. What's the next problem?'[20]
At the conclusion of his lecture Bill got a standing ovation; such was
its intellectual vigour it was later assimilated into US Marine Corps
training manuals and formed the basis of a documentary made for
training purposes years later.

Back in London in mid-April, Bill was immediately swept up in
finalising a comprehensive review of Britain's defence policy, which
had been ordered by the Prime Minister. Between 28 April and 2

May, the three Chiefs of Staff cloistered themselves in the Royal Naval College at Greenwich, away from the distractions of their busy offices, to work on the final draft of what would become the most highly regarded British defence document of the post-war period.

'The Report on Defence Policy and Global Strategy' was hailed as an 'important innovation in military thought' and praised by Churchill as a 'state paper of the greatest importance'. Central to its argument was the prospect of a protracted Cold War promulgated by a Soviet Union bent on 'world domination' which could best be countered by the nuclear deterrent – 'the knowledge on the part of the Kremlin that any aggression on their part will involve immediate and crushing retaliation'. It called for a high state of readiness for land and air forces in Western Europe and would set the foundations of British strategic policy for many years to come.[21]

Although he was not due to relinquish his position as CIGS until November, Bill was already embroiled in a protracted wrangle with the Treasury over his pension, the ramifications of which fill a bulging file[22] at the National Archives. At issue was £250 per annum – Bill was convinced he should get £2,000 a year, the Treasury was equally convinced the correct figure was £1,750. It was for Bill not just a matter of principle: he was still desperately hard up. He was never quite sure where the money went, only that it went. Letters flew back and forth for months as Bill fought for the extra cash. The two sides differed on the interpretation of the terminology in letters agreeing the original terms of his contract. Bill went so far as to employ a counsel for an opinion supporting his argument, obliging the Treasury to similarly seek legal advice. He even pulled strings and appealed directly to the Chancellor, 'Rab' Butler, to intervene on his behalf, finally meeting Butler personally to put his case. It was one battle he was destined to lose – the Treasury stuck by its guns and Bill had to be satisfied with £1,750.

He was by then 61 years old and could hardly expect to be inundated with job offers when he left the War Office. But on the other side of the world, in Australia, the term of the Governor-General, Sir William McKell, was coming to an end. McKell, a former boilermaker and union official turned Labour politician, was only the second Australian to be Governor-General. Robert Menzies, with his great reverence for the monarchy and Britain, wanted to revert to the tradition of appointing a distinguished Briton as Governor-General of Australia, partly to discourage Australians from thinking that the Governor-Generalship was just another 'job for the boys'.

During a visit to Britain towards the end of 1952, Menzies raised the issue with the young Queen Elizabeth II, who had acceded to the throne on the death of her father, King George VI, in February. As Prime Minister, Menzies had the constitutional right to nominate the next Governor-General but required the approval of the monarch. Menzies suggested to the Queen, and to his host, Lord Salisbury, with whom he was staying at Hatfield House, that they should each write down the names of three suitable candidates to take over as Governor-General and then compare their choices. Returning to Buckingham Palace two days later, Menzies discovered the same name was at the top of all three lists – Field Marshal Sir William Slim.

Menzies was delighted. With the authority of the Queen to offer Bill the post, he was driven straight to the War Office, where he winkled Bill out of a conference and said, 'Sir, I gather that you are about to finish your term as Chief of the Imperial General Staff.' 'That is so,' Bill replied. 'Under these circumstances,' Menzies continued, 'I have the authority of the Queen to ask you whether you would care to be Governor-General of Australia.' Bill's response was typical. 'Are you serious?' he said.

20

Governor-General

On 18 February 1953, Winston Churchill sent a top-secret message to Bob Menzies in Australia, seeking a favour. The Middle East was in turmoil, following the overthrow of King Farouk in Egypt the previous year, and Britain and the United States were still pursuing the idea of setting up a Middle East Defence Organisation to protect the Suez Canal and provide security in the region. Churchill explained to Menzies that he was going to propose personally to President Eisenhower that each country should send to Cairo 'two military men of the highest standing, who, by their prestige and their personal capacity', will carry the greatest possible weight negotiating with General Mohamed Naguib, leader of the Egyptian revolution.

'We are all agreed,' Churchill continued, 'that, on the Commonwealth side, there is no man who, in knowledge, prestige and capacity, could match Field Marshal Slim for this most important task. I have spoken with the Field Marshal who, with characteristic selflessness said, that if this is the considered opinion of both our Governments that this is the best service he can render, he is ready to undertake the task.'

The problem, the Prime Minister finally admitted, was that the field marshal was due to leave for Australia within a matter of days to take up the post of Governor-General. 'I know well the temporary difficulties this involves for you ... All arrangements are made for his reception and inauguration in Australia. A delay in his arrival has many inconveniences. I trust, however, that you will agree the disadvantages are overridden by the critical situation in the Middle East, and the unique service he can render to both our countries at this time ... I sincerely trust that our minds may be in accord and that we may go forward together.'[1]

Menzies, of course, agreed. Churchill suggested that no mention should be made of Bill's mission until President Eisenhower had appointed the US military representative and so preparations for Bill and Aileen's departure ostensibly went ahead even to the extent, as a cover, of loading their luggage on to the SS *Himalaya* waiting at Tilbury docks to depart for Australia. But inevitably the news leaked out and guests who had attended a farewell luncheon for the Slims at the Savoy Hotel in London had the bizarre experience of leaving the hotel to find newspaper billboards in The Strand shrieking 'SLIM FOR EGYPT', while at Tilbury John Swinton, a young Guards officer who had been appointed one of Bill's new ADCs, was attempting, with difficulty, to supervise the unloading of all their bags.

During the course of the next six weeks Bill attended innumerable meetings and briefings at the Foreign Office to prepare him for the difficult negotiations anticipated with 'the dictator Naguib', as he was routinely referred to in official papers, but it all came to nought: Eisenhower prevaricated and Bill's departure for Australia could be delayed no longer. (In the end, nothing ever came of the Middle East Defence Organisation proposal.)

Aileen and Bill finally set sail on 26 March in the considerable comfort of a first-class stateroom on board the P & O liner RMS *Strathnaver*. 'We are very sad at the thought of going away from England,' Bill wrote to a friend, 'we had planned a nice, quiet retirement at Greentops [their home in Surrey] with me doing one or two odd jobs which would have brought in sufficient money to keep the wolf from our newly painted front door ...'[2]

Over the next few years the Slims' lives would be utterly transformed. Each of them would forthwith be addressed as 'Your Excellency', they would exchange their modest house in Surrey for two imposing official residences, in Canberra and Sydney, both with a large domestic staff. They would travel by Rolls-Royce in a motorcade with police outriders and would frequently be called upon to entertain visiting heads of state from around the world.

Although many Australians believed that the Governor-General should be one of their own, not some 'pommy bastard' imposed on them from Britain, and there were stirrings of unrest about the monarchy in general along with increasing talk of the country becoming a republic, Bill's appointment was widely welcomed and there was an enthusiastic crowd waiting to greet them on the quayside when the *Strathnaver* docked in Sydney in May 1953. On his side was not just the fact that he was an authentic war hero, but that he had fought side by side with the Diggers at Gallipoli in the Great War (a legendary battle still etched vividly on the Australian psyche and celebrated by a public holiday, Anzac Day). As he got to know Australia and Australians got to know him, what worked most in his favour was that he remained, well, Bill. Despite the panoply of his office he was still a blunt, no-nonsense, rugged soldier and absolutely the kind of man that blunt, no-nonsense, rugged Australians could relate to. He became, very quickly, extraordinarily popular.

Affectionate stories about him (some undoubtedly apocryphal) rapidly circulated on the bush telegraph ...

How, invited to inspect his escort of police outriders after arriving in Sydney he told them: 'When I looked at your uniforms I thought you had been cleaning your motorcycles with them – until I saw your motorcycles.'

How, entering the bar of an outback hotel in his field marshal's uniform (he eschewed the ornate ceremonial regalia of a Commonwealth Governor-General), one of the drinkers took one look at him and exclaimed, 'Jesus Christ.' 'No,' Bill shot back, 'Bill Slim.'[3]

How, when implored by a photographer to smile, he snapped, 'I am smiling, dammit.'

How, travelling in civilian clothes with Sir Arthur 'Artie' Fadden, the Australian Treasurer, they stopped for a break in a bar outside Canberra and fell into conversation with one of the customers. When Fadden disappeared to the men's room Bill's new friend asked, 'I seem to know that chap's face. Who is he?' After Bill explained he said: 'Christ. Fancy him talking to two poor bastards like you and me.'

Bill's arrival in Australia was somewhat blighted by Aileen, who was then 52 years old, suddenly falling seriously ill and being rushed to hospital with a haemorrhage which very nearly cost her her life. She was still on the danger list and hence, to his great disappointment, not by his side when he was sworn in as the 13th

Governor-General of Australia before the Parliament in Canberra on 8 May 1953.

When Aileen's health was fully restored, she set about organising improvements at Government House in Canberra and Admiralty House in Sydney, both of which had become rather shabby and run down under Bill's predecessor. (Bill complained to Menzies that he did not have enough ADCs to stand over the holes in the carpet in the reception area at Government House.) Set in 54 hectares of parkland in the Canberra suburb of Yarralumla, Government House began life as a homestead on a working sheep station in 1891 but was extensively enlarged over the years, after it was taken over as the official residence of the Governor-General and became generally known as Yarralumla. Nearly 300 miles to the north-east, Admiralty House, the Governor-General's Sydney residence, was a handsome Italianate mansion with a colonnaded verandah perched on the tip of Kirribilli Point with sweeping views over Sydney Harbour, but it, too, was in need of refurbishment.

Aileen quickly ran into bureaucratic problems when she tried to restore both houses to a semblance of viceregal glory. She planned extensive renovations, redecorating the entertaining rooms and bedrooms, choosing new wallpapers, chintz for upholstery and paint colours. Government departments had to be consulted, every item of expenditure, no matter how trivial, had to be approved, estimates drawn up ... it drove Aileen to distraction. Money was the issue, of course. Unlike previous Governors-General the Slims had no private means and had to get by on a comparatively modest salary, adequate for someone 'with a few chips' (personal funds) but not without. Bill raised the matter with Menzies, who was sympathetic and recognised that it was inappropriate for Australia to conduct public affairs at Yarralumla on a shoestring. Increasing the Governor-General's salary would have involved constitutional problems but Menzies was able to persuade the Cabinet to authorise a new, more flexible system under which all the Governor-General's official expenses, including entertainment, transport and maintenance of the official residences, were billed directly to the government's general account. At the same time Menzies warned Bill he should not expect to be able to look out of the window, decide something must be done and immediately order a gang of labourers to get to work, as he had been able to do as a soldier. Later, when an auditor complained that Bill was the most expensive Governor-General Australia had ever had, he quipped: 'Yes, I know, but as the lady said to the sailor, you can't have the Fairy Queen for fourpence.'[4]

Before she left England Aileen had asked Zara Gowrie, the wife of the Earl of Gowrie, who was a notably successful Governor-General of Australia for nine years from 1936 to 1945, to talk her through life as chatelaine at Yarralumla and Admiralty House. Zara suggested she should meet Ethel Anderson and her daughter, Bethia Foott, who were said to know everyone worth knowing in Australia. Anderson was a well-regarded painter, poet and writer who, in her later years, was rarely seen without an ear trumpet. When Aileen had recovered from her operation, she invited Ethel and Bethia to tea at Admiralty House and asked them if they could put together a list of interesting people it would be nice to entertain. 'I think we are going to love the Slims,' Bethia wrote in her diary that night.[5] Ethel Anderson and her daughter would become regular visitors to Government House.

'In many ways Yarralumla was like a superior boarding house,' Bethia Foott recalled, 'catering for strangers, the famous or the would-be-so's, some zooming in for just one night, from England, America, or Singapore, tired after their long flights, all needing different and singular attention. One old friend, Clem Attlee, turned up, to be instantly devastated by toothache which meant a sudden switch in his schedule, ending with plans hastily made for him to have his dinner in bed (for he was an old man) – a plan he instantly refused, coming down instead to keep us all in gales of laughter.'[6]

Bill took his responsibilities as the personal representative of the Queen very seriously. Outside of his ceremonial duties – receiving visiting heads of state, conducting investitures, opening each new session of Parliament and the like – he went to great pains to familiarise himself with Australia and the realities of Australian politics. He liked to walk in the garden at Government House with eminent visitors, particularly if they were members of the Australian Club, and quiz them about political developments and what people were thinking. The Australian Club, at Macquarie Street in Sydney, was founded in 1838 and was said to be the oldest gentlemen's club in the southern hemisphere; Bill tested his views on members by demanding: 'What will the Australian Club think of *that*?'

As Governor-General he was required to remain above politics but all his life he had been a man of strong opinions which he was rarely reluctant to voice and it was perhaps inevitable he would soon find himself in hot water. It happened when he addressed the National Congress of the Returned Sailors', Soldiers' and Airmen's Imperial League of Australia (now the RSL) in October. The League had become a highly politicised veterans' lobby group as much concerned with the alleged menace of Communism within its ranks as the welfare of its members. Bill deeply disapproved and used his speech to urge the League to return to its roots. He even suggested that perhaps the time had come for veterans to cease pleading for special treatment from the government – a proposal no politician, conscious of the powerful veteran vote, would have dared put forward. The speech caused an uproar and Bill was booed as he left the Congress. Bill Yeo, a Gallipoli veteran and League firebrand, accused the Governor- General of speaking on behalf of the government, a clear breach of his responsibilities as the Queen's representative. That row had not long been smoothed over when Bill offered his rather forthright – and far from flattering – views on modern architecture to a conference of architects at which he confessed that he still thought it 'rather indecent' to sleep on the ground floor.

When Bill made a speech during a tour in the north of Australia criticising the government's defence policy, the Secretary to the Prime Minister's Office sent a note to Menzies: 'The Governor-General seems to me in his speeches to deal more freely with current issues of policy than is desirable and I suggest you should consider whether he should not receive some guidance from yourself on these matters.' Menzies was the Governor-General's principal constitutional adviser and as such Bill was under some obligation to accept his advice, but Menzies knew Bill well enough to recognise he was not the kind of man to react well to 'guidance'. Although he was irritated by Bill's penchant for what he (Bill) described as 'the odd, small, calculated indiscretion', it soon became clear that most Australians were not the slightest bit bothered about the Governor-General candidly articulating a few home truths and in fact admired his guts for doing so.

Menzies admitted in his memoirs that he never went into Bill's presence without feeling nervous. While it was inevitable that there would be occasional tension between the two men and they some-times disagreed at their monthly meetings, their mutual regard for each other's intellect and integrity was such that any differences between them were soon forgotten. Menzies, for example, would have been happy for all future Governors-General to be British, whereas Bill often referred in speeches to his belief that his job should be done by an Australian. (From 1965 onwards all Governors-General have been Australian.)

Old soldiers, naturally, remained close to Bill's heart. When he arrived for a civic reception at Melbourne Town Hall he noticed that the one-armed lift operator was wearing a Victoria Cross ribbon on his uniform and stayed to talk to him at length while the accompanying dignitaries were left waiting in a corridor. His name was Bill Jackson and he had been awarded the VC at the age of 19 for rescuing wounded comrades marooned in no-man's-land at Armentières during the battle of the Somme in 1916. On his second foray, a shell blew off his right arm but he managed to get back to the trenches where an officer applied a tourniquet and he returned once more to no-man's-land for another half an hour to ensure there were no further wounded men left on the battlefield. Jackson was the first Australian, and the youngest, to win a VC on the Western Front.

Some urgency was injected into effecting the continuing improvements at Yarralumla and Kirribilli Point when it was announced that Queen Elizabeth and Prince Philip would be making their first official visit to Australia in early 1954. In a letter to Philip Pratt, Aileen said that as the date of the royal visit neared there were, at times, '20 workman hammering all over the house'.[7] On 3 February 1954, Bill and Aileen were waiting nervously at Farm Cove, Sydney, as Queen Elizabeth II became the first reigning monarch to set foot on Australian soil to the wild cheering of huge crowds waving Australian and Union flags.

The Queen and Prince Philip stayed at Yarralumla for five hectic days. 'I loved every minute of it,' Aileen wrote to Philip Pratt after the visit. 'They were such fun and so easy and yet so wonderful to watch in all they did. A terrific programme each day – we took in 19 extra bodies of both personal and domestic staff, we never sat down with less than 24 to lunch and 50 was nothing for dinner. And we had a happy little garden party for 3,800. So it took some thought, but it was fun and we loved it and I have been treading on air ever since.'[8]

The 56-day tour was a spectacular success. For those many Australians who still considered Britain to be their homeland and proclaimed unwavering loyalty to British culture and values, the visit had particular significance. The royal couple travelled all over Australia, attended a rally of 70,000 ex-servicemen and women at Melbourne Cricket Ground and visited 70 country towns in addition to all the capital cities except Darwin. (Bill ensured that the man given the honour of unfurling the royal standard as the Queen stepped from her car at Melbourne Town Hall was Bill Jackson VC; he also arranged for Jackson to be invited to a state dinner given for the royal couple in Sydney.) By the end, the Queen and Prince Philip had logged more than 30 flights covering 10,000 miles and travelled 2,000 miles by car on more than 200 journeys – as a result, it was estimated that 75 per cent of the population had been able to see the Queen at least once.

The Queen was followed at Yarralumla by a seemingly endless succession of visiting dignitaries, all of whom had to be accommodated and entertained. The Slims reintroduced a certain pomp and formality at both Yarralumla and Admiralty House which they felt more adequately reflected the dignity of the office of Governor-General. Curtseying, which had been dismissed by Bill's Australian predecessor, unsurprisingly, as an outdated anachronism, was reintroduced, probably by Aileen who liked everything to be done properly. 'There would be 30 people to dinner quite regularly,' recalled Simon Weber-Brown, one of Bill's ADCs, 'and at the end of the dinner the ladies would withdraw and as they reached the big double doors they would all turn in pairs, face the gentlemen and curtsey. Of course, the younger ones found it a bit easier to get up again. The Field Marshal would just incline his head in acknowledgement.'[9]

Aileen was such a perfectionist that most of the domestic staff at Yarralumla and Admiralty House were said to be terrified of her. She laid down strict rules for dinner parties, for example, which were organised with great precision. Before the event, Aileen and Bill would be briefed on the guests and when they went in to dinner they would sit opposite each other in the centre of a long dining table. Aileen's first dinner party rule was not to talk across the table as it left the guests on either side with no one to talk to. She and Bill would first talk to the guest to their right and then, after 20 minutes, they would turn and talk to the guest on their left. Secretaries and personal staff around the table would wait for this cue and engineer the switching of conversation so that no one was left out. When the ladies withdrew, Aileen's personal secretary would stand by the doors and remind them to curtsey. Then, when the gentlemen had joined the ladies, Bill and Aileen sat in separate parts of the room and received small groups of three, four or five people arranged by the personal staff who discreetly consulted scraps of paper on which the composition of the groups had been noted. In that way, every guest got to talk to the Governor-General or his wife before the end of the evening.

Such occasions could sometimes be torture for Bill since he was not by nature socially gregarious and was not good at small talk. Give him an ammunition box to stand on and an army to inspire and he was in his element; he'd have the men cheering in no time. But it was something of a challenge for him to sit at a dinner table with a woman on either side and make entertaining conversation; Aileen constantly nagged him to try harder and look more cheerful. In his defence, he was still in frequent pain from his war wounds and suffering somewhat from the vicissitudes of his years. 'He is becoming older,' Aileen wrote to Pratt, 'and has much discomfort from his arthritic neck. So nasty for him, for he gets headaches. His doctors despair of him, for he will NOT do what they tell him.'[10]

Friends noticed there were periodically signs of strain between Bill and Aileen during their time in Australia and occasional quarrels, often because Bill expected Yarralumla to be run like a military unit; Aileen complained that he simply could not comprehend how difficult it was to organise everything efficiently. In some respects Aileen was very different from her husband. Despite her strict upbringing as the daughter of a minister in the Scottish Presbyterian Church (or possibly as a consequence of it) she loved a party. Before the Slims left England she had suggested it might be a good idea to hold a ball for 600 people within 72 hours of their arrival in Australia, only to be rather brusquely informed that Government House could not accommodate anything like that number of people.

Largely at Aileen's instigation the Slims initiated a tradition at

Yarralumla of throwing a Christmas party for all the staff and their husbands or wives. Supper was served in the dining room and afterwards there was a dance with a hired band at which an enthusiastic Aileen and a less enthusiastic Bill danced with various members of the staff. Betty Jackson, Aileen's personal secretary, recalled that her employers were exceptionally generous and gave everyone wonderful presents. It was the thoughtfulness of the Slims that also touched individual hearts – Aileen's insistence that her dressmaker was on the invitation list for the Queen's garden party; remembering to send a Christmas card every year to the family of the man who came every week to groom their beloved wire-haired terrier, Susie; Bill paying a special visit to his barber at the Australia Club to thank him for his services before they left Australia.

Bill was happiest at Yarralumla on the rare occasions when the family was visiting or when they were able to entertain close friends informally – they would play riotous charades, or push back the furniture for carpet bowls, or engage in ferocious battles of croquet on the lawn in front of the house. (Bill said he enjoyed croquet because it was 'the only English game you don't have to play like a gentleman'.) When the Slims' daughter, Una, visited with her first child, Bill could occasionally be seen in the garden sitting in the shade of a deodah tree writing a speech on his knee and carrying on a conversation – incomprehensible to both parties – with his year-old granddaughter, Sarah, in her pram. Una had married a captain in the Grenadier Guards shortly before her parents left for Australia. Her brother, John, was only an occasional visitor as he had joined the Special Air Service in 1952 and was involved in clandestine operations in Malaya, where a bitter little guerrilla war was being fought against Communist insurgents. Inevitably, it was an extra worry for his parents. 'He [John] went back to Malaya for a last special operation,' Bill wrote in a letter to Pratt dated July 1957. 'I'm always a bit nervous about "last" operations but he cabled us to say that this one had been "successful", whatever that means, but he had been rather bruised "where Daddy got shot last". So I suppose he landed in the trees with a bit of a bump.'[11]

Among the many duties ascribed to the Governor-General and his spouse was the requirement to 'accept patronage of many national charitable, cultural, educational sporting and professional organisations'. Aileen became patron of the Australian Red Cross, the Country Women's Association and the Girl Guides and spent a great deal of her time visiting schools and hospitals, although she was reluctant to accept invitations if it required making a speech, which she did not enjoy. One of her great strengths was that she had an extraordinary facility for remembering names and faces and family details. She would revisit a hospital or school and astonish the people she met by recalling previous conversations as much as a year earlier and asking after their families by name.

It was in some ways unfortunate for Bill that one of his interests was Fairbridge Farm School in Molong, New South Wales, which he visited for the first time in July 1953 to open a new wing. Fairbridge Farm School had been established in 1934 to accept orphans and disadvantaged children from Britain and prepare them for a new and better life in Australia. Bill liked young people and on his first visit he instructed his chauffeur to give the children rides around the grounds in his official Rolls-Royce, a typical Bill gesture, while he was meeting the staff. He had no way of knowing that the regime at Molong was a lot less benign when a viceregal visit was not taking place. Years later ex-pupils at Fairbridge spoke out and told harrowing stories of endemic physical and sexual abuse and Dickensian lives of hard labour, devoid of affection.[12] All this was concealed from their important visitor: Bill formed the view that the Fairbridge people were doing an excellent job and after leaving Australia accepted chairmanship of the London Fairbridge Society.

Throughout his first years as Governor-General Bill worked, whenever time allowed, on his magnum opus, *Defeat Into Victory*, a history of the Burma campaign. He had started writing it before he left Britain, but the major portion was written in Australia with the help of his old 14th Army stalwart, Brigadier Michael Roberts, who by chance and good fortune was attached to the Historical Section at the Cabinet Office in London helping to compile *The Official History of the War Against Japan*. As Bill completed a draft of each chapter, he sent it to Roberts for fact checking, along with long lists of questions he needed answering. Most writers require long periods of uninterrupted concentration to produce a book, particularly something as complex as a military history; that Bill was able to complete such a magisterial work with a full diary of engagements and distractions, often working late at night in his up-stairs study at Yarralumla, was a tribute to his extraordinary powers of concentration.

In July 1955 Bill wrote to Nigel Bruce, his ADC at 15 Corps: 'Do you remember how years ago I said I would some day write a book about the Burma war and that when I did I should ask you to illustrate it? Well, I've now written the book and Cassell are going to publish it but alas, it will be illustrated only by maps. But there will be a dust cover. Would you do it? ... The book "Defeat Into Victory" – I hope you like the title – is my personal account from the Retreat in 1942 to the end of the war. It is meant to be a serious and reasonably dignified but, I hope, not too dull military work designed for the general reader. So the dust jacket can't be a bosomy Burmese beauty leaning on a pagoda, but a bit more sober ...'[13]

Bill added that he did not want any letters after his name on the dust jacket because 'I think they always look stupid'. He had by then acquired quite a few letters: the previous year he had attained the rare distinction of being awarded 'the four Gs' – a GCVO being added to his GBE, GCB and GCMG. Only a KG – a Knight of the Garter – remained and that would be bestowed on him before he left Australia.

Defeat Into Victory, dedicated to 'Aileen, a soldier's wife who fol-lowed the drum and from mud-walled hut to Government House made a home', was a publishing sensation – the reviews were uni-versally admiring and the initial print run of 20,000 copies sold out in the first week, an almost unprecedented demand for a non-fic-tion book by a new author. The *Evening Standard* called it the 'best General's book of World War Two', the *Observer* described it as 'a vivid and deeply moving story of endurance and heroism', to *The Times* it was 'a magnificent tale' and, in the *Field*, Major General D. R. Bateman, an Indian Army officer, went completely over the top: 'Of all the world's greatest records of war and military adventure, this story must surely take its place among the greatest. It is told with a wealth of human understanding, a gift of vivid description, and a revelation of the indomitable spirit of the fighting man that can seldom have been equalled – let alone surpassed – in military history.'

When *Defeat Into Victory* appeared in the United States, the critics were similarly enthusiastic. The *Journal of Modern History* judged it to be 'an outstanding example of the best of British military memoirs' while *Time* magazine pronounced it 'a minor masterpiece of war reporting' and went on to portray the author as a 'master of the English language' and (perhaps not entirely to his liking) 'an amiable blend of Colonel Blimp, Pukka Sahib and strategic genius'.

What set the 375-page book apart as a military memoir, apart from its lucid, robust prose and occasional flashes of dry humour, was its disarming humility. Here was an unusual (almost unknown) species among military commanders – a general ready to admit his mistakes, often assailed by self-doubt and more than willing to attribute his success to others. His modesty was exemplified in a letter of thanks he sent to Michael Roberts in which he said he had had two comments on his book so far – one from a lady who wanted to get a copy as it was a solid enough volume to throw at her husband and the other from his son John who moaned that it would be 'another bloody book to read for the Staff College'. 'So,' he concluded, 'it ought to suit all tastes.'

Bolstered by the success of *Defeat Into Victory*, in the following year he produced an anthology of his speeches under the title *Courage and Other Broadcasts*, which he predicted in a letter to Pratt would probably not sell to 'anyone except a few maiden aunts who may give it to their reluctant nephews'. He was not far off the mark but he returned to form in 1959 with the publication of *Unofficial History*, a collection of light-hearted short stories originally written for magazines describing his adventures in the Great War and on the North-West Frontier between the wars. It was acclaimed in the *National Review* as 'one of the most delightful and amusing books about modern campaigning I have ever read'. *The Scotsman* thought it was 'perfectly delightful' while Bernard Fergusson, who had served under Bill as a Chindit, suggested in the *Sunday Times* that it offered a 'real clue to the esteem in which this particular general was held by soldiers of so many different races'.

In November 1956 Lord Carrington, a future Foreign Secretary in the government of Margaret Thatcher, arrived in Australia with his wife and three young children to take up an appointment as High Commissioner. Although his responsibilities were quite separate from those of the Governor-General, he recalled Bill as being enormously kind and helpful. 'By the time I arrived he was tremendously popular, absolutely revered, and an important figure in the life of Australia.'[14] Bill and Aileen naturally invited the Carringtons to the Christmas dinner party they held every year at Government House. It proved to be a memorable occasion: nine-year-old Virginia Carrington decided to fill a brief lull in the conversation by inquiring of the table, in a clear, piping voice: 'Do you know who Daddy hates most in Canberra?' After dinner, Aileen suggested a game of hunt the thimble for the children. As soon as a thimble was produced, Virginia delightedly grabbed it and, searching for a suitable hiding place among the other guests, rammed it down Ethel Anderson's ear trumpet. 'Before we left for Government House,' Peter Carrington sighed, 'we were terrified the children were going to behave badly.'

Throughout his time in Australia, Bill was in great demand as a speaker. (He joked to Philip Pratt that he was 'cheaper than a conjuror'.) In April 1957 he delivered a lecture entitled 'Leadership in Management' to the Australian Institute of Management in Adelaide in which he demonstrated how leadership techniques in the military could be adapted and applied in civilian life. It would foreshadow the advice of legions of management 'experts' in the years to come. Indeed, nearly 50 years later, in 2003, a transcript of the lecture was published in the *Australian Army Journal* with a note: 'It is amazing to consider how many of the ideas in this article have been sold in recent books as novel new approaches.'

Later that year Bill was reluctantly obliged to receive the credentials of the newly appointed Japanese ambassador. He warned Australian officials he had no intention of removing the samurai sword he had taken from General Kimura at the end of the war and kept as a souvenir of the war prominently displayed in the entrance hall at Yarralumla. When the ambassador and senior Japanese diplomats arrived in morning dress they walked impassively past the sword as if they had not seen it, but Bill was gratified to observe two secretaries at the rear of the procession nudge each other and furtively gesture towards it. Bill received the ambassador with strict formality and wearing an expression which Aileen described as his 'There are Japs at the bottom of our garden face'.

During his term in office Bill logged 949 flying hours across the length and breadth of Australia, even though he was frequently in pain and still found it difficult getting in and out of aeroplanes. (In 1957 he had to spend a week in hospital in Melbourne, having damaged his back.) Sergeant Taffy Aveling, who had been a general transport driver in Imphal and later joined the RAAF, volunteered to be the flight steward on the Governor-General's aircraft – a Dakota or a Convair of the 34th Special Transport Squadron in Canberra – and had many happy memories of his travels with Bill and Aileen. On trips into the far reaches of the outback they would load their aircraft with sweets for the children, newspapers for the men, magazines for the women and fresh bread. When they landed the children would often run up to greet them shouting 'Uncle Bill, Uncle Bill'.

Aileen sometimes undertook engagements independently – she toured Papua New Guinea alone – but whenever she was away she always fretted about her husband's health, and his diet in particular. Taffy Aveling remembered her lecturing Bill not to eat steak and onions, one of his favourite dishes, while she was on a visit to the family in the United Kingdom. It was, Taffy said, the first meal he ate after she had left and one he then enjoyed regularly until she returned. But Aileen found out about it when she got home and, according to Taffy, gave the Governor-General 'hell'. On another occasion Simon Weber-Brown was present when Aileen, on the eve of another trip, pleaded with Bill not to eat or drink too much while she was away. After she had gone, Bill turned to his ADC and said, with a twinkle in his eye, 'I didn't hear Lady Slim say anything about eating or drinking, did you, Simon?' 'No, sir,' he replied. 'Not a word.'

By their travels the Slims got to know Australia better than most Australians and Menzies' decision in 1958 to ask Bill to stay on for two more years as Governor-General – the usual term of office was five years – was warmly welcomed. The general view was that Bill could be forgiven for being a 'pommy bastard' because he was such a thoroughly good bloke. The extent to which he had become accepted as 'an honorary Australian' was demonstrated when, during a visit to the Fossil Downs cattle station in Kimberley, Western Australia, local Aborigines took him, alone, to their ancient burial ground, presented him with a message stick and revealed the mysteries of their tribal rituals – an extraordinarily rare honour, rarely bestowed on a white man.

Bill's popularity also helped cement Australian cultural ties to Britain at a time when those ties were being challenged by a number of factors: Australia was asserting a new nationalism following the success of the 1956 Olympic Games in Melbourne, which had fostered a great sense of national pride; there was an influx of American culture through film, radio and television; and an increasing number of immigrants were arriving from countries other than Britain, notably Italy and Greece. After British Prime Minister Harold Macmillan paid an official visit to Australia he wrote to Bill thanking him for his hospitality at Yarralumla and added: 'I know what a wonderful job you have done in Australia and I realise how much you have contributed to the respect and affection which they feel for us.'[15]

What most appealed to Australians about their Governor-General was his obvious humanity and his complete lack of stuffiness and self-regard. When he was asked to present the Gold Cup at Canberra Jockey Club, the recipient, a local farmer, launched into a long and tedious speech at the end of which he turned to Bill and said, 'Thank you very much for presenting me with the Cup, Sir William ... er ... the name is Slim, isn't it?' The horrified silence was broken by Bill, who smiled and confirmed that his name was, indeed, Slim. Afterwards the chairman of the Club tried to apologise but Bill assured him it was unnecessary. 'I had to ask his name,' he said, 'so why shouldn't he ask mine?'

For a man approaching 70, not in the best of health, the ceaseless grind of public duties was undoubtedly exhausting. Aileen offered a brief glimpse into their lives in a letter to Philip Pratt: 'We are quite hectic as usual. I have managed (how I know not) to give 6 dinners and 3 lunches within 15 days (the dinners are usually in the thirties). As well as that we have each opened three affairs, and seen the Melbourne Cup. Yesterday we flew back to Melbourne – Bill was given the Freedom at the Lord Mayor's Banquet. It was memorable and moving for us both. Now we have just flown back. I am doing cards before preparing to go to Sydney tomorrow where Bill opens the Pacific Rehabilitation Conference. Home for tea to receive five Guide State Commissioners who come to stay while attending their

Federal Council which I open on Tuesday: and then we attend the Cenotaph ceremony ...'[16]

The Slims' final days in Australia were marked by a round of receptions and dinners, fulsome speeches, lavish tributes in the Australian press and cheering crowds lining the streets to wish them Godspeed. When he came to say farewell to Taffy Aveling after their 949 hours flying together, Bill presented him with a silver tray and made a little speech, addressing him by his nickname for the first time: 'We've three things in common, Taffy – I shall call you Taffy for once. We're both Pommies, which we won't say too much about here. And we're both servicemen, though there's some difference in our rank. But above all, and this is something no one can take away from us, we're both Fourteenth Army.'

Bill and Aileen finally left Australia on 26 January 1960, setting sail from Melbourne on the P & O liner *Arcadia*. 'Thousands of Australians,' the *Melbourne Age* reported, 'farewelled their retiring Governor-General, Sir William Slim, and Lady Slim, with cheers and streamers at Station Pier.' A naval guard of honour was drawn up on the pier, which the field marshal inspected before he boarded the ship. As the *Arcadia* slipped its moorings at precisely six o'clock and edged away from the pier, a flight of RAAF jets swooped low across the water and a 21-gun salute echoed across the bay.

21

A Secret Mission to Nepal

The Slims returned to London with a minimum of fuss. Aileen was ill again, having suffered another, although less serious, haemorrhage on the month-long voyage home. They rented a flat near Battersea Bridge and soon had the welcome news that Robert Menzies had arranged for them to receive a pension from the Australian government. 'Such a man,' Menzies contended about his former Governor-General, 'should not be left languishing in a London boarding house or reduced to attending official functions in a taxi.'

Bill got back in time to attend the great spring reunion of the Burma Star Association at the Royal Albert Hall, his first for eight years, and he received a tumultuous welcome from the thousands of 14th Army veterans who had converged on London from all over the world for the event. Their respect, affection, even love, for Uncle Bill remained undiminished by the years and the fact that he was now back in their midst made the 1960 reunion a very special occasion. In his speech he paid moving tribute to Edwina Mountbatten, who had died a few weeks earlier in North Borneo while on a tour for the St John Ambulance Brigade:

'Lady Louis, Lady Louis Mountbatten, is not here tonight on this platform as we have so often seen her. She has given her life, as so many of our comrades gave theirs, on active service. She died in the front line of unselfish and unsparing service to the weak, the sick, the poor and the desolate. She went to their help wherever they were; no journey was too arduous, no conditions too hard for her. Thousands all over the world, and not least the countries of South-East Asia that we knew, mourn her.

'But with us, who wear the Burma Star, she had a special link and our hearts kept for her a special affection. There can hardly be one of us who, when things were toughest, has not seen her vital, graceful figure in her trim St John's uniform, moving from bed to bed in a *basha* hospital, standing on a sunbaked airstrip to meet the wounded, lurching about the sky in an old Dakota on some errand of mercy, passing down a muddy jungle track, reaching, ahead of most of us, the ghastly prison camps. Wherever we saw her she brought us courage, hope and practical help.

'The other day, after her Memorial Service as I paid off my taxi, the driver asked me if I had been to the Abbey. When I told him I had, he said, "A woman like that ought never to die" ... She won't. She will live in all our memories and still, I know, inspire us with something of her own courage, vitality and unselfishness.'

Bill's success and achievements as Governor-General of Australia were officially recognised four months after he returned home with his elevation to the peerage, on 15 July 1960, as Viscount Slim of Yarralumla in the Capital Territory of Australia and Bishopston in the City and County of Bristol. (There was considerable anger among 14th Army veterans when Mountbatten was made Viscount Mountbatten of Burma, a title they believed belonged indisputably to Uncle Bill.) Among other laurels he collected no fewer than 11 honorary doctorates, was made a Freeman of the City of London, a Liveryman of the Worshipful Company of Clothworkers and an Honorary Fellow of the Royal College of Surgeons in Edinburgh. When he travelled to Edinburgh for the conferring ceremony he began his speech by emphasising how honoured he was but then added, in typical Bill fashion, that when he was wounded in Mesopotamia he only survived because no doctor came near him for four days. His hosts, fortunately, presumed he was joking – although he wasn't.

By then his experience, diplomatic skills and common sense were much in demand in company boardrooms. Before he left Australia he had already accepted, in principle, an invitation to become a director of ICI, the chemical conglomerate. Alexander Fleck, the then chairman of ICI, had met Bill in Australia and had been greatly impressed by his 'capacity to take a broad view and to make sound judgements about important issues which had nothing to do with military matters'. Fleck recommended to his successor, Sir Paul Chambers, that Bill be sounded out to join the ICI board. Bill indicated he would be delighted to accept once his tenure as Governor-General had ended, as protocol demanded.

Other companies followed ICI, seeking not just the prestige of Bill's name but his acumen and authority – the National Bank of Australasia, London Assurance, Edger Investments, Dalgety & New Zealand Loan and British Home Entertainment – the latter a company set up to market 'pay television' by John Brabourne, his old ADC at Allied Land Forces South East Asia. Bill did not view his directorships as sinecures but considered he was morally obliged to 'earn his pay'. Thus it was that the case for pay television was argued before a select committee at the House of Commons not by some thrusting young entrepreneur or music industry mogul but by an elderly field marshal in his capacity as chairman of British Home Entertainment.

In September 1962, at the age of 71, he embarked on a gruelling 15-day tour of East Africa on behalf of the Dalgety & New Zealand Loan Company. His mission was to report on Kenya, Tanganyika and Uganda as they moved towards independence. In Tanganyika he dined with President Julius Nyerere, whom he found to be 'by far the most attractive of African politicians'. In Kenya he gave a speech at the Royal Agricultural Show urging European farmers to stay, despite their fears of a resurgence in violence from the Mau Mau. Things would improve, Bill privately thought, if Jomo Kenyatta (who was destined to become the first prime minister of the newly independent country) was out of the way. 'In spite of the hazardous state of the economy and potentially grave internal security risks,' Bill wrote in his final report. 'I left East Africa more hopeful than when I arrived. I would strongly recommend the Board hold its determination to remain. I would suggest we all, and our staff in East Africa, should mentally regard ourselves as a new company starting business in a new country.'[1]

While he was in Kenya, Bill also had a meeting with Noel Irwin, the officer with whom he had had such an angry confrontation after the 1942 retreat and who had later tried to sack him and had himself been sacked. Irwin had retired to Kenya and the two old soldiers reminisced amiably about the war and past times and agreed to let bygones be bygones. (Bill had earlier had a similar rapprochement, in England, with Leese, the second officer who had tried to sack him.)

In early 1963 he found himself back in hospital being treated for a damaged backbone caused, he said in a letter to a friend, by the fact that 'some 40 years ago I thought I could ride better than I really could'. A few months later he was globe-trotting again, this time to Nepal, on a secret assignment for the British government so 'cloak and dagger' that he was required to travel under an assumed name as 'Mr Pitts'. Harold Macmillan's Conservative government had decided to curb defence expenditure by reducing the strength of the Brigade of Gurkhas over three years from 14,600 to 10,000. The Secretary of State for War, John Profumo (soon to be engulfed in the scandal that would be known as 'the Profumo Affair' and lead to his resignation in disgrace) was due to make the announcement in the Army Estimates debate in the House of Commons on 13 March 1963, but it was suddenly realised towards the end of February that no agreement had been reached with the king of Nepal, a grave discourtesy, if nothing else.

An emissary was urgently needed to fly to Kathmandu and persuade the king of the need to make the cuts and to obtain his approval. Who better than the most distinguished Gurkha officer alive? Bill agreed to go even though he bluntly told Profumo that he thought it was 'crackers' to suggest reducing the strength of the Gurkhas. 'I am so very relieved and encouraged that you have agreed to carry out this mission,' Profumo wrote to Bill in a 'Personal and Secret' letter dated 28 February 1963, 'for I now have every hope that the exercise will be a successful one ... With warmest wishes and gratitude, for I know very well at what personal inconvenience you are going on this journey.'[2]

An aide-mémoire attached to the letter provided Bill with a full briefing of what was expected of him. Widespread rumours about the future of the Gurkhas had turned the whole issue into a political concern, he was informed, and therefore it was vital that the proposed cuts were agreed in advance by the king. 'You will know,' it continued, 'the best way to impress upon the King the very high regard in which Her Majesty's Government and the British Army hold the Brigade of Gurkhas and our hope that the traditional partnership will continue.' He was to convey news of the king's attitude by telegram from Kathmandu as soon as possible and certainly before the debate in the House.

The secrecy surrounding his mission was worthy of James Bond. The cover plan was that Bill was an official touring ICI factories in India. He was warned that the true nature of his mission was not be revealed either to the Military Attaché in Kathmandu or to any officer in the Brigade of Gurkhas. 'As far as the press is concerned you will be visiting India on business. When it becomes unavoidable, you can say the King has asked you to pay an informal courtesy visit.' (Although why the king of Nepal would invite an 'ICI official' to visit him in Kathmandu was not explained.)

Bill flew to Kathmandu via Calcutta and had an audience alone with the king, arranged by the British ambassador, on the afternoon of his arrival on 7 March. The meeting was less tricky than Whitehall had imagined it might be. Bill explained in detail the British government's proposals and the king listened carefully, his face expressionless. After Bill had finished his presentation, the king raised no objection; indeed, he said he was relieved that the reduction in the Gurkhas was not as severe as some rumours had indicated and he appreciated the fact that the cuts would be spread over three years. Neither the king, nor any of the senior officers in the Nepalese Army, made any counter-proposals to the British government's plans. Bill's task was certainly not hindered by the fact that the Commander-in-Chief, the Chief of Staff, the Quartermaster-General and the Adjutant-General of the Royal Nepalese Army had all served under him as junior officers.

Bill was able to signal London the complete success of his mission in plenty of time for the debate and when he returned to Britain he found a handwritten note from Profumo waiting for him at home. 'Dear Field Marshal,' it began, 'I hope perhaps this letter may arrive to greet you on your return, for I want to take the earliest chance of congratulating you on your great success with the King and the Nepalese Government. A most skillful performance which, as I do hope you know, has made all the difference to what was a most difficult operation . . .'[3] (Only a few weeks later Profumo admitted that he had lied to the House about the nature of his relationship with Christine Keeler and was forced to resign.)

That summer Bill and Aileen moved from Battersea to Windsor – to Windsor Castle, to be precise, where Bill had been appointed Deputy Constable, an honorary position dating to the eleventh century which was unpaid but came with rent-free accommodation – an apartment in the Norman Tower with sweeping views across parkland and the Thames valley. It was a welcome perk for a man still plagued by money worries, despite his City directorships and pensions.

Living at Windsor Castle greatly appealed to Bill's keen sense of history: the castle was built by William the Conqueror after the Norman invasion and had been used as a royal residence since the time of Henry I. His study, where he hung his samurai sword, his CIGS car pennant and many photographs of old friends, was the old guard-room and was said to have been the room in which King James I of Scotland was imprisoned and from where he first glimpsed his future bride, the daughter of the Earl of Somerset, walking in the garden. Carved into the room's stone walls, still perfectly legible, are the names of five Cavaliers held captive there during the Civil War in the seventeenth century.

St George's Chapel, just a few steps from the Norman Tower, is the spiritual home of the Knights of the Garter, the highest order of chivalry in England and into which Bill had been inducted as a companion in 1959. Membership of the Most Noble Order of the Garter is limited to the Sovereign, the Prince of Wales and 24 companions, personally appointed by the Queen. It was instituted by Edward III in 1348 in commemoration of his victory at Crécy: 'Tie about thy leg for thy renown this noble Garter; wear it as the symbol of the most illustrious Order, never to be forgotten or laid aside ...'

Bill, who became Constable and Governor of the castle the following year, liked to tell friends that the Queen was 'the best landlord I have ever had'. This was confirmed by the Duke of Edinburgh at a Gurkha Brigade Association dinner when he turned to Major General Taffy Davies and said he was not sure if he liked the field marshal, who was sitting on his other side, because he couldn't get anything done to his quarters at Windsor Castle as the Queen had decreed that no one's quarters were to be improved until the Slims had everything they wanted.[4]

As Constable and Governor, Bill was nominally in charge of the castle and the garrison on behalf of the Queen and was required to meet her whenever she arrived to take up residence, but he also played a full role in the community life of the castle and helped raise

funds for St George's House, a college within the castle walls established by the Duke of Edinburgh and the then Dean of Windsor in
1966 to explore contemporary issues in government and industry
and 'effect change for the better in our society'.

Bill liked to socialise with the Military Knights of Windsor, who
were all old soldiers like himself – distinguished retired officers
granted a pension and accommodation at the castle. When the artist
Terence Cuneo was commissioned to paint the procession from the
Chapel after the annual Garter ceremony, Bill was particularly concerned that the oldest of the Military Knights should be featured.
There had been a dispute about whether the Yeomen of the Guard,
who also took in part in the procession, should be more prominent
in the picture at the expense of the Military Knights and Bill was
determined it would not happen. Cuneo was working from colour
photographs of the procession in which Bill's face was obscured by
the Queen Mother's hat (he was never as successful as other generals, he remarked wryly, at getting his picture taken) and so he had
to visit Cuneo's studio for his likeness to be added to the painting. When he arrived he was appalled to discover that the Military
Knight he particularly wanted to appear was blocked by a Yeoman.
Bill protested but Cuneo insisted that there was nothing he could
do about it. 'Yes there is,' Bill retorted, 'you can paint the bugger
out.' He stayed until it had been done.

One of Bill's regular visitors at Windsor was his old Indian Army
chum Lieutenant General Sir Reginald Savory, who had commanded the 23rd Indian Division in Burma. On 20 January 1967,
Savory found his friend in a gloomy mood and kept a note in his
journal of their conversation:

'Windsor Castle … Had quiet tea with Bill and Aileen. Yarned
together and then he said, "I won't be here much longer."

'"Why not?"

'"Can't afford it, Reg. I have spent too much on doing the place
up and now I have the bills to pay and besides I cannot live on my
income as there is so much entertaining to do. True, I have an entertainment allowance of £400, tax free, but that doesn't go very far."

'"What about writing another book or two?"

'"I am writing one now [presumably his unpublished memoir],
but I am not as energetic as I was and I tire very quickly. Besides, my

brain isn't as good as it used to be, I cannot concentrate as I could."

'"Yes, but surely if you want money a man with your worldwide reputation would be commissioned by any firm of publishers to write a book and they would pay you handsomely in advance?"

'"Yes, I know and I have already been approached but I am not going to write anything which is not really first class; and frankly, Reg, I am beginning to doubt I have it in me now. I'm worried, I don't mind admitting it. I am older than Aileen and I am likely to die before her. Then she will have to clear out of this place. I have no capital and my pension will die with me. All she will have is her Army pension and what she gets from the Indian Army Widows and Orphans Fund …"'[5]

(His money worries were real: after his death his estate was valued at only £12,249.)

About this time Bill's health began to fail. In June 1967, he suffered a small stroke which left him with impaired eyesight – 'a most damnable nuisance,' he wrote in a letter to a friend. Savory visited for lunch the following month and, when Bill had retired for a post-prandial nap, Aileen asked him to stay on and chat. 'Poor dear, she is worried about Bill, as well she may be. His arteries are very hardened; he tires very easily; yet he tries still to do too much. His mind wanders. There must be a touch of distantly approaching senility in all this, poor old chap. At times he is his old self and then tails off. Aileen is remarkably cheerful, but she has no illusions as to what the future will hold. There is no doubt that Bill relies on her a great deal and always has done. She is sad and rather hurt, she admits, at the often spoken accusation that it has been she, all along, who has been the social butterfly who has led him along social paths for which he had no real liking. I admire her immensely. Bill, despite his desire to continue to fulfil his obligations, is I sense more resigned than when I saw him last … It is all sad, to see this great man in the grip of Time and watch him going without complaint and in full, though unspoken, knowledge of what it all means … He came to see me off. This meant walking down the stairs and into the courtyard where my car was parked. He stood for a while talking and reminiscing just like his old self. Then I left. "Come again, Reg" he said as I moved off "and as often as you like".'[6]

Bill's Christmas 1967 message to members of the Burma Star

Association was an exhortation for them to keep alive the spirit of the 14th Army: 'What better friends could men ever have than our old Burma comrades? So let all us old Burma sweats get together as much as we can, renew the old comradeship, swap old yarns of how we won the war. Here's to us and a Merry Xmas to us all. Bill Slim.'

Over the coming months Bill's condition deteriorated further and in the summer of 1968 his speech became impaired. He continued to attend ICI board meetings regularly but Sir Paul Chambers, the chairman, was increasingly concerned about him, particularly after he failed to show up for a meeting when Chambers knew he was in the building. 'I looked round as usual to see whether all Directors who were expected were in their places. Only Lord Slim's seat was empty, so I waited a minute or so and in answer to a question I replied that as he had already been at a meeting which had just finished I knew that he would not be more than a minute or two. [Bill was found, very confused, wandering around in a corridor.] At a later stage of that meeting I asked him for his opinion on a matter on which I thought his opinion would be valuable. He made no reply and I realised at once that he was "not with us". So without comment I turned quickly to another Director. He attended Board meetings subsequently after that but made little contribution to our discussions or decisions. Nevertheless he was very upset when, having discussed the matter with colleagues, I suggested that perhaps the time had come for him to retire from the Board.'[7]

'Bill has been quite ill for the past six weeks,' Aileen wrote to their friend General Sir Richard O'Connor in January 1969. 'He was in Millbank [hospital] for a couple of weeks. He has had another slight stroke which has affected his speech and has very great difficulty putting thoughts into normal words ... Doctors hope that with speech therapy and patience things will improve over the next few months. It is quite hard for Bill and he gets desperately frustrated as his brain is clear ...'[8]

'Bill is very blind,' she wrote in another letter a few months later, 'but in some astonishing way he now contrives to read more. He has just finished Wellington and is plunging into Winston's Marlborough ...'

At the beginning of 1970, Bill's Windsor doctor noted that his powers of comprehension were slowing. Bill could have ended his days at Windsor Castle but his strong sense of morality, of what was right and proper, forbade it – he insisted he should be allowed to relinquish his position on health grounds and on 30 June 1970 an announcement was made that 'Lord Slim will retire from his appointment as Constable and Governor of Windsor Castle'. The Military Knights of Windsor turned out in full uniform for a special farewell parade as the Slims left the castle for the last time, but by then Bill was more or less blind.

Bill and Aileen moved into a comfortable flat in Eaton Mansions, near Sloane Square, in London, where Bill received a constant stream of visitors and well-wishers, friends and old comrades. Montgomery telephoned every day to ask after him. Aileen strictly rationed the time visitors could spend with him to avoid overtiring him. Among the last visitors was Dickie Mountbatten; as usual, they spent time reminiscing about their glory days together in Burma. When Aileen quietly entered the bedroom to warn Dickie it was time for him to leave Mountbatten was leaning over the bed. Her husband had grabbed the younger man's arm and Aileen heard him whisper: 'We did it together, old boy.'

On 7 December 1970, Bill was admitted to the King Edward VII Hospital for Officers in Marylebone after another stroke at Eaton Mansions. John was with him as he was carried down the stairs to a waiting ambulance. As he was being made comfortable, he whispered to his son, 'Tell them not to use the siren – I don't want to be a nuisance.' They were the last words he spoke. Uncle Bill died seven days later, at the age of 79.

Epilogue

Field Marshal The Viscount Slim KG, GCB, GCMC, GCVO, GBE, DSO, MC, KStJ was accorded a funeral with full military honours at St George's Chapel, Windsor, on 22 December 1970. Thousands gathered to pay their respects as a horse-drawn gun carriage bearing his coffin passed through the town en route to the castle that had once been his home.

On 24 April 1976 Bill joined the famous British figures commemorated in the crypt at St Paul's Cathedral when Aileen unveiled a remembrance plaque placed there by the Burma Star Association. Admiral Lord Mountbatten addressed the congregation at a thanksgiving service. 'Whenever leadership is spoken of, or written about, tribute is regularly paid to his supreme qualities,' he said, 'as the finest leader of fighting men in the Second World War.'

In 1990 the Queen unveiled a statue of Bill erected on Whitehall outside the Ministry of Defence, alongside those of Montgomery and Lord Alanbrooke.

In 2011 the National Army Museum in London conducted a poll to discover who merited the title of 'Britain's Greatest General'. A field of 20 candidates was finally narrowed down to a short list of five contenders – Oliver Cromwell, the Duke of Marlborough, the Duke of Wellington, Douglas Haig and Bill Slim. After a day of debate during which each candidate was championed by a celebrity speaker, the result was a tie. It was agreed that the Duke of Wellington and Bill Slim were the greatest generals in British history.

APPENDIX A

Defeat Into Victory vs the Chindits

Many former Chindits were furious when *Defeat Into Victory* was published in 1956 and accused Bill of not only betraying their revered leader, Orde Wingate, but of slandering his memory with lies. The particular passage that caused most offence was Bill's description of Wingate going to pieces at Lalaghat airfield in March 1944 when he was shown pictures of the Piccadilly landing site blocked by felled trees.

A number of Wingate's admiring biographers pointed out that none of the other officers present at Lalaghat that day supported Bill's version of events. This is not quite true. None of those who have written their own memoirs mentions Wingate having a breakdown, but none says he did not. Wingate asserted in his report after the operation that he never wanted to abort the mission, but in correspondences with the official historian after the war Bill insisted his recollection was absolutely clear – that Wingate was convinced the operation had been compromised and wanted to pull out. And Wingate's claim that he made the final decision to go ahead was obviously untrue, as confirmed by Tulloch.

It is certainly true that Bill inexplicably got the name of the airfield wrong – he wrote that it happened at Hailakandi – but it is impossible to believe that his memory would play him false over such an extraordinary event or that he would have deliberately lied to damage Wingate's reputation. Bill admired Wingate as an inspiring leader and a soldier with innovative ideas, although he recognised the many flaws in his character.

Ex-Chindits also complained that Bill paid generous tribute to Wingate after his death but then stabbed him in the back in his book by describing him as 'strangely naïve when it came to the business of actually fighting the Japanese'. They felt that Bill had belittled the achievements of the two Chindit expeditions and were offended by his suggestion that the regular infantry could have performed just as well as the Chindits.

Actually, Bill never made any secret of the fact that he generally disapproved of specialist 'private armies', not least because they tended to make disproportionate claims on resources.

The final cavil, that Bill never gave Wingate credit in *Defeat Into Victory* for his contribution to Operation Extended Capital, perhaps has some substance. On 13 March 1944, Wingate had proposed in a report[1] to Bill and the Supreme Commander using a reserve brigade to cross the Irrawaddy at Pakokku and attack the Japanese at Meiktila. The idea was not taken up because it did not fit in with the overall strategy at the time, but it certainly foreshadowed Bill's plans for Extended Capital and he probably should have made a reference to it in his book. That he did not do so can only be down to an oversight. Throughout his career Bill was always ready to give credit where it was due, often at the expense of his own standing; unlike almost every other general in the war he never felt the need to burnish his reputation or bolster his ego.

Notes

The following abbreviations are used in the notes:

BL British Library
CAC Churchill Archives Centre, Churchill College,
    Cambridge
DIV *Defeat Into Victory*
IWM Imperial War Museum, London
LHCMA Liddell Hart Centre for Military Archives, King's
    College London
NA   National Archives, Kew
NAM National Army Museum, London

1: Onslaught

1 All Japanese names are printed in the Japanese style, with the
surname first.
2 Churchill, *The Second World War*, Vol. IV.
3 Lieutenant General Sir Henry Pownall, Wavell's Chief of Staff.
4 Smith, *Singapore Burning*.
5 Smyth's decision would be the subject of bitter controversy for
years; he was subsequently relieved of his command and replaced
by 'Punch' Cowan.

2: Playing at Soldiers

1 SLIM 5/2/2, Unpublished memoir, CAC.
2 Unpublished memoir, CAC.
3 Ibid.
4 Ibid.
5 Ibid.

6 RLEW 3/6, CAC.
7 Slim, *Defeat Into Victory*, p. 550 (hereafter referred to as *DIV*).
8 Unpublished memoir, CAC.
9 Ibid.
10 Ibid.
11 Ibid.

3: A First Taste of War

1 Unpublished memoir, CAC.
2 Ibid.
3 SLIM 6/8, CAC.
4 Rhodes James, *Gallipoli*.
5 Unpublished memoir, CAC.
6 Interview Viscount John Slim.
7 Philip Pratt, 'Care For His Men', *British Army Annual*, No. 2, 1955.
8 Unpublished memoir, CAC.
9 Ibid.
10 *Warwickshire Advertiser*, 27 November 1915.
11 Unpublished memoir, CAC.
12 Slim, *Courage and Other Broadcasts*.
13 Unpublished memoir, CAC.
14 SLIM 1/1, CAC.
15 Unpublished memoir, CAC.
16 Interview Viscount Slim.
17 SLIM 6/8, CAC.
18 Ibid.
19 Slim, *Unofficial History*.
20 Ibid.
21 Interview Viscount Slim.

4: A Premonition of Death

1 James Morris.
2 Slim, *Unofficial History*.
3 Ibid.
4 Slim, *Courage and Other Broadcasts*.

5 SLIM 5/2/2, CAC.
6 SLIM 1/6, CAC.
7 Slim, *Unofficial History*.
8 SLIM 12/1B, CAC.
9 Unpublished memoir, CAC.
10 Ibid.
11 SLIM 12/4, CAC.
12 Unpublished memoir, CAC.
13 Buck, *Simla Past & Present*, Letter to Colonel Churchill, 1832.
14 Ibid.
15 SLIM 5/1/1, CAC.
16 Ibid.
17 Hamilton, *The Full Monty*.
18 SLIM 2/1, CAC.

5: A Recruit for the Gurkhas

1 *British Army Review*, No. 88.
2 SLIM 5/1/1, CAC.
3 Ibid.
4 Slim, *Unofficial History*.
5 Ibid.
6 SLIM 5/1/1, CAC.
7 Ibid.
8 Evans, *Slim as Military Commander*.
9 RLEW 3/6, CAC.
10 SLIM 5/2/2, CAC.
11 SLIM 1/2, CAC.
12 SLIM 13/2, CAC.
13 SLIM 5/1/1, CAC.

6: Bill in Love

1 SLIM 13/2, CAC.
2 Information provided by Viscount Slim.
3 Interview George Mathewson.
4 SLIM 1/2, CAC.
5 Interview General Maxwell Dyer, SLIM 13/8, CAC.

6 SLIM 2/1, CAC.

7 Interview 'Punch' Cowan, SLIM 13/2, CAC.

8 Interview Viscount Slim.

9 Ibid.

10 Interview Lt Gen. Phil Vickers, RLEW 3/6, CAC.

11 Interview George Mathewson.

12 Interview Lt Gen. Phil Vickers, RLEW 3/6, CAC.

13 SLIM 2/1, CAC.

14 Gibbs, *Historical Record of the 6th Gurkha Rifles*, Vol. 2.

15 Smyth, *Milestones*.

16 Ibid.

17 Evans, op. cit.

18 SLIM 2/1, CAC.

19 Interview Major Gen. Davies, SLIM 5/4, CAC.

20 SLIM 2/1, CAC.

21 SLIM 1/3, CAC.

22 SLIM 5/1/1, CAC.

23 SLIM 1/3, CAC.

7: A Battle in the Sudan and a Bullet in Eritrea

1 Brett-James, *Ball of Fire*.

2 Evans, op. cit.

3 SLIM 9/1, CAC.

4 Ibid.

5 Slim, *Unofficial History*.

6 Ibid.

7 Six months later the battalion was back fighting with distinction in Syria and Iraq.

8 Slim, *Unofficial History*.

9 Ibid.

10 Brett-James, op. cit.

11 Unpublished memoir, CAC.

12 Ibid.

13 L/WS/1/535, BL

14 File 199, Auchinleck Papers, John Ryland Library, University of Manchester.

8: An *Opéra Bouffe* in Persia

1 Masters, *The Road Past Mandalay*.
2 Slim, *Unofficial History*.
3 Ibid.
4 Ibid.
5 Ibid.
6 Masters, op. cit.
7 Slim, *Unofficial History*.
8 Ibid.

9: The Corps Commander

1 *DIV*, p. 23.
2 Ibid., p. 27.
3 Fraser, *Quartered Safe Out Here*.
4 Ultra was the code name adopted by British military intelligence for breaking encrypted enemy communications at the Government Code and Cypher School at Bletchley Park, an operation that remained top secret until 1974.
5 *DIV*, p. 27.
6 RLEW 3/6, CAC.
7 Hutton papers, IWM.
8 Rodger, *Red Moon Rising*.
9 *DIV*, p. 39.
10 Unpublished memoirs of Lt Col. I. C. G. Scott, 698697/36/1, IWM.
11 Lunt, *A Hell of a Licking*.
12 Unpublished memoir, MSS EUR d1223/2 South East Asia Collection, BL.
13 *DIV*, p. 50.
14 Hedley, *Jungle Fighter*.
15 Wagg, *A Million Died*.
16 Moser, *China, Burma, India*.
17 Ibid.
18 Stilwell, Stilwell Papers.
19 Lewin, *Slim the Standard Bearer*.
20 *DIV*, p. 53.

21 Ibid., p. 64.

22 Wagg, op. cit.

23 Private information from Bruce Scott's son, Ken.

24 *DIV*, p. 69.

25 Unpublished memoirs of Colonel Bill Amies, 459681/21/1, IWM.

26 Carmichael, *Mountain Battery*.

27 SLIM 5/4, CAC.

28 After the war Mains met Bill – for the first time – at a Gurkha reunion dinner and confessed to his role in the blowing up of the fuel. Bill, he reported, was 'still not amused'.

29 Rodger, op. cit.

10: A Hell of a Beating

1 *DIV*, p. 91.

2 Slim was referring to an 'old soldier' anecdote: 'And we says to him "Jump and we'll hold the blanket". And he jumped and there weren't no blanket.'

3 *DIV*, p. 92.

4 Burma Star Association website.

5 *DIV*, p. 97.

6 Report of General Sir Harold Alexander on Operations in Burma, 5 March 1942–20 May 1942, HMSO.

7 Slim, *Courage and Other Broadcasts*.

8 Unpublished memoirs of Colonel Bill Amies, op. cit.

9 SLIM 13/2, CAC.

10 Thompson, *Forgotten Voices of Burma*.

11 Unpublished memoirs of Colonel Bill Amies, op. cit.

12 *DIV*, p. 102.

13 Ibid., p. 108.

14 *Army Quarterly*, January 1956.

15 *DIV*, p. 107.

16 Evans, op. cit.

17 *DIV*, p. 110.

18 SLIM 3/9, CAC.

19 SLIM 5/4, CAC.

11: The Arakan Debacle

1 MSS EUR d1223/2, South East Asia Collection, BL.
2 SLIM 13/2, CAC.
3 *DIV*, p. 113.
4 Calvert, *Fighting Mad.*
5 Evans, op. cit.
6 Interview Mrs Una Rowcliffe.
7 *ITMA* (*It's That Man Again*) was a popular BBC radio comedy programme starring Tommy Handley which ran from 1939 to 1949.
8 SLIM 13/8, CAC.
9 *DIV*, pp. 142–3.
10 Ibid., p. 141.
11 Irwin Papers, IWM.
12 *DIV*, p. 155.
13 Ibid., p. 157.
14 Irwin Papers, IWM.
15 Ibid.
16 Alanbrooke correspondence, LHCMA.
17 Irwin Papers, IWM.
18 Lewin, op. cit. This signal no longer exists. There are a number of differing accounts of Bill's supposed sacking, but Lewin's is thought to be the most reliable.
19 Alanbrooke Papers, LHCMA.
20 Brett-James, *Report My Signals.*

12: Army Commander

1 Greenwood, *Auchinleck.*
2 MSS EUR d1041/3 BL.
3 Greenwood, op. cit.
4 File K261 Mountbatten Papers, Broadlands.
5 No relation to the disgraced Noel Irwin.
6 SLIM 3/9, CAC.
7 Ibid.
8 Speech by Mountbatten at Slim's Thanksgiving Service, St Paul's Cathedral, 24 April 1976.

9 RLEW 3/5, CAC.

10 *DIV*, p. 164.

11 CAB 106/170, NA.

12 RLEW 3/5, CAC.

13 Masters, op. cit.

14 Ibid.

15 *DIV*, p. 186.

16 Davis, *A Child at Arms*.

17 McKie, *Echoes from Forgotten Wars*.

18 Moran, *Winston Churchill: The Struggle for Survival*.

19 Greenwood, op. cit.

13: The Turning Point

1 SLIM 9/2, CAC.

2 *DIV*, p. 226.

3 Roberts, *Golden Arrow*.

4 Messervy 5.3, LHCMA.

5 Maule, *Spearhead General*.

6 *DIV*, p. 235.

7 'Tokyo Rose' was actually a generic name given to about a dozen English-speaking female broadcasters disseminating Japanese propaganda.

8 SLIM 13/2, CAC.

9 *DIV*, p. 246.

14: The Chindits

1 Bill did not mention Ultra in *Defeat Into Victory* as it was still secret at the time of publication.

2 *DIV*, p. 232.

3 Bond (ed.), *Chief of Staff*.

4 Tulloch, *Wingate in Peace & War*.

5 Bond (ed.), op. cit.

6 Unpublished memoir, IWM.

7 Tulloch, op. cit.

8 Calvert, op. cit.

9 Tull 1/9, LHCMA.

10 *DIV*, p. 260.

11 See Appendix A.

12 CAB 101/184, NA.

13 Ibid.

14 Much later it was learned that the landing site had not been obstructed by the Japanese, but by Burmese loggers, who had dragged the teak logs into the open to dry.

15 *DIV*, p. 261.

16 Tulloch, op. cit.

17 After the war Cochran served as the prototype for a dashing airman in an American comic strip *Terry and the Pirates*.

18 Kirby, *Official History of the War Against Japan*, Vol. III.

19 CAB 101/185, NA.

20 Ibid.

21 *DIV*, p. 269.

15: An Attack on the Raj

1 *DIV*, p. 293.

2 Ibid., pp. 296 and 324–5.

3 Ibid., p. 285.

4 SLIM 3/9, CAC.

5 Evans, op. cit.

6 *DIV*, p. 305.

7 Ibid., p. 309.

8 *SEAC*, August 1944.

9 Lewin, op. cit.

10 Tulloch, op. cit.

11 Allen, *The Longest War*.

12 Wilson, *The Sum of Things*.

13 Thompson, op. cit.

14 Wilson, op. cit.

15 *SEAC*, August 1944.

16 *DIV*, p. 325.

17 Kirby, *Official History of the War Against Japan*, Vol. III.

18 *DIV*, p. 332.

19 Interview with Dame Vera Lynn.

20 Allen, op. cit.

21 Box C247A, Mountbatten Papers.
22 Smith, *The Emperor's Codes*, p. 296.
23 SLIM 8/1, CAC.
24 Fraser, op. cit.

16: The Pursuit

1 *DIV*, p. 385.
2 Fergusson, *Trumpet in the Hall*.
3 Later General Sir Mike West, a witty and unconventional soldier with a taste for partying and jazz.
4 Fergusson, op. cit.
5 Lewin, op. cit.
6 Hawkins, *Drury Lane to Dimapur*.
7 Greenwood, op. cit.
8 When MacArthur was ordered to leave the Philippines in February 1942 by President Roosevelt he made a famous speech in Australia promising to return.
9 Author's interview.
10 *DIV*, p. 385.
11 Ryder, *Oliver Leese*.
12 Ibid., p. 369.
13 Ibid., p. 367.

17: The Master Plan

1 Kirby, *Official History of the War Against Japan*, Vol. IV.
2 *DIV*, p. 401.
3 Ibid., p. 410.
4 Evans, op. cit.
5 *DIV*, p. 429.
6 Ibid., p. 444.
7 Ibid., p. 447.
8 Ibid., p. 468.
9 RAF Museum AC/76/32. This line was deleted from Vincent's draft memoirs before publication.
10 Fraser, op. cit.
11 Masters, op. cit.

12 *Slim, Courage and Other Broadcasts.*
13 Some versions claim the word was EXDIGITATE.
14 1219703/22/1, IWM.

18: Sacked

1 Ryder, op. cit.
2 Hill, *China Dragons.*
3 Kirby file, NAM.
4 SLIM 2/3, CAC.
5 Lethbridge Papers, LHCMA.
6 SLIM 2/3, CAC.
7 Ibid.
8 NAM 7603-893-64-71.
9 SLIM 2/3, CAC.
10 Kirby file, NAM.
11 SLIM 2/3, CAC.
12 Kirby file.
13 SLIM 2/3, CAC.
14 Ryder.
15 Box 3, Leese Papers, LHCMA.
16 Christison's unpublished memoirs, IWM.
17 'Operations in Burma from 12 November 1944 to 15 August 1945', *London Gazette*, 6 April 1951.
18 *DIV*, p. 532.
19 Itagaki was executed for war crimes, among them allowing the inhumane treatment of POWs, in 1948.
20 *DIV*, p. 534.

19: From Railwayman to Field Marshal

1 *Dekho*, the magazine of the Burma Star Association, Spring 1998.
2 Lethbridge Papers, LHCMA.
3 He was being sarcastic – V cigarettes were widely loathed.
4 RLEW 3/9, CAC.
5 Lewin, op. cit.
6 L/ML/14/2720 BL.
7 SLIM 2/5, CAC.

8   Unpublished memoir, CAC.

9   O'Connor 11/22, LHCMA.

10 Ibid.

11 Chester, *The Nationalisation of British Industries*, p. 852.

12 Brooke conjoined his name when he was elevated to the peerage in 1945.

13 Montgomery *had* told Crocker he would be succeeding him as CIGS. Similarly, when Montgomery was appointed CIGS he told Major General Sir Francis de Guingand that he would be his deputy, leaving de Guingand in an embarrassing position when his appointment also was not ratified.

14 Unpublished memoir, CAC.

15 RLEW 3/9, CAC.

16 Unpublished memoir, CAC.

17 Shortly afterwards, after the outbreak of the Korean War, it was increased to two years and remained unchanged until National Service was abolished in 1960. This author was one of the last National Servicemen.

18 RLEW 3/9, CAC.

19 Dimoline 12/3, CAC.

20 SLIM 18, CAC.

21 John Baylis and Alan MacMillan, 'The British Global Strategy Paper of 1952', *Journal of Strategic Studies*, Vol. 16, June 1993.

22 T213/472, NA.

20: Governor-General

1   PREM 11/704, NA.

2   SLIM 1/7, CAC.

3   This story was verified by Simon Weber-Brown, one of Bill's ADCs at the time.

4   SLIM 3/2, CAC.

5   RLEW 3/2, CAC.

6   Foott, Ethel and the Governors' General.

7   SLIM 1/4, CAC.

8   Ibid.

9   Author's interview.

10 SLIM 1/4, CAC.

11 Ibid.

12 Long after his death, Bill was implicated in the scandal. Much
to the distress of his family, he was accused of molesting a boy
at the school in the back of the official Rolls-Royce. No one who
knew him believed it for a moment.

13 SLIM 7/1, CAC.

14 Author's interview.

15 SLIM 10/1, CAC.

16 SLIM 1/4, CAC.

21: A Secret Mission to Nepal

1 SLIM 6/1, CAC.

2 SLIM 2/7, CAC.

3 Ibid.

4 SLIM 5/4, CAC.

5 NAM, 7603-893-64-71.

6 Ibid.

7 RLEW 3/2, CAC.

8 LHCMA'Connor 10/30.

Appendix A

1 WO 203/187, NA.

Bibliography

Abhyankar, Col. M. G., *The War in Burma* (Natraj Publishers, Delhi, 1955)

Allen, Louis, *The Longest War, 1941–45* (J. M. Dent, London 1984)

Arnold, Ralph, *A Very Quiet War* (Rupert Hart-Davis, London, 1962)

Baillergen, Frederick A., 'Field Marshal Slim and the Power of Leadership' (Army Command and General Staff College, Fort Leavensworth, Kansas, 2005)

Barker, A. J., *The March on Delhi* (Faber & Faber, London, 1963)

Bayley, Christopher and Harper, Tim, *Forgotten Armies: Britain's Asian Empire & the War with Japan* (Allen Lane, London, 2004)

Belden, Jack, *Retreat with Stilwell* (Knopf, New York, 1943)

Bhattacharji, Romesh, *Lands of the Early Dawn; North East of India* (Rupa & Co., New Delhi, 2002)

Bidwell, Shelford, *The Chindit War. The Campaign in Burma 1944* (Hodder & Stoughton, London, 1979)

Bond, B. (ed.), *Chief of Staff, The Diaries of Lt General Sir Henry Pownall*, Vol. II, *1940–44* (Leo Cooper, London, 1974)

—— and Tachikawa, Kyoichi (eds), *British and Japanese Military Leadership in the Far Eastern War 1941–45* (Frank Cass, London, 2004)

Bower, Ursula Graham, *Naga Path* (John Murray, London, 1950)

Brett-James, Anthony, *Report My Signals* (Hennel Locke, London, 1948)

—— *Ball of Fire: The Fifth Indian Division in the Second World War* (Gale & Polden, Aldershot, 1951)

Buck, Edward J., *Simla Past & Present* (Thacker, Spink & Co., Calcutta, 1904)

Burleigh, Michael, *Moral Combat: A History of World War Two* (Harper Press, London, 2010)

Callahan, R., *Burma 1942–5: The Politics and Strategy of the Second World War* (Davis-Poynter, London, 1978)

Calvert, Mike, *Prisoners of Hope* (Jonathan Cape, London, 1952)

—— *Slim, War Leader* (Pan/Ballantine, London, 1973)

—— *Fighting Mad* (Pen & Sword Books, Barnsley, 2004)

Carew, Tim, *The Longest Retreat: The Burma Campaign 1942* (Hamish Hamilton, London, 1969)

Carmichael, Pat, *Mountain Battery* (Devin Books, Bournemouth, 1983)

Carver, Michael, *The War Lords: Military Commanders of the 20th Century* (Little, Brown, Boston, 1976)

Chester, Sir Norman, *The Nationalisation of British Industries* (HMSO, 1975)

Cloake, John, *Templer, Tiger of Malaya: The Life of Field Marshal Sir Gerald Templer* (Harrap, London, 1985)

Collis, M., *Last and First in Burma* (Faber & Faber, London 1956)

Colvin, John, *Not Ordinary Men* (Pen & Sword Military Classics, Barnsley, 1994)

Connell, John, *Wavell, Supreme Commander* (Collins, London, 1969)

Coulthard-Clark, C. D. (ed.), *Gables, Ghosts and Governor-Generals* (Allen & Unwin, London, in association with the Canberra District Historical Society, 1988)

Davis, Patrick, *A Child at Arms* (Hutchinson, London, 1970)

Dorn, Frank, *Walkout: With Stilwell in Burma* (Thomas Y. Crowell, New York, 1971)

Dulat, J. S., *Partners in Victory – Mountbatten, Slim and the Campaign in Burma* (ABC Publishing, Delhi, 1983)

Edwards, Leslie, *Kohima, the Furthest Battle* (The History Press, Stroud, Gloucestershire, 2009)

Evans, Sir Geoffrey, *Slim as Military Commander* (Batsford, London, 1969)

—— and Brett-James, A., *Imphal: A Flower on Lofty Heights* (Macmillan, London, 1962)

Fergusson, Bernard, *Beyond the Chindwin* (Collins, London, 1945)

—— *The Wild Green Earth* (Collins, London, 1946)

—— *Wavell: Portrait of a Soldier* (Collins, London, 1961)

—— *The Trumpet in the Hall* (Collins, London, 1970)

—— 'Slim' (*Army Quarterly*, Vol. 4, 1971)

Foott, Bethia, *Ethel and the Governors' General: A Biography of*

Ethel Anderson (1883–1958) & Brigadier General A. T. Anderson (1868–1949) (Rainforest Publishing, Sydney, 1992)

Fowler, William, *We Gave Our Today* (Orion, London, 2010)

Fraser, George MacDonald, *Quartered Safe Out Here* (Harvill, London, 1992)

Gibbs, Lt Col. H. R. K., *Historical Record of the 6th Gurka Rifles 1919–1948* (Gale & Polden, Aldershot, 1955)

Goodall, Felicity, *Exodus Burma: The British Escape through the Jungles of Death 1942* (The History Press, Stroud, 2011)

Grant, Maj. Gen. Ian Lyall, *Burma, The Turning Point* (Leo Cooper, London, 2003)

—— and Tamayam, K., *Burma 1942: The Japanese Invasion: Both sides tell the story of a savage jungle war* (The Zampi Press, Chichester, 1999)

Greenwood, Alexander, *Field Marshal Auchinleck* (The Pentland Press, Durham, 1991)

Hamilton, Nigel, *The Full Monty: Montgomery of Alamein 1887–1942* (Allen Lane, London, 2001)

Hastings, Max, *Nemesis: The Battle for Japan* (Harper Press, London, 2007)

Hawkins, Doreen, *Drury Lane to Dimapur* (Dovecot Press, 2009)

Heathcote, Tony, *The British Field Marshals, 1736–1997* (Leo Cooper, London, 1999)

Hedley, J., *Jungle Fighter* (Tom Donovan, Brighton, 1996)

Hickey, Michael, *The Unforgettable Army: Slim's XIVth Army in Burma* (Spellmount, Kent, 1992)

Hill, David, *The Forgotten Children* (Random House, London, 2007)

Hill, John, *China Dragons: A Rifle Company at War, Burma, 1944–45* (Blandford Press, London, 1991)

—— *Slim's Burma Boys* (Spellmount, Stroud, 2007)

Keane, Fergal, *Road of Bones: The Epic Siege of Kohima 1944* (Harper Press, London, 2010)

Keegan, John, *Churchill's Generals* (Weidenfeld & Nicolson, London, 1991)

Kirby, Maj. Gen. S. W. (supervising ed.), *The Official History of the War Against Japan*, (5 volumes, Naval and Military Press, Uckfield, 2004)

Latimer, John, *Burma, The Forgotten War* (John Murray, London, 2004)

Leese, Lt Gen. Sir Oliver, *Operations in Burma from 12 November 1944 to 15 August 1945* (HMSO, London, 1951)

Lewin, Ronald, *Slim the Standard Bearer* (Leo Cooper, London, 1976)

Leyin, John, *Tell Them of Us: The Forgotten Army, Burma* (Leyins Publishing, Stanford-le-Hope, Essex, 2000)

Lunt, J., *A Hell of a Licking* (Collins, London, 1986)

—— *Jai Sixth: The Story of the 6th Queen Elizabeth's Own Gurkha Rifles 1817–1994* (Leo Cooper, London, 1994)

Lyman, Robert, *Slim, Master of War: Burma and the Birth of Modern Warfare* (Constable, London, 2004)

—— *Japan's Last Bid For Victory* (Pen & Sword Books, Barnsley, 2011)

Lynn, Dame Vera, *Some Sunny Day* (Harper Collins, London, 2009)

Mackenzie, Compton, *Eastern Epic* (Chatto & Windus, London, 1951)

Mains, Lt Col. Tony, *The Retreat from Burma* (W. Foulsham & Co., Slough, 1973)

Manson, Michael, *The Hidden History of St Andrews* (Tangent Books, Bristol, 1995)

Masters, John, *The Road Past Mandalay* (Michael Joseph, London, 1961)

Maule, H. *Spearhead General: The Epic Story of General Sir Frank Messervy in Eritrea, North Africa and Burma* (Odhams Press, London, 1961)

Maung Maung, Dr, *To a Soldier Son* (U Htin Gyi, Rangoon, 1974)

McKie, Ronald, *Echoes from Forgotten Wars* (Collins, Sydney, 1980)

McLynn, Frank, *The Burma Campaign: Disaster Into Triumph, 1942–45* (The Bodley Head, London, 2010)

Mead, Richard, *Churchill's Lions: A Biographical Guide to the Key British Generals of World War II* (Spellmount, Stroud, 2007)

Menzies, Sir Robert, *Afternoon Light* (Cassell, London 1967)

Moberley, F. J. *Military Operations Mesopotamia*, Vols II and III (HMSO, London, 1997)

Moser, Don, *China, Burma, India* (Time-Life Books, Alexandria, Va., 1978)

North, John (ed.), *The Alexander Memoirs 1940–45* (Cassell, London, 1962)

Nicolson, Nigel, *Alex: The Life of Field Marshal Earl Alexander of Tunis* (Weidenfeld & Nicolson, London, 1973)

Nunneley, John, *Tales from the Burma Campaign* (Burma Campaign Fellowship Group, Petersham, 1998)

Pearson, Michael, *End Game Burma 1945: Slim's Masterstroke at Meiktila* (Pen & Sword Military, Barnsley, 2010)

Pocock, Tom, *Fighting General* (Collins, 1973)

Potter, John Dean, *A Soldier Must Hang* (Frederick Muller, London, 1963)

Redding, Tony, *The Wilderness War* (Spellmount, Stroud, 2011)

Rhodes James, Robert, *Gallipoli* (Batsford, London, 1965)

Roberts, M. R., *Golden Arrow: The Story of the 7th Indian Division in the Second World War 1939–1945* (Gale & Polden, Aldershot, 1952)

Rodger, George, *Red Moon Rising* (The Cresset Press, London, 1949)

Rooney, David, *Burma Victory: Imphal, Kohima and the Chindit issue, March 1944 to May 1945* (Arms and Armour Press, London, 1992)

—— *Wingate and the Chindits: Redressing the Balance* (Arms & Armour Press, London, 1994)

—— *Stilwell the Patriot: Vinegar Joe, the Brits and Chiang Kai-Shek* (Greenhill Books, London, 2005)

Royle, Trevor, *Orde Wingate, Irregular Soldier* (Weidenfeld & Nicolson, London, 1995)

Ryder, Rowland, *Oliver Leese* (Hamish Hamilton, London, 1987)

Seaman, Henry, *The Battle at Sangshak* (Leo Cooper, London, 1989)

Slim, Sir William, *Defeat Into Victory* (Cassell, London, 1956)

—— *Courage and Other Broadcasts* (Cassell, London, 1957)

—— *Unofficial History* (Cassell, London, 1959)

Smith, Colin, *Singapore Burning* (Penguin/Viking, London 2005).
Smith, Brig. E. D., *The Battle for Burma* (Batsford, London, 1979)

Smith, Gen. Dun, *Memoirs of the Four-Foot Colonel* (Cornell University Press, Ithica, New York, 1980)

Smith, Michael, *The Emperor's Codes* (Bantam Press, London, 2000)

Smyth, Sir John, *Before the Dawn* (Cassell, London, 1957)

—— *The Only Enemy* (Hutchinson, London, 1957)

—— *Milestones* (Sidgwick & Jackson, London 1979)

Smurthwaite, D. (ed.), *The Forgotten War: The British Army in the*

Far East 1941–5 (National Army Museum, London, 1992)

Stilwell, General Joseph W., *The Stilwell Papers* (Schocken Books, New York, 1972)

Swinson, Arthur, *Four Samurai* (Hutchinson, London, 1968)

—— *North-West Frontier; People and Events 1939–1947* (Hutchinson, London, 1967)

—— *Kohima* (Cassell, London, 1966)

Tanner, R. E. S. and D. A., *Burma 1942: Memories of a Retreat* (The History Press, Stroud, 2009)

Tamayama, Kazuo and Nunneley, John, *Tales by Japanese Soldiers* (Cassell, London, 2000)

Taylor, A. J. P., *The War Lords* (Hamish Hamilton, London, 1977)

Thompson, Julian, *War in Burma, 1942–45* (Sidgwick & Jackson, London, 2002, in association with IWM)

—— *Forgotten Voices of Burma* (Ebury Press, London, 2009, in association with IWM)

Tuchman, Barbara, *Stilwell and the American Experience in China* (Macmillan, New York, 1970)

Tulloch, Maj. Gen. Derek, *Wingate in Peace & War* (Macdonald, London, 1972)

Vincent, Stanley, *Flying Fever* (Jarrolds, London, 1972)

Wagg, Alfred, *A Million Died: A Story of the War in the Far East* (Nicholson & Watson, London, 1943)

Warner, P., *Auchinleck, The Lonely Soldier* (Sphere Books, London 1988)

Webster, Donovan, *Burma Road* (Macmillan, London, 2004)

Williams, James Howard, *Elephant Bill* (Rupert Hart-Davis, London, 1950)

Wilson, Charles McMoran, *Churchill: Taken from the Diaries of Lord Moran* (Houghton Mifflin, Boston, 1966)

Wilson, David, *The Sum of Things* (Spellmount, Stroud, 2001)

Wingate, Ronald, *Lord Ismay: A Biography* (Hutchinson, London, 1970)

Wright, Denis and Hyde, John, *Bishopston: The Early Years* (Bishopston, Horfield & Ashley Down Local History Society, 2010)

Ziegler, Philip, *Mountbatten: The Official Biography* (Collins, London, 1985)

Acknowledgements

This book would not have been possible without the enthusiastic support and help of the current Viscount Slim, Bill's son, who gave generously of his time, read every draft chapter, made numerous helpful suggestions and saved me, I hope, from making too many mistakes. I would also like to thank, more or less in the order in which they became involved in the research, the following: the Honourable Mrs Una Rowcliffe, Bill's daughter; the distinguished military historian Robert Lyman; the staff at the Archive Centre, Churchill College, Cambridge, particularly Madelin Terrazas; Eric Morris; David Baynham at the Royal Regiment of Fusiliers Museum, Warwick; Father Paul Chavasse, archivist at St Chad's Cathedral, Birmingham; Ranald Leask of the Commonwealth War Graves Commission; John Hinchcliffe; Mark Eccleston, University of Birmingham; Professor John Baylis; Alison Wheatley of King Edward's School, Birmingham; Doctor Sekhar Raha, Dehraduhn; Julia and Simon Dams; Valerie Karatzas, secretary of the Bishopston Local History Society; Andy Buchan, chair of Bishopston, Horfield & Ashley Down Local History Society; Khaing Tun, Rangoon; Neisatuo Keditsu and Lucy Angami in Kohima; Angus Moncur, an enthusiastic amateur historian whom I met on the road in Nagaland; Burma veteran Patrick Burgoyne; Royston Slim, historian of the Slim family; Enid Slim, wife of Charlie's son, Arthur, and her son George, both in New Zealand; Robert Stephens in Canberra; Robert Rowlands QC; Gavin Edgerley Harris and Major Gerald Davies, archivist and curator respectively at the Gurkha Museum, Winchester; the helpful staff in the research room at the Imperial War Museum; George Mathewson, son of Kashmir missionary Dick Mathewson; Alistair Massie at the National Army Museum; Phil Crawley, Burma Star Association; Rosie Llewellyn-Jones at the Royal Society for Asian Affairs; Ken Scott, son of Major

General Bruce Scott; ex-Chindit John Riggs; Dame Vera Lynn; John Rouleau, Japanese expert; General Sir John Swinton and Major Simon Weber-Brown, both ADCs to the Governor-General in Australia; Burma veteran Mr E. G. W. Browne CBE; Barbara and the late Laurence Goss; Lord Peter Carrington. My good friend Philip Norman introduced me to Viscount Slim and suggested I should take on this project and my incomparable agent, Michael Sissons, and my editor Alan Samson of Weidenfeld & Nicolson, made it happen. Finally, as always, I must thank my wife, Renate, for living with me uncomplainingly for so long when my mind was often elsewhere and for travelling with me through Burma and India in not always the most comfortable circumstances.

Index